SOUNDINGS IN ST. AUGUSTINE'S IMAGINATION

SOUNDINGS
in
ST. AUGUSTINE'S
IMAGINATION

by

ROBERT J. O'CONNELL, S.J.

Fordham University Press
New York

Library of Congress Cataloging-in-Publication Data

O'Connell, Robert J.
Soundings in St. Augustine's imagination / by Robert J. O'Connell.
  p. cm.
Includes bibliographical references and index.
ISBN 0–8232–1347–1 : $40.00. — ISBN 0–8232–1348–X : $19.95
1. Augustine, Saint, Bishop of Hippo. Confessiones.
2. Augustine, Saint, Bishop of Hippo—Style.   3. Christian
saints—Algeria—Hippo (Extinct city)—Biography.   4. Catholic
Church—Algeria—Hippo (Extinct city)—Bishops—Biography.   5.
Hippo (Extinct city)—Biography.   6. Imagination—Religious
aspects—Christianity—History of doctrines—Early church, ca. 30–
600.   I. Title.   II. Title: Soundings in Saint Augustine's
imagination.
BR65.A62026   1994
270.2'092—dc20   93-11257
                                                                CIP

Contents

For John J. O'Meara
In friendship and esteem

Acknowledgments

For one's first or second book in a given field, acknowledging one's scholarly indebtedness can be a rather straightforward business. But it is a more challenging matter to dredge up memories of debts which go back, some of them, more than thirty years. How is one to recall accurately where, and with whom, one first contemplated the seed of an idea which came to flower only ten or twenty years later? How many a stimulating conversation have I enjoyed with the warm and kindly scholar to whom I dedicate this book; but how seldom can I pinpoint whether it was he, or someone to whom memory has errantly assigned his voice and manner, who casually tossed out this or that suggestion which subsequently laid bare some rich vein for research.

I am obliged, then, to limit myself to what I know, and beg advance indulgence for any grevious omissions. The reader will find that my Introduction already spells out a record, admittedly incomplete, of authors I am sure have presided, remotely or otherwise, over the long gestation of ideas finally developed in this book. But I must add to that list the name of Fr. G. Richard Dimler, S.J., who, as editor of *Thought*, solicited and published the earliest core-version, which grew into the study included here, of Augustine's maternal God. I must also thank the authorities of Marquette University, and especially my friendly critic-advocate, Fr. Roland J. Teske, S.J., for having conspired to elicit the kernel of this book, in the form of the Aquinas Lecture for 1986, on Augustine's melding of "Imagination and Metaphysics." For fraternal help over occasional interpretive rough spots, my thanks to Frs. Thomas V. Bermingham, S.J., and Joseph T. Lienhard, S.J. And I must pay homage, once again, to those two of my Jesuit professors, Frs. Joseph A. Slattery and W. Norris Clarke, who were (unwittingly, perhaps, and therefore blamelessly!) most responsible for pointing down the road I have chosen to travel here.

In addition I must thank the authorities of Fordham University for having accorded me the Faculty Fellowship year which facilitated bringing the substance of this work to completion. Finally, it would be ignoble to omit mention of my superb editor, Dr. Mary Beatrice Schulte, and those others of the cordial and efficient staff of Fordham University Press, for laboring so assiduously to make this book the kind of beautiful production for which they have become distinguished.

Abbreviations

For Research Instruments:

AM	*Augustinus Magister.* Acta of the International Augustinian Congress. 3 vols. Paris: Études Augustiennes, 1954)
RA	*Recherches Augustiniennes*
REA	*Revue des Etudes Augustiniennes*

For the Works of St. Augustine:

Acad	*Contra Academicos*
Adim	*Contra Adimantum Manichaei discipulum*
Civ	*De civitate Dei*
Conf	*Confessiones*
En(n)	*Enarratio(nes) in Psalmos*
EpJo	*Tractatus in Joannis Epistulam*
GenLitt	*De Genesi ad litteram*
GenMan	*De Genesi contra Manichaeos*
InJo	*Tractatus in Joannis Evangelium*
Lib	*De libero arbitrio*
Ord	*De ordine*
Quant	*De quantitate animae*
Retr	*Retractationes*
S(S)	*Sermo(nes)*
SC	*Sermo Caillau*
SD	*Sermo Denis*
SG	*Sermo (Morin) Guelferbytanus*
SMa	*Sermo Mai*
SMo	*Sermo Morin*
Sol	*Soliloquia*
SW	*Sermo Wilmart*
Trin	*De Trinitate*
Ver	*De vera religione*
Vita	*De beata vita*

In cases where Augustine produced two versions of an *Enarratio* on a particular Psalm, the citation includes the term "version" followed by the appropriate version and paragraph numbers in arabics; thus: *En 8*, version 2, 3. The same principle is followed, using the term "sermon," when several sermons were preached on (i.e., normally on consecutive portions of) the same Psalm; thus: *En 118*, sermon 11, 2.

I have profited where possible from the texts made available in the Bibliothèque Augustinienne series. In other cases I have employed the texts recommended by Eligius Dekkers and Aemilius Gaar in their *Clavis patrum latinorum*, 2nd ed. (= *Sacris Erudiri* III), published in Steenbrugge in 1961), or those published subsequently (such as Vol. XXVII, Luc Verheijen's edition of the *Confessions*) in the CCL series. All translations are my own.

Despite the uncertainties surrounding the chronology of Augustine's preached works, I have tried to bear in mind the chronological indications to be found in the following:

For the *Sermones*: *Études critiques sur les sermons authentiques de saint Augustin*, by Pierre-Patrick Verbraken, Instrumenta Patristica 12 (The Hague: Nijhoff, 1976).

For the *Enarrationes in Psalmos*, as well as for the *Tractatus* on both St. John's Gospel and his First Epistle ("*Ad Parthos*"), *L'Aventure de la raison et de la grâce*, by André Mandouze (Paris: Études Augustiniennes, 1968), pp. 591–663, including notes and references.

Introduction

One can understand why a student of rhetoric or poetry might set himself to exploring the workings of St. Augustine's imagination, but why should the subject interest a philosophical interpreter? Some years ago, that question was put to me by a renowned Augustine scholar, in rolling, sepulchral terms that insinuated, unmistakably, that the burial service they announced was my own. I had presented for scholarly discussion a series of preliminary excavations into the imaginative sub-cellar that, to me at least, appeared to underlie Augustine's account of his conversion in A.D. 386. That sub-cellar, or, as I came later to conclude, that catacomb-network of sub-cellars, seemed to wind tortuously in a labyrinth of crazy configurations, snake about into a number of dust-piled nooks and cobwebbed corners, where an occasional acrid reek hinted that old bones might lie concealed.

Alas, I was much younger then, fresh (and, yes, green) from the heady excitements of graduate studies in Paris; my mistake was to think that I might communicate my baroque Sherlockian suspicions contagiously enough to provoke this particular circle of Augustine scholars to, ah well, not quite *sit up*, but at least blink fitfully as they dozed through my exposé. Hubris, indeed. I ended my presentation in a burst of voluble enthusiasm; a cloud of pipesmoke gradually cleared; then that voice, round and sonorous as Big Ben's tolling through a London fog, solemnly pronounced sentence upon this most recent recruit to the inexhaustible battalions of great Hippo's heretical interpreters. "This," the Voice intoned, not angrily, but sadly, disappointedly, "has much more to do with *scientia* than with Augustinian *sapientia*."

Nothing truly significant, then, was to be found by dissecting Augustine's imagery. Wordless nods all around; a brief but perfunctory discussion, doubtless for courtesy's sake. After a decent interval the jury rose, its members exchanged a few congenialities with each other, wished each other good evening, and departed into the night.

Time was when a comparable attitude prevailed in the interpretation of Plato's Dialogues. Skip over the mise-en-scène, the introductory banter, the artful delineation of the characters engaged in the discussion, and get to the argumentative parts; only there was the philosophical "meat" of Plato's thinking to be found. More recent interpretation has come to stress that Plato was a consummate philosophical artist, a "dramatist," as the title of John Herman Randall, Jr.'s study puts it, "of the life of reason"; the artistic bits and argumentative bits were undivorceably interwoven. The setting, literary touches, the myths and drama of character, were more than mere stage-scenery for the reasoned argument; the "philosophy" could not be rightly appreciated if surgically excised from its artistic embodiment, any more than the human being can be adequately understood from studying a skeleton shorn of the muscles, tendons, and organs that once constituted its enfleshment.

But Augustine was every bit the philosophical artist that Plato was; one reading of his *Confessions* puts paid to any doubts about that. There is something of an irony here; few thinkers have inveighed against the dangers of imaged thinking more fiercely than he, or than the one who came closest to being his philosophic "master," Plotinus. Yet closer inspection quickly reveals that both of them repeatedly transgressed their own strictures on imagery, and with a brilliance and power that never cease to amaze.

It was, in fact, that connection with Plotinus which first whetted my interest in Augustine's imagery. It puzzled me that at the dramatic high-point of his *Confessions* (7.20) two distinct images collided: a head, and a hand that simultaneously turned that individual head (*fovisti caput*) and, oddly, upheld (*manu veritate*) the entire created universe! And all this occurred within the magnetic field, as it were, of God's integral Omnipresence. I have described elsewhere the mental processes that brought me to conclude from that image-complex, that Augustine's thinking on integral omnipresence derived from Plotinus' double treatise on the that same subject (*Ennead* 6.4–5). There, the presence of the same images— or the same "pattern," rather, of thought, image, and affect— argued that Plotinus, not Porphyry, was their "source" or, better, their inspiration.

After that experience, it would have been impossible to study the "theory of man" contained in Augustine's early works without stumbling again and again upon the feminine image of God's maternal "care" which, on closer inspection, knitted Plotinus' and Augustine's "hand" and "head" images together. Stumble I did, and repeatedly; gradually it dawned on me that a broader study of Augustine's imagery, in and for itself, might turn out to be richly revealing of some facets of his thought and expression which still puzzled the scholarly world. So, I decided to start with what I had come to call Augustine's *fovere* image. A number of accidental finds persuaded me to focus that probe more narrowly by investigating Augustine's exploitation of Isaiah's maternal images of God.

The results were encouraging; so, when invited to give the Aquinas Lecture at Marquette University in 1986, I was emboldened to expand the range of my explorations, and to inquire into how the metaphysics embodied in Augustine's image of the "weighted universe," the hierarchically structured *Omnia*, consorted (or conflicted) with the metaphysics implicit in his *fovere* image. The research one does on a narrower topic invariably turns up a wealth of materials that do not relate to that initial topic; at the same time, they may suggest a dozen other topics beckoning for attention. And so it was; by this time, I realized I had gradually become committed to prosecuting a full-scale exploration of Augustine's imagery, *tout court*. This volume presents the first-fruits of that exploration.

The images examined in the first part of this study (though perhaps "image-clusters" would be a more exact description) function, I am now convinced, as the three "basic" image-clusters supposed by all the "secondary" image-clusters Augustine wields in his thinking. First, the image of the *Omnia* furnishes the picture of the total universe which constitutes the backdrop for the two subsequent images: it provides the geography (or "cosmography") of all human history, which Augustine envisages (second) as a *peregrinatio animae*, a "wayfaring of soul," which first plunges from the heights of the created universe downward into its depths, and then, rescued by God's *fovere* action (the third image), by His (or Her?) omnipresent providential "care," returns to those primordial heights again. These three images once in place, it becomes possible to plot the workings of the numerous "secondary" image-clusters Augustine employs.

It would be arrogant to understimate how much the work of other scholars contributed to the views expressed here. I shall have more than one occasion to acknowledge those many debts. But before going further, I must first of all avow a new burst of admiration for the mentor whom I had already come deeply to admire, Henri-Irénée Marrou. His brilliant and careful study of Augustine's "culture" once again turned out to be extremely revealing on how the mind of this professional *rhetor* worked. Later on, Kenneth Burke's study of the *Rhetoric of Religion* as exhibited in Augustine's *Confessions* encouraged me to hope that it would be fruitful to push his investigations deeper into the imaginative subsoil, as it were, from which that rhetoric sprang. Partial confirmation of that hope came from diverse studies produced by Henri Rondet, Pierre Courcelle, Jean Pépin, Huguette Fugier, Leo C. Ferrari, and others, all of them illuminating various themes, or (as I would call them) "image-clusters," that Augustine exploits in his *Confessions*, and in other works that furnish valuable stage-lighting for the *Confessions*. My debt extends, directly and indirectly, to others, certainly; I suspect that one day I shall come to recognize the sizable debt I have come to owe, for this study quite as much as for others I have worked on, to the invaluable illumination Mlle Anne-Marie La Bonnardière's numerous writings have shed on Augustine's use of the Bible and on the enormous stock of images it furnished him. And now, although I came to study her thesis only when my own research had reached substantial completion, it is clear that we shall all henceforth stand in similar debt to Suzanne Poque.

In this same connection, finally, I must again confess that I have seldom been more grateful for any piece of advice than the one which that perfect gentleman Romano Guardini gave me in a memorable conversation years ago. I was about to embark on a graduate thesis focused on Augustine's aesthetic theory; I was already uncomfortable with that theory, having found it every bit as Henri-Irénée Marrou had once characterized it, a rationalistic blend of Neoplatonism and Neopythagoreanism, an analysis that succeeded less in explaining art than in explaining it away. Ah, interjected Guardini, but if he were I, he would concentrate much more on what Augustine the artist *does* than on what he *claims* to be doing! My subsequent research led me to conclude that on this point, as on so many others, Guardini was unerringly perceptive; Augustine's poetic artistry, particularly as exhibited in his *Confessions*, turned out to be a stunning refutation of his theory of art.

One by-product of that graduate thesis was a lifelong sensitivity to Augustine's masterful way of wielding poetic imagery. Eventually, a question began to emerge: Which was the more authentic register Augustine chose for saying what he most deeply wanted posterity to understand about the human condition? Did his message come across in the language of what is customarily considered "philosophical analysis"—the *sapientia* my interlocutor referred to—or did he convey the more intimate and contagious pulsations of his message in the language of poetic imagery? Obviously, he could shift from one register to the other; we may take it, for the moment, that he meant to convey the identical views, now in one, now in the other register: the evidence accumulated throughout this study will confirm that this was his intention. But is it a foregone conclusion that his hopes in this connection were perfectly fulfilled? Do the two registers really follow the same logic, obey the same dynamics of development, really *say* the same thing?

It would be tempting to suppose that the answer to that question can be expressed in the metaphor used above, in reference to Plato; in that case, Augustine's reasoned view of reality would stand to his imaged view as a skeleton stands to the flesh it supports. Both would present essentially the same shape; his reasoned view would be more like a monochrome x-ray in neutral black-and-white, whereas his imaged view provided the more graceful contours that betray the skeletal structure, both concealing and revealing it, at the same time lending that variety of flesh-tones that contribute charm and emotional warmth to the visible human body.

That comparison, in fact, quite satisfactorily fits the first image-cluster we are about to study, the *Omnia*. I apply this term to Augustine's image of the universe, both spiritual and corporeal, as a structured hierarchy of "all things." Compare its structure and dynamics with those described (quite accurately) in Vernon Bourke's presentation of Augustine's more "philosophical" or reasoned view of reality, and the match is near-perfect. There is only one point, I think—better call it a "seam"—to which the imaged view ascribes far greater importance than does the reasoned view; but beyond that, Augustine's imagery principally contributes the vivid coloration and emotional tonalities that its more abstract, conceptual counterpart could never hope to rival.

That coloration and emotional tone represent no small contribution, of course; I suspect, in fact, that it is precisely this kind of utterance that identifies Augustine as uniquely, even incomparably, himself. That fact provides ample justification, surely, for the plethora of literary studies devoted to his work. But the properly "metaphysical" fallout from analyzing the *Omnia* image is relatively slight; with few exceptions, we simply relearn what studies of the reasoned system have already taught, or, at least, should have taught us.

And yet, tracing the dynamics of the *Omnia*, Augustine's bedrock "foundational" image-cluster, contributes significantly to resolving a nest of problems in translating Augustine's Latin. Ironically, that contribution all too often consists in warning us of something we should already have realized: that this professional *rhetor*'s Latin should always be translated exactly as it stands. Then, if we find the result difficult to comprehend, our business should be that of stretching our minds to grasp *his* meaning rather than substituting an inaccurate translation that we find more congenial to *our* twentieth-century thought-ways.

There is another, even more substantial contribution that analysis of the *Omnia* image-cluster makes: it lays bare certain lines of force, highlights certain priorities and emphases in Augustine's world-view, which even assiduous study of his reasoned view would rarely bring to light. In doing so, it prompts us to detect where those emphases and priorities collide with, or at least run cross-grained to, the characteristic lines of competing image-systems, which sometimes conduct Augustine's thinking along different pathways. Even among the three "foundational" images studied here, we shall detect a number of such mutual interferences, counter-pressures, differences of emphasis. In my Aquinas Lecture on *Imagination and Metaphysics in St. Augustine* (Milwaukee: Marquette University Press, 1986), for instance, I tried to show that the logic of the *Omnia* image would tempt us to think of our souls as realities moving inexorably, it would seem, in accordance with their spiritual "weights"; the *fovere* image, on the other hand, the third foundational image we shall study here, accentuates the unaccountability of God's parental care for His chosen ones. That unaccountability should result, *de jure*, in canceling all the inexorabilities suggested by the conception of an *Omnia* as a universe ordered by spiritual "weights." Probe this rift at the image-level, and you may account more satisfactorily for the corresponding rift as it shows up, albeit more discreetly, in Augustine's reasoned views.

For we shall come to see that each of Augustine's image-clusters manifests an associational "logic" all its own. Think of earth, and (if you are Augustine, and familiar with the physics of the ancient world) you may be brought to think of its companion elements, water, air, and fire, arranged in the cosmos from lowest to highest according to their "weights." Or you may think of the feeling of firm stability that earth provides, particularly when one disembarks from bobbing on a river or tossing on a sea. Or, still another possibility, earth may bring you to think, paradoxically, of the insubstantial dust that flits about aimlessly in the slightest breeze. One basic element, and yet its image prods this man's mind to travel any number of pathways, each of them with its own imaginative "logic."

Similarly, think of the sun, and, like Augustine, you may think of the fiery heat and "lightness" that place it in the highest station in the visible world; then go on to think (especially if you are an African) of its cruel inescapability, its power to sear and wither, the sufferings its burns can cause. But, in another mood, you may find yourself thinking of that same sun's power to warm, thaw, comfort, heal; or you may be led to think, by the logic of contrast, of that antithetical scheme of associations: of cold, iciness, and the numbness, discomfort, and suffering they bring with them.

But when Augustine thinks of the sun, he also thinks of its light, brightness, clarity; this leads him to think of the sharpness of vision, the knowledge and confident sense of secure control that comes with that clarity. Or he thinks of sun and is led to think of moon, of waxing and waning, changeability, dimness, night, uncertainty, then . . . lostness, danger, hopelessness.

Whatever path his imagination strikes out on, however, it normally follows that path's direction, and if it veers, it veers off only into the natural branchings that path provides for it. Imagination may not follow the logic of reasoned thought, but it has its logic, nonetheless. Freud's conviction was not entirely amiss: "free" association may be counted on to disclose the pathways imagination takes, and takes with a considerable measure of inevitability.

Each image-system has, then, its own peculiar logic. But differing image-systems, each pursuing its own inherent logic, may move along avenues that "intersect" with each other. To illustrate "intersection": take an example from two distinct systems studied here. One facet of the logic peculiar to Augustine's *Omnia* image is this:

it depicts the universe as arranged in levels that correspond, *grosso modo*, to the levels of the "weighted" world of ancient physics. That is to say, bodies characterized by light, fire, and heat belong in the highest, those characterized by darkness, earthiness, and cold in the lowest reaches of the physical cosmos. Below the sun and stars in the lofty ether, accordingly, we find the air; farther down, the humid clouds, vapor, and the waters of rivers and seas. Heaviest, and therefore lowest of all, we find the rocks and soil of earth.

But consider the highest region of sun and light as the natural "place" our souls' "weight" tends toward, and the inferior realms, both of "earth" and the "waters" of river and sea, become ("logically") places where the soul is a foreigner, an "alien"—in the language of the second image studied here, an *anima peregrina*, a "wayfaring soul." But the journey of the wayfarer must have a setting, a geography or, better, a "cosmography." The wayfarer can, for instance, journey overland (as the Prodigal did) or across the sea (as both Odysseus and Aeneas did): in the language of Aristotle's four elements, he may travel on "earth" or on the "waters."

At this juncture, the logic of Augustine's *peregrinus* image "intersects" with that of his *Omnia* image: the description of the "journey" must submit to the logic of the *Omnia* image. A sea-voyage must be depicted in accordance with the properties and behavior the *Omnia* scheme confers on "sea" and "waters" more generally: instead of stressing the jostling, bumping, parching, and dust-choked discomforts of road-travel in the ancient world, Augustine will more naturally, logically, lay emphasis on the rolling, the pitching, the stomach-wrenching storms, the constant uncertainties and unremitting menace involved in voyaging over the capricious and hostile ocean deeps.

But that evocation of the sea-voyage suggests a second peculiarity of Augustine's image-logic: two image-systems, each obeying its own proper logic, may do more than merely "intersect"; they may run "parallel" over a certain distance; more, they may actually "fuse" with each other. Consider the three wayfarers already mentioned: the Prodigal, Odysseus, and Aeneas. We shall come to see that all three figure in Augustine's imagination as types of the *peregrinus*. But the experiences of those two sea-voyagers, Aeneas and Odysseus, are often so similar that Augustine can begin by describing an experience proper to Odysseus, and in the very next phrase allude—in "parallel"—to a seafaring experience that is more proper to Aeneas. And yet, the reader can detect, the two remain two: Odysseus remains identifiably Odysseus, and Aeneas, Aeneas: their experiences (and identities) remain parallel but distinct from each other.

But in other instances they can do more; they can actually "fuse." The evocation of Aeneas can imperceptibly slide into becoming an evocation of Odysseus: so imperceptibly, that we abruptly realize that the image of Aeneas has at some point in the process become identical, actually "fused," with the image of Odysseus. But, even more remarkably, a comparable fusion can occur between the Christian Prodigal and the pagan Odysseus (less often Aeneas), so that we wonder how the land-journey Augustine started with has all at once turned into a sea-voyage, or vice versa! Then, as if to complicate matters even further, the sea-voyager can suddenly turn into Christ, or the apostles, tossed about on the lake of Galilee, or into the typical Christian, clinging for safety to the "wood" of the Cross as Odysseus once clung to his raft. Hence, we may not think of these images as hermetically distinct and sealed off from one another: unlike Cartesian ideas whose very clarity ensures that they also remain distinct from one another, images act much more like osmotically porous cells of a living organism, capable in an instant of combining with a neighbor image.

The phenomenon of "fusion" suggests a third property of Augustine's image-logic which must be borne in mind: his imagination does not observe the same principle of contradiction as conceptual thought obeys. Conceptual thought would insist that the wayfaring *peregrinus* must be Odysseus, *or* Aeneas, *or* the Prodigal—*or*, for that matter, the lost sheep, or the man who "went down from Jerusalem to Jericho." Augustine's imagination (and the poetic imagination more generally?) replies: "Nonsense." To the "either-or" of conceptual thinking, this man's poetic imagination obstinately flings back its defiant "both-and."

Consequently, a corresponding both-and relationship must govern any search for the "sources" or "inspirations" for this or that Augustinian image. His exegetical practice repeatedly shows that Augustine was both delighted and stimulated when he found the same image occurring in two or more loci, and the "farther apart" those loci the better! Finding the same image operative in two neighboring Psalms could be moderately exciting; but finding and then being able to ring the changes on the same image as it occurred in a Gospel, a Pauline Epistle, the prophecy of Isaiah (say), and Plotinus' *Enneads*—now that, for Augustine, was happiness indeed!

One final "law" of Augustine's image-logic I shall refer to under the rubric of "recession." To be precise, however, this phenomenon directly affects, not the image itself, but the linguistic expression that originally triggered or accompanied the image-complex. For the evidence shows that the great majority of Augustine's images are triggered by some particular linguistic turn, most often from Scripture.

The imaginative workings of his *Omnia* image, for example, seem to have evolved principally out of his meditations on Wisdom's affirmation that God created all things according to "number, measure, and weight," a teaching he was able to flesh out in accord with the Plotinian image of the "two worlds," along with the Aristotelian physics of "weights." Similarly, the Gospel texts depicting the lost sheep and the Prodigal Son account for the frequency with which his "wayfarer" image signals its presence by the use of such terms as "wandered off" or "departed" for a "far country." And Paul's self-depiction to the Thessalonians as a "nurse," lavishing her "care" on her infant children, seems to have been the linguistic correlate that eventually impregnated the term *fovere* (which the Latin translators of the Pauline letters used in this connection) with all its rich associations of maternal tenderness.

Now, when Augustine begins to evoke and develop any particular image, he regularly quotes the Biblical text that inspired it and, more often than not, quotes it in full. It is as though he felt obliged to remind both himself and his readers (or hearers) of his Scriptural warrant for exploiting the image suggested by the text. As time goes on, he may feel free merely to paraphrase the Biblical text in question, or to quote no more than a word, or a few key words from it. His appeal to the linguistic correlates that originally inspired his resort to this or that image can become more and more allusive, to the point that he eventually feels free to supply no more than a single word from the original text. This tendency for the linguistic correlate of any image to become gradually more discreet, until it almost reaches a vanishing point, I refer to as "recession."

It would be a serious mistake, however (and this is one of the fallacies implied in adhering to purely linguistic "parallels" when attempting to understand this extraordinarily imaginative thinker), to conclude that the original image has become less operative in Augustine's imagination in the same measure as the linguistic correlate has become recessive; indeed, the evidence will show that the very opposite is more often true. As Augustine gains confidence in exploiting a particular image, as it gradually takes its place as a familiar and trusted implement both of thought and of expression, it brings to his mind a number of other Scriptural texts, evoking the same or similar imagery; it then attracts those texts into a cluster about the original text, each of them adding some facet to the original image so that it "grows" into an ever-richer image-complex. At the culmination of the process, Augustine may evoke one, two, or as many facets of the complex as suit his purpose, but his masterful economy of expression will often permit him to represent each distinct facet by no more than a single word, or even a synonym of some word drawn from the appropriate tributary text of Scripture. Hence, the paradoxical rule: precisely in the measure that any image comes to function more powerfully in the subterranean reaches of Augustine's imagination, the linguistic correlate of this or that particular image-facet may, and regularly does, become increasingly "recessive."

This volume represents the first installment of a probe that could easily extend to an indefinite number of Augustine's images. I begin by focusing here on the three image-complexes which, I am persuaded, are foundational for the entire superstructure of Augustine's imaged thought. It would be logical to follow with a study of the entire array of images making up that superstructure, at least a representative sampling of them. I begin to doubt, however, that enough years are left to me to pursue that more complete study. But since those superstructural images would certainly include two of his most important derivative images of the *anima peregrina*, the Prodigal and Odysseus, and since both those images are variants on the more generic *peregrinus* image, I have chosen to study them in the second part of this volume.

But there is an additional reason for including the study of those two images here: limiting this initial exploration to Augustine's three basic images would have left all three of them rather colorless and schematic; whereas exploring the unpredictable sinuousities of both the Prodigal and, even more especially, the Odysseus images manages to fill out the *peregrinus* image with those flashes of vivid detail which tell us much about the pathways, tortuous sometimes and even slightly bizarre, which Augustine's imagination often delights in following. I myself was delightedly surprised at how rich the Odysseus image turned out to be, and how much it revealed about the byways of Augustine's imaginative thinking.

Were we to remain insufficiently attuned to those thought-ways, we should never be able to credit our interpretive judgment when it stubbornly tells us that Augustine plainly meant to say what our common sense resolutely refuses to accept as the fact of the matter. For this, I am increasingly convinced, is true of certain crucial passages of the *Confessions*: we are both enabled and obliged to interpret them far more cogently than hitherto if only we become more sensitive to the workings of Augustine's imagination.

There is one particular feature of Augustine's thinking which is thrown into much sharper relief by studying his imagery than by analyzing his more speculative thought. This claim will scarcely come as a surprise: I am referring to his theory of the human being as "fallen soul." Several scholars have suggested that if Augustine truly espoused this view of the human, he was being very discreet, even (as one writer put it) "secretive" about it. Certainly, there came a time when he was compelled to wrestle with St. Paul's reminder (in Romans 9:11) that neither Esau nor Jacob—and therefore, by extension, none of us—could be held guilty of having committed some pre-natal sin; hence, the main-spring of the "fallen soul" theory appeared to shatter. The force of that text, I have tried to show elsewhere, did make Augustine very guarded, for a time, about advocating his former theory. But his nervousness in that regard set in at a precise time, even if we can date its onset only approximately, somewhere in the neighborhood of A.D. 417. Furthermore, the textual evidence argues that his nervousness abated greatly, even if not entirely, in something less than two years (at the very outside, I suggest). That was the span of time it took Augustine to gain confidence in applying the distinction which, he felt, restricted the application of Romans 9:11 to the *propria vita* each of us individually lives, thus leaving open the possibility that we could have fallen in "common."

When Augustine does return to holding something very like his earlier "fallen soul" view, he has been scalded in the meanwhile, and the texts in which he discloses his renewed preference for that view can scarcely be viewed as super-confident proclamations of it. Discreet they may be, but I would never call them "secretive."

All this, however, has to do with Augustine's more technical writings. What analysis of his sermon-imagery reveals is this: before and after his temporary quandary over Romans 9:11, in years of preaching to his fellow-Africans, whether brother-bishops or ordinary faithful from Hippo, Carthage, and elsewhere, Augustine felt no constraint in deploying a skein of images whose import his hearers could hardly have misunderstood: that we are all wayfaring souls, having turned our backs on our Heavenly Home and plunged down to the lowest region of the *Omnia*; now, with the help of God's fostering "care," we strive to "re-turn" (quite literally) to where we originally came from. That view of human existence, powerfully conveyed in his three basic images of the human predicament, is etched even more clearly in the versatile ways Augustine exploits the Prodigal and Odyssey images. Nothing secretive here, nothing conspiratorially discreet. All of which suggests that the problem has rather been ours: in reading his works, whether preached or otherwise, we simply have not opened our eyes and paid careful, unprejudiced attention to what the man was saying, and, for readers and auditors of his time, saying with quite unmistakable directness.

There are, however, limitations to this study, and it would only be fair to warn the reader about them from the outset.

The first such limitation has to do with the twin problems of chronology and development. My explorations here have focused, primarily but not exclusively, on Augustine's preached works: sermons, Psalm-interpretations, and explanations of St. John's Gospel and First Epistle. But we still have much to learn about the chronology of all those works. A glance through Patrick Verbraken's heroic *Études critiques sur les sermons authentiques de saint Augustin* (The Hague: Nijhoff, 1976) will illustrate the problem as it touches Augustine's *sermones*. Adalbert Kunzelmann, writing in 1930, was often obliged to "date" a number of Augustine's *sermones* as vaguely as "before [or after] 400," or "On a Sunday," or "During Lent." Subsequent efforts have frequently been compelled to remain equally vague. Where Kunzelmann thought it

possible to assign more precise dates, scholars since have sometimes agreed with him, but in other instances their conjectures can
differ from his and from each other's, sometimes wildly and by a
matter of decades. And the problem regarding Augustine's other
preached works is quite comparable: not a year goes by without
some scholar's arguing for some readjustment in the accepted
chronology.

I had originally hoped to take chronology as a *prima facie*
indication of how each of Augustine's image-clusters started off
and then "grew," but I soon realized how formidable, indeed,
how forbidding, such a project would be. Only rarely, accordingly, have I been confident enough to claim that I have succeeded
in analyzing any particular image-cluster "developmentally"; insisting on the "best" in this as in so many human ventures would
have been the "enemy of the good." The image of the Prodigal
(Chapter 4) is an exceptional case: I was hoping to situate the
moment when Augustine suspended his earlier interpretation of
the Prodigal's "first garment" as referring to his pre-lapsary
spiritual body; that attempt, it will be seen, was only moderately
successful. And the same would have to be said of the similar
attempt with respect to the *deliciosae lassitudines* image.

In the majority of instances, then, I have adopted a compromise
solution. It involves, first, the negative step of never proposing a
developmental interpretation that entails contradicting the chronological conjecture of a reputable scholar, even if that conjecture
swims against the dominant scholarly tide.

My second canon respecting chronology is this: I have made my
own judgments, ranging from tentative to firm, on the basis of
what scholars have suggested about the chronology of the works I
have explored; then I have assigned a chronological niche to each
of those works, and have ordered my exposition of them by
following that chronology. But only in a minority of instances,
and only when the chronological footing seemed firm enough to
warrant it, have I argued from chronology to make explicit
developmental claims; and, each time I did so, I have alerted the
reader to that fact by mentioning the dating I was assuming.
Particulars of the chronological studies on which I have relied will
be found both listed among Research Instruments and referred to
when appropriate in my footnotes.

But that cautiousness about chronology is just one specific instance of a more generic methodological caution I have adopted throughout this study. Years of having to battle phalanxes of outworn scholarly myths have persuaded me that it is far wiser to abstain from taking a firm position on shaky grounds than to risk an erroneous suggestion that could set up just one more roadblock to clutter the highways of Augustinian scholarship. That caution is especially fitting in a field of study as young as Augustinian image-research. It behooves us all to acknowledge that we do not yet know our way about in this business. So, it is important that we not leap prematurely to ill-grounded conclusions that (inevitably, for this is the rhythm of progress in ideas) it will take one or two generations of scholars to dismantle, when they never should have encumbered the field in the first place. Equally important is it that we not begin by reposing too much initial trust in grand assumptions thinkers may have spun out, concerning the image *qua talis* or the symbol *qua tale*—or concerning such systematic divisions as images "diurnal" *vs*. images "nocturnal"— in short, we must not allow *general* theories of how the human imagination *must* work to dictate, and very possibly obscure, the way we look at that very particular and perhaps consummately individual imagination that was Augustine's. So, we would be well advised to go slowly, carefully testing each successive step, like a mountaineer traversing an unfamiliar snow-field.

I would hope that merely pointing to the dangers of starting from untested general assumptions, or leaping prematurely to sweeping general conclusions, might render the reader indulgent toward the resolute particularity of this study. For the moment it is quite uniquely *Augustine's* imagination I mean to explore; I hope to map the workings of *his individual* imagination. I do not wish to clutter the lens of observation with generalizations about "the imagination" drawn from others, whose imagination may or may not have worked the same way as that possessed by this quite unique fifth-century North African *rhetor*, son of Patricius and Monica, once Manichee turned Catholic bishop, etc., etc., etc. (how individual can one get?). Nor do I want to draw back too soon from scrutinizing this individual imagination, out of some anxious desire to draw general conclusions, "the way philosophers are supposed to do." I want to present the data as as "raw" and pre-suppositionless as possible, so that the reader may behold it as fresh and undistorted as he can.

My point in all this is not to deny that Augustine's imagination *may* have worked very much like that of other poetic minds in the Western tradition. But any such assumption can, after all, be called into question by competing assumptions, and I simply do not wish any such clash of interpretive biases to interfere with the unclouded inspection of how Augustine's individual imagination actually did work.

Nor would I question that the study of Augustine's own *theory* of the imagination holds both interest and importance; but it would be more appropriate if the reader concerned with that range of questions addressed himself to a work (perhaps even my own?) on Augustine's aesthetic theory, or to Cornelius Mayer's multi-volume study of Augustine's theory of signs. Augustine's theory of the imagination is not my concern here.

For (it is time I admitted it) the real purpose of this inquiry is more pragmatic than speculative. It is intended precisely to clear the ground for a subsequent interpretation of how Augustine's imagery works, and of what his imaginative language imports, in that baffling poetic masterpiece the *Confessions*. To accomplish that task, it is essential that I first decode the language of Augustine's own imagination, distilling it "neat," as it were, as purified as possible from alien ingredients. That propaedeutic intention, however, will also explain a few instances where I promise a study of some particular image, but postpone delivery on that promise until that interpretation of the *Confessions*. The promises are entered here to assure, but not, I fervently hope, to annoy the reader overmuch!

Citations from Augustine's works (see my list of "Abbreviations") regularly occur in the text itself, at the end of the paragraph or section exposing what I take their content to import. I have followed my usual practice of simplifying citations from the *Confessions* to Book and arabic paragraph-number, dropping out the small-roman "chapter" number. All translations from Augustine's text are my own.

I must close these remarks by conceding something to my pipe-smoking critic: in one important respect his attitude may have been more authentically "Augustinian" than mine. For Augustine himself, I suspect, would probably have taken a somewhat jaundiced view of this, or of any study like it. Imagine, he might have exclaimed, a grown man so fervidly tracking down these images of stormy deeps and falling snows, journeys, shipwrecks, perils of night and parching deserts by day; images of God as Father, Doctor, Nurse, and Mother. Indeed, Augustine could have depreciated such image-hunting by adducing one of the most moving images we are about to encounter: of God, as nursing mother, condescending to the infant understanding of those carnal "little ones" who must suckle at the breast of Mother Church because they are still too spiritually immature to arise to spiritual "understanding." How often, even in his preaching to quite ordinary folk, did he insist that his flock "grow up," think of God in a way that left all such images behind, truly come to "know" God as God. To the end of his life he never forgot the lesson the great Plotinus had hammered home in his treatise on Omnipresence: that bodily images were the enemy here; true understanding must lunge and stretch into a realm beyond all such imaginative thinking.

Yet most of us, I think, would fight shy of being all that "Augustinian." We would prefer not to follow him onto those chilly theoretical uplands. We find it comforting to dwell in these lowlands that, his theory insists, are not our home—even while his heart cannot disguise his human affection for them: for care-ridden doctors and solicitous nurses; for anxious brooding-hens and bleeding pelicans; and for mothers, especially mothers, who fondle, blandish, and tenderly suckle their squalling infants.

The fact is, though, Augustine may have granted us a stronger warrant for abiding here than he realized. It is piquant, in an ironic way, to monitor the moves he makes to think out that central theme of his theologizing, God's Omnipresence: for, very like Plotinus, he employs the power of an extraordinary imagination to transcend imagination's more pedestrian workings. His chosen technique of the "dynamic image," moreover, is not unlike another process we shall meet with in these pages: when asked whether God be maternal or paternal in character, Augustine, like a bright-eyed schoolboy with a pixie grin, calmly answers: "Yes." Paradoxical, that answer is also true: as true for the mind as it is for the imagination—and the heart. For only beyond that clash of mutual exclusives lies the One of Whom, our properly schooled imagination knows, everything earthly speaks: mothers, doctors; storm and clearing; sun and snow and warm south-winds; hens and pelicans, sparrows solitary on the housetops; and, leaping upward in a flight that mimics the heart's thrill when at last we glimpse the face of Augustine's God, madcap skylarks that climb, climb, climb until, still singing, they vanish into the Sun.

I • BASIC IMAGES

1

The *Omnia*: "All Things"

SOME YEARS AGO, Vernon J. Bourke proposed an elegant version of *Augustine's View of Reality*.[1] Everything existent, Bourke explained, found its place in a universe structured in three distinct tiers. The framework of that structure derived in the first instance from the distinction that is most fundamental to all of Augustine's metaphysical thinking: between changeable beings and the Being that is absolutely unchangeable (as only God is). But the class of changeable beings in turn divided into two further strata, consisting, on the one hand, of those spiritual beings that are changeable in temporal but not in spatial terms (angels and human souls), and, on the other, of bodily realities, whose changeability is both temporal and spatial.

AUGUSTINE'S "IMAGINED" UNIVERSE

One can go a good distance in understanding Augustine's thought in terms of that three-tiered universe. But I suggest that, to understand him more adequately, one must recognize that alongside his metaphysical view of reality Augustine more often thinks in terms of an imaginative "picture" of the universe.[2] Or perhaps it would be more accurate to envisage this imaginative picture as clothing or "fleshing out" the skeletal structure of his metaphysics. For while the imaginative picture does not stand in contradiction to the intelligible construct Bourke outlines, there are, nevertheless, nerve points where it "works" in response to slightly different dynamic principles, and, so, "operates" in accord with a somewhat altered set of priorities. In that world-image, God and the "all things" He created are accorded their appropriate "places" as in the following diagram:

Unum, Summum, The One, Highest	**GOD**	*Aeternum, Immutabile* Eternal, Unchangeable
Superiora, altiora Betters, Highers	*Angels and Souls*	*Spiritualia*: Spirituals (even bodies)

Above this line: *Invisible, suprasensible, Intelligible realities:*
i.e., *"Heaven"* and *"Truth"*

Below this line: *Visible, sensible, "opinative" realities:*
"Earth" and *"Vanities"*

Multa, Inferiora *Mutabilia* The Many, Lower and the *Infima, Extrema* Lowest, "Last"	Sun (Heat) Air (Dryness) Water (Dampness) Earth (Coldness)	*Temporalia,* Temporals, Changeables *Corpora,* Bodies

The diagram already suggests a shift in priority from the more metaphysical construct Bourke has outlined. Notice that the critical dividing line in this world-image occurs between "lower" sensible realities and supra-sensible "higher" realities, between bodily and spiritual beings. These, Augustine often reminds his hearers, are the *duae regiones*, the "two regions" of primary interest to the Christian. "Our region is earth; the angels' region, heaven. Our Lord came, therefore, to this [*istam*] region" of death and toil "from that other region," of life and happiness (*SG 9* 1). (Augustine's use of *iste* is invariably depreciatory!) Men desire to be happy here, but they quest for it in the "region" where it cannot be had, a "region of wretchedness" (*regio miseriae*) (*SG 12* 2). Much as in Plotinus' "emanation" image, the *Omnia* that God made consists of these two, "the intelligible heavens and the visible earth," where "spiritual" and "carnal" creatures dwell, respectively (*Enn 135* 5–6; *134* 15–16).[3] But we must "raise up our hearts, not allow them to make their home here, for this is an evil region" (*non hic habitandum corde: mala regio est*) (*En 39* 28). But Bourke is correct: the change–unchange contrast is the touchstone for discerning these two "regions"; for here we are born and die, change and are changed, so that we can never be assured of firmly possessing what would make us happy. The happiness we all long for must be sought in that other, higher "region," a timeless world where all is eternal and unchanging. But, one might ask, if our life in heaven is to be an unalterable happiness, what becomes of the soul's "natural" mutability?

One way of answering that question lies in Augustine's interpretation of a text he obviously cherished: St. John's assurance in his First Epistle (3:2) that "we shall be like Him, for we shall see Him as He is" (*sicuti EST*). That "is," Augustine insists, refers to God's absolute Immutability. For what is "called IS, and not merely called, but truly is such, is unchangeable, always remains [the same: *semper manet*], cannot change." And as for us, "we shall see a vision." But in seeing it, Augustine asks, "what shall we *be*? What is promised us? 'We shall be like Him,' Scripture answers, 'unchangeable as He Himself IS' " (*EpJo* 4 5–6). But "we already exist," Augustine objects to his own thesis, *jam sumus*, and yet John assures us "we shall be something [else]" (*aliquid erimus*). "But what more shall we be than what we now are? Listen," Augustine exclaims: "we shall be like Him" (*InJo 40* 9; *S 117* 15). The same is true of the unfallen angels: seeing God, they become "like" Him precisely in His manner of Be-ing (*sicuti EST*). Every creature in that higher world, in fact, whether angel or blessed soul, has somehow had its natural susceptibility for change suspended, as it were; everything there shares in God's own Immutability.

The speculative view of metaphysics is one thing, therefore, but from the salvational point of view the crucial dividing line sets these "two worlds," timeless and spiritual *vs.* temporal and corporeal, off against each other. The lower world is made in the shadowy image of the higher, and so boasts a certain "likeness" to it; but Augustine's more favored ways of expressing their relationship run to the antithetical characterizations used above: temporal *vs.* Eternal, visible *vs.* Intelligible, insubstantial "vanities" *vs.* solid "Verity," Truth.

ETERNITY AND UNCHANGE: TO BE, IN AN ALWAYS NOW

Notice, further, that Augustine's primary way of characterizing God's perfection is by pointing to His absolute Unchangeability. Above and beyond all change, God is therefore Eternal. By this Augustine does not mean that God is "everlasting," His existence stretching indefinitely into both past and future, for that would place Him in Time, even if He were imagined as occupying a unique status among temporal beings. To be Eternal in Augustine's meaning of the word is to be totally beyond and above time, to have no "before" or "after" whatever, to be unchangeably "now." This is what God meant by saying, in Exodus (3:14), that His Name was "I AM." In God "nothing is past, as though it no longer existed; nothing is future, as though it did not yet exist. There is only IS there . . . whatever is there simply IS" (*En 101*, sermon 2, 10; cf. *S 7* 7).

In another of his favorite expressions, God is the *Idipsum* the Psalmist speaks about, the utterly "Selfsame" Who truly "IS" the "Eternal" One. Thus, when Scripture speaks of "standing," we must understand the term as regularly implying a "standing *still*," an absolute "stability" in being which excludes every slightest suggestion of change or temporality. God's "years do not fail" but "stand" (*stant*); His "one day" neither comes to be nor passes away, "has neither rising nor setting, begins from no yesterday, is bounded by no tomorrow, but simply *stands* forever" (*En 121* 5– 6; cf. *Enn 23* 3–4, *146* 11).[4] The term "remain" (*manere*) regularly connotes the same stability, but adds the nuance of enduringness, abidingness: "Past and future I find in every changing being; in the [Divine] Truth Which remains [the same: *manet*] I find neither past nor future, but only present" (*InJo 38* 10). *Esse, stare, manere*: when used without further qualification, these three terms signify, for Augustine, the kind of plenary, unchangingly stable, and "abiding" or "enduring" being proper to the Eternal God. But we shall come to see that, in a slightly different image-context, the verb *stare* will also convey the further nuance of "standing solid," being "firmly established."

THE DIS-TENTION OF TEMPORALITY

We temporal beings, in contrast, experience our existence as "stretched out," "dis-tended," into moment that follows moment; our lives *transeunt*, each segment of them coming to be and then "passing," in the sense of passing away as it dissolves into the succeeding segment. Unlike God's, our existence *non stat, non manet*; it has no "stability," no enduring "abidingness." We do not, in other words, possess the entirety of our reality at "once," in the incredibly intense unity of a single super-distilled "now." Hence, it cannot be said of any being so dispersed through the transient "flow" of time that it ever truly "IS." Temporal existence inexorably implies an uninterrupted sequence of not-being what one will become, and becoming what one formerly was-not; it is a type of existence undivorceably wedded to non-existence. We temporal beings both "are" and "are-*not*"; we do not fully "exist." Only in the Eternal God are all "befores" and "afters" so perfectly "in-gathered," present in His "now," that they are not truly "befores" or "afters" in the first place! Only of a God so perfectly "One" can it be said that He truly "IS."

THE POEM OF TIME

From the sixth book of his *De musica* onward, one of Augustine's very favorite illustrations of this temporal "flow" focuses on what happens when we recite a line of verse, like Ambrose's hymn *Deus creator omnium*. He resorts to that illustration, and to that very hymn, in his discussion of eternity and time in Book 11 of his *Confessions*. Preaching on Psalm 76, he takes a similar tack: we begin by pronouncing the first syllable, the *De-* of *Deus*. While we are pronouncing it, he would have us notice, the second syllable does not yet "exist." That second syllable can come into "existence" only at the moment when the first goes out of existence, the third only when the second no longer exists, and so on. Each succeeding syllable lives its "life," as it were, only at the price of its predecessor's "death," then itself "dies" in turn so that its successor may enjoy its momentary life (*En 76* 8). But the analysis can be pushed even further: even the very first syllable takes "time" to pronounce. Or take a one-syllable word like *est*: the "e" must have begun and ended before the "s" can be sounded. Indeed, it takes "time" to pronounce even the initial letter "e" (*En 38* 7)! Can one ever carry the analysis to such a point as to reach some absolutely elemental unit of sound that is not further divisible? The answer, Augustine aims to convince us, is no; there is no such thing as an "indivisible in-stant," a truly "stand-ing" moment in the temporal continuum.

Allow me a "science fiction" analogy for what Augustine is driving at: had we a kind of metaphysical "time camera" with which we hoped to take a snapshot of an "indivisible instant," we would be forever frustrated. For no matter how infinitesimally short we set the "exposure time," we would always be snapping a moving target; the picture would inevitably turn out blurred!

We shall have occasion to see that Augustine represents this absolutely continuous nature of temporal reality in Heraclitus' classic image of the ever-flowing river: the image implies that the hope of locating a static temporal in-stant is as illusory as trying to locate an unmoving droplet in the current of a river. The image of a river will become, accordingly, one of his favorite metaphors for temporality; indeed, almost any image of flux or flow will suggest to Augustine the transient quality, the irremediable "instability," of our temporal existence.

THE "HEAVEN OF HEAVEN"

But we noticed earlier that the "higher" spiritual beings dwelling in that invisible world are given an extraordinary privilege: they "participate" in God's own eternal unchangeableness. They dwell in what Scripture refers to as the "Heaven of Heaven": not the heaven of this "earth," this lower world, with its sun and moon and stars that any bodily eye can see, but the highest realm of that true "Heaven," that higher invisible world to which only the mind can attain. It should come as no surprise that he locates the angels as dwelling there; but Jean Pépin has shown that impressive scholars like Gilson and Guitton were mistaken in claiming the "Heaven of Heaven" was the exclusive abode of angelic spirits, for human souls dwell there as well.[5] How are we to understand that affirmation?

The most obvious answer is that human souls, after their life in the lower corporeal world, are introduced into the same beatitude as the angels enjoy: doesn't the Gospel assure us that they will be like angels in heaven? So, Augustine invariably places them there with their risen "spiritual" bodies. But when speaking of this "Heaven of Heaven," Augustine explicitly tells us that both angels and human souls "flowed down" from it: *defluxit angelus*, he exclaims, *defluxit anima hominis* (*Conf* 13.9). Did human souls, then, dwell in this contemplative bliss even *before* they entered this lower world? Pépin quotes this text, but seems to balk at drawing that obvious conclusion.

"FLOWING DOWNWARD": THE METAPHORS OF "EMANATION"

What, though, one might object, does Augustine mean by the term *defluere*? To start with, call to mind what we have already seen, that the highest reality in the lower, visible world is, for Augustine's imagination, the sun. But the sun radiates both light and heat, and the farther "down" or "away" from the sun any lower reality is situated, the less light and heat it receives; the lowest reaches of the corporeal world, then, are both its coldest and its darkest portions.

That sun metaphor, however, also operates for the entire spectrum of higher and lower worlds taken together: Augustine accepts this Neoplatonic image for the highest of realities, the One, and applies its properties to God. The Neoplatonists "pictured" the One as the source from which all lower realities "emanated," or "poured forth," much as light-beams pour downward from the sun in the visible world. This imaginative scheme sometimes conveyed the implication that the light of the sun dwindled and became less powerful the farther down it traveled: the higher world was almost sheer light, but the lower image-world displayed a spectrum of gradations of brightness, moving downward toward the ultimate darkness of non-being, or pure Matter.

This sun image, though, frequently yielded the palm to another: the One was then imagined as a "fountain" of being from which lower realities "flowed" downward—*defluxerunt*—in cascading fashion. That "flowing" image also makes it way into Augustine's thinking, but it carries peculiar resonances.

THE SPATIO-TEMPORAL "MANY"

To identify those resonances, note that below the line dividing the higher world from its shadow-image, Augustine would have us see the *multa*, the "many," his term for the manifold variety of the lower world. He does not mean to imply that the higher world was totally "one," for angels and souls are in a real sense "many." To get inside his thinking, take "many-ness" as entailing that each unit-reality is its own "proper" self, to the exclusion of each and all other realities (which are in their turn "proper selves," to the exclusion of every other); so, for instance, *this desk* is itself and necessarily *not this chair*. Such mutual exclusivity manifests itself most plainly in the world of sensible, bodily beings by the fact that each such being occupies its own "exclusive space," a "space" distinct from, "exterior to," the spaces occupied by its neighbors.

THE GRADES OF MUTUAL EXTERIORITY

Augustine would have us notice, however, that "spiritual" realities, whether angels or human souls dwelling in that higher world, are not nearly so "exterior" and mutually "exclusive" to one another as are the bodily realities of our lower world. For even if they possess bodies, as Augustine thinks they do, their bodies are so "spiritual" as to be totally transparent to one another (*SS 252* 7; *243* 5); the result is that spiritual creatures can "enter into" one another's thoughts and sentiments in an even more perfect way than our opaque and mutually impenetrable bodies permit us earth-dwelling humans to do (*InJo* 77 1–2, 4).

We humans can, of course, use language, gestures, all manner of communicative symbolisms in order to "get around" the mutual opacity, exteriority, and "exclusivity" that makes us "many." By doing so successfully, we can come to experience something *like* the intimate unity those higher creatures can naturally enjoy with one another. Although they are naturally "many," Augustine would claim that, compared to beings of our lower world, they are "more one than many"; indeed, in that higher world every "part" is equivalent to the "whole" (*Ord* 2.51). But this higher spiritual unity is even further intensified: for these beings are all contemplatively attached, adhering, cohering, to the One Eternal God, and, so, participate in the even higher form of Unity represented by His Eternity.

Now, compare this unity with the multiplicity that separates even human beings of the lower world, to say nothing of brute animals and plants and stones, and Augustine's rather blunt characterization—"the many"—makes greater sense. And to anyone who has experienced that transport of joy which can come from having entered so completely into the thoughts and sentiments of somebody wonderful and very dear that it seems as though two persons momentarily had only one mind and heart between them, Augustine's further conviction makes sense: that mutual unification and unity among beings is a more perfect state of affairs than permanent exteriority and alienation from one another. It followed, then, for both Plotinus and Augustine, that beings capable of such spiritual unification must be superior to those whose natures did not equip them for it.

The ladder of ontological perfection, then, the scale of reality from less to more perfect, runs from lesser to greater unity. The more unified a being is in itself, the more capable it is of unification with others. But, by the same token, the more self-unified a being is, the more perfectly and intensively it must be said to "exist." In image-terms, the "higher" an entity is on the ladder of being, the closer its self-unity resembles that of Plotinus' absolute One, and Augustine's God—and precisely because it is more closely united with the One Highest Reality in both men's worlds. We shall shortly see, accordingly, that in its most perfect condition a spiritual being would be so intimately united with the Eternal Source of its reality as to be itself "eternalized," its temporal distention "in-gathered" and "collected" into a perfectly concentrated "now."

But were that spiritual being somehow to snap that bond of unity and break away, as it were, it would (in a kindred sense of that term) inevitably "flow downward," *defluere*, from the Highest into the lower realm of the "many," and into the flux of temporal existence proper to that inferior world of restless multiplicity.

THE AMBIVALENCE OF "EMANATION"

At this juncture we come up against what is probably the most irreducible ambiguity in emanationist metaphysics; for the process whereby the "many" emerge from "One" can be regarded in two fundamentally antithetical ways. Most brutally put: it can be hailed as a good thing, or regretted as something that should never have happened.[6] It can be viewed optimistically, as revealing the incredible generosity of the One which is also a Goodness so unbounded that It necessarily, by the very law of Its being, "diffuses" Itself, pouring Its ontological riches outward (and downward) in a cascade of inferior realities which, at the same time, results in no diminishment of Its own perfection. Or that downward flow, that emergence of the "many," can be regarded more negatively, as resulting from some kind of "fault" on the part of those lower realities that successively turn and break away and stream downward from the One.

Plotinus employs a central term to express that fault: *tolma*. By that he means a restless, insubordinate move toward self-assertion, an "audacious" will to break away, to be and to act independently of whatever higher principle—be it the One, Noûs, or All-Soul—to which the "tolmatic" lower principle should (in some obscure sense of "should") have remained subordinate and attached. *Tolma*, therefore, prompted Noûs to break away from the One, All-Soul from Noûs, and our individual souls from All-Soul.

Plotinus was convinced that both these views, optimistic and pessimistic, rooted in Plato's own Dialogues. Let other followers

of the Master choose one view to the exclusion of the other: not
Plotinus. It is a hallmark of his personal view that he clings
resolutely to both sides of this seeming contradiction and strives
somehow to reconcile them.

There are excellent reasons for thinking that a similar tension
marks Augustine's estimate of the soul's *defluxio* from the "Heaven
of Heaven." But tension or no, we shall see that Augustine
unquestionably believed that our "downflow" from that contemplative abode was the inexorable consequence of "pride," *superbia*.
And *superbia*, as Augustine will describe it, bears more than one
resemblance to Plotinus' fault of *tolma*.

If Augustine did draw his *defluxio* image from Plotinus, he
would have felt in excellent intellectual company. But let the
Plotinian character of Augustine's theory remain a secondary issue
for the moment; our primary question should remain precisely
this: Did Augustine himself intend the image of *defluxio* to convey
the sense outlined above?

The elements we have thus far surveyed suggest a positive
answer to that question; but notice that they are all of a metaphysical order. They all follow from Augustine's view that unity as a
mark of "being" is superior to multiplicity, just as eternal being is
metaphysically superior to temporal being. In order to gauge the
complete resonances of the *defluxio* image, however, it will be
necessary to examine more closely how Augustine's image of the
physical universe eventually harmonizes with those metaphysical
evaluations. We shall be better positioned to do that somewhat
further on.

The "Grades" of Being in Scripture

Reading Scripture through the lens of this theory of being, Augustine can occasionally produce interpretations that seem curiously
baroque. Commenting on Christ's words to the apostles, for
example, "Have faith, it is I": *Fidite, ego sum* (Mt 14:27), he takes
that *sum* as implying Christ's claim that He "existed" in the
plenary, divine sense. He then proceeds to gloss that interpretation
by adducing St. Paul's declaration (2 Cor 1:19) that in Christ there
was no *Non*, only *Est*. What Paul intended was that Christ totally
"affirmed" God's promises to Israel; the Latin *est* and *non* mean
simply "yes" and "no." But Augustine's metaphysical interpretation of Exodus leads him to interpret Paul as saying that Christ,

as divine, was unalloyed "Being" without any trace of non-being (*S 75* 8)!

This same view of temporal existence will entitle Augustine to make occasional statements that initially shock. If asked the perfectly unqualified question, for instance, whether we human beings "exist," and obliged to answer yes or no, Augustine's answer is a simple "no." These changing realities all about us "so exist as not to exist" (*sic sunt ut non sint*). He senses that his auditors will find this hard to digest: *Quis ergo hoc capiat?* he exclaims (*InJo 2* 2). So, he frequently takes steps to make them more receptive to the notion. He reminds them that they are accustomed to think of things as more or less "good," so that they have no difficulty accepting what Christ meant by claiming that "No one is good, except God" (Mt 19:17). No one save God, Christ intended us to understand, is perfectly good: truly, absolutely good in the plenary sense of that term; all other realities derive what share in goodness they have from His Goodness, and must be looked on as only more or less good. But the same holds for that term "to be" or "to exist": when God gave His Name to Moses, He meant us to understand that He "IS [*est*] in such wise that in comparison with Him created things are not [*non sunt*]. For truly to be is to be unchangeably," and that is true of Him alone. "He is *est* in the same sense as [He], the Goodness of all things good, is good" (*Est enim est, sicut bonorum bonum, bonum est*) (*Enn 134* 3–4; *38* 10).

Oh, Augustine will grant, if we fail to compare our being with God's, we may feel entitled to say that we do, after all, "exist." And it is true that we exist, in a limited sense and to a certain degree. But a little reflection will make us aware that our existence is a more-or-less affair, an alloy of existence and non-existence. So the Idithun of Psalm 38 comes to perceive: looking upward contemplatively, he glimpses what truly "is." But then, turning his attention to "all the things which are below" (*infra omnia quae sunt*), he sees that "in comparison with that Being, they are not." Then, says Augustine, Idithun declares that "he himself does not exist" (*et se non esse dicebat*) (*En 38* 22).

Augustine was aware, therefore, that his hearers might find that insight into grades of be-ing hard to swallow; he had to get their minds used to the notion. A similar awareness showed in the text (*InJo 40* 9) we saw above: to illumine his hearers, Augustine objects to the logic of his own development and protests: we already exist, how can St. John say that we shall exist "more" than we do now?

But even the ablest of his modern translators seem to have suffered a comparable shock. In Book 7 of his *Confessions*, for example, Augustine is outlining the series of insights he came to after reflecting on those "platonist books" that had so enflamed him. In paragraph 16, he writes that God had "lifted [him] up" to "see" something or other, which he expresses in the phrase *ut viderem esse quod viderem*. The phrase translates literally as: "so that I saw that what I saw existed." What we have already learned suggests that one should write that *esse* in capitals: Augustine has come to an insightful understanding into God's reality as the "I am Who AM" of Exodus.

But this was precisely the sort of truth he had been unable to credit before reading the "platonists"; he had formerly been tempted to think that whatever he could not grasp through sense perceptions or imaginative images of a corporeal variety must be a "nothing" with no reality-value attached to it. Now, he assures us, he has come to the intelligible insight that a higher realm of spiritual reality, beyond what all such Manichee phantasms permitted him to attain, truly *existed*. Hence, the force of the literal translation given above; we need only trust Augustine's ability to express in accurate Latin what he means to express. God had empowered him to "see" that "what he saw existed," and, indeed, *truly* existed.

Can We Hope to "Exist"?

But Augustine adds a further phrase. He tells us that he also saw *nondum me esse qui viderem*. Trust Augustine's Latin once again, translate it literally, and he is saying that he saw "that I, who was seeing, did not yet exist." But precious few translators seem to have found such a statement making any sense; and, so, they doctor their translations by inserting all manner of qualifying—and traitorous—expressions.

One of the most frequent ploys consists in inserting (mentally) terms like *talem* or *idoneum* before that final *qui viderem*. This produces the self-contradictory translation: "so that I might see that I was not yet *such* as, or *able*, to see." But had Augustine wanted to say precisely that, he could very easily have inserted a *talem*, or an *idoneum*, himself. It is a fact that he does insert such qualifying expressions in other loci where he is depicting an "ascent" like the one he is describing here, but that does not justify our supplying such a qualifier here when Augustine quite plainly chose to omit it. Quite the contrary. We must respect the manuscript tradition and exert our minds to uncover what sense this professional *rhetor*, this trained expert in writing correct Latin, intended us to glean from the expression he deliberately chose to employ. And one should hesitate before interpreting such a careful thinker as saying that he saw what he was unable to see!

Augustine's real intention becomes plain from the moment one bears in mind his disconcerting claim about the grades of "being": he is saying that he came to see that he "did not exist" in the true and plenary sense of that term. But we must be more accurate than that: he is saying precisely he "did not *yet* exist." What can he mean by that?

THE PROMISE OF JOHN'S EPISTLE

The reference we saw to St. John's Epistle gives a glimmer of the answer: we are "promised" that we *will* "be" even "as He IS." Hence, one surmises, the force of Augustine's "not yet." Following that lead, we notice that although the spiritual creatures dwelling in the "higher" region of the *Omnia* are indeed, as Bourke points out, "naturally" susceptible to change, "should," *de jure*, be involved in change, they are, nevertheless, *de facto* unchanging.

How to explain this apparent discrepancy? As his career proceeds, Augustine must resort to a variety of shifts to justify his enduring conviction *that* the facts are so. But his explanation of *how* those creatures come to be unchanging seems to have remained fairly constant.

THE SOUL'S ORIGINAL HOME

Their dwelling place, first of all, is described in terms consistent with his *Omnia* image; it is what Psalm 113:16 refers to as the "Heaven of Heaven" (*Conf* 12.2, 9–23; 13.9). This, Augustine interprets, is not the visible "heaven" of this lower world, the "heaven of earth." To locate this "Heaven of Heaven," our eye must move upward and cross that divide setting the visible world off against the invisible. The Heaven of Heaven is not "*this* [*istud*] visible heaven, filled with luminaries of the sort these [bodily] eyes can see," but the loftiest realm of that higher world, the heaven to which only the insight of the mind can attain, "compared to which, whatever fleshly eyes can see must be called 'earth' " (*En 113*, sermon 2, 11).

It is scarcely surprising that this is the dwelling of the angels; they are undisturbedly rapt in beatific contemplation of the Divine Splendor. At the same time, Augustine's "not yet" clearly supposes that we humans, also, may aspire to that same contemplative happiness. For in the resurrection, as Matthew's Gospel puts it, we shall be "like the angels in heaven."

Just as clearly, though, Augustine refers to that abode of angels and blessed souls as God's "house" (*domus*) and equates that "house" with God's own "Eternity" (*aeternitas tua*) (*Conf* 13.13; cf. 4.31).[7] Though we are naturally mutable, accordingly, in the resurrection we shall somehow become "eternalized." How will this transformation be effected? We shall come to that question in time, but first we must more fully explore the resources of the *Omnia* image which Augustine employs to answer it.

Before we leave the topic of the "Heaven of Heaven," though, another disturbing question begs for attention. Not only does Augustine tell us that our souls, and risen bodies, *will* dwell there with the angels, but he also seems to imply that they were once originally there, and "fell" into this lower sphere of the *Omnia*. *Defluxit angelus*, he writes, *defluxit anima hominis*: "the angel flowed down, the soul of man flowed down" from that eternal dwelling (*Conf* 13.9). What can Augustine mean by this? Again, a more adequate understanding of his *Omnia* image may provide the answer.

THE LOWER WORLD OF THE "MANY"

To turn our attention once again to what lies below the line dividing higher world from lower: Augustine would have us notice the manifold variety of that lower world: the *multa*, the "many." He does not mean to imply, as we saw, that the higher world is totally "one," for angels and blessed souls are in a real sense "many"; they still preserve their individuality. And yet, their bonds of communion are far more intimate than any we humans experience in our earthly lives. Indeed, his early *De ordine* roundly declares that "in that intelligible world, each part is as though it were the whole" (2.51).

THINKING OF UNITY AND MULTIPLICITY

But his stress on the unity of the higher world is only part of a more generalized perspective; Augustine would have us beware of thinking of spiritual realities as once he strove to do: in the gross images drawn from the world of sensible reality. It is easy to understand why. We have already seen that in the spatio-temporal world of sense experience we differentiate *this* desk from *that* chair because both are extended, "diffused in space" Augustine will say, and as such mutually exclude each other from occupying the identical space. Their "otherness" from each other is one of strict mutual "exteriority." The only way they can be made "present" to each other is by being brought into such close physical contact that each of the several extended parts of one of them is contiguous with corresponding parts of the other; even then, however, extended sensible realities can be present to each other only through this "part to part" contiguity with each other. Their presence to each other is limited to their lying "alongside" each other, still mutually excluding each other, never becoming truly "one" with each other. Bodily realities, precisely as bodily, are incurably "many."

The case is different for angels, however, and also for human souls dwelling in the higher world. They are in no way so "exterior" to, so mutually exclusive of, one another as bodily realities are. Even their "celestial" or "spiritual" bodies are totally transparent (and, it would seem, interpenetrable) to one another; their "hearts" are "open" and their "consciences public" to one another (*S 252* 7); they can "comm-une," can "see" one another's "thoughts" and share one another's sentiments in a way our opaque and mutually impenetrable bodies prevent us earth-dwelling humans from doing (*S 243* 5; *InJo* 77 1–2, 4). So intimate is their community, they possess and enjoy all spiritual goods "in common" (*InJo 67* 1).

We humans, in this lower sphere of the *Omnia*, share ambiguously in the characteristics of both higher and lower worlds. When applying the omnipresence insight he learned from Plotinus, Augustine thinks of our mind-souls as present *to*, but not truly "in," our bodies (*Quant* 24.5–8). And yet, he also employs a whole distinct register of images depicting the body as a "vestment" or "dwelling" surrounding the soul. In this image-register, Augustine imagines us as "wearing" or "carrying about" bodies that "cloak" our thoughts and sentiments from one another; this is why we can lie and deceive one another (*SS 252* 7, *166* 2; *InJo 23* 10). Further, we can selfishly choose to ap-propriate the material objects of our enjoyment and make them our "own" (*proprium*), our "private" possession; we can jealously refuse to share them, can refuse to raise the sights of our affection to the spiritual goods that can be shared in "common" without reducing the portion possessed by each of the sharers (*SS 28* 1–5; *47* 30; *85* 6). We can, in short, choose to remain "many" rather than strive to become one. Or we can redirect our love to those spiritual goods like mutual understanding, peace (*S 357* 1–2), wisdom (*En 75* 17–18), and, above all, the God Who can supereminently be "enjoyed" in common (*S 28* 5; *InJo 13* 5). Even in our earthly condition, we can use language, gestures, all manner of communicative symbolism in order to "get around" the mutual opacity and exteriority that makes us "many" (*InJo 23* 8–9). If we succeed, we can come to experience something *like* the intimate unity of minds and hearts those higher creatures enjoy with one another. All of this supposes, of course, Augustine's tacit conviction that mutual unification and "community" of beings is a more perfect state of affairs than permanent exteriority and alienation from one another.

But again, one of Augustine's central concerns in all such discussions is to warn us not to apply the kind of thinking appropriate to bodily realities when striving to understand how soul is present to body, or, more generally, how any reality from the higher spiritual world can be present to the realities of the lower, visible world. For the power those higher beings have of unifying with, being "present" to, one another, and indeed to all their fellows at once, is paralleled by their power of being present, and totally, undividedly present, to each and every being of the lower world. This is sublimely true of God.

How to Think About the Omnipresent and the World

Here we come to the dominant motive for Augustine's meditations on such questions. He is eager to help us think correctly about that relationship which had long baffled him: God's "integral Omnipresence" to His creation. He raises that problem in the opening pages of his *Confessions*, comes back to it repeatedly, and claims to have resolved it only with the aid of those "platonist" readings he did at Milan (*Conf* 7.16–26).

The fundamental flaw in his previous thinking, he tells us there, had been to think of the relationship between God and the other beings of the created *Omnia* as the Manichees implicitly encouraged him to "imagine" it: in terms appropriate to bodies that are extended, "diffused in space." For anyone employing this style of thinking, whatever is "real" must be spatially extended; talk about "spiritual" realities as having no such extension, and the Manichee hooted that you must be talking about a "nothing." So, Augustine imagined Divinity as a gigantic ocean of Light, bounded by the evil realm of Darkness which cut into it like a quarter-slice of cosmic pie.

How to Think About Good and Evil

This cast of thought in turn related to the central issue that had originally made him, and subsequently kept him so long, a Manichee: image-thinking induced him to picture Evil as a sub-stantial reality over against Divinity, and to picture the "presence" of Divinity to its Evil counterpart in terms of spatial, part-to-part juxtaposition. The crucial art his "platonist" readings taught Augustine was that of thinking of spiritual realities in more appropriate terms. By doing so, they enabled him to think of God's "presence" to His creatures as an "integral omnipresence": He is present *integrally*, that is, with the totality of His Being, both to the created universe as a whole and to every single one of His creatures in both higher and lower worlds (*SS 12* 12, *120* 2; *Enn 94* 2, *138* 10–12; *InJo 2* 10, *35* 4, etc.).

But the same thing is true of the angels' presence to the individual beings of the sense-world: the angel has no need to be present to one such being in a way that excludes its presence to others, even to all others. A similar law holds for human souls even while they are dwelling in this lower world: though in some mysterious way they have committed themselves to be especially present and attentive to one individual body, they are "integrally omnipresent" to every part of that body (*Quant* 58–63; *S 256* 7)!

Observe, however, the careful turn of phrase: a spiritual creature can be present *to* its various inferior bodily counterparts, but precisely on condition that it never becomes present *in* that body. Perhaps a somewhat crude comparison will help: the sun of our solar system can illumine each of the planets only on condition that it "keep its distance" from all of them; it must never come so close as to devote itself exclusively, so to speak, to one of them to the exclusion of the others. In a phrase Augustine loves to repeat, the Omnipresent must, to be truly omni-present, "remain in

Itself" (*manere in seipsa*) (*S 117* 3; *Enn 33*, sermon 2, 6; *138* 8). To
be truly "immanent"—integrally present to each and all—It must
at the same time be thoroughly "transcendent": ontologically
"above and beyond" each and all.

THE SOUL'S IDEAL "MID-POSITION"

This notion of "immanence from a distance," as it were, helps to
understand how Augustine depicts the soul's ideal position in the
hierarchy of reality. Inferior in nature only to God, and superior
to lower, corporeal realities, the soul was established in the beginning in an appropriate "mid-rank" position "below" God and
"above" the world of bodies. It was God's creative intention that
it remain so. Gazing upward toward the Divine Splendor in a
contemplation that filled it with bliss, it was to exercise, at the
same time, the "active" function of governing the entire sensible
universe below it, without that governing activity's ever being able
to distract it from its contemplation! Had it remained subject to
God, the total sensible universe would have remained subject to its
ruling power; the soul would, in the phrase from Genesis, enjoy
"dominion" over all lower creation. One can see why, in this ideal
situation, the soul's doing what it *ought* would perfectly coincide
with doing what it most profoundly *desired*, doing what made it
happy (cf. *Lib* 1.30–32).

THE SOUL'S INSUBORDINATION: AVERSION AND INVERSION

But the soul had the power of choosing to close the "distance"
between it and the sense-world, which it ruled most effectively by
ruling it "in common" with other souls and "from afar." Such a
choice is tantamount to abandoning its total contemplative ab-
sorption with, its complete subjection to, God; it implies that the
soul has yielded to an "audacious" desire to "appropriate" some
single "part" of the sense-world—this or that body, say—and
make it a kind of kingdom of its "very own" (*proprium*). That
"appropriated" portion of the sense universe the soul would aspire
to rule "on its own" and "out of its own power," no longer
subordinate to God: the soul, in effect, has striven to become its
own "God," imitating Him "perversely" in that bid for independence and self-supremacy. The ironic result of this "per-version,"
Augustine tells us, is an "in-version"—the soul has quite literally
turned things upside down: no longer subject to the God above it,

it finds to its dismay that realities below it—beasts and plants, even the body it has fastened on as its "very own"—no longer remain subject to the ruling power it once so easily exercised over them.[8]

THE PARADOXES OF OMNIPRESENCE

The seeming paradox, that genuine immanence requires equally genuine transcendence, Augustine delights in orchestrating with all manner of striking expressions: God remains present to us even when we have turned our backs and chosen to be absent from Him. He is never far from us, even when we wander off, far from Him; we may try to flee, but we can only flee from a loving God to that same God, but angry (*S 69* 4; *Enn 94* 2, *74* 9, *138* 10–11, etc.). Had Augustine held on to only the former member of such phrases, stressing God's nearness, then God's presence to every item in the lower world would have obliged him to scrap the image of the universe represented in our opening diagram: all images and notions of "distance" and "separation" would have to be banished from our thinking; depicting God as "on high" and the "lowest and last" of beings as "furthest down" the ontological scale would involve us in sheer metaphysical nonsense.

But keep both ends of the Omnipresence paradox intact, and the above diagram visually represents a side of Augustine's thought that he never tires of calling to our minds: that we are truly alienated from God, "far" from Him, not spatially, but in terms of our hearts' loves, our deepest affections. We must devote a special chapter to Augustine's most fundamental image of human life as a *peregrinatio*, a "wandering away" from, and "wayfaring" back to, God. There, we shall see that he attributes our alienation to our having chosen to love "earth" and things "earthy," and so been confined to this earthy lower world, this "region of unlikeness" to God.

Augustine constantly reminds us that this "distancing" from God must not be understood spatially: the spatial separations in his imaginative diagram of the universe are intended to *mean* and be *understood* as suggesting this spiritual and moral "distance." He does not want us to be tricked and led astray by such spatial, bodily images; and yet, his practice implicitly admits, and his theoretical works explain why, we "fallen" humans need to convey and receive our notions of the spiritual through just such bodily imagery (*Mor* 1.11; *Ver* 79).

The result is ironical: few philosophical thinkers have more fervently warned their readers and hearers against the dangers of thinking about spiritual realities by using corporeal imagery, but none has ever surpassed Augustine in extravagantly exploiting the power of such imagery. And it is by wielding that imagery, by fleshing out the bones of his metaphysics with stirring evocations of the earthly landscape of our human everydays, that Augustine so often succeeds in touching our hearts, playing masterfully on our fears and dreams and aspirations, electrifying us with the very same *feel* he has for the world about him.

The "Weighted" Universe

One of the most pervasive images Augustine applies to the sensible world is drawn from the ancients' way of depicting the physical arrangement of the bodily realities about them. They looked out and saw how stones and mud would sink to the bottom of ponds and lakes, felt the airy breezes brush their hair and cheeks, beheld far above them the sun by day and the burning stars by night. Stones and mud, they generalized, had "earth" as their dominating element; earth was heavier than water, and so it was natural that earth-dominated things should sink and settle at the bottom of that lighter element. But water in its turn was heavier than air, and air in its turn heavier than fire; hence, the general distribution of physical realities we all can see: the fiery sun and stars above the rest, the slightly heavier air below those fiery realities, water at the next tier down, and finally, last and lowest of all, earthy realities. In ways this scheme anticipated what the science of a later epoch came to call "specific gravity"; Aristotle expressed it rather more simply by saying that the physical universe was arranged in accord with the "weights" of its various elements (*De caelo* 3–4), and regularly counted those elements as four: fire, air, water, and earth. Each of those elements possessed a property specifically characterizing it: fire possessed heat; air possessed dryness; water, dampness, and earth, cold.

Augustine accepted this version of the physical universe, along with the somewhat anthropomorphic manner the ancients had of describing its operations: they often projected an almost human psychological drive into the physical elements, an "appetite" that stirred each element to "seek its proper place," move upward or downward toward its "natural" place of "rest."

Readers of the *Confessions* will recall Augustine's vivid evocation of this physical picture in paragraph 10 of Book 13. Every physical body, he reminds us, "tends by its weight" to its proper "place." For "weight" should be thought of as merely bringing things down, not to the "lowest" realm, to the *ima*, but to the place appropriate to them. "Fire," for example, "tends upward, a stone downward: they are acted upon by their weights [*ponderibus suis aguntur*] and seek the places that are theirs. When less well-ordered [*minus ordinata*], they are restless [*inquieta*]; brought to good order, they come to rest": *quiescunt*.

Immediately Augustine makes that famous application to the spiritual world: "My weight is my love; by it I am borne to wherever I am borne": if our love be earthy, we are borne downward to be "ordered" among earthly realities; but if the Holy Spirit "enflames" us, "sets us on fire," alters our spiritual "weight," we are borne upward until we come to "rest" on high, where we truly belong. For our presence among earthly realities is an "ordered" presence, perfectly appropriate to the "weight" of our earthly love; but here we are *minus ordinata*, "less well ordered" than we should be, since our love itself is not an "ordered" love. Our "proper" place is on high, among those spiritual realities; only there can we be "well-ordered" and ever find genuine "rest." Here, needless to say, we have the background image for understanding the "restless heart" motif (*inquietum cor*) which peals through the opening bars of the *Confessions*.

Augustine's preaching plays upon this physical metaphor repeatedly (e.g., *SS 125* 5, *217* 2–3; *Enn 7* 19, *51* 10, *93* 16; *InJo 1* 13–15). Indeed, there comes a moment when his habitual appeal to it seems to trouble him: it may furnish arms to the enemies of the resurrection of our bodies (*S 242* 5–10)! But the implications of this "weight" image will bear closer examination.

CHANGE, ACTIVITY, AND RESTLESSNESS

First of all, it becomes clearer now how "motion," meaning any sort of change, came for Augustine's mind to be symptomatic of "restlessness," of the changing being's "disquiet" at not being in its natural place of "rest." The whole point of motion was, for him, to arrive at fulfillment, at the satisfaction of desire which was "rest." And since all "action" implied change, and every changing being "took time" to move from one place or state to another, he came to associate the very fact of being in time with a restless "busy-ness" (*neg-otium*), an immersion in "action" which negated the "rest" (*quies, requies*) toward which action tended by its very nature. Since all activity is naturally ordained toward "rest," then it follows that wise human beings will direct all their *negotium* toward enjoying philosophical "leisure" (*otium*) and contemplative "stillness" (*vacatio*).

Augustine's strongest statement of this idea-complex may be found in his *De vera religione* 65, but it threads its insistent way through his preaching as well. Its influence is as pervasive as its applications are varied. It inspires his interpretations of the Martha–Mary story (*S 103* 3–6), the Transfiguration scene (*S 78* 3), the Sabbath "rest" (*S 8*, 4), the "peace" required for hearkening to the Word (*En 84* 10), the "vision" that lies at the term of our earthly *peregrinatio* (*En 146* 4), the meaning of death (*En 114* 6), and the radical contrast between "this" life and the immortal life we must long for: "one" is a life of "faith, the other of vision, one a *peregrinatio* through time, the other an abode in eternity, one a life of toil, the other of rest . . . one engaged in the work of action, the other reaping the reward of contemplation . . ." (*InJo 124* 5).

Those contrasts, finally, provide a series of clues for unlocking one of the hidden dynamics at work in the second phase of his Milanese conversion, from the *negotium* of secular "action" to the *otium* and *vacatio* of the contemplative life, which Augustine describes in Book 8 of the *Confessions*. But it also illuminates aspects of that conversion's necessary prolongations, all of which lead up to the rapturous anticipation of our Eternal Sabbath "rest" in Book 13. Significantly, the *Confessions* begins with the private plaints of a "restless" individual soul and ends with a hymn to the common "rest" promised all the saved.

CHANGE, DEATH, AND NOTHINGNESS

But we have not finished with Augustine's evaluation of change. We have seen that it implies, for him, that the changing being must be an ever-shifting alloy of being and non-being. But alongside his conceptualization of it, Augustine has several ways of imagining this non-being: he envisages it as a "death" (*mors*) from which change emerges and into which it passes (*InJo 38* 10). In another image, it implies a kind of void or hollowness (*inane*), nesting at the very core of changeable realities, an inner emptiness imagined as a kind of residual symptom of the "nothingness" from which God created them (*Enn 123* 5; *118*, sermon 24, 6).

Emilie Zum Brunn, in her careful study of the *nihil* idea in Augustine, shows how he figures sin as a descent away from God, the Highest,[9] a descent that would logically terminate in nothingness, but is inhibited from doing so by the power of the being's God-given form. Despite that inhibition, however, she translates the term *inanescere*, which Augustine regularly uses in this connection, by the French "s'anéantiser." I suggest that "se vider" or "s'évacuer" would be more faithful to the image Augustine is employing; for in its fall from the Eternal God into the temporal world the sinful soul does actually "empty itself," "spill forth" its interior riches (*projecit intima sua*) (Eccli 10:10), though never so completely as to "nothing-ize" ("s'anéantir") itself.

Vanitas

For these connected reasons, all changeable beings are, to Augustine's eyes, *vanitas*. When compared to the solid durability of *Veritas*, they are ephemeral and radically insubstantial (*S 157* 4–5; *En 143* 11). From that, it is an easy step to viewing them as sham realities, illusory, to be valued only by persons who are equally "vain." *Vanitas vanitantium* read the earlier translation of Ecclesiastes 1:2 which Augustine long favored, "vanity of those who are vain," empty things that only the empty would take seriously.[10] That same text encourages him to situate those vanities in terms of his cosmic image, for Ecclesiastes tells us that they are all *sub sole*, "under the sun," just as the *Omnia* image requires. It comes as no surprise, then, that those who are *graves corde*, "heart-heavy" by reason of earthy affections, are attached to these "lowest" of realities (*Enn 4* 3, *118*, sermon 12, 1).

His favorite images compare "vain" or "empty" realities to a mere shadow, a vapor, or a smoke-cloud; however large and pseudo-impressive they may seem, we quickly realize they are all "mendacious" kinds of "nothing," outwardly pretentious but without the slightest "inner" solidity to them (*En 61* 15–16). That image becomes a versatile one, moreover, applying not only to changing beings (*En 143*, 11), but also to idols (*En 36*, sermon 2, 12), spiritual phenomena like lying (*S 231* 4, *En 61* 15), pride (*S 22* 8), and sin more generally (*InJo 1* 13), as well as to the humans who exhibit all such traits. All these Augustine views as profoundly illusory, posing as what they "are not"; they are sheer façade with nothing of substance behind them.

Vanitas, EXTENSION, AND DISTENTION

That image of inner vacuity parading as pretentious grandeur readily associates with Augustine's depreciation of all spatial extension as a kind of *tumor* (*Quant* 24), whereas temporal "distention" assumes the guise of a "swelling outward" (*foras*) (*Conf* 11.39) which manifests comparable insinuations of "sickness." Central to his *De quantitate animae* is the insight (70–79) that the soul's true *quantitas*, true "greatness," lies neither in spatial extension nor in temporal distention, which are both dismissed as illusory, as connected species of the "weaker greatness" of Plotinus' paradox. But his favorite target for the *tumor* epithet is unquestionably pride; for what is more truly a diseased tumor than this distended self-inflation of a creature made from nothing, yet pretending to be God?

THE INSUBSTANTIAL SPIDER

Psalm 38 suggests the "spider" as still another symbol of vanity, the reason being, Augustine explains, that spiders (as he knew them, anyway) collapse under the slightest pressure and disintegrate—they prove to be as insubstantial as their webs (*Enn 122* 6, *38* 17–18). And so have our souls become in their fall from God. For "when first created [*conditus*], man was made to become like [*similis factus est*] the *Veritas*," Which is "ever enduring and never failing"; but through sinning he has "become" or "been made" (*similis factus est*) like the vanities, "gliding and flowing by," which now surround him in this world "under the sun." In vain, accordingly, do we seek among them the beatitude we can find only in that higher world of Truth (*Enn 143* 11; *118*, sermon 12, 1).

VANITY *vs.* VERITY, FLUX *vs.* SOLIDITY

Over against this insubstantiality of changing reality, Augustine loves to depict Truth, meaning the Divine Word in the higher world, as solid, supportive, a genuine "firm-ament" on which to rely and take one's "stand" (*Enn 1* 4, *24* 14, *121* 3, 6). And so we have come back to the characterization of True Being as "stable" and "enduring," but by another imaginative route than we took previously. The confluence of those two paths, however, one starting from the transitoriness of change, the other from the radical insubstantiality it betrays, helps us appreciate the aptness of another of Augustine's cherished images: that changing reality is a "river" (*flumen, fluvius*) incessantly flowing (*En 136* 3–4), or an ocean "flood" (*fluctus*) restlessly heaving and subsiding (*SS 76* 1, *251* 3; *En 23* 2). Both river and ocean images capture simultaneously the transitory quality of time, along with the lack of solidity proper to changing realities: what man with any sense would expect to "stand still" in, and receive "firm support" from, the waters of a river or the waves of the sea?

But the sea image adds the further note of risk and menace, storm and shipwreck (*SS 75* 2, *63* 1–2). The saltiness of sea water, moreover, makes it an excellent symbol for the "embittered" spirit (*amaricans*) of those who have plunged into it (*En 32*, version 2, sermon 2, 10).[11]

Defluxio: "FLOWING DOWNWARD"

We have already seen how that term *fluere*, to "flow," can appear in the compound form *defluere*. We have seen, as well, two of its metaphysical implications: *defluxio* imports a diminishment in the soul's unity and very "be-ing," and a fall from its "adhesion" to the Eternal One to a wearisome pursuit of the temporal "many." But now we are in a better position to appreciate its more physical and imaginative implications. The term means to "flow downward," and suggests the kind of "liquefaction" whereby a "solid" reality loses its solidity, so that it then pours downward from some higher position onto, or into, what formerly lay below it. In this way, souls, in love with mortal realities, "flowed down" into the regime of mortality (*En 51* 2).

Augustine can be ultra-vivid in explaining this image of *defluxio*. *Defluxit terra*, says Psalm 74:4. "Why does it flow downward," Augustine asks, "except on account of sins [*peccata*]? For that reason they are called *delicta*, for *delinquere* connotes a downflow from some liquid [state] or other, down, that is, from the stability of the firmament [*firmamentum*] of virtue and justice. . . ." That image of *firmamentum* throws him slightly off stride for a moment: it is, he tells us, as though the foundations (*fundamenta*) had suddenly been removed, and some building formerly supported on them plunged downward through the hole left by their removal

(*et aliquid . . . hiatu quodam demersum est*). But the next moment
sees him back on the original track: think of liquefaction as a
sudden seizure of weakness—even we moderns say, for example,
"I felt my knees turn to water"—then "Just as love for higher
things strengthens the soul, so does lust for lower things liquefy
it" (*En 74* 6).

And so it was with us: we were once (*olim*) told to "do no
iniquity," but we "did not heed [that command], we fell, we
became mortals, were born as mortals" (*defluxit terra*) (*En 74* 7).
Facti, geniti: Augustine's choice of words makes it clear that we
had *olim*, "once," been other than the mortals we "became" in
consequence of our "delinquency." For (to combine the two
images he employs here) we were once supported, "stabilized,"
by that "stable firmament" which is divine "Truth and Power,"
His strength and solidity communicated to us by reason of our
love for the "higher things" of that upper world; but somehow
the lust (*cupiditas*) for "lower things" came over us, "liquefied" us,
and we "flowed downward" into this inferior region of "mortality" (*En 74* 7).

But that "becoming" mortal somehow coincides with our
having been "born" or "begotten" (*geniti*) from Adam, or from
Adam and Eve. For "no human of that mass of mortals which
flowed down [*defluxit*] from Adam" (*S 176* 2) or "flowed forth
[*profluens*] from Adam and Eve" (*En 70*, sermon 1, 15), can claim
innocence of sin. Again and again, when he is speaking of our
fall, that image of "flux" leaps to Augustine's mind. "Behold how
the human race flowed forth [*fluxisse*] from the death of that first
man" (*S 153* 14).

The movement of *defluxio*, therefore, is a movement of "fall"
from the ontological solidity and stability we once enjoyed amid
"higher" realities into the flux and *fluvium* of mortal, temporal
existence. As such, it associates closely with the image Augustine
embodies in the term *labi*: a once "standing" and "stable" being
has somehow become a reality "falling" and "fallen" (*labens,
lapsus*) and, consequently, "labile" (*labile*); having "slipped down"
from the lofty firmament, it now slides and glides its slippery way
through time (*En 72* 8). And both expressions connote that we
who once possessed the God Who is "stable" and One now chase
wearily after the passing "many."

CONTINENCE, CHASTITY, AND RETURN FROM *Defluxio*

That antithesis between the One and the many becomes the leitmotif in Augustine's prayers for "continence." For he thinks of continence, on one level of his understanding of it, as the virtue that delivers us from the fragmented mode of being into which our primordial *defluxio* has poured us, and restores us to the contemplative collectedness we once enjoyed. But, the Book of Wisdom (8:21) pointedly reminds us, continence is God's gift; no one can be continent without receiving it as a gift (*Conf* 10.40; *SS 160* 7, *283* 1–2). This prompts Augustine, on another level of interpretation, to look on *Continentia* as a hypostatic reality that, on closer inspection, is identical with the divine *Virtus* God gave us, the Eternal Son Who is (in Paul's phrase: 1 Cor 1:24) God's *Virtus et Sapientia* and is symbolized as God's "right hand" (*dextera*) (*Conf* 10.42, 65–66). Continence, then, is simultaneously a virtue that we possess and the effect of God's *dextera* "gathering" or "collecting" our splintered being into one.

In any case, continence seems at once closely related to, and yet distinct from, "chastity," as Augustine subtly implies by confessing that he used to pray both for "chastity *and* continence, but not yet" (*Conf* 8.17) For continence seems to include (while also extending more broadly than) chastity (*Conf* 6.1). Augustine, as we know, attributes the soul's *defluxio* to the triad of sins St. John speaks of in his First Epistle as "concupiscence of the flesh, concupiscence of the eyes, and secular ambition"; he envisages chastity as aiming at repairing the effects of fleshly concupiscence, whereas the healing powers of continence appear to extend to the effects of all three sins in the triad (*Conf* 10.41, 66). Hence, he can refer to continence as a generalized "turn away from evil" (*S 108* 2). True, Augustine frequently blames our *defluxio* from on high on "concupiscence," while also depicting unchastity in images of "flow" and "outflow" whose sexual associations are quite transparent (*Enn 74* 6, *77* 13; *InJo 15* 16). But he sees it as equally true that pride and "curiosity" also succeed in spiritually distending us, deflecting our love from the "One" and consequently "scattering" our interior riches in greedy pursuit of the "many" (*Conf* 10. 65–66). Thus, continence brings us back to love of the One God from the generalized "love of this *saeculum*," from clinging to the temporal many instead of to the One God (*Conf* 13.29; *S 125* 7,

9, 11). The same association in distinction is conveyed by Augustine's explanation of the term *fornicatio*; for there is a generalized "spiritual" type of fornication which consists in loving the "many" in preference to God, and continence delivers us from this. But he more regularly thinks of the "special" kind of fornication, involving the body and fleshly concupiscence, as a sub-class of the above, and chastity's task is to deliver us from it (*S 343* 7, 9).

This association of *defluxio* with the "many" precisely as many accounts for the need Augustine expresses in his *Confessions* to have his "scattered [powers]," those *intima viscera*, "gathered together" (*colligar*) (10.65, 11.39, 12.23) so that "cleansed and liquefied by the fire of [God's] love" he may "flow back together" from his scattered state (*donec in Te confluam purgatus et liquidus igne amoris Tui*) (11.39). But the original physical logic of the imagery immediately reasserts itself: that unifying "liquefaction" is preliminary to his becoming "stable" and "solid" in the divine Truth (*stabo atque solidabor in Te*) (11.40). For while the fallen soul begins its ascent from its "earthy" condition, and moves "upward" as it were through the watery "clouds" into the upper "air" of the spiritual world toward the Divine "Fire" which has warmed and lightened it for that ascent, Augustine can picture its ultimate destination as that higher and heavenly "earth" which Scripture calls the *terra viventium*—not the lower earth proper to "mortals," but the "land" (or earth) of the "living" (*En 26*, version 2, 22). This is the *terra* promised to the "meek," and it is equivalent to that pristine *stabilitas in Deo* which our souls lost by sinning (*En 1* 4).[12]

The *Confessions* fills out this picture generously. The soul's *defluxio* is toward "these" (*ista*) beings of the lower world (12.10; cf. 13.2–3); it is prompted by a paradoxical "desire for cares" (*amore curarum*) (13.8) and "wretched disquiet" (13.9) that Augustine regularly associates with the life of "action," among the "many things" Martha was concerned with (*SS 103, 104*); it prompts the soul's departure from the "Heaven of Heaven" where its contemplative union with God in "chaste love" placed it in a rest (*requiescat*) beyond all change (12.19), beyond all care and disquiet (13.9). That portion of the "Heaven of Heaven" which remained in contemplative bliss would itself have yielded to its natural tendency toward "vagabond *deliquia*" had it not been converted to the radiance of the Divine Splendor (13.6, 9). But, clearly, some portion of that "Heaven of Heaven" did fall, and it included both "the angel" and (mysterious phrase) the "human soul" (13.9). We are left to glean occasional hints about the precise relationship of our fallen souls with the fallen Adam, but once again it would appear that Adam stands for the entire human (or human-to-be) portion of the Heaven of Heaven which fell, and that we subsequent humans came forth from his loins in the course of history. Thus, Augustine can say that "had Adam not fallen, the saltiness of the sea" which stands for embittered sinful humanity "would not have poured forth from his womb" (*non diffunderetur ex utero eius*) (13.28).

Defluxio FROM THE HEAVEN OF HEAVEN

Here, then, we have finally assembled the materials for answering the question that, we saw above, Jean Pépin for some reason left hanging: What does Augustine mean by saying that "angel" and the "soul of man" both "flowed downward" from the Heaven of Heaven? It is clear, first of all, that Augustine describes the Heaven of Heaven as a "community of holy spirits" whose natural tendency to change has been neutralized by their timeless contemplation of the timeless God (12.19–21). We have already seen that when first "created" (*conditus*) man underwent a transformation that "made" him "become like" the unchanging Truth he gazed upon (*Veritati similis factus est*) (*En 143* 11). But *defluxit angelus, defluxit anima hominis*. Now Augustine is telling us that change somehow inserted itself into angels and human souls—or *the* (collective) human soul?—and they "flowed downward" into the realm of time and constant flux; they fell from eternity into time. For while terms like *labi* and *cadere* can express the notion of a "fall" in its most general sense (*SS 96* 2, *142* 2–4; *Enn 93* 19, *134* 26), Augustine's preaching and his *Confessions* harmonize in showing that *defluxio* is one of his favorite ways of characterizing that fall precisely inasmuch as it brings the soul down from eternity into time, from unity in-gathered to splintered multiplicity, from the restful and unchanging contemplation of the One God to the care-ridden life of action among the inferior and temporal "many." From the metaphysical point of view, we saw earlier, that descent implies a diminishment in the soul's very "being." But now we are in a position to appreciate how Augustine "images" that diminishment: the density, the ontological "solidity" that the soul formerly derived from its adherence to Eternal Truth, becomes "weakened," "liquefied"— thinned out, as it were, into a solution blending the being and non-being of changingness. Like a once-brilliant color paled by dilution, the soul now exists in a less intensive way than formerly.

Number, Weight, and Order

It should be remarked that in all Augustine's characterizations of inferior, changing reality, bodies "naturally" tended to act the way they acted; it was a characteristic that went with the very "nature" of earth as earth, fire as fire, and so forth. A Christian thinker like Augustine would briskly draw the conclusion that God, the creative Author of all such natures, had implanted those tendencies so that everything should act in a regular manner and so contribute to our dwelling in an "order-ly" universe. Didn't the Bible assure us that God had disposed everything in accord with "number, measure, and weight"?[13]

That notion of "order" held a powerful fascination for Augustine. "God loves order; He truly loves it" (*Ord* 1.17): Augustine would have found it utterly sacrilegious to suggest that the universe could be less than perfectly ordered, for the "order" God loves is none other than the "Order," with a capital "O," which is Augustine's code-name for the creative Word "through Whom all things were made."[14] Only a flawlessly ordered universe could worthily reflect the beauty of God's Eternal Son.

That notion of order, then, from Augustine's earliest post-conversion writings, has an unmistakable religious and ethico-religious flavor. Hence, the strength of his conviction not only that it is a *fact* that all things operate in orderly fashion, but also that it is *best* for them so to operate, and, further, it is the way they *ought* to operate. And since Augustine thought of the order of our universe as hierarchical, consisting, that is, of grades of being ideally arranged with those of superior being-quality and worth "above" their inferiors, it was a small step to conclude that it was for the best that "higher" beings should govern and direct those "below," and inferior beings remain "subject" and "subordinate" to their superiors (*SS 214* 2, *37* 23; *Enn 7* 19, *51* 10; *InJo 1* 13–15). Thus, it went without saying that all creatures ought to accept their subjection to God the Highest, while creatures proper to the lower world, like the human body, ought to remain subject to the command of their immediate superior, the spiritual soul (*SS 273* 1, *169* 1; *InJo 2* 14, *23* 5). And since the soul is naturally the equal of the angels in dignity (having become their inferior only by reason of its having sinned), its only rightful superior is God Himself (*Quant* 78).

THE PHYSICS, PSYCHOLOGY, AND ETHICS OF "WEIGHTS"

But one might object that value-terms like "best," "should," and "ought" are more appropriate to ethical discussion than to physics. For to "act for the best" ordinarily implies that the agent has some "view" of what is best and "intends" to attain or achieve it by his or her action; similarly, to "do what one ought" ordinarily implies that one "sees" where one's "duty" lies and "intends" to fulfill it by this or that action (or abstention from action, as the case may be). Terms like these suppose, accordingly, that the agents being talked about are conscious, reflective, and able to deliberate about their actions, adapting means toward the achievement of ends-in-view. Such ethical discussion further supposes, ordinarily at least, that the agents involved are to some extent "free" to choose one course of action over its competitors. We instinctively hold such agents accountable for their actions, saying, for instance, that they "should have done 'x' rather than 'y' "; we consider some of their actions "praise-worthy" but others of them "blame-worthy."

This is not the place to test the truth of the various suppositions alluded to above; the point for now is this: that Augustine accepted all those suppositions, that ethical agents are reflective, deliberative, free, and accountable. But the motion of stones and fire, air and water, he knew, was "spontaneous, as it were, without mind or sense knowledge" to goad or guide it (*En 29*, version 2, 10). Such beings move into action without either consciousness or deliberation; they are "determined" by their very natures to act in set and necessary ways. And yet, he adopts this physical model with all its deterministic overtones and boldly transposes it in order to portray the actions of free and conscious ethical agents.

METAPHOR AND "SPIRITUAL INTERPRETATION"

In making that transposition, Augustine frequently warns us that he is giving a "spiritual interpretation," or, as we might prefer to put it, he is speaking only "metaphorically." We do much the same thing when we first use a "simile," for example, "he came at me like a lion," and in the next breath eliminate the "like" and so make the simile a "metaphor": "But he was a real lion, I tell you, a *real lion!*" Neither we nor our hearer is deceived by this process. We both understand the expression to convey the frightening ferocity, say, of the onslaught being described. We do not go on to assume that the man in question had four legs and a flying mane. We do not, in other words, usually take a metaphor "literally"; we quite readily "see" that it implies a certain likeness or set of likenesses between the man and the lion, but a certain unlikeness as well. Every metaphor, like every analogy, "limps" a bit; it implies a kind of "sameness," but it always admits of a kind of "difference" too.

But we have known people who are apt to take our metaphors "literally"; when they do, we are tempted to exclaim, "Oh, don't be so literal-minded!" We also know of cases where an expression was coined as a metaphor at some time in the past, and we can employ it without consciously adverting to its metaphorical character. "He really has an earthy sense of humor," we can say, and scarcely advert to why, and with what implications, that term "earthy" originally came to function in the context of describing a person's manners, tastes, or sense of humor. And, whether we know it or not, we may be just one step away from forgetting that the metaphor is a metaphor, and on the brink (another metaphor!) of taking it literally.

These were among the dangers Augustine was courting when he adopted the image of the "weighted universe" of ancient physics and applied it to the world of free ethical agents. We can take him more "literally" than he meant to be taken; or, conversely, he could slip inadvertently into forgetting his metaphor was exactly that, and begin to take the wrong aspects of it more literally than he should have. We must stay alert to both those dangers in what follows.

"WEIGHTS" AND THE SPIRITUAL WORLD

How, then, does Augustine make his transposition of the "weighted world" of physics apply to the actions of spiritual creatures? Consider the metaphor of "earthiness" mentioned above; then combine it with a commonplace of ancient thought: that every lover becomes "like" his or her "beloved." Augustine frequently depicts love as a way of becoming "attached" or "glued" to, of "adhering" or "sticking" to, the beloved person or object (*Enn 62* 17, *121* 1; *Trin* 10.11). In a further step, he imagines love as an "umbilical" bond (*Conf* 2.8), so that the process of "becoming like" the beloved begins to suggest a kind of "union by osmosis" whereby the natural characteristics of the beloved being seep into and become characteristics of the lover. "Each of us is such [*talis*] as his love is. Do you love earth? Then earth you will be. Do you love God? What shall I say, that you will be God?" Yes, indeed, Augustine replies, for Scripture says no less than that. Love God, therefore, "and as God is eternal, you will abide eternally also" (*sic et vos maneatis in aeternum*) (*EpJo 2* 14; *Trin* 11.5; *En 96* 10).

This transforming power of love, then, can turn the soul into a cosmic voyager, moving up and down the scale of being depending on the level at which it fixes its dominant affections. Thus, Augustine tells his hearers, impure love "summons the soul to a desire of earthly goods . . . and plunges it down toward the lowest of realities . . . whereas holy love lifts the soul and inflames it toward higher, eternal things" (*En 121* 1). Hence, he can counsel them, "Yoke yourself [*junge te*] to God's eternity . . . for when your heart sticks [*adhaeserit*] to the Highest, all mortal realities will be below you" (*En 91* 10). And since, as we have seen, "higher" realities exist in a more intensive way than their lower counterparts, it follows that we ourselves "exist" in lesser or greater fashion depending on the being-quality of the realities we most love. Love earthly realities, accordingly, and you take on the "weight" of those realities: you necessarily plunge downward to the lowest possible level of existence, just this side of sheer nothingness. But fix your love on God, the Sun of the spiritual world, and His "heat" will "warm" you, set you aflame and thereby make you as "light" as those tongues of fire we see always leaping upward to regain their natural place alongside the sun and burning stars; the "ardor" of your loving desire for union with God will make you soar upward (*SS 234* 3, *170* 11; *En 83* 10). Ultimately, you will "cleave" or "stick" to God, become osmotically transformed by God's own Unity and Eternity, and so "exist" in the fullest possible fashion. We shall see presently how this cosmic image explains one of Augustine's favorite metaphors for the action of the Holy Spirit, Who "warms" and thereby "lightens" us to rise from earthly loves to spiritual love of God;

for (in the Psalmist's words) what is true of the visible sun is equally true of God's Son and Spirit, "no one can hide from His Heat" (*En 18*, sermon 2, 7).

DIVIDING THE TWO WORLDS: THE CLOUDS

Observe that this metaphorical application of the weighted universe is not confined to the lower, visible world; it spans both higher and lower worlds, and applies to everything, from the "earth" that is lowermost in the visible, to the divine spiritual "Sun" that is highest in the unseen world. That Sun is both Light and Heat, brightens and warms both the spiritual heaven and, in more attenuated fashion, the lower world as well. But there is a crucial divider between those worlds: just above "earth" is water, and it puts Augustine in mind of those rain-clouds that so frequently gather overhead, blocking our view of the "airy" heavens that rise beyond them to the sun and stars, and obscuring the sun's rays as they stream downward to our earth.

Those "heavens," Augustine tells us, "are above the clouds, and the clouds beneath the heavens." The "clouds," in other words, constitute a kind of boundary-line between the lower and the higher worlds. "Heaven" is "above," containing "the dwellings of the angels" who "praise God, gazing upon the very face of Truth, with no beclouding of their vision, no intervening falsification" (*En 56* 17).

The clouds, accordingly, can first of all be imaged as blocking our view of the higher world of spirits and of the Divine Sun that dominates that world. But their function can also be imagined more positively: as receiving and actually transmitting the light of the Sun, albeit in filtered, "nebulous" fashion, to the world below them. Augustine sees the clouds in this latter capacity as standing for the various agents, like prophets (*S 79*, 1), apostles and evangelists (*S 135*, 8), and preachers (*En 56* 17), who mediate the radiance of God's Divine Splendor to the "earth," which stands for us dwellers in this lower world. Those clouds cannot empower us to glimpse that radiance directly and in all its purity. Even while enabling us to glimpse the Light beyond them, they necessarily "becloud" our vision to some extent; they filter the Divine Radiance like an intervening medium, partially revealing and partially veiling, "falsifying," very much the way language, images, and symbols do (*En 56* 17). Sometimes both functions join:

"You see a cloud in a sky cloud-filled and darksome; it envelops in itself something hidden. If that something shines forth from the cloud, it flashes brilliantly; you may have contemned it before, but now something leaps forth from that cloud to make you gasp with dread." So did Christ send forth His apostles, ordinary men, weak, enfleshed, unlearned; and people despised them, as we ourselves customarily depreciate the clouds, "before," that is, "that something leaps forth from them and bedazzles you with wonder" (*En 96* 8; cf. *En 103*, sermon 1, 7–10).

THE "NOCTURNAL" WORLD

But in contrast to the bright radiance of the spiritual "heavens," Augustine normally depicts this lower world, beneath the clouds, as a "nocturnal" (*SS 219; 210* 6; *En 118*, sermon 15, 7–8) or, at very best, a "twilight" world. It would be total "night" were it not dimly lit by those luminous "clouds," or (in another image) by those human "lamps" (*lucernae*) like John the Baptist (*En 76* 4). Those lamps are not themselves "the Light" that God is, but catch their light from Him and thereby "give testimony" that His Light truly exists, even though we cannot gaze on it directly (*InJo 2* 5–7).

THE IMAGE OF "INTEL-LIGENCE"

Ordinarily, our only access to that Divine Light is through such filtering clouds: we discern Its radiance much as a reader discerns what is "written between the lines" of a text. Here, it would appear, Augustine is playing on the etymology (*inter-legere*) which *The Oxford Latin Dictionary* gives of the Latin term "to understand."[15] That etymology already suggests the image of "reading between." Augustine frequently "imagines" understanding as a gaze that discerns, *through* a screen or latticework of mediating realities, some meaning that pierces, half-hidden but half-revealed, through that screen. The screen may be one of linguistic or symbolic terms, or bodily gestures, that half-express, half-distort the inner workings of the mind or will (*InJo 34* 4); it may be the flesh by which Christ's Divinity both hides and discloses Itself (*Conf* 13.18); or it may be the human messengers, prophets, apostles, and preachers, who relay God's truth to us (*Enn 56* 17, *134* 17).

Or the cloud image can be set in its cosmic framework. Then it stands for the entire panoply of inferior, visible reality "through" which the mind may glimpse the supernal radiance of the creative Word Who is also Light (*S 135* 8; *InJo 19* 5). In this context, Augustine imagines the act of understanding as an upward gaze toward the clouds which largely conceal but also dimly disclose the radiance of the Sun, gilding and occasionally piercing through them. One of his favorite quotations in this connection is St. Paul's assertion from the Letter to the Romans (1:21) that (literally translated) "the invisible things of God are caught sight of [*conspiciuntur*] through the things that are made understood" (*per ea quae facta sunt intellecta*). One might be tempted to assume that the term "understood" is meant to modify "the things that are made," but Augustine does not interpret St. Paul's sentence that way. Especially when he quotes this text somewhat freely and in abbreviated form it becomes evident that it is the "invisible things of God"— His "Power and Divinity"—that are being "understood," that is, "caught sight of" in the cloud-filtered way described above. So, in *Sermo 241* 1, he explains that the *Illa* he has been speaking about, meaning the *invisibilia Dei*, are "caught sight of, understood, through *haec*," meaning the *ea quae facta sunt*. And he goes on to add that Paul means by those *invisibilia Dei* the "*virtus [Dei] et divinitas* which, he implies [*subaudis*], are caught sight of *as understood*"; it is these invisible divine attributes, not the "things which have been made" which the "eye" of understanding catches sight of (*intellecta conspiciuntur*) (cf. *S 126* 3; *SMa 126* 5).

THE "NIGHT" OF FAITH

This imaginative scheme, accordingly, provides Augustine additional encouragement to picture us, who dwell on "earth," below the "clouds," as living in the "dark" of "night" (*InJo 2* 11, *3* 5). Were it not for the light discernible through the clouds, or the illumination provided us by those flickering "lamps" who witness to the invisible Light, we would be totally "blind." But (here the two images converge) those lamps direct our eyes upward, assuring us that the Light is there for us to behold; they urge us to leave behind our semi-blind stage of merely believing that the Light shines unseen behind the clouds, and pass upward to "understanding," that is, to a higher stage of discerning Light's radiance as filtering through those clouds. To the "understanding" eye, therefore, the clouds that formerly occluded now positively mediate the radiance of the Light (*En 96* 8). We must begin by believing, but then pass upward from belief to understanding.

Analysis of his *fovere* image will presently show that Augustine is equally serious about both members of this claim. We must begin with belief in order to understand; but, no less important, we must strive to pass upward from simple "blind" faith to the measure of "spiritual understanding" God has appointed for each of us. For Augustine considers understanding an intermediate stage in normal spiritual growth, an upward progress from the faith we begin with, toward the direct, immediate "vision" we all profoundly long for.

To remain content with simple faith would be comparable to resigning oneself to living in the depths of nocturnal darkness, refusing to mount toward the sunlit uplands that beckon so invitingly. "Flee the darkness," Augustine urges; "Approach Him, and be enlightened" (*S 225* 4). Nothing could be more unnatural than passing one's life entirely in darkness, for, as Paul reminds us, "We are children of light, children of day: we are not of the night, not of the darkness" (1 Thess 5:5; cf. *S 230*).

This is the line of argument one fully expects Augustine to unfurl in urging the passage to understanding. There are, it is true, hints of it in his earlier works (*Mor* 1.3). And yet, as time goes on, he seldom if ever fully pursues the logic of his *Omnia* image along these precise lines.

THE NIGHT OF SINFULNESS

One reason for his not pursuing that logic may have been this: Augustine traces our presence in the darkness of this lower world to our having sinned; hence, he prefers to depict our ascent toward the Light as entailing a "conversion" movement *away* from the sinfulness that *accounts for* our blindness and consequent need of faith. That preference shows in features of the *Omnia* image we have already seen: sinfulness "weighs us down" with sluggishness and somnolence. So, we are like drowsy slugabeds, inclined to postpone Light's invitation to awaken and rise to greet the day; we drift back instead into darkness and slumber, murmuring "in a little while, a little while" until that little while becomes a long, long while indeed (*SS 87* 11, *262* 3; *Conf* 8.12)!

FROM "MILK" OF FAITH TO "FOOD" OF UNDERSTANDING

This, therefore, is how the nocturnal image operates to portray the soul's conversion from the slumbrous torpor of sinfulness. To

depict the soul's refusal to pass upward from the darkness of faith
to the sunny heights of understanding, we shall see that Augustine
prefers an image drawn from a different register entirely: he
compares the one who declines the quest for spiritual understanding to a spiritual "infant" who petulantly insists on sucking
"milk" at the maternal breast well beyond the age when weaning
is appropriate. For the very point of maternal breast-feeding is so
to nourish the growing child as to make it capable of leaving the
maternal breast behind in order to share the "adult food" (*cibus
grandium*) served at the "*father's* table." That *fovere* image and its
implications we shall study further on; suffice it to say for now
that Augustine interprets the "food of grown-ups" provisionally
as the "solid food" of mature "spiritual understanding," but
ultimately as the heavenly "Bread" of "vision" for which our
minds incurably hunger. Understanding is, in a word, an interim
stage in our spiritual growth, the God-appointed halfway house
leading from simple faith to crowning vision.

Had Augustine chosen to envisage this progress from faith
through understanding to vision as an ascent from lower to loftier
cosmic levels of the *Omnia*, that choice would have led him to lay
even greater stress on the "nocturnal" reaches of the *Omnia* as
representing the "lower" life of blind faith. Even as things stand,
we have seen that this image-logic represents one sense in which
the lower world of our mortal lives is a single long "night,"
relieved only by the glimmers of those "lighted lamps" or "luminous clouds" that serve to guide our faltering steps.

NIGHT, SLEEP, DREAMS AND ILLUSIONS

But "night" has other associations for Augustine, and they derive
quite directly from the cosmic implications of the *Omnia* image.
We have already seen, for example, that "night" is the time when
the sinful "heaviness" and "lethargy" of "sleep" weigh us down.
But Augustine can orchestrate that image masterfully: beyond
being sleepy sluggards who turn a deaf ear to the voice that tries
to awaken us, we are like people "sickly" and feverish, overpow-
ered by languorous longing for the comfort of our beds (*SS* 87
11, *40* 6).

Now he takes that image a further step: if we take this temporal
world too seriously, we become like delirious "dreamers" who
interpret the illusions of dream-life for the real world (*En 131* 8).

We are like beggars who dream they are rich (*S 345* 1; *En 75* 9–11); maddened by fever, we take unreal "vanities" for realities (*En 39* 8); famished, we die of starvation, deluded by phantom feasts enjoyed only in our dreams (*En 7* 11). Here we have the most extreme characterization Augustine gives of *vanitas*, of the hollowness, the insubstantiality of lower image-realities: compare them with the solid substantiality of *Veritas*, True Being, and they threaten quite literally to "evanesce"; so much dream-stuff, the coming of day reveals them as sheer illusion.

But night is also the time when dangers of every shape prowl the darkness. It is when thieves break in to steal and murder, when "the beasts of the forest hunt, and the mighty lion roars in search of prey" (*En 118*, sermon 15, 8), when predatory kites attack, when snakes and dragons slither insidiously toward the kill, and the lurking enemy's arrow flies unseen (*En 90*, sermon 2, 2, 9). In short, nameless fear and danger choose the night to stalk the earth. Our "mortal life" in this lower world, Augustine reminds us tirelessly, is just such a night, dangerous and fearful: one unbroken series of trials, battles, ambushes—an unremitting warfare (*SS 57* 9, *84* 2, *210* 5; *Enn 42* 4, *76* 4).

How Did We Come Here? The Manichee Reply

By what cruel trick, then, did we happen to be born into this nocturnal lower world? As long as he was a Manichee, Augustine thought he could explain our presence here by a kind of primordial catastrophe: our souls, all pure and lightsome, sparks of the Divine Light itself, once dwelt peacefully and joyfully in the world above, while down below the vile and ugly "race of darkness"—a kind of Anti-God called *Hulē*, Matter—gazed upward in an agony of jealousy at our beauteous bliss. That race of darkness attacked, invaded the divine region, and carried our souls back into captivity in this lower world. What each of us needed, now, was to be "awakened" by some messenger of the "saving knowledge," who would remind us that our nature was truly divine, blameless and pure, and teach the Manichaean way of "return."[16]

The evils that beset us in this lower world, therefore, are simply explained: this is the domain of that thoroughgoing Evil, that very substance of Evil that is the "race of darkness." Whatever fleeting hints of goodness and beauty can be discerned in this hellish place are owing to the efforts Divine Light has made to rescue our souls, innocent fragments of Itself imprisoned here. For mark it well, completely innocent those fragments were, and still remain: whatever evil acts we might be thought to commit are not our doing, but the products of the alien *Hulē* that imprisons us.

We live, then, the Manichee insisted, in a "lower world" that should never by rights have become a "world" in the first place. Were it not for that primordial catastrophe, it would have remained the totally repulsive, the smoky and cacophonous pit of Darkness that it was before. We are right, accordingly, to hate this world of our temporary imprisonment, to long for deliverance from it. What blasphemy on the part of those Jewish writers of Genesis, who taught that the all-good God was responsible for the creation of this visible world; they have perversely interpolated their obscene imaginings into what was once the pure word of God, which originally transmitted the message of Mani as presented here. And how pathetic of Catholic Christians to be duped by their deceitful tactics, and to claim that God was "Creator of the visible and the invisible." For we Manichees are the genuinely enlightened "Christians," certain of the truth that this visible world should never have existed in the first place!

Birth of the *Omnia* Image

Evidently recalling his own days as a Manichee, Augustine admits in his *Confessions* (7.19) that he once thought that same way: *non essent ista*, these lower realities should not even exist. But after reading those "books of the platonists" that so influenced his conversion, he learned to think of higher and lower realities as constituting an *Omnia*, the "all things" that the God of Genesis found to be not merely "good," but "very good." Granted: he still thought of "higher" realities as "better" than their lower counterparts; nonetheless, it was "better" that there exist both higher and lower realities than higher realities alone.

Augustine's reason for that claim is this: he argues that a combination of higher and lower worlds permits of the full panoply, the completest possible graded hierarchy of beautifully ordered archetypal and image-realities. His reasoning is unmistakably aesthetic in character.[17]

But it took him a certain amount of time and reflection to formulate this position fully. It does not make its appearance in either of his first two commentaries on the Book of Genesis, but

is first articulated in the third book of his anti-Manichean work
De libero arbitrio (3.12–31); that book seems to have been finished
only in the year 395, nine years after his conversion at Milan. But
from that moment onward, the notion of the *Omnia* is regularly
and repeatedly aimed at justifying God's having created a lower
visible world, as beautiful in its own way, and on its own inferior
level, precisely because it faintly mirrors its model: the perfectly
ordered beauty of the higher, spiritual world.[18]

THE *Omnia* AND ORIGENISM

In taking this position, Augustine (though he was not yet aware
of it)[19], had already separated himself from the theory proposed
by that earlier great Platonizing Christian thinker Origen of
Alexandria. Writing more than a century before Augustine, Origen had imagined that God had first created the higher, invisible
world of spiritual creatures, made up of angels and human souls.
Some of those spirits sinned, thus bringing God to create the
lower visible world as a "prison" for their punishment and purification. Origen went on to explain that the "prison" for each
sinner was one perfectly proportioned to the gravity of the sin
that accounted for his "fall" from the higher world, some being
incarcerated in lower and viler, others in higher and purer reaches
of the visible universe. Only one such creature seems to have
sinned so splendidly as to be accorded a sun as its dwelling place,
thus accounting for the fact that there is only one sun in the sky!

So, at least, Augustine will later be informed about Origen's
teaching, and he will make mocking sport of it.[20] But there was a
final feature of Origen's system which Augustine found thoroughly repelling. It claimed that all the spirits who had sinned and
fallen would, without exception, be purified and eventually reintegrated into their original heavenly bliss; but then, horror of
horrors, this theory portrayed the created universe as an endless
series of such cyclical falls and returns! That souls, once returned
to the heavenly world, should never be assured of everlasting
happiness—that, for Augustine, was the height of the unthinkable.

HOW DID WE COME HERE? AUGUSTINE'S REPLY

But how did our souls enter this lower world in the first instance?
The question clamors for an answer, since Augustine emphatically
views our souls' presence in this world as a profound alienation,

quite literally a dis-location. Darkness, misery, trial, warfare, his
characterizations of what he calls "this mortal life, this living
death," are scarcely that different from the Manichees' or from
Origen's. The fuller answer to that question will come only after
we have studied other features of Augustine's imaginative landscape of our human world; we have begun with his portrait of the
Omnia because it furnishes the indispensable backdrop for that
landscape.

But even while we restrict our focus to the *Omnia* motif, our
attention is caught by some fascinating expressions. Our souls, he
tells us, have become "weighed down" by these "mortal" and
"corruptible" bodies (*InJo 23* 5); we "bear them about with us,"
or "wear" them like an oppressive garment; those bodies are
"earthy," and like earth seek their natural place amid the "last and
lowest" of things (*S 242* 5; *EpJo 3* 11); hence, they cannot but
"press us down," keep our souls from flying aloft to their more
natural place, their appropriate place of "rest" in the higher
spiritual world (*S 180* 3; *En 83* 9–10). As mortal and corruptible,
they contrast with those immortal and incorruptible bodies that
clothe the angels and risen saints in the Heaven of Heaven: their
bodies are lightsome, thoroughly transparent, perfectly suited to
the upper realms (*SS 241* 7, *264* 6; *En 145* 3–5). Such are the
bodies promised us after that "angelic mutation" of the resurrection (*SS 242* 11, *243* 5). But did we wear bodies of that sort
"before" our miserable lives here?

Augustine comes close to answering that question when commenting on Psalm 147:15, which tells us that God's Word "runs
swiftly," indeed, he assures us, is "very swiftness itself." That
property he now explains in terms familiar from ancient physical
theory: "Swiftness, though, is fervent; everything is swifter the
more fervent it is, and everything slower the colder it is." The
ordered universe, moreover, places light and heat on high, but
cold is the characteristic of that lowest and most inertial element,
earth. "We, therefore, are frigid with the slowness of the body,
burdened by the chain of this corruptible life." Does that mean
the all-creating Word has "deserted us . . . pressed down as we are
by our body to the lowest [*infima*] of realities?" No, for did He
not "predestine us before we were born in this mortal and sluggish
body"? Certainly. But then, as the Psalm goes on to say, He "gave
snow" to the earth. Mysterious words! What can they mean? Just
this: "Look: we sluggish ones upon the earth, we have, as it were,

become frozen together here. It's as it happens with snowflakes: on high, they freeze, and fall down to where it is lowest: just so with [our] human nature, its charity grew cold and it fell down onto this earth, was wrapped around with the sluggish body, and became like snow." Predestined though these snows are, they are not yet "fervent with the spirit of charity"; the "weight" and sluggishness they have taken on by freezing prevent them from flying upward to whence they came (*En 147* 22–23; cf. *En 125* 10).

"This passage," Fr. Henri Rondet comments, "which has received too little notice, is sheer Origenism, with this difference: that for the fall of souls there is substituted human nature in its entirety."[21] But that, as we shall have occasion to see further on, is precisely how Augustine thought of the "fall of souls."

The grounds for that assertion will become plainer when we have examined how Augustine imagines our relationship to Adam, and how that relationship accounts for the mortality and corruptibility of the bodies we now bear about us. To anticipate for a moment: he will assure us that we once bore bodies that were spiritual and incorruptible, that we sinned "in" the sin of Adam, and so, with him, were clothed with the "animal skins" of "mortality" God wove for us—our present mortal bodies—and were "dis-missed" from the paradise we once enjoyed (*GenMan* 2.32).

THE WEIGHT OF "DISMISSAL"

But that term "dis-missed" *(dimisit)* inspires Augustine's most elegant application of the "weighted universe" motif. It was the word Genesis (3:23) used to describe God's action with respect to Adam and Eve when they had sinned, and Augustine finds the choice of that exact word rich in doctrinal content. For, he bids us note, God did not "send" or "expel" them from paradise, but precisely "dis-missed" them. What is the difference? Again, the former *rhetor* delights in exhibiting his feel for the exact use of language. We may "send" someone away when he would rather stay; when we "expel" someone, the supposition is that he is reluctant to go. Both those terms would have implied that God drove our first parents out of paradise against their wills. But when a visitor, say, looks at his watch and observes that it is time he got going, we *fall in with his desire* to leave: this is precisely what is meant by saying that we "dismiss" someone. St. Paul

implies the very same thing when he tells us, speaking of unbe-
lieving pagans, that God "gave them over [*tradidit*] to the desires
of their hearts" (*GenMan* 2.34). That interpretation of "dismissal"
turns up frequently in Augustine's preaching (*S 55* 5; *Enn 5* 10, *93*
17), as does the corresponding exegesis of Paul's *tradidit* (*S 57* 9;
Enn 54 25, *80* 17, *106* 14). Augustine gives the same interpretation
to the expression from 1 John 2:19 "They went out from among
us [*a nobis*], but they were not of us" (*ex nobis*). God did not "cast"
them out (*non enim ego te ejicio*), but He says (in the imperative)
"you, you go out" (*exi tu*). It is just the way it happened with our
first parents, who "were already moving downward out of their
own weight: [God] dismissed them from paradise; He did not
drive them out" (*dimisit . . . non exclusit*) (*S 285* 6; *En 106* 14). This
became one of Augustine's most cherished insights, and tracing
its fortunes in his works would be a fascinating project.

Augustine tacitly hopes that an illustration from the universe of
weights may help us understand this "dismissal" notion. We may
wonder, when a stone falls to earth, if the falling was the action of
the stone, or the working of the natural, hence the Eternal Divine
Law. A little reflection shows that both explanations are equally
true, for it is precisely God's doing, through the working of His
Divine Wisdom ordering all things, that stones not only do, but
must inevitably, fall if their "weight" is greater than that of the
surrounding medium.

Similarly, when "we" (as present in Adam) yielded to the love
for "earthly things," we immediately took on the "weight" of the
objects we chose to love, and "fell" from the heavenly paradise of
the higher world. We fell because as "weighted" beings we simply
had to fall; the Divine Wisdom that orders the entire universe could
not but decree from all Eternity that such an "earth-weighted"
being would be "out of place" everywhere except in the earthly
region it chose to love. Hence, God did not need to "send" us
down, or "expel" us from the Heaven of Heaven; He could not,
without violating the Wisdom of His own Eternal Law, do anything else than "give us over" to what had become the "desires of
our hearts," and "dismiss" us to go where we had chosen to go.
The interlock between free spiritual choice and necessary natural
law is seamless, Augustine feels; there is no reason for the Manichees to impugn God's justice, when we have simply been granted
exactly what we freely and sinfully chose. All the evils that we
must *endure* from the harsh and menacing denizens of this lower

world are necessary consequences, perfectly "in order," of that primal evil we *committed* (*Conf* 7.5; *S 171* 3–4).

Iniquitas: THE PLUNGE TOWARD NOTHINGNESS

Augustine's most frequent term for that primal sin is *iniquitas.* Surely its frequent occurrence in the Bible had much to do with his preference for it. But one may also wonder whether its similarity to another Latin term had something to do with that choice as well. For in one of his earliest dialogues (*Vita* 8.30–31), he chooses the term *nequitia* to express the same idea (cf. *Ver* 21). An excellent expression, he tells his companions, for it is compounded from *ne* and *quidquam*, hence means "not-anything" or "no-thing." Thereby it elegantly suggests the movement involved in all sinning: a plunging movement from the loftier regions of the hierarchically graded universe,' downward toward (though never reaching) very nothingness.

Pro iniquitate erudisti hominem, Augustine sums up our alienated condition in his *Confessions* (7.16): "You have corrected man for his iniquity." But what, he goes on to ask, is this "iniquity"? He answers with the same downward movement: like *nequitia*, iniquity is a turning away from "God, the Highest of substances, to the lowest": from the *Summa* to the *infima*. The residues of that primal iniquity now account for Augustine's inability to remain in vision-contact with the "invisible things of God" which he has glimpsed, *intellecta*: he is borne downward again by his own "weight," *pondere meo*. "For the corruptible body weighs down the soul" (*adgravat animam*) (7.22–23). The perfectly ordered *Omnia* has once again executed its inexorable law.

Peregrinatio: THE WAYFARING SOUL

It would appear, therefore, that our presence in this lowest stratum of the *Omnia* is the consequence of God's having "dismissed" us from the higher, spiritual world. But that dismissal answered perfectly to the sinful desire for earthly realities, a desire that "weighed" us down so that we naturally, inevitably plunged into the cold and darkness of "this" world. We have become "alienated" from God, quite literally so; for whereas we were once securely "at home" in the region of the universe which perfectly suited us, we now find ourselves "wayfarers," "foreigners," "strangers"—in a word, *peregrini*. No cluster of images better epitomizes Augustine's somber evaluation of our human condition than those evoked by that single term.

NOTES

1. (Villanova, Pa.: Villanova University Press, 1964), pp. 3–7.

2. For some anticipations of this treatment of the *Omnia* image, see my *Imagination and Metaphysics in St. Augustine* (Milwaukee: Marquette University Press, 1986) (henceforth: *Imagination*). Compare A. H. Armstrong's account of Plotinus' emanationist metaphysic (which can readily be translated into imaginative terms) in "Plotinus," *The Cambridge History of Later Greek and Early Mediaeval Philosophy*, ed. A. H. Armstrong (Cambridge: Cambridge University Press, 1967), pp. 236–58. Huguette Fugier has attempted to synthesize this cosmic image in such a way as to "fit" a number of other Augustinian images within it; see her study of "L'Image du Dieu-Centre dans les *Confessions* de saint Augustin," in REA, 1 (1955), 379–95. My remarks in the Introduction about the "particularity" of Augustine's individual imagination may explain why I find her effort somewhat reductionist; the *peregrinatio* and *fovere* images strike me as operating along lines quite distinct from those of the *Omnia* register, even if they relate (as I would insist they do) to the *Omnia* register as to their cosmic backdrop.

3. For the greater portion of his career, Augustine equates *caro* ("flesh") with the "mortal body" of our experience, implying that its mortal quality is the consequence of our original "fall." The Pelagian controversy will eventually sow some doubts in his mind about the adequacy of that equation.

On these two "regions," compare *Le Langage symbolique dans la prédication d'Augustin d'Hippone* by Suzanne Poque, 2 vols. (Paris: Études Augustiniennes, 1984) (henceforth: *Langage symbolique*), esp. I, 299–324 (on the Earth–Heaven couple) and 257–79 (on the Light–Darkness couple).

4. Poque's systematic division of images in her Introduction (pp. xvii-xxxv) leads her to deal only with what she terms Augustine's "diurnal" or "heroic" images; so, she sets her treatment of the term *stare* in the context of the "soldier of Christ" image (I, 37–68), which in turn suggests the soldier's "standing firm" in battle as the term's primary image. She does admit (I, 50–51), however, that Augustine employs the term with a certain "originality," for *stare* "betrays that nostalgia for attaining to 'what does not pass [away].' " Augustine does, as Poque is able to show, employ the term *stare* with this military import; but I question whether her method permits her to judge which import is truly primary for his imagination.

5. See his "Recherches sur le sens et les origines de l'expression

Caelum caeli dans le Livre XII des *Confessions* de saint Augustin," *Bulletin du Cange*, 23 (1953), 185–274, esp. 191n1 and 201n2.

6. For this "tolmatic" side of emanationist doctrine, see Armstrong's treatment of "Plotinus" cited in note 2, above, pp. 242–43.

7. Compare *Conf* 4.31 (*domus nostra, aeternitas tua*), and the later explanation of that term at 12.22 (*domus dei . . . aeterna in caelis*, etc.).

8. See my *St. Augustine's Early Theory of Man, 386–391 A.D.* (Cambridge: The Belknap Press of Harvard University Press, 1969), pp. 146–83 (henceforth: *Early Theory*), for Augustine's more technical treatment of these issues, chiefly in his *De Genesi contra Manichaeos* and *De libero arbitrio*. For his more pastoral observations, all implying that background theory, see *SS 117* 3, *152* 5, *142* 2–5, *163* 3–4; *InJo 23* 5, *25* 15–19.

9. See her "Le Dilemme de l'être et du néant chez saint Augustin" in RA, 6 (1969), esp. pp. 57–75. Ruth Namad, in the English translation, *St. Augustine: Being and Nothingness* (New York: Paragon, 1988), uses the term "nihilated"; see pp. 49–68. A number of such blurry imprecisions, in translations of Augustine's Latin, only emphasize the value of Henri-Irénée Marrou's remarks on the lasting effects that Augustine's education as a *rhetor* wrought on his "exact" use of words (and, I would only add, his instinctive respect for the image-freight those words conveyed). See *Saint Augustin et la fin de la culture antique*, 2 vols. (Paris: Boccard, 1938, 1949), esp. I, 54–83, 125–28 (henceforth: *Culture*).

10. See Louis Chevalier and Henri Rondet, s.j., "L'Idée de vanité dans l'oeuvre de saint Augustin," REA, 3 (1957), 221–34. The authors see *vanitas* as stemming from (a) man's involvement in time, and (b) his fallenness. Despite their demurrals on pp. 221 and 234, at note 87, the similarity to Origen's "fall" theory is real, though Augustine's version is stripped of those attendant features which he found either ludicrous or repulsive. For both Augustine and Plotinus, our presence in time is the consequence of a "fall" that is somehow our "fault"; see the references in note 5, above, and *Ver* 43: *saeculorum vero partes* damnatione *facti sumus*: "we have become [or: "been made"] parts of the ages [i.e., the temporal process] by reason of [our] damnation [for sin]"; also *Mus* 6.30, *eorum* [scil., *temporalium*] *ordini* pro meritis nostris *assuti sumus*: "we have been sewn into the [fabric of the] temporal order on account of our [sinful] merits."

11. See the texts included in the excellent study by Henri Rondet, s.j., "Le Symbolisme de la mer chez saint Augustin," AM II, pp. 691–701. Cf. the less precise account in Robert A. Markus, *Saeculum: History and Society in the Theology of St. Augustine* (Cambridge: Cambridge University Press, 1970; repr. 1988), esp. pp. 9–10. I would amend to say that God creates human souls as "naturally" changeable and therefore *de jure* temporal, but they do not actualize that temporality except by "falling" from the higher to the lower world.

12. Mlle Anne-Marie La Bonnardière has shown the startling (and "illogical") ambiguity of the "earth" (*terra*) image in Augustine's *Enarrationes* (an ambiguity that holds, I submit, for his other preached works as well). Earth can image solidity/stability in contrast to "water," but it can also symbolize sinfulness by evoking the transitory and weightless properties of "dust." See "Le thême de la 'terre' dans le Psautier d'après les *Enarrationes in Psalmos* de saint Augustin," in the *Annuaire* of the Ecole pratique de Hautes Etudes, Section V, 78 (1970/1971), 293–96. See my remarks in the Introduction on the frequently divergent lines of "logic" which Augustine's imagination follows in treating various particular images, along with those of Jacques Fontaine, in "Sens et valeur des images dans les *Confessions*," AM I, pp. 117–26.

13. For the importance of this text (Wis 11:21) in Augustine's thought, see Olivier DuRoy, *L'Intelligence de la foi en la Trinité selon saint Augustin: Genèse de sa théologie* (Paris: Études Augustiniennes, 1965), esp. pp. 279–81 and 421–24.

14. See ibid., pp. 135–37 for this identification and its implications.

15. (Oxford: Clarendon, 1982), p. 936.

16. See Henri-Charles Puèch, *Le Manichéisme, son fondateur, sa doctrine* (Paris: Civilisations du Sud, 1949); the whole of the *Contra Faustum* is worth reading in this connection.

17. It is important to bear in mind the "strong" sense beauty conveyed to the ancient-world mind: it was heavily laden with value implicits, aesthetic in our modern sense, but moral and metaphysical as well. This was especially true for Plotinus and Augustine, as I have tried to show in *Art and the Christian Intelligence in St. Augustine* (Cambridge: Harvard University Press, 1978).

18. From A.D. 395 onward, this becomes regularly Augustine's point in stressing the *Omnia* motif; see, for example, *Conf* 7.18–19, *Oros* 9, *Civ* 11.22–23.

19. Both Pierre Courcelle and Mlle Anne-Marie La Bonnardière have observed that Orosius' description of Origenism, in the year 414, seems to have struck Augustine with the force of a surprise revelation. See my "St. Augustine's Criticism of Origen in the *Ad Orosium*," in REA, 30 (1984), 84–99.

20. See *Civ* 11.23.

21. See his *Original Sin: The Patristic and Theological Background*, trans. Cajetan Finegan, O.P. (New York: Alba House, 1969; repr. 1972), pp. 118–19 (pp. 139–40 in the original [Paris, 1966]). Rondet's affirmation holds for the pre-existing soul's sinful fall, but not for the attendant features of Origen's view; to these, Augustine always strenuously objected. See my *The Origin of the Soul in St. Augustine's Later Works* (New York: Fordham University Press, 1987), esp. pp. 74–90, 139–49, 160–66, 291–94.

2

Peregrinatio Animae: The Wayfaring Soul

SOME THIRTY YEARS AGO, Georg Nicolaus Knauer published a remarkable article under the above title.[1] It extended a number of themes he had already explored in his provocative book-length study of Augustine's citations of the Psalms in his *Confessions*.[2] One of those ideas Knauer saw as answering to a problem that has bedeviled interpreters of that work for decades and perhaps centuries: Is the *Confessions* a truly unified composition, a "book" rather than a series of disconnected fascicules strung together and published, somewhat arbitrarily, as though they constituted a single work?

One needs only a single exposure to the *Confessions* to acknowledge that the question is a real one: for why in the world is Book 10, with its meditation on "memory" and its lengthy "examination of conscience," patched on to the "autobiographical" section represented by Books 1 to 9? And what prompted Augustine then to veer off, in Books 11 to 13, into that tortuous commentary on the first and second chapters of Genesis? It is scarcely any wonder that more than one eminent scholar has concluded that the search for some genuinely unifying thread holding these disparate pieces together was simply misguided, indeed, quixotically futile.[3]

But Knauer had been persuaded that there was a pattern in Augustine's citation of certain Psalms, one that argued for a unity of conception running from Book 1 right through Book 13. His article was an attempt to show that the unifying thread knitting the work together was a thematic one; Augustine wished to portray his life as a *peregrinatio animae*: translate (for now) the story of his "soul's wayfaring." That theme was the, or at least *a*, fundamental motif running through the entire work, Knauer argued; it furnished the ground-bass, as it were, for the entire array of subsidiary themes Augustine announces, develops, allows to subside and open out again, chord with others and still others, recede into the background, but only to re-emerge, again and still

again, in ever more fully orchestrated form. And only with the
thirteenth book does Augustine achieve the final orchestration he
was aiming at from the very first.

I have expressed Knauer's insight in terms of the "musical
metaphor" so genially coined by that great Augustinian scholar
Henri-Irénée Marrou,[4] but it works no distortion on the claim he
made; indeed, it fits his case admirably well. Immediately,
though, it raises the question other scholars have also asked: Is the
peregrinatio animae theme powerful and pervasive enough to furnish
the unifying ground-bass Knauer thought it did? Or are there too
many elements in the *Confessions* which the notion of *peregrinatio*
leaves unexplained, still dis-unified, like so many foreign bodies
unaffected by its magnetic field?

"Ways" and "Deeps"

Consider, for example, two thematic images to which Knauer
calls attention early in his article, and promptly subsumes under
the *peregrinatio* image. Augustine, he tells us (p. 218*n*1), frequently
speaks of having traveled, wandered, or strayed along a variety of
"ways" (*viae*), all of them "bad" (1.24, 2.1), "difficult" (3.5),
"broad" (6.24), and "tortuous" (6.26), because they were "his
own" (*meae*) rather than God's (3.5). The result of God's action in
bringing about his conversion was, understandably enough, to
"set" Augustine in "His" ways—or, more precisely, as things
turn out, "His Way" (6.16), in the sense of making him a follower
of His Incarnate Son, the Christ Who is Way and Truth and Life
(7.24).

Now, I submit that there is no difficulty whatever in accepting
this "image of the way" (as Knauer himself calls it) as constituting
an integral "part" of the more comprehensive *peregrinatio* image;
the image of wandering or wayfaring calls naturally to the image
of roads, lanes, or "ways" to wander along.

But the imaginative transition is not nearly so simple when we
are asked (p. 218*n*2) to associate the human *peregrinatio* with
images of "deeps" or "lower depths," whether their "darkness"
and "blinding" character be the effect of "mist" or "seawater."
Certain of these associations, I suggest, derive just as much, if not
more, from Augustine's having imaginatively set the human *peregrinatio* within the framework of his *Omnia* image. Knauer is
partially correct; it was entirely natural that Augustine should

choose to portray the soul's journey as taking place not only on land (as the Prodigal's did), but across ocean depths as well (the familiar stories of Odysseus and Aeneas come to mind). And yet, we have already seen how the terms of the *Omnia* image naturally call for "lower" realities to be dark, foggy, and restlessly moving like the sea. The "imaginative reason" why the notion of *peregrinatio*, precisely as such, should evoke such murky associations seems at first blush somewhat less compelling, and yet there is some imaginative reason for it. We have here another instance where two image-systems "intersect" in Augustine's imagination, so that the characteristics of the first "run" over into the other, as pigments do in a watercolor painting.

In attempting to account for so many properties as deriving uniquely from the *peregrinatio* motif, however, Knauer is anticipating a weakness in his case which becomes more noticeable to the reader further on: for while the *peregrinatio* image, aided by its natural cousin, the "way" image, unmistakably succeeds in bonding the first seven books of the *Confessions* tightly together, that precise thematic image slips almost completely into the background in Books 8 and 9 (Knauer, pp. 231–34), appears only very discreetly in Books 10 and 11 (Knauer, pp. 234–41), makes a momentary but dramatic re-appearance in Book 12, only to recede into the background once again in Book 13. Knauer himself admits, in fact (p. 239), that the unifying power of this precise motif is markedly reduced from Book 10 on. But that same admission would hold for Books 8 and 9, and seems to me less applicable to Book 12. This remains true despite Knauer's stalwart efforts to persuade us to consider a number of secondary images— like the "depth" image—as organically linked with the *peregrinatio* image. But just as the "depth" image finds a more natural place in the *Omnia* complex, so too, I suggest, a number of the images Knauer finds active in Books 10 to 13, and strains to graft onto the *peregrinatio* image, are better understood in other connections. They find their more natural place, I further suggest, either as integral to the *Omnia* or to the *fovere* image which we shall treat of shortly, or as deriving, unsurprisingly, from both those image-complexes simultaneously, or from the intersection and occasional fusion of all three!

My contention here will be, accordingly, that Knauer was sometimes tempted to place too much weight on, claim too much unifying power for, the single image-complex that had captured his attention. But that is a far cry from saying that his insight went entirely astray. For there is no single theme, I think, that sums up more compellingly Augustine's view of human life than this: we are all *peregrini*, souls on *peregrinatio*.

THE MEANING OF *Peregrinatio*

But what does Augustine mean by those terms? Once again we are reminded that we are dealing with a professional *rhetor* who had a near-pedantic respect for the exact meaning of the words he used. Consult, for example, *The Oxford Latin Dictionary*, and it is almost like reading his mind: for the word *peregrinatio* conveys the condition of the *peregrinus*, the foreigner, the one who is traveling or perhaps residing "abroad" and hence in alien surroundings, "not at home"; so, it comes to mean one who "feels like a foreigner," experiences the pang of being far from one's native city or homeland, one's *domus*, *civitas*, or *patria*.

Augustine seems to have had a keen personal sensitivity to what all of that implied. We are informed, first of all, that he abhorred travel, sea-voyages especially, but overland journeys as well. We moderns have to exert our imaginations in order to picture the jolting hardships, as well as the real dangers, of travel in the ancient world. The rigors attached to going on a journey in his time, combined with his own frail bodily constitution, account for much of Augustine's aversion. But one also senses in him a certain restlessness with being "away," a hankering to "be home again."[5] During his sojourns in Rome and in Milan, he remained a foreigner, whose accent betrayed him as a North African provincial (*Ord* 2.45; *Conf* 1.29). Jerome caustically reminds him that grain-producing Africa was regarded as the "breadbasket of the Roman Empire," the implication being that this country hick from Thagaste might better stick to such rustic tasks than presume to discuss intellectual matters with Roman-educated Jerome. There must have been a number of similar occasions when Augustine was made to feel like an insecure outsider, target of that thinly veiled hostility that is the perennial lot of the foreigner, or, the contemporary equivalent, the "displaced person."[6]

WAYFARING AND MELANCHOLY

Accordingly, *peregrinus* and *peregrinatio* were, for Augustine, far from happy words. Quite the contrary. All associations stemming from the streamlined joys of modern tourism must be set firmly aside. Even the medieval terms "pilgrim" and "pilgrimage," especially with any jocund Chaucerian connotations we might be tempted to associate with them, will not serve as translations; we are best advised to make do, however awkwardly, with "wayfarer" and "wayfaring."[7] For Augustine is forever reminding his fellow-*peregrini* that they are not at home in "this" mortal life, this lower region of the *Omnia:* our home is not "here" but "there," *sursum* (*S 111* 2); we must continually "sigh" after it, keep alive that nostalgic sense of *nondum,* "not yet" (*SS 38* 11, *103* 1).

The Christian, in fact, has almost a duty to cultivate that nostalgia, for whoever finds wayfaring sweet, does not love his homeland:

> if his homeland be sweet to him, then wayfaring is bitter, and tribulation the whole day long. When will we be without tribulation? When we experience the delight of being in our homeland. . . . Then will toiling and groaning be no more; no longer will we need to pray, but only praise [*En 85* 11].

At least two other terms play a similar role in Augustine's thinking: we are merely *incolae* in this lower world (*En 119* 6), or, more emphatically, *inquilini,* pensioners in a "tent" from which the landlord can expel us with a gruff and peremptory "*migra*": "move on." Our greatest mistake would be to confuse that temporary dwelling with a "home"—a *mansio* in the Biblical sense—in which we are entitled to "stay": *manere* (*Enn 60* 6, *38* 21, *118,* sermon 8, 1; *InJo 40* 10).[8] As long as we dwell in such temporary shelters, Augustine tells his parishioners, "we groan, but when arrived at home, we will praise. And why?" His answer is disarmingly direct; the reason is quite simply that "groaning is what wayfarers do, but praise is proper to those at last residing permanently in their homeland" (*in patria commanentium*) (*En 131* 10).

A Variety of Wayfarers

Augustine illustrates our wayfaring plight by referring to a number of figures, Biblical and otherwise. Knauer points out that we are like that "younger son," the Prodigal of St. Luke's Gospel, or like the sheep of the parable that "wandered away" and got lost. He correctly traces one of Augustine's clichéd expressions—that the Prodigal's traveling was not by means of feet, or horses, or chariots or ships (1.28, 8.19)—to Plotinus' *Ennead* 1.6; yet he somehow fails to follow up on that connection and to remark on how often Augustine (significantly) makes the Prodigal resemble the classical wanderer Plotinus was evoking, Homer's Odysseus. They may be less important omissions, perhaps, but Knauer might also have sharpened his portrait by observing that the "wayfarer" is sometimes figured by the apostles (as well as by Odysseus, or is it Aeneas?) tossed about on the stormy sea (*S 63* 1–2), or by that man of Luke's Gospel who "descended" from Jerusalem to Jericho, fell among robbers, and was rescued by that "foreigner," the Samaritan (*En 121* 7). That "man," we are told elsewhere, was "the entire human race" (*totum genus humanum*), whereas the Samaritan was Christ (*S 171* 2). Each one of these symbolic figures adds its individual brushstroke to sharpen Augustine's portrait of the wayfaring soul; but each of them, alas, is rich and suggestive enough to merit an independent study in and for itself. We must content ourselves here with sketching, as accurately as possible, the family features of Augustine's more anonymous "wayfarer."

WANDERING IN THE DESERT

Unsurprisingly, Augustine also finds our *peregrinatio* most unmistakably symbolized by the stories of the Israelites as exiled captives in an alien city, Babylon, or, more frequently, as departing from Egypt to wander in the desert for those forty years. The number forty regularly reminds him of this desert symbolism: our forty days of Lenten fasting, for example, should call to mind this entire *saeculum*, this temporal existence through which we journey incessantly, from moment to moment and year to year (*SS 205–209*). "This life" (*ista*) in the *saeculum* is one long desert, "full of the worst of cares, and fears, and dangerous trials," when compared to the eternal bliss awaiting us at home (*S 252* 11; *En 126* 1). "Evil, the desert," Augustine exclaims; parched and trackless, it is "fearsome and horrifying" (*En 62* 8).

OVER WATERY DEEPS

But since our *peregrinatio* takes us through the country of our exile, the lower "region" of the *Omnia*, it can also summon up a series of associations evoked by that motif: our life in the *saeculum* is lived in the "depths" (*Conf* 2.5, 4.20, 11.3) or in the *profunda inferi*, the "depths of the lower world" (3.11); those depths Augustine can variously describe (as Knauer points out, p. 218*n*2) as "misty (3.19), "darksome" (13.9, 49), or "blinding" (8.9); then as the "depths of the sea" (6.1), as a "whirlpool" sucking him down (1.30), or as a series of battering waves that threaten to drown him (7.5). Here, obviously, images from the *Omnia* register have interwoven and fused with those of traveling, but notice (once again) how regularly the traveler in question is an endangered sea-voyager, a Christian Odysseus, or Aeneas!

Through the Darkness

This "lower world" Augustine further images as one long night, a night of unremitting toil (*SS 210* 5, *259* 3; *En 76* 4). It is also a sleep, *somnum* (*S 189* 2), which threatens to make us "forget" the homeland, the true *patria* that alone answers to our soul's longing (*S 362* 4; *En 125* 1; cf. *En 32*, version 2, sermon 2, 6). More darkly yet, the domain of time is a "land of death," a land peopled by the constantly "dying" (*SS 108* 5, *45* 4, *346* 1).

Forever Restless

Hence, the mood of the *peregrinus* must remain an unrelieved, a near-obsessive, "restlessness." He must constantly fight the great temptation, or multiple forms of temptation, which Augustine expresses by the term *manere*. For example, everything we see about us in "this life," *ista vita*, is transient and passing; we ourselves, accordingly, must be forever transients, forever passing onward (*S 38* 11), never tempted to "settle down" and "stay behind": *manere* (*SS 111* 2, *254* 4).

That theme of restlessness is even more poignant when Augustine pictures us as sea-wanderers. No sane person would hope to find a *mansio*, a secure "resting place" on the treacherous seas of time (*S 76* 1, *251* 3; *Enn 23* 2, *64* 3) or on this ever-flowing river of carnal existence (*S 119* 3). The only point in voyaging over these waters is to reach the farther shore; our only hope for doing so is to cling to the "wood" of the Cross, the "boat" in which Christ keeps us company (*SS 75* 2, *63* 1–2).

Using This Alien World

We must, then, not only act but also feel like the travelers, *viatores*, we are. That means we must use the goods of the temporal world in order to pass beyond the boundaries of that world (*S 157* 4–5); we must regard all its amenities as the traveler regards the inn, the *stabulum* in which he passes the night, only to set out refreshed for the next day's journey (*SS 177* 2, *111* 2; *En 125* 15). We must literally "pass" the night there, never confusing the inn with our *domus*, the "home" where we hope, eventually, to "abide," to settle down to a permanent "stay": *manere* (*S 50* 11; *Enn 126* 3, *121* 2, *60* 6).

Or, in a companion image, we must treat this world as a "tent," the kind of *tabernaculum* soldiers inhabit while campaigning; for (Augustine untiringly reminds his flock) this life of ours is a warfare (*Enn 14* 1, *131* 10, *42* 4) in which we are constantly on campaign, compelled to fight against enemies both within us and without (*S 57* 9, 11), enduring tears and tribulations of every kind (*S 31* 5).

Toward Home, Fatherland, Native City

Augustine is unrelenting in his efforts to stir up this restless nostalgia for the *domus*, the "house of God" (*S 50* 11), the *patria* or "eternal homeland" (*SS 91* 9, *205* 2, *31* 5) that he sees as the destination of all our wayfaring. He would have us be, like Paul, forever "on the stretch," *extenti*, like runners racing toward the tape and never looking back (*SS 169* 18, *170* 11), ex-tended upward, toward God, the One, rather than "dis-tended" horizontally, through scattering attention to "the many" (*S 255* 6).

But the term he most frequently uses for describing our destination is *civitas*; for Scripture tells us repeatedly that we are bound for that "heavenly city," the "heavenly Jerusalem" (*S 157* 6). She is our "eternal homeland," our *aeterna patria* (*S 31* 5), where we shall enjoy "eternal life" in the blissful "vision" of God (*S 170* 10–11). There, after our busy temporal labors, we shall find the fulfillment of what Martha's sister briefly tasted, the unbroken *quies*, unending "rest," for which our restless hearts incurably long (*S 255* 1; *Enn 86* 1, *134* 26). *Aeterni erimus*, Augustine cries, "we shall be eternal, the equals" of those fellow-citizens of ours, "the angels of God" (*S 213* 9).

Peregrinatio in the Confessions

Up to this juncture, the evidence from Augustine's preached works agrees substantially with the interpretation of *peregrinatio* which

Knauer succeeded in extracting from the *Confessions*. That at least confirms what common sense would lead us to expect: whether he is preaching or writing, Augustine's imagination works along consistent paths. Knauer, too, made the same assumption when citing the preached works to buttress his interpretation of the *Confessions*.

But, as I suggested above, the variants on the "wayfaring" motif are even more numerous than Knauer seems to have noticed. "Not on foot or across spatial distances": Knauer makes much (p. 219) of this virtual quotation which Augustine lifts (1.28) from *Ennead* 1.6.8. He notes that Augustine applies Plotinus' remark—one does not need ships or chariots for this journey—to the Prodigal Son; yet he must also have noticed that Plotinus himself is speaking of Homer's pagan Odysseus!

The Interweave of *Odyssey* Imagery

Had he followed that thread, Knauer might have been compelled to notice how artfully Augustine has prepared us for this seafaring image: so, for example, having learned to use language as a child, Augustine depicts himself as a young Odysseus, "entering," in consequence, "more deeply into the stormy society of human life" (1.13) and later, breasting its "waves of temptation" (1.18). Or is he thinking of Aeneas, whose "wanderings" he was later obliged to study and memorize (1.20, 22)? Or is he, once again, combining and then actually fusing two, or even three, images, derived from various sources?

Omnia Images

Knauer then traces the *peregrinatio* image through Book 2 (p. 220), where Augustine was "swept" (in another seafaring image) by the power of his awakening passions "over the crags of desire, and plunged . . . into a whirlpool of shameful deeds," and "wandered" even farther from God (2.2). Augustine develops his lengthy meditation on the famous theft of pears, and then *Defluxi abs Te*, he ends Book 2, "I flowed down away from You, my God, and wandered away [*erravi*] too far astray from Your *stabilitas*" and "became unto myself a land of want" (*regio egestatis*). Knauer is correct in pointing to the "lost sheep" allusion in Augustine's *erravi*, as well as to the Prodigal allusion in that "land of want." But Augustine has also combined these with an image from the

Omnia register: his soul, once aloft in the spiritual world, and supported by the unchanging *stabilitas* of Divine Truth, has "flowed downward" into the realm of change and "vanity." The vanities of this lower world are, however, too empty and insubstantial to feed a soul that was meant to be nourished on Truth; hence, the appropriateness of that "land of want."

Once arrived in Carthage, Augustine finds himself swept away once again, on "immense surges" of lusts (3.3), an "unhappy sheep wandering away from [God's] flock" (3.4). "Amid terrible dangers" he "wandered, . . . loving [his] own ways, not [God's]" (3.5), until, suddenly, he came upon a book that he would never afterward forget: Cicero's *Hortensius*. It changed his heart dramatically. Knauer is again correct in noting (p. 220*n*3) that Augustine characterizes his response to that reading in a pair of Lucan phrases from the Prodigal parable: "I was beginning to rise up, in order to return to You": *Et "surgere" coeperam, ut "ad Te redirem"* (3.7).

That apparently pluperfect form is deceptive, of course; the verb *coepi* being defective, *coeperam* represents its imperfect tense. So, scholars are quite correct in speaking of this as Augustine's "first conversion." The language of the parable's imagery leaves no doubt: like the Prodigal, Augustine has gone as far away from God as he ever will; now he has reversed his life direction and pointed his steps—however hesitantly, uncertainly—"homeward." True, he will later tell us (3.11) that, deceived by Manichee confabulations, he "was wayfaring far away from [God]" (*longe peregrinabar abs Te*) and was even kept from "eating the husks" he (like the Prodigal) fed to swine—by such "degrees was I led down into the depths of the lower world" (*profunda inferi*)—but it is seriously doubtful, as we shall see, that these expressions should be understood as claiming that the Manichees brought him even *further* away from God.

More *Omnia* Interweaves

Again, Knauer sees (pp. 221–25) that the account in Book 4 of Augustine's young friend's death, and of his own sorrowful reaction to it, plays subtly, but demonstrably, on the "wayfaring" motif. Yet once again, the picture may be more complex than he paints it, for several of its features derive from image-complexes other than that of the "wayfarer." Notice, first, the "weight" image: Augustine sighed and wept, but could find no "rest" (*requies*); he "carried about [his] soul . . . unwilling to be carried by me [*portari a me*], but I could find nowhere to put it." Tears alone provided "a little rest" (*requies*). He knows now that he ought to have "lifted [his burden] up" to God, to be "cared for" (*curanda*) by Him, but if he "put it there, so that it might rest" (*ut requiesceret*), it came hurtling back at him, leaving him "an unhappy place [*infelix locus*] where [he] could neither remain nor depart." But even were he to depart, whither could he go? His "heart" could not flee his "heart"; nor his self flee his sorrowing self. Finally, futilely, he "fled from [his] native town [*de patria*] . . . and came to Carthage" once again (4.12). Augustine soon returns to that suffocating predicament of having no "whither" to flee to; the larger paradox involved obviously delights him. For if God "made heaven and earth" and "fills all things," then how can the soul effectively forsake God; for "whither does he go, or whither does he flee, except from [God] well pleased to [that same God] wrathful" (4.14)?

Now, this is a genuinely fascinating cluster of images. First, observe with Knauer (p. 222) that the *patria* Augustine fled is skillfully meant to suggest not merely his "outer" native town, Thagaste, but also the "inner," spiritual "fatherland" of his erring soul. Clearly, the *peregrinatio* image is at work here.

But is that equally true for paradoxes involved in trying to "flee" the omnipresent God, and for the allusions to "carrying" and to striving to find a "place" to put his "heart"? Here, manifestly, Augustine took delight in erecting a façade of "travel" imagery, but closer inspection will show that it was a mock façade, though provocative for all that. The contradictions involved in "fleeing" from the omnipresent God, however, as though we could leave Him "behind" us by "traveling," derive their power much more from the *Omnia* than from the *peregrinatio* image-register. Or better, perhaps, their power comes from the way the *peregrinatio* image, with all its spatial connotations, has been squeezed, as it were, into the space-defying Omnipresence register.

But the fact that Augustine cannot find a "place" to "put" his heart, a place where his heart will find "rest" (he harps on this *requies* theme in 4.11, 12, and 15), is also explained by *Omnia* imagery, for (as Augustine insinuates, a trifle archly) the human heart's *locus naturalis*, the only place where it will find rest, is "on high," with God, to Whom he should have "lifted it up" to be "cared for." This, then, is why his own self, in this lower world, can only be an *infelix locus* for his heart—and why that heart is "intolerant" of being "carried" by him, when all the while the "caring" God Isaiah speaks of is silently screaming "I, I will carry you!" and "I shall be your rest!"

ISAIAH'S MATERNAL GOD

But that last feature, we shall come to see, derives largely from the third foundational image Augustine employs: the *fovere* image of the tirelessly caring God. So Augustine can exclaim with Isaiah 46:8 (as Knauer notes, p. 223): *Redite, praevaricatores, ad cor*, and (in an equally Isaian image, one which Knauer has missed) "stand with Him, and you shall stand; rest in Him, and you shall find rest" (4.18). Why do we sinners "walk such hard pathways," Augustine complains, seeking bliss in this "region of mortality"? Again, as Knauer (p. 223) points out, we have a reminiscence of Isaiah 9:2, in this, and yet one that performs double duty in echoing the *regio egestatis* of the Prodigal parable. And Augustine has once more succeeded in adroitly combining images from two distinct registers.

Augustine next applies the *peregrinatio* image toward the end of Book 4. He has told of having composed his first book, *De pulchro et apto*; he was also able, he recounts, to master Aristotle's *Categories* (in translation, doubtless) without any outside help; and yet, he now asks God, what did all this avail him? "For I strove [like the Prodigal] to keep so good a portion of my substance in my own power. I did not 'guard my strength for You,' but set forth from You to a far country, in order to waste [that substance] in whorish lusts" (4.30).

The final paragraph (31) of Book 4 is a brilliant display of imaginative fireworks, rare even for Augustine. *Tu portabis, Tu portabis*, Augustine cries, "You, You will carry us; You will carry us, both as little ones and to our gray hairs; You, You will carry us." We shall have to analyze this image more at length in our next chapter, but for now take it that Augustine has drawn it from Isaiah. He continues, still addressing God, "when You are our strength [*firmitas*], then is it [genuine] strength; but when it [our strength] is our own, it is but weakness."

"OUR HOME, YOUR ETERNITY"

But the final sentence of Book 4, Knauer must confess (pp. 224–25), baffles him. What does Augustine mean by saying that "our good lives forever with You" (*apud Te*), and that we "fell to ruin from there" (*quia nos inde ruimus*). But "in our absence our house, Your Eternity, has not fallen into ruin" (*nobis autem absentibus, non ruit domus nostra, aeternitas Tua*). Knauer admits he is temporarily stumped by this identity between "our" *domus* and God's *aeternitas*; we shall be wise to postpone dealing with this puzzle, returning to it when Augustine himself returns to it, in Book 12 of his *Confessions*.

Almost an entire book goes by before we come upon the next serious candidate Knauer can propose (p. 226) as instancing the *peregrinatio* theme: Augustine observes (5.23) that, on his arrival at Milan, Ambrose "welcomed" (*dilexit*) his *peregrinatio* "in episco-pal-enough fashion." Once again, Knauer astutely points to the pregnant ambiguity of that term *peregrinatio*: it refers to Augustine's "outward" voyage to Milan, surely, but at the same time alerts the reader to the fateful change in direction Ambrose will provoke in the young man's "interior" journey.

Toward Conversion

Book 6 begins with a summary of Augustine's spiritual state: he was "walking through darkness and on a slippery way," but a moment later and his journey is no longer over land; in despair of finding the truth, he "had come down into the depth of the sea" (6.1). "O tortuous ways," he exclaims, but finishes Book 6 (see Knauer, p. 227) with the familiar motif from Isaiah 46:4: God alone is *requies*, and He will "place us on His Way," will "console" us, and say: "Run, I, I will bear you and I will lead you there, and even there, I will bear you [up]" (6.26).

Book 7 bristles with imagery drawn mostly from the *Omnia* register. The *peregrinatio* theme is briefly sounded when his readings in Plotinus prompt Augustine to identify the Lucan "region of want" (*regio egestatis*) he has been living in with the Neoplatonic *regio dissimilitudinis*, the "region of unlikeness" to God (7.16). But Augustine's depiction of where his Neoplatonic experience had left him is couched unambiguously in *peregrinatio* terms: he has come to "see," with the eye of understanding, a number of truths about the higher, spiritual world, truths that he had formerly been commanded to "believe." But how profitable was that achievement, after all? He is like a man who has caught sight of his

beloved *patria* from a hill that lay along his homeward road; but
he must now experience the vital "difference between those who
see whither [*quo*] they must journey, but do not see the way [*qua*]
to it, and those who do see the Way [*Viam*] that leads, not only to
beholding, but also to dwelling in, our blessed *patria*" (7.26). He
will come in time to realize that the Church's "little ones," who
have never "seen" what he has been privileged to see, but who
nonetheless "keep to the Way," following Christ in humble faith,
are sure to arrive in the "homeland of peace." They are better off,
therefore, than any brilliant Neoplatonist who may well have
"seen" the spiritual homeland of our souls, but proudly refuses to
follow the "Way" Whom God has appointed to lead us there
(7.27).

From this point on, Augustine's employment of *peregrinatio*
imagery slackens off considerably. He presents himself to Simpli-
cianus, he tells us, for help in deciding whether he should "walk
in [God's] Way" as a celibate or a married man (8.1); but the
allusion to the Prodigal parable in 8.6 illustrates the joys of
homecoming, and has very little to do with the *peregrinatio* motif
as such. Knauer's efforts to find *peregrinatio* material in Book 9 are
strained, to say the least: except for Augustine's terminal reflection
depicting his parents as "fellow-citizens in the eternal Jerusalem"
to which the *peregrinatio* of God's people longs to "return" (9.37).
Books 10, 11, and 13 are woven out of imagery drawn almost
entirely from different registers.

But in Book 12 Augustine's identification of the "Heaven of
Heaven" with the "eternal Jerusalem," makes it clear, as Knauer
(p. 243) correctly shows, that this has been the "goal" of his and
our journeying from beginning to end. Book 12, accordingly, is
quite as rich in *peregrinatio* imagery as Knauer claims (pp. 240–
44).

KNAUER'S UNANSWERED QUESTIONS

But in the course of his article Knauer found himself obliged by
the text of the *Confessions* to raise several questions, only to leave
them curiously half-answered. The first of these (p. 234*n*2) might
appear relatively minor: Did Augustine understand *peregrinatio* as
having only the general sense conveyed by the German *Wanderschaft*, or did he think of it as having as one of its senses the more
special meaning of *Pilgerschaft*, religious "pilgrimage"? A first
answer to this has been given by Perler: his wider survey of

Augustine's employment of the term convinces him that Augustine does not use it in that more modern specialized sense.[9]

But latent in Knauer's German is another question. For *Wanderschaft* can mean "traveling" or "journeying" toward a known destination and with a sense of direction, but it can also mean "wandering" in the more aimless sense of "roaming," "rambling," or "straying." Now, it may be an even more interesting question whether Augustine consciously uses the term in these two senses and expects his reader to differentiate between them. For if he did, he would be intending that we detect a difference of "flavor" between those usages, a difference that would imply a shift in the force we ought to read into the term.

We saw, for instance, that one of his Biblical figures for the *peregrinus* was the sheep of the parable who "went astray" and so became "lost." The *Confessions* frequently describes Augustine's plight in similar terms: *erravi sicut ovis perdita*, "I went astray like the lost sheep" (12.21), was like "an unhappy sheep wandering off [*aberrans*] from your flock" (3.4), "a sheep that had gone astray" (*erraverat*) (8.6). One cannot help thinking, in this connection, of Augustine's dramatic evocation of our human situation *before* we knew the "goal toward which we are now tending": "We did not know the way. . . . We did not know how to go: the way was full of all sorts of twists and turns; it was thorny, rocky, extremely painful": *spinosi, lapidosi, omnino graves. . . . Aberravimus enim*: "for we had gone astray." Clearly, he is depicting us here as sheep, lost, baffled, and disheartened by all the panicking obstacles of the mountainside. And his point is that *before* Christ came to be our "Way," our *peregrinatio* was of a different sort from what it has now become: we had no *finis*, no sense of destination or direction; we were wandering helplessly, hopelessly, aimlessly, until He "made Himself into our Way" (*ipse . . . fecit se viam*) (*SD 20* 9).

That text, however, is the furthest thing from an *obiter dictum*. The desert figure provokes a similar reflection: Psalm 62 speaks of it as *sine via, sine aqua*, "trackless and waterless." This, Augustine tells us, refers to *saeculum istud*: "this temporal world." Then:

> O would that there were a way in the desert! Would that man could enter it and know how to exit from it! He can see no other comforting human figure, can see no way of being free of the desert. And so, he turns off for lodging [*ibi divertit*]. Evil is the desert . . . fearsome and horrifying! And yet, God took pity on us,

and made a Way for us in the desert, our Lord Jesus Christ Himself [*En 62* 8; cf. 6; cp. 8.8].

It is God in His mercy who calls those who "of themselves were unable to return" (*per seipsos redire non possent*). He "graces" the impious so that "he returns like the lost sheep . . . which was able by its own choice to wander off and become lost" (*redeat ovis perdita . . . quae se perdere potuit dum sponte vagaretur*). We had the power to wander off, but once lost, we were unable to return (*En 77* 24; *InJo 7* 21). We roamed about, no "way" before us, as the Israelites thought they were roaming about in the desert, though they could not go truly astray with God as their guide (*errabant . . . sed duce Deo errare non poterant*) (*En 124* 3; *EpJo 7* 1; cf. *10* 1). And the same sense of lostness was experienced by that "younger son," the Prodigal (*En 77* 24).

Augustine, then, imagines *peregrini* as falling into two classes: first, there are those who have wandered away—from God, from the Father's "house," from the "flock"—and have not yet found (or been found by!) the "Way" Who is the Incarnate Word (*SS 346* 1, *91* 1; *Enn 62* 8, *66* 5; *EpJo 10* 1). These, like the lost sheep, or the man lost in the trackless desert, have neither destination nor sense of direction; they roam about aimlessly, pointlessly. *Peregrini*, they may not even realize that they are wayfarers! But then there are those who have come to know the Way, and realize that they have strayed far from home and homeland: these no longer roam or wander, but direct their steps along the Way that they know will lead them home—again.

The Identity of Our "Home"

For there, I submit, we have Augustine's reply to a final question which Knauer has raised, but left only half-answered. We saw above that in his analysis of the *Confessions* Knauer came upon the marvelous coda which ends Book 4 and spills over into the first two paragraphs of Book 5. After depicting himself as the Prodigal who had "departed from [God] to a far country, and dissipated [the good portion of his substance] among harlots," Augustine goes on to say that "we do not fear that there will be no place for us to return to [*quo redeamus*], on account of our having fallen from it to our ruin [*quia nos inde ruimus*]; though we be absent, our *domus*, Your Eternity, has not fallen into ruin" (4.31). "What 'house' is being described" here, Knauer queries, "out of which men have fallen, and to which they desire to return? Doubtless it is also the Father's house, hence God's, where He keeps the indefectible 'good' safe for the [Prodigal] son on his return." The parallel between the *domus* and God's *aeternitas*, however, prompts the conjecture (pp. 224–25) that one should look toward "some even more precise interpretation."

It is somewhat surprising that Knauer never fully pays off on the promise he seems to be making his reader here, and all the more surprising in view of his central thesis. His main contention is that the *Confessions* is a unified composition, which demands that the reader hoping to understand its message may not stop at the end of the "autobiographical" portions, but must plunge bravely onward through Books 10 to 13. That contention is, I am convinced, perfectly correct: for Augustine does make it clear in those later books what his answer would be to this question of Knauer's. And, paradoxically, Knauer should have been the last person in the world to miss it.

Knauer has obviously detected that the ending of Book 4 implies nothing less than this: that Augustine, like the Prodigal, once dwelt in the Father's "house," which is identical with God's own "Eternity"; this is precisely what the *Omnia* image already suggests. He "departed" from that house, "flowed downward" from it (*defluxit*), wandered off into the "far country" which, Knauer has also seen (pp. 223, 229–30), corresponds to the "region of unlikeness." Now the Prodigal yearns to "return" to the very house from which he once departed. The implication is clear enough, even if one attended only to Book 4; but instead of bravely drawing it from the text, Knauer balks, and postpones dealing with the issue.

Now, this reaction may well have been precisely what Augustine hoped to prompt from the attentive reader: the autobiographical books of the *Confessions* appear to comprise a series of provocative puzzles, calculated to "exercise the mind" (one of Augustine's favorite teaching techniques) until the reader himself is as struck as Augustine had become by that *grande profundum, homo*, the "vast depths of the human" that had made him into a "great question," *magna quaestio,* to himself (4.9, 21).[10]

But Knauer's own theory on the unity of the *Confessions* requires that Augustine eventually furnish answers to the queries he has artfully inserted into his reader's mind. So, when he comes to Augustine's depiction in Book 12 of that *domus Dei*, the "house of

God" which is one with the Heavenly Jerusalem, we become especially alert for Knauer's answer to the question he himself has raised. He sees that Augustine has artfully woven together a number of evidential strands that he had, until now, deliberately left somewhat loose-ended. But he also sees that we are now entitled to conclude this much: that the *domus* of Book 4 is identical with that portion of the *domus Dei*, the Heavenly Jerusalem, which never went on *peregrinatio*, and so remains beyond all time and change (12.13). So, Knauer gives expression to his conclusion: "Here, therefore, for the first time, [Augustine's] life's wandering [*Wanderschaft seines Lebens*] up until his conversion, finds its true goal: it is the *domus Dei*, which in contrast to Augustine, did not need to wander, in order to exist eternally with God" (p. 243). We are assured, accordingly, that this unity of "goal" confers the desired bond of unity between the "biographical" and the "exegetical" books of the *Confessions*.

The Journey of "Return"

As to the unity of the *Confessions*, I am in perfect agreement; but I think that the case can and ought to be made even stronger than Knauer makes it. But notice how elusively he has replied to the question about the *domus Dei*. Augustine has finally identified it as the "goal" of all his "wanderings"; there is little doubt about that much. But Knauer himself phrased the question raised by the mention of the *domus Dei* in Book 4, and it contained, not one, but two puzzling features that Augustine includes in his specification of that "house of God." Not only do our wandering souls long to "go back" there (*zurückkehren*), but our souls "fell down from there" (*hinausgesturzt sind*); *nos inde ruimus*, Augustine expressly puts it. The implications could scarcely be clearer: if we long to *zurückkehren*, to "go *back*" there, we must have *been there before*; that implication is confirmed beyond cavil by Augustine's claim that we (in Knauer's term) "hinausgesturzt sind" from there: "we fell from there." Augustine is unmistakably saying that his and our "wandering" began when we left that *domus Dei*. But, *pace* Knauer, neither we nor Augustine did that in our "lifetime." We must, therefore, have done it at some mysterious "time" before "this life" of ours. Book 4 makes it clear, and Knauer's paraphrase makes it just as clear, that the "goal" of the human *peregrinatio* is identical with its original starting point!

To the "Heaven of Heaven"

If there were any doubt on that conclusion, Augustine dissolves it by returning to the topic of the "Heaven of Heaven" in Book 13. This has not escaped Knauer's notice, either. He strives bravely (pp. 241–43) to interpret those dense and difficult paragraphs in which Augustine describes the original creation-and-conversion of intellectual creatures (perhaps creation *by* conversion would be more accurate: the metaphysic here is thorny beyond imagining), but he allows a crucial phrase to get buried in a footnote. It is the very expression Pépin had emphasized as indicating that the Heaven of Heaven must be the abode not only of angels, but of human souls as well (*defluxit angelus, defluxit anima hominis*).[11] Not only did angels "flow downward" from that changeless state into the *ista*, the *multa* of this ever-flowing temporal world, but men's souls—or (again) is it one soul that is equivalent to "humanity" entire?—did so as well. But, clearly, to flow downward from that abode, they must previously have been "there."

Now, we have seen that Augustine leaves no doubt possible on the accuracy of Knauer's underlying contention that the goal, the destination of the human being's *peregrinatio*, is the celestial Jerusalem, the "house of God," the "eternal homeland." And the fact that in composing his *Confessions* Augustine so deliberately teases our minds with hints and allusions to this effect, and discloses his full intention only in Books 12 and 13, strongly confirms Knauer's principal conclusion that the work represents an artfully conceived but definitely unified whole. But his preached works leave just as little doubt that Augustine plainly thought of that ultimate destination as identical with our starting point: "in our end," as Eliot puts it, is quite literally "our beginning."

The most numerous clues in that direction are linguistic ones: here, once again, we must take seriously this professional *rhetor*'s passion for using the exact term. We have seen him speak of himself as a "lost sheep" that had *gone* astray (*erravi, errabam*). But we have also seen examples when he tells us he had "strayed away," "away from [God's] flock" (*aberraveram*). There is a difference, and Augustine would have expected us to give him credit for knowing that difference; for "straying away from the flock" clearly authorizes the inference that the sheep in question originally belonged to that flock. Indeed, as Augustine well knew, this seems to be implied if one takes the exact term of the Lucan parable

(*perierat*) as seriously, and literally, as Augustine's regular exegetical method tended to do.

But there are a number of similar linguistic clues. Clearest of all
are Augustine's reminders that we are all *peregrini* "from" (*ab*) the
homeland we now sigh after (*En 121* 2, 5). But aside from
reminding us that this homeland is our "whither" (*quo*), Augustine repeatedly describes it as the *unde*, the *inde* "whence" we have
come (*S 189* 2; *Enn 148* 4, *86* 1, *93* 6). The force of that "whence"
is made doubly certain on occasions when he combines it with
terms like *recesseramus* or *deseruimus*: we "deserted" or "withdrew
from" that celestial abode (*Enn 90*, sermon 2, 1; *94* 2, *119* 6).
"There," in that "city," he tells us,

> the angels also are our fellow-citizens; but because we are *peregrini*,
> labor is our lot; they, however, await our arrival in that city. And
> from that city, whence [*unde*] we are *peregrini*, letters have come to
> us. . . . The King Himself has come down and become a Way for
> us in our *peregrinatio*, so that, walking in it, we shall not go astray.
> . . . [He has become our] Mediator in order to reconcile through
> Himself those who had withdrawn [*recesserant*]. . . . We had
> withdrawn from God's majesty, and offended Him by our sin
> [*peccato nostro*]. The Son was sent to us, the Mediator, . . . to give
> us back to Him and reconcile us to Him [*redderet nos ei et reconcili-*
> *aret*]. . . . He is God . . . God to create, but man to re-create us;
> God to make, but man to re-make us [*En 90*, sermon 2, 1].

This text, besides exhibiting the interrelationship of a number
of themes we have been examining, unveils another set of linguistic
clues Augustine is fond of deploying. Notice the insistent multi-
plication of verb forms beginning with *re*: *reconciliaret*, *redderet*,
recrearet, *reficeret*, all pointing to Augustine's conviction that the
religion of the Incarnation was designed to *re-ligare*, re-tie a
relationship with the Father which has been snapped, but which,
before having been snapped, once obtained.[12] The same device can
be detected elsewhere (*Enn 100* 3, *101*, sermon 2, 8, etc.), but the
term that most frequently figures is, understandably, the journeying term *redire*: we are not merely "going" to the Heavenly
Jerusalem, but going "back" to it (*S 75* 2; *Enn 29* 6; *126* 1, 3; *119*
7; *121* 5; *64* 3; *49* 22; *62* 6; *66* 5; *77* 24; *85* 11).[13] Augustine could
scarcely speak more plainly: we dwelt in that Heavenly City before
going "astray."

> She [Jerusalem] is our mother, after whom we sigh and groan in
> this *peregrinatio* of ours, that we may go back to her [*redeamus*].

Erraveramus ab ea: we had wandered away from her, and we had no way: her King came, and became the Way for us, so that we might be able to go back to her: *ut ad illam redire possimus*. . . . . She it is where "our feet were standing" [since we enjoyed] "participation in the Selfsame" [scil., the Unchanging God]. Those who dwell there, accordingly, "will not be moved for all eternity." But those who dwelt in this [earthly] Jerusalem were "moved" [*moti sunt*], first in their heart, then in their exile. When they were moved in heart and fell [*ceciderunt*], then they crucified the King of the supernal Jerusalem. . . . And He ejected them from His city, the eternal Jerusalem, that is mother of us all, which is in the heavens [*En 124* 3].

We were all once dwellers in the heavenly Jerusalem therefore, "standing," and, so, sharing in the eternal "stability" of the God Who is ever the same (*Idipsum*).[14] Though we were changeable by nature, that participation exempted us from change (*motus*). We had a change of "heart," however, an alteration in the object of our love, and the consequence of that heart-change was our consignment to this lower world of time. We became "exiles" from the heavenly and eternal Jerusalem, consigned to "this" (the *ista* of contempt) earthly Jerusalem, where change can take the darkly sinister form of murdering the very Way that has come to lead us back home again. But, Augustine is careful to note, when we return to that eternal city, no further change will occur (*non movebuntur in aeternum*).

Augustine's thought is unmistakably clear on this. In the seventh and final "day" of the *saeculum*, "we shall go into that life and rest" of which Paul tells us that no eye has seen nor ear heard. That "going" will, though, be like a "going back" to Christ our Head (*velut ad caput reditur*), for we shall "go back [*rediemus*] to that immortality and bliss from which man fell [*de qua lapsus est homo*]. . . . But meanwhile, until we enter into that rest, during this time when we are in labor and in night . . . and journey through the desert until we arrive in the heavenly Jerusalem . . . let us do good works" (*S 259* 2–3).

We are the part of that heavenly Jerusalem that went on *peregrinatio*: *non in angelis, sed in nobis peregrinatur*, and that city's "better part" awaits the part that is returning (*En 131* 21). "Not all of Jerusalem was being held captive in this temporal Babylon, for the angels are also her citizens" (*En 136* 1). Those angels

rejoice in seeing God in that great, wide, heavenly city; God Himself is the object of their vision. But we are on *peregrinatio* from that city, expelled by sin so that we could not remain there [*ne ibi remaneremus*], and weighed down by mortality, so that we could not go back there. But God looked down on our *peregrinatio*, and He who is the builder of Jerusalem, restored the fallen part [*restituit lapsam partem*]. . . . For a certain part fell [*cecidit*] and became *peregrina*: that *peregrina* God beheld with mercy, and went seeking those who were not seeking Him" [*En 146* 4].

We "fell" from that city, therefore; we "sold ourselves" by "sin" into the Babylonian captivity we now endure.

Who sold us? We ourselves [*nos ipsi*], we who gave consent to the Seducer. We were able to sell ourselves, but not to buy ourselves back.

How then is Sion both eternal Sion and captive Sion? Eternal in the angels, captive in men. For not all the citizens of that city are captives; but those who made *peregrinatio* from it [*inde*], those are captives. Man [*homo*] is citizen of Jerusalem, but, sold through sin, has become *peregrinus*. From his progeny was born the human race, who filled the earth with the Sion of captivity [*En 125* 1–3; see also *En 62* 6).

What is the relationship with Adam that is implied here? That question merits a full-scale treatment; but for now let it suffice to say that Augustine thinks of that relationship in terms that warrant his saying that "we" sinned, that "we ourselves," *nos ipsi*, sold ourselves into captivity. *We* "deserted," and *we* are now "returning" (*En 117* 23). Once dwellers in that heavenly city along with the angels, we long to return to their company. The length of our journey has "perhaps" made us "forget" that it was once our homeland, but the Gospel reminds us that that is indeed the truth (*En 32*, version 2, sermon 2, 6). Adam did it; but that does not preclude, but seems positively to imply, the fact that "we" did it; indeed, "we did it" and "Adam did it" seem to come down to the same thing!

The same conclusion follows from consideration of that other *peregrinus*, the "man" who "descended" from Jerusalem to Jericho. That man, Augustine tells us, is Adam, inasmuch as he represents the entire human race (*ipse Adam intelligitur in genere humano*). The Jerusalem he left was "that heavenly city of peace," from whose beatitude he fell: *lapsus est*. Jericho means our "mortality." The Samaritan, the "guardian," is of course Christ the Lord, while the *stabulum*, the "inn" to which He confided the half-dead traveler stands for the Church, "where voyagers returning from their *peregrinatio* to the heavenly homeland, are refreshed." Originally fallen, *lapsi* (in Adam), we are all now heading back to our eternal fatherland (*redeuntes in aeternam patriam*). That exegetical base is laid down in Augustine's *Quaestiones in Evangelium* (2 19), but the interpretation, as one might expect, runs through his preaching as well. Had that man of the parable not "descended" from the heavenly Jerusalem to Jericho, "from immortality to mortality," he would never have fallen among robbers. Adam it was who "descended," but in fact "we are all Adam" (*omnes enim nos Adam sumus*). "If we have descended, and were wounded, let us ascend, singing; let us walk onward, so as to arrive" (*S 31* 4–5; *Enn 88*, sermon 2, 5; *121* 7; *125* 11; *118*, sermon 15, 6; *InJo 41* 13).

The same circularity of departure and return is encased in that archetypal story of fallen humanity, the Prodigal. The same must be said of Augustine's interpretation of Homer's Odysseus. But again, Augustine's interpretation of both those figures is so rich and suggestive as to merit special studies for themselves.

CONCLUSIONS: HUMAN LIFE AS *Peregrinatio*

For the present, though, it is clear that Augustine's preaching supports the contention Knauer drew from his *Confessions*: his commanding metaphor for our human life sees us as *peregrini*, wayfarers, journeyers, but journeying laboriously through a country that is alien, comfortless, even hostile. We begin that journey, most of us at least, as Augustine did: as wanderers, aimless and lost like someone in a trackless desert. But then we may find a way, or, better, the Way may find us. We are awakened to our plight, reminded of the homeland, the native city we had perhaps forgotten. From that moment our journeying takes on a new quality: we now have a destination, a sense of direction; we can be confident that the Way is leading us back "home." We must never stop stoking the fires of our nostalgia, must "use" all the goods and amenities of the desert as *viatores* do the tents or inns they pass their nights in; we must not slip into the error of taking them as *mansiones*, lasting homes, places of terminal "enjoyment." We must walk onward, or preferably, as Paul depicts himself as doing, run: always on the stretch for that final rest in the homeland we sigh and groan for.

But, something Knauer failed to grip firmly enough, that homeland, that heavenly city beyond all time and change, was where we started from. We deserted, wandered away from it; but there the unfallen angels, the "better part" of Jerusalem's citizenry, await our return.

Or, in the language of the *Omnia* image, we were once aloft with those angels, in the Heaven of Heaven, rendered changeless by the vision of the God Who is ever the "Selfsame." But a change occurred, a sinful change of "heart," and we "fell" from that lofty world into this change-ridden region of want. Our *peregrinatio* must therefore be not only an onward, but the upward, one David chanted in his Psalms of "Ascent"; our Pauline *extensio* must be forward into further journeying, but upward also, from this lower region into which we fell, to the higher realm we once inhabited. To summarize in Augustine's terms, here is how he comments on the words of Psalm 136:

> Everyone who has learned from the holy Church should know whence we are citizens, and whither we are journeying, and that the cause of our *peregrinatio* is sin, the cause of our return [*reversio*] being the gift of forgiveness of sins and justification through the grace of God. . . . It is not the whole of Jerusalem that is held captive in Babylon, for the angels are also her citizens. . . . But this very day we chanted: *Super flumina Babylonis, ibi sedimus et flevimus, cum recordaremur Sion.* What, therefore, are these "rivers of Babylon," and what does it mean that we "sit and weep in remembering Sion"? . . . The rivers of Babylon are all the things that we love, here, and that are forever passing. . . . But the citizens of the holy Jerusalem understand their captivity. . . . [They] do not enter into the rivers of Babylon, but sit "over" them [*super*] and weep over the rivers of Babylon, or over those who are swept away by them, or over themselves, who have merited to be [captives] in Babylon. . . .
>
> O holy Sion, where everything "stands" [unchanging], and nothing "flows," what has precipitated us into these realities [*ista*]? Why did we dismiss your Establisher and your society? Behold, ordered as we are among these ever-flowing and -passing things, it is hard for anyone to escape, swept away by that river, [even] if he can cling to the wood! . . . Let us therefore sit "over" that river, not in the river, or under it: but sit, sit humbly, and do not speak as though you were in Jerusalem. For there you shall stand, for another Psalm speaks of that hope, and sings: "Our feet were standing [*stantes*] in the courts of Jerusalem." There you will be exalted, if you humble yourself here by doing penance and confessing [*En 136* 1–4).

Our presence in this nocturnal region, then, our "wayfaring" life in this lower portion of the *Omnia*, is the result of our having "wandered away" and become *peregrini* from the lofty home we once enjoyed. Our only hope, accordingly, is to find the "way" that will lead us home again. Or, more accurately, we must hope that the "Way" will deign to find us.

That hope is far from groundless, though, for the God Whom we deserted never deserts us. He—or is it She?—is like a mother anxiously fretting over her straying child; her care pursues him tirelessly, stubbornly, no matter where he wanders. This brings us to the third of Augustine's foundational images of the wandering soul and its cosmic situation: the image of God's activity, providential, but at the same time omnipresential, of "caring" for us fallen souls.

NOTES

1. *"Peregrinatio animae*: Zur Frage der Einheit der augustinischen KONFESSIONEN," *Hermes*, 85 (1957), 216–48 (henceforth: *Peregrinatio*). We shall be dealing with studies of Augustine's more particular *peregrinus* images (the Prodigal, Odysseus, Aeneas) in subsequent chapters.

I was unable to profit from M. A. Claussen's "*Peregrinatio* and *Peregrini* in Augustine's *City of God*," *Traditio*, 46 (1991), 33–75, which actually appeared only in 1993.

2. *Psalmenzitate in Augustins* KONFESSIONEN (Göttingen: Vandenhoeck & Ruprecht, 1955).

3. See, for example, Pierre Courcelle, *Recherches sur les* CONFESSIONS *de saint Augustin*, 2 vols. (Paris: Boccard, 1950), pp. 20–26 (henceforth: *Recherches*); the claim is repeated in the second edition (Paris: Boccard, 1968), pp. 20–26. See also John J. O'Meara, *The Young Augustine: The Growth of St. Augustine's Mind Up to His Conversion* (London: Longmans, Green, 1954), pp. 13, 16.

4. See his *Retractatio* (the second volume of *Culture*), pp. 665–72.

5. See Othmar Perler, *Les Voyages de saint Augustin* (Paris: Études Augustiniennes, 1969), pp. 13–21, 45–47 (henceforth: *Voyages*).

6. See Peter Brown, *Augustine of Hippo* (Berkeley: University of California Press, 1967), pp. 68–72.

7. Ibid., pp. 323–24.

8. Perler, *Voyages*, p. 43, notes that the term *mansio* could also refer to the more elaborate lodgings for travelers of the *cursus publicus*, and wonders about Augustine's infrequent use of the term in this meaning. I suggest that this omission may have much to do with the *manere* nuance he could have chosen to reserve for our more permanent "home."

9. *Voyages*, p. 45.

10. See Marrou, *Culture*, pp. 299–328; see also my *Saint Augustine's* CONFESSIONS: *The Odyssey of Soul* (Cambridge: The Belknap Press of Harvard University Press, 1969; repr. New York: Fordham University Press, 1989), pp. 15–16.

11. *Peregrinatio*, pp. 244–45, esp. 244*n*1, where Knauer observes that the term *defluo* in the various examples he quotes is obviously being used "terminologisch," meaning, I assume, that it has technical import for Augustine. But he does not say how he understands that import. For my understanding of it, see above, chap. 1, pp. 26–46.

12. *Ver* 113 begins with an allusion to this etymological sense.

13. The term *revolare* ("to fly back": see *Conf* 3.8), despite its clear *peregrinatio* resonances, I intend to treat of in a later chapter, in the context of the *fovere* image: it represents a "fusion" of these two image-registers.

14. For the meaning Augustine attaches to the terms *stare* and *Idipsum*, see above, chap. 1, pp. 23–24.

3

Fove Precantes, Trinitas: God's Omnipresent Care

THE IMAGE OF THE *Omnia* furnishes the necessary backdrop to all of Augustine's other images. That is natural enough. The universe of "all things" is the theater in which the entire drama of cosmic history is played out. At the center of that story, we have seen, Augustine places the soul's "fall" from the Highest into the "lowest" region of the *Omnia*, humankind's *peregrinatio* from, and return to, the "Heaven of Heaven." But that "return" to the contemplative peace we once left behind could never reach home did the Trinitarian God not envelop us with the unremitting "care" that makes it possible.

Augustine's literary skill is never more masterfully displayed than in producing the luxuriant bouquet of images depicting God's poignant care for fallen humanity. And it testifies to his imagination's amazing fertility, as well as to its dominantly literary character, that so many of those images seem to have been triggered by a single Latin word—*fovere*.

His partiality toward that word is clear from the frequency of its occurrence in his early writings. The climax of his *De beata vita* (paragraph 35) is punctuated, for instance, by Monica's quotation of a line from Augustine's own favorite Ambrosian hymn, the *Deus Creator omnium*; to show that she has divined the Trinitarian bearing of her son's remarks, she murmurs: *fove precantes, Trinitas*. But the term *fovere,* along with its associated imagery, runs like a refrain through those early works, from Cassiciacum forward. By studying its occurrences, one can track the imaginative process whereby an entire family of related images come to cluster about it, one calling to a second, the second associating with a third, perhaps even a fourth, until the mind runs back to the first—and the process can then begin over again![1]

And yet, in his poetic masterpiece, the *Confessions*, the term occurs only twice, and never once before that central book, Book 7, and the very central section of that book.[2] When finally Augustine explicitly resorts to the term, its abrupt appearance has been so artfully prepared that it explodes upon our minds like a pyrotechnic display.

In *Confessions* 7.20 Augustine is spelling out the world view to which his readings in the "platonists" introduced him. He has come to the most agonizing question he had wrestled with throughout his younger years: the mystery of evil. Describing God's action on his behalf, he expresses it with a common Latin verb: *fovisti caput nescientis,* he says. It is clear that he is portraying himself as an "un-knower": a *nesciens.* Clearly, too, he is telling us that God did something or other to his head: *caput.* But what was that something or other?

A TRIAL FOR TRANSLATORS

Translators of the *Confessions* differ in answering that question. Sampling the best known among them, the reader soon comes on "bathe[d]" (V. Bourke), "soothed" (Pusey, J. K. Ryan), "mis un calmant [sur]" (Tréhorel and Bouissou). Sheed seems to be playing odd man out with "caressed." But his daring is tame when compared to Pierre de Labriolle's apparently wild stab, "Vous avez tourné ma tête contre Vous."

Consulting the Latin dictionary seems, initially, to offer little help. The first meaning of the verb *fovere* is to "warm"; but like so many common Latin terms, it turns out to be amazingly polyvalent; warming activity can be applied by so many diverse agencies, can take so many forms, serve so many different purposes. But patience is rewarded: *The Oxford Latin Dictionary* (p. 729) illustrates one of the word's frequent contexts with expressions like "bathe, foment." Obviously, the context here is medical, and recalls the action whereby a doctor treats a wound or swelling with some "soothing application" that, originally, was warm. That medicinal action would, of course, closely relate to other typical expressions, like "give comfort, soothe, relieve." And so we have lexical justification for the first three translations listed above.

Yet search a bit further and Sheed's "caressed" can also be defended: in certain other contexts *fovere* can mean to "fondle, caress," to "hug" someone, or to "nurse" someone's wounds, or even (more metaphorically still) someone's "sorrows." Examine some typical expressions listed—*sinu,* or *gremio fovere,* to cherish or embrace against one's breast, or on one's lap—and de La-briolle's image of a mother tenderly turning her child's head against her comforting breast suddenly leaps into focus as a definite possibility for the translator. By now the word's elasticity is becoming almost visible, as it stretches to further meanings (and associated images) like: to "foster, nurture," "watch over the growth of" a child, for example, an animal, or a nestling chick.

Augustine's professional feel for words would have permitted him, therefore, to intend any of the above senses when using the term at this central point in his *Confessions*. Which of them, though, did he intend us to understand? Or, more in line with our purposes, which of the images associated with the term did he want us to uncover in this crucial employment of the expression? What did this versatile word convey to his lively imagination?

A CLUE FROM AUGUSTINE HIMSELF

As luck would have it, Augustine himself has shed some light on this question, although in another work entirely. In his *De Genesi ad litteram* (1.36), he has come to the phrase portraying the "Spirit of God" as "borne over the waters." His first instinct is to warn us against interpreting that expression in some "carnal," corporeal sense; God's ways of acting cannot be comprehended by such crass metaphors. Rather, he reminds us, the Creator works through those immutable forms and "reasons" contained in His co-eternal Divine Word. But that is not the end of it: God also works "by a kind of incubating action [*fotu*], if the expression be permitted me, of His equally co-eternal Holy Spirit." That term *fotus*, derived from the same root as the verb *fovere*, presents us with a daring metaphor, Augustine acknowledges. But he has been reliably informed that the Syriac language, which is much closer to Hebrew than either Latin or Greek, employs an expression for this action of God's Spirit which implies that the Spirit "warmed [*fovebat*] [the primeval waters] by setting [on them]."

The first image the term suggests, then, is the "warming" action of a mother-bird, incubating her eggs to bring forth living chicks. But Augustine is not finished. We should not, he warns us, interpret that *fovere* action in the equally familiar medical sense, as intimating the curative action whereby doctors *fovent* "tumors and bodily wounds by [bathing, or "fomenting" them with]

water, either cold, or appropriately tempered with warm." No,
Augustine prefers us to think that the incubation metaphor is
more apt here, particularly since the mother-bird's "warmth
contributes somehow to the formation of the chicks by a kind of
feeling that is, in its way, a form of love" (*dilectionis affectum*).
Augustine's imagination may have been influenced here by the fact
that the Holy Spirit is symbolized as a dove; but more to the fore
is his conviction that He (She?) must always be thought of as the
Spirit of God's love.

But we must not think of God's creative working in terms of
such "carnal" and bodily images, Augustine warns again. For the
point of Christ's coming in order to "gather us children of
Jerusalem under His wings, as a hen does her chicks," was not to
leave us forever "little ones" (*parvuli*) who took such earthly
imagery literally; no, He meant us to grow up to a more adult
"understanding" of His spiritual reality and activity. Even while
issuing that warning against imagination, though, Augustine has
explicitly evoked the very image Christ used of Himself: that of a
mother-hen, gathering her chicks beneath her wings, but now, in
order to shelter and protect them. This was another familiar
image, summoned up to the Latin speaker by the word *fovere*. But
that maternal image of the hen, showing her care for her chicks
by sheltering and defending them, found its natural partner in the
equally familiar image of a human mother doing much the same
thing, but as human mothers do: by taking her child into her arms
or onto her lap, fondling it against her breast, calming it by
"cooing," caressing, perhaps even suckling it.

ASSOCIATIONS DERIVED FROM THE *Omnia* IMAGE

It seems clear that it was the broad generality of its abstract
dictionary meaning, "to warm," which permitted the term *fovere*
to flower forth into this exuberant cluster of sub-meanings and
associated images. We shall have further occasion to note how
sensitive Augustine's imagination was to all of them.

But to stay, for the moment, with that most general meaning
of the term: Augustine conceives of God as constantly "warming"
us. What does that import for him? The answer lies in the
implications of his more fundamental *Omnia* image, for (again)
both *fovere* and *peregrinatio* images operate within the larger frame
of his image of the two-tiered universe.

Consider, for example, his remarkable interpretation (in *En 147* 22) of the Psalmist's expression *currit Verbum Ejus usque in velocitatem*. He understands this as referring to God's Divine Word, so that we must translate: "His Word runs unto swiftness [itself]," meaning (Augustine goes on to explain) "to the very utmost" of swiftness. This "swiftness itself" refers to the Word's Omnipresence, which permits God's subsistent Wisdom to be everywhere simultaneously, to "reach from end to end mightily" (Wis 8:1). Why do we humans experience such difficulty in getting our minds around such a notion? Because, Augustine replies, "the body which is corrupted," as Wisdom 9:15 reminds us, "weighs down the soul" (*aggravat animam*). And we are back to the *Omnia* theme of "weights."

Once back to that theme, Augustine continues with it: for earth, the heaviest and lowest of the four elements, is "cold," while "heat" is proper to the highest and lightest, fire. He assumes his hearers' familiarity with these basic insights of ancient physics, and goes on to their "spiritual" corollaries: "We on earth, therefore, are cold. For swiftness is fervent. All fervent things are swifter, whereas cold things are slower. We are slow" in understanding divine realities like Omnipresence, "hence cold. But that [Divine] Wisdom is . . . most fervent," so that, like the Sun of Psalm 18:7, "no one can hide from His heat."

Now Augustine continues (*En 147* 23) with his "spiritual physics" lesson: he links the slowness of our "frigid body" with our having been "burdened" (*onerati*) with the "chain of this corruptible earthly life." And yet the Divine Wisdom has not "deserted us, thrust down [*depressos*] though we have been by the body into the lowest of realities," into the *infima*. For He "predestined us, before we were born in this mortal and sluggish body" (*antequam in isto mortali et pigro corpore nasceremur*). This, he assures us, Psalm 147:16 insinuates by saying that God "gave snow to the earth," the snow that is "our very selves" (*ipsos nos*).

Did we, then, exist in some other condition before being born in these burdensome bodies? We have already seen part of Augustine's answer: he explains that we are rightly called "snow" because "snow, while in the upper regions, freezes," and, by the laws of the *Omnia*, "falls down into the lower regions. So human nature," he now makes the application, "its charity growing cold [Mt 24:12], fell down [*decidit*] to this earth, and, wrapped in sluggish bodies, became like snow" covering the earth. This

explains why, "sluggish on this earth, we froze together here."
Though still predestined from before our fall, we are "not yet
fervent with the spirit of charity." But "let not the snow despair";
God does not abandon those whom He has predestined. He will
"send forth His Word," that "Sun" from Whose "heat" no one
can hide, and the snow "will liquefy, will dissolve." He will
"breathe forth His Spirit," also, and the "waters" from that
melted snow "will flow." For "the Spirit is fervent, which is why
that other Psalm [125:4] says 'Convert, O Lord, our captivity, like
a torrent in the southlands.' Captive Jerusalem had frozen solid, as
it were, in Babylon: but the South-Wind blows, and the hardness
of that captivity is loosened, and the fervor of charity runs" like a
torrent to—or back to—God (24–26).

We have already remarked[3] on Henri Rondet's accurate characterization of this sort of thinking as "sheer Origenism"; Augustine
is unmistakably thinking of the entirety of human nature as once
having dwelt in the "upper regions" of the *Omnia*, before our
"charity grew cold" and like the snows we "fell" to our appropriate place in the "lower regions," indeed, in the lowest—*infima*—
stratum of the universe, "this earth." That fall occurs in accord
with the spiritual "physics" of the *Omnia*: our corruptible bodies
act as "burdens" or "chains" to bring us downward to "this
earth," but our "coldness"—the quality proper to "earth"—has
the identical effect. But those same laws of spiritual physics explain
why we now stand in need of the "warming" and "melting" (and,
by implication, the enflaming and "lightening") action of the
Divine Sun's "heat," and the Divine Spirit's "fervor." Both of
them are types of the redemptive "care" embodied in God's *fovere*
activity toward us, though Augustine, remarkably, never mentions the term itself; both are required to bring us aloft once again
to the higher regions from which we fell. *Fove precantes,
Trinitas.* . . .

Rondet has also pointed out that Augustine repeats the essentials
of this interpretation in *Enarratio 125* 10–12, but this time when
explaining the fourth verse of Psalm 125 which he quoted to
support the exegesis we have just examined. He cites the verse
from Ecclesiasticus (3:17) which seems to have furnished the
explicit inspiration for his equating "cold" with sinfulness: "Just
like ice in the fair warm weather, your sins will melt away." That
text implies that "our sins were binding us . . . as frigidity binds
water [and prevents it] from flowing. So we, bound up by the

frigidity of sins, we froze." But the Auster the Psalmist speaks of "is a hot wind [from the South]. When the Auster blows, the ice liquefies, and the torrents are filled." "Convert our captivity," verse 125:4 prays. "We had, therefore, become frozen in captivity; our sins held us bound; the Auster, [meaning] the Holy Spirit, blows, and . . . we are loosed from iniquity's frigidity; like ice in fair warm weather, our sins are dissolved [or loosed: *solvuntur*]. Let us run to the fatherland, like torrents of the South."

But this frigidity may not have been our original condition: "Human life itself, into which we have entered [*quam ingressi sumus*], is miserable and toilsome." We observe that every child issues from the womb crying, never laughing. Why? "Because he has begun to set forth into this life" (*in istam vitam*). The implication that there was another life the child enjoyed before "this" life—the depreciatory *ista* is eloquent—is not so clear as in *Enarratio 147*; but the parallelism of the two interpretations suggests that one may legitimately illumine the one by its partner. God's "care" for us, in any event, is exercised through a "warming" *fovere* action which, once again, obeys the universal laws of the *Omnia*.

Sermo 273 4–5 illustrates that Augustine can elicit essentially the same image-dynamic from a variety of Scriptural materials. The fidelity of martyrs, he tells his flock, illustrates God's merciful regard toward unworthy mortals, and so fulfills the "prophecy" expressed by the Canticle of Canticles (4:16): "Arise, you North-Wind [*Aquilo*], and come, you South-Wind [*Auster*], blow through my garden, and let its aromatic spices flow." That verse recalls to Augustine's mind the Canticle's phrase (1:3) that "we shall run after thee to the odor of thy ointments," which links up, in turn, with 2 Corinthians 2:14, where Paul speaks of the "good odor" of Christ; but the resulting amalgam, ingenious though it is, could almost have been predicted from what we have seen already. The *Aquilonia* evoked by mention of the "North-Wind" is, Augustine reminds his hearers, "the cold part of the world. Under the devil [and his prompting], as though by a North-Wind, souls grew frigid, lost the warmth of charity, and froze over." This is why the author of the Canticle calls on God, identifying Him with the South-Wind: "Arise, *Auster*," as though to urge Him, "it is enough that You incubate, that You take possession, that You bend low over us prostrate ones." For God, Augustine assures us, now in the familiar "warming" register, is like a "South-Wind from the region of light and fervor," and His blowing on us will melt our iciness and so release the "flowing ointments" of "Christ's good odor."

A Father's or Doctor's "Care"

This last text shows Augustine's imagination effecting what I have already described as a "fusion" of images. The most general meaning of the term *fovere* is represented by God's "warming" action, even though the result of that action is portrayed in terms commanded by a cluster of texts evoking associations of odors and aromas. But now Augustine has linked the more cosmological agencies of "warming"—Sun and South-Wind—with agencies of a markedly different sort. *Incubare, possidere, super prostratos incumbere*: incubation recalls, of course, the bird or mother-hen images referred to earlier; but "bending low" evokes its human counterpart, the image of a mother stooping down to a helpless child who has fallen "prostrate." What, though, does Augustine have in mind when asking God to "possess" or "take possession" of us? The possibilities are several, at least; perhaps we shall glean more light on that question as we go on.

God's "Paternal" Care

We shall shortly come to see that, to Augustine's imagination, God's *fovere* action can have distinctly maternal overtones. But for the moment notice that Augustine frequently imagines God's activity of dissolving, and freeing us from our sinfulness, as displaying more properly paternal characteristics. He envisages that paternal activity as an exercise in what has come to be called "tough love," for, like Hamlet, our Father must often "be cruel to be kind." Clearly, Augustine found encouragement for this view in the author of Hebrews' reminder that the Lord "chastises" every son He truly loves; but that conviction surely emerged, as well, from reflecting on how God had employed pain and sufferings to effect his own conversion.

God's *fovere* action is, we saw, frequently a "warming" action. But that warming activity can also become a painfully "burning" one: *Enarratio 18*, sermon 2, 7 stresses that the Spirit came as tongues of "fire" in order to "burn away our fleshly straw, melt down and purify [us like] gold" in a furnace; and "no one can hide from His heat." Indeed, in an earlier commentary on the same Psalm, Augustine teaches that our purification takes, in the end, the form of death. For when He "took up our death, the Word made flesh did not permit a single mortal to excuse himself from its shadow. But even [death] the heat of that Word has penetrated" with redemptive value (*En 18*, sermon 1, 7).

God's warming action can sometimes become a positively "burning" one; indeed, the Psalmist prays God to "burn my loins and my heart," by which he means "apply a medicinal purgative [*purgatorium*], like a fire, to [his] thoughts and delights," lest he be consumed in "that fire" reserved for the ultimate punishment of the wicked (*En 25*, version 1, 3). His second commentary on the same Psalm (*En 25*, version 2, 7) embroiders that message somewhat; God's "fire" (*ignis*) is personified in the Christ Who came to "cast fire upon the earth," while His "heat" (*calor*)—"from which no one can hide himself"—has now become the Holy Spirit. Augustine's imagination has its own rules for adapting to his exegetical task, but there is a fundamental consistency there, nonetheless.

Sometimes God's "heat" can not only become a punishing "fire," but also slip over quite naturally to take the stern form of *flagellatio*, "whipping." Then, just as quickly, the movement can reverse itself, as it does in *Sermo 22* 3. Augustine is commenting on Psalm 67:3b: "As wax melts in the presence of fire [*ignis*], let the wicked perish in the presence of God." All the sufferings and tribulations of "this life," Augustine insists, are "God's whip [*flagellum*] to correct anyone willing [to be corrected]." Hard they may be, and grievous, but they are "small," in fact "nothing," in comparison with the future "eternal fire" (*ignis*). God is striving to spare us by "correcting" and "admonishing" us now. Let none of his hearers claim that they were left in ignorance of that Sun of Justice Who came to save us, thereby fulfilling the Psalmist's prophecy: "And no one shall hide himself from His heat." "Now His heat is [embodied] in His Word: [permit yourself to] be changed by His heat, and you will not melt like wax in His fire."

Or the *flagellatio* image can stand on its own. While commenting on Psalm 138, which he found so rich a meditation on God's Omnipresence, Augustine asks why the Prodigal had to suffer "want" and even be reduced to feeding pigs? He answers: it must have been that "His father wished to flagellate him [while he was at a distance], in order to bring him close enough to receive him back." The *peregrinus* is also a *fugitivus*: "a fugitive being pursued,

God's rightful vengeance forever dogging him." And so God acts with each of us, "wreaking vengeance on our affections, wherever we go and however far we have gone away" from Him. Augustine attributes this exigency, once again, to our charity's having "grown cold," and then, recalling his own conversion, goes on to thank the Omnipresent God "Who searched me out when I was a fugitive, Who striped my back with whippings, Who called me, and, by calling, called me back from ruin" (*revocabat*). For when we pray God to "illuminate our darkness," we must not forget that He does so precisely by not allowing "our sins to remain unpunished. He whips us amid these toils of ours, and [thereby] instructs us." *Erudit nos*: Augustine would never have us forget that God's punishment is His way of caring for us; the sufferings He sends are always, if we accept them in the proper spirit, "instructive."

GOD THE PHYSICIAN

In a different metaphor now, he immediately adds that the "miseries" about which we so often complain are "medicinal." Augustine's imagination has forged an intimate association of God as Father with God as medical doctor (*medicus*). The associative bridge, of course, was the fact that both these agencies so regularly achieve their benevolent ends by inflicting pain. And so do judges! It would be more accurate to describe that associative "bridge" as a kind of osmotic bonding, for it permits one image to leak into another, then into a third, then, often, back again to the first, with marvelous ease. Observe, for example, how Augustine artfully brings the above remarks to a close by fusing the images of father, judge, and (more subtly) doctor: we ought, he concludes, humbly to "acknowledge that we stand under [God's] punishing whip, and bless the Lord Who mingles [as a doctor's presciption might?] bitterness with the sweetness of our temporal life." For His purpose is to keep us on the stretch with "desire of eternal delights." Let the whipping we have merited from God as our Father actually "become sweet" to us, therefore, "lest His sentence on us, as judge, be a bitter one" (*En 138* 5.14–15).

But Augustine really surpasses himself when ringing the changes on the image of God as doctor, or (more frequently), Christ as *medicus humilis*. Fr. Rudolph Arbesmann's studies on this theme have rightly become cameo classics.[4]

HEALING OUR SPIRITUAL EYES

One line on which the *medicus* image runs implies that our fallen condition has left our souls with "eyes" that are sickly, enfeebled, hence unable to "see" spiritual realities. We are like Philip, whose spiritual eye was not yet "healthy" enough to "see" the Father when looking upon His Incarnate Son. Hence, Christ must sometimes resort to painful scalding lotions which act as "medicinal fomentations" (*fomentis*) to "heal and strengthen" them (*S 88* 4). (The term "foment," needless to say, has the same root as *fovere*.)

This weakness of spiritual sight is our condition while on *peregrinatio*, Augustine reminds his hearers. To help us eventually to see aright, God has placed us in the Church as into a *schola*, our *magister* being Christ. Our business here is to be eagerly studious (*studiosi*), "learning each day" from the "precepts, examples, and *sacramenta*." They have been placed at our disposal as so many "medicaments" and "fomentations" to foster our "studies" (*SD 20* 1). True, the *collyria* the divine *medicus* applies to enhance our vision may at first be painful, but we must believe Him when He tells us of the splendid vision awaiting us when our eyes have been healed (*InJo 18* 11). For in order to strengthen our spiritual sight, it is necessary for Him "not only to care for [us] gently, but also to cut and to burn" (*non solum fovere, sed et secare et urere*) (*En 85* 9).

GOD THE SURGEON

We have already glimpsed instances where the *medicus* acts as a surgeon. In this capacity, he may be obliged not only to "burn," but also to "cut" (*En 40* 6; *EpJo 9* 4). We may be tempted to resist His ministrations, even, maddened by the pain, attempt to slay Him (*En 34*, sermon 2, 13; *SG 9* 2–3). But we must bear up under these salutary sufferings (*En 91* 1). When our *medicus* refuses to heed our tormented cries, we must persuade ourselves that He is paying heed to our deeper desire to be healthy again (*En 90*, sermon 2, 6), that He knows what is for our good, while most times we do not (*Enn 21*, version 2, 4; *47* 4; *40* 6; *SS 137* 3; *354* 7; *EpJo 6* 8), that He hates the disease He is attacking, but is acting out of love for His patient (*S 49* 6).

GOD OUR *Susceptor*

We must, then, confide ourselves to this *medicus* with unreserved trust in Him, for only then will He "take up" our case. The term

Augustine regularly uses in this connection is *suscipere*. Its primary sense is to "catch from below" and so prevent something, or someone, from falling; but from this primary meaning it expands to its more general sense, to "take up," to "support" or "uphold." But that general sense permits it, like the term *fovere*, to fan out into a variety of meaning families. A Roman father was said to "take up" a child either to "adopt" it or to acknowledge it as his own, the cruel alternative being to "expose" the infant instead. A person of influence could receive someone into the shelter of his home, take him under his protection; or, in a wider sense, he could make himself responsible for someone needing his help, make that needy person's interests and concerns his own. Notice that each of these meanings exhibits the same cluster of associations as Augustine found in the term *fovere*: all of them imply that the *susceptor* in question has resolved to "care for," "take care of," the child, or adult, he has "taken up."

TRUSTING OUR *Susceptor*

Two particular applications of the term *suscipere* are especially interesting. When a Latin speaker was in legal difficulties, he could present himself to a lawyer, explain his problem, and ask the lawyer to "take up his case." The same would be true of a sick person asking for the services of a medical doctor. We are about to see that Augustine is fond of interpreting these various forms of "taking up" as implying that the person in difficulty is willing to trust, "cast his cares" upon, his father (natural or adoptive), his doctor or lawyer, who in turn responds to that trust with the pacifying assurance that he will "take care" of him, "take his cares" upon himself—make his dependent's cares "his own." "Don't you worry any more," we can hear the professional say, "just follow my instructions and let *me* do the worrying."

The parents of the man born blind, for instance, were "afraid of being cast out of the synagogue" (*SMa 130* 4). But not so the blind man himself, for there was always "Christ the *susceptor*, so that [the blind man] could say: 'Because my mother and my father have abandoned me . . . but the Lord has taken me up' " (*assumpsit me*). Augustine never tires of invoking this verse (Ps 26:10), behind whose key term, *assumpsit*, he regularly discerns the action of "our *susceptor*, the God of Jacob" (from Ps 45:12). "Come, O Christ," Augustine exclaims, "take them up [*assume*]. They cast themselves upon You; do Thou take them up" [*suscipe*]. The Pharisee in the temple showed just the opposite attitude: "he did not say, 'Come to my aid,' did not say 'Have mercy on me, because my father and mother have abandoned me'; he did not say 'Be Thou my helper, do not abandon me.' " No, he lacked the humility that inspired the Publican to cast himself on God's mercy (*SMa 130* 2).

Enarratio 45 9–15 constitutes a lengthy section interweaving a number of *fovere* motifs. The Psalmist's phrase that God is "in the midst of us" inspires Augustine to launch into his favorite Omnipresence theme. We must not imagine Him as though He moved about from place to place, or literally "stooped down" (*incumbit*) over us, or were "supported" by us. Instead, "He uplifts you [*sublevat*], so that you exist" and find your support in Him (9). Hence, "let us be without care [*securi*] and tranquil" for " 'the God of Jacob is our *susceptor*.' However great your infirmity, behold Who it is that takes you up [*suscipiat*]. Someone is sick, say, and employs a doctor. The doctor tells the sick person that he has personally taken him up" (*susceptum suum dicit*). But the human *medicus* can himself become ill; not so the Divine *medicus*, the God of Jacob, our *susceptor*! And now Augustine depicts the Publican's "humility" in a striking image: "Make yourself a tiny, tiny infant, of the sort that parents take up." He now recalls the cruel Roman alternative to adoption:

> Those not taken up are given over to be exposed; those taken up are nourished and cared for. Think you that the Lord has taken you up the way your mother took you up as an infant? Not so. He has taken you up for all eternity. Listen! hear your own voice in the Psalmist's: "My mother and my father have abandoned me, but the Lord has taken me up" [11].

"Make yourself a tiny, tiny infant" (*infantem parvulum omnino*). How humble, helpless, and utterly trusting can he ask us to become? Yet our temptation, like that of the Pharisee, is to consider ourselves genuine adults and to trust in our own virtue, our own powers. So too, the Israelites were frequently tempted to trust in their swords and chariots to protect them. But God has ways of shattering all our weapons, so that "You remain disarmed, and, in yourself, powerless. But the weaker you are, with no arms of your own, so much more powerfully does [God] take you up." You were confident of your own strength, and in consequence,

you wound up "full of dismay." But "put down your arms" and
say with the Apostle Paul "when I am weak, then I am strong,"
not in your own strength, but in God's.

At this point, in what seems to have only the remotest surface
connection with the Psalm he is interpreting, Augustine veers off
into an excursus on God's Omnipresence. How shall we "come"
to Him, he asks? He answers in that famous tag from Plotinus'
Ennead 1.6.8: "Not by foot, surely, not by ship or on wings, not
astride a horse. Insofar as spatial distances are involved, don't
think you must bustle about, or get all disturbed" (*ne satagas, ne
conturberis*). "Why do you want to come to Him by traveling the
earth, when He fills the earth entire?" Instead of requiring that
you go to Him, "He comes to you." Indeed, "behold, He is
coming now; wake up" (*evigila*); or, as Paul insists, "Rise, you
sleeper, and rise up from among the dead, and Christ will enlighten you" (12; cf. *Conf* 1.28).

Vacate: "Be Still, and Know That I Am God"

This concise summary of God's initiative in converting each of us
soon brings Augustine around to expressing the total trust God
requires of us in a pregnant term from Psalm 45:11: *Vacate*. "Be
still," our modern translations render it, "be still and know that I
am God." That means, Augustine tells us, "Not You, but I, I am
God." He goes on to remind us of how Isaiah chided the Israelites
who thought that their troubles proved that God had abandoned
them: Augustine repeats the sequence of *Ego . . . Ego . . . Ego . . .* ,
contributing a near-strident emphasis to the prophet's proclama-
tion: "*I* created you, *I* shall re-create you; *I* formed you, *I* shall
re-form you; *I* made you, *I* shall re-make you" (see Is 43:7).

Alas, Augustine reflects, "the human soul when in the tumult
of contentiousness," arguing and "arming itself, as it were," to
fight against God Himself, cannot understand that God alone "is
God." Our trust in ourselves brings us only "insecurity," renders
us simply incapable of making all "contention" cease, of pacifying
the "tumultuous disturbance" that lacerates us. To bring ourselves
to *vacare*, we must first "ask of [God] all that [we] once presumed
we could provide for ourselves" (14). Then, if we trust Him
completely, we shall be able to *vacare*, "take leave" of all our
frantic exertions, "take a vacation" from the nagging self-concern
that fuels our frantic activity, "be still" and "in tranquillity of

heart acknowledge that God is the author of all His gifts," our *susceptor* in every danger and anxiety (15).

Enarratio 67 6 forges a similar connection between God's fatherly *susceptio* (though that precise term does not occur) and our liberation from all disturbance. "Those who trouble you" (*turbant*), he assures his hearers, "will themselves be troubled in the presence of Him Who is father of orphans and judge of widows" (Ps. 47:5–6). Though "destitute" and perhaps separated from all your loved ones, even "abandoned" by your own father and mother, be sure that those who cause you tribulation will themselves "be troubled," while you have the "consolation" of knowing that the "God of Jacob" has "taken [you] up" (*assumpsit*).

But Augustine's second *Enarratio* on Psalm 26 is one of his richest orchestrations of the *susceptio* motif. Woven into it are reminders of our *peregrinatio* and God's continual "presence" to us wherever we go; but the "arms" we once trusted in have now become the "freedom of choice" on whose power we might wrongly "presume." We must never cease praying, rather, that God be our "helper" and "not abandon us" (17). " 'Because my father and mother have abandoned me,' " Augustine quotes verse 10, our former father being the devil, our former mother the evil city of Babylon; Augustine, here as elsewhere, dwells fondly on this theme, calling on his flock to recognize that God (frequently in the person of the Incarnate Christ) has deigned to become their father, whereas the Church, the new Jerusalem, has become their mother (*SS 216* 7; *37* 1, 7; *121* 4).

But there are times when, as here (*En 26*, version 2), he is even bolder. He calls attention to what the Psalmist has implied by this verse: "He has made himself a little one [*parvulum*] before God; has made God Himself his father," but now, even more remarkably, "he has made God Himself his mother," as well! But how can the one and the same God be simultaneously father and mother? God "is Father," Augustine explains, "because He created us, because He calls us, because He commands and rules over us": *condidit, vocat, jubet, regit*, all "masculine" functions, as Augustine sees them. But He is also "She," God is also our "mother," Who exercises these more feminine functions: [She] *fovet* [that term again], *nutrit, lactat, continet*. Augustine seems to be referring to the characteristic tenderness exhibited by a mother's "care" and "nourishment" and "suckling" of the child she once "enveloped" in her womb, as God "envelops" us by His Omnipresence; it is noteworthy how frequently the term *fovere* evokes the notion of Omnipresence to Augustine's imagination. Our mortal mothers and fathers, Augustine goes on to say, may depart this life and leave behind their living successors, but this Omnipresent God will never "depart" from us, so let us not "depart" from Him (18). Indeed, Augustine asks in one of those ironies of Omnipresence-doctrine he loves to play upon, whither could we "depart," except from a God Who is "content" with us (*placato*) to that same God "angry" with us (*iratum*) (19)?

We shall have occasion to note the comparable boldness that characterizes Augustine's depictions of Christ, as well as of Paul, Moses, and even himself: all of them are simultaneously father and mother of the people for whom they exercise their care.

THE HAND THAT RAISES US UP

Before we follow the lead Augustine has given us, and examine more closely his image of God as both "father" and "mother," a parenthetical remark is in order. We have seen that Augustine can launch into substantially the same imaginative fugue, whether the term that launches him is *suscipere, assumere,* or *sublevare.* The reason is that all three terms (and several others, including the term *erigere*) evoke the same *image.* (This is just a further clue to the relative futility of tracking the workings of Augustine's mind by attending solely to the words he uses, while prescinding from the thoughts, images, and associated affects they express.) But when anyone "takes up," "supports," or "upholds" another, what is the *physical image* implied by the literal sense of all these terms? One feature of that physical image would surely be this: the *susceptor* uniformly holds the one he "takes up" *in his hands.*

However banal that observation may seem, it goes far to explain why Augustine so regularly attributes this "upholding" action to the "hand," or "right arm" (*dextera*), of God and why the image of God's "hand" crops up so frequently in connection with other forms of God's *fovere* activity as well. Certainly, Augustine found encouragement for this in Scripture: both Psalms 17:36 and 62:9 depict God with the expression *dextera tua suscepit me,* and Isaiah 41:10 has God speaking of Himself in identical terms. But, just as certainly, it was the activity of Augustine's exegetical imagination which brought him so unquestioningly to interpret Scripture's evocations of God's *manus, brachium,* or *dextera,* His "hand," or "arm," or "right" hand or right arm, as referring to His creative Word, whether Eternal or Incarnate (*S 212* 1).

The second sermon of *Enarratio 101*, for example, argues at considerable length that the working of God's "hand" or hands" refers to the creative "power" (*virtus*) He exerts in and through the Eternal *Verbum* (12). And once created, all those works continue to exist only because they are constantly "upheld" by that same omnipotent, omnipresent, and *Omnitenens manus*, that "all-holding Truth" (*En 114* 3). Augustine later explains that the Latin *omnitenens* is equivalent to the Greek *pantokrator* in referring to the Eternal Son as sharing in the Father's Omnipotence (*InJo 106* 5).

THE HAND OF THE PHYSICIAN

But God's "right hand" has also reached down, as it were, into our lower, temporal world, in order to "take us up," much as the shepherd lifted the lost sheep onto his shoulder. It is striking how frequently that "hand" belongs to Christ as *medicus*.

As early as the year 391, *Sermo 20* 1 depicts the Psalmist as "prostrate from his fall" and imploring "God's medicinal *dexteram* to heal what sin had wounded," just as we in our sinfulness must "look for a *medicus*." "His right hand [*dextera*] has healed . . . and His holy arm," Psalm 97:1 affirms. "What is this *brachium*, this holy arm?" Augustine asks, and replies: "Our Lord Jesus Christ. . . . [He] therefore is the arm, and the right hand of God," and for that reason the Psalmist says "He healed" (1). Indeed, "God's right hand, God's arm, God's saving power, God's justice"—all these are Scripture's titles for "our Lord and Savior, Jesus Christ" (2). No illness is beyond His power of healing, Augustine assures his folk. "You must only allow yourself to be cared for [*curari*]; do not push away His hands [*manus ejus ne repellas*]. He knows what He is doing. Do not take delight only when He cares gently for you [*fovet*], but bear up under it when He cuts," as a surgeon sometimes must. We must endure the work of the "Physician's hand" even when He inflicts "salutary pain," so we shall come to discern in all the trials that beset us "the hand of the Physician Who cuts, not the sentence of the Judge Who punishes" (*S 278* 4–5). "Bear up under this medicinal suffering," Augustine urges, for (in the tag we already noticed as coming from Isaiah 43:7) the God "Who created you knows how to re-create you, the God Who formed you knows how to re-form you." He is not like some

fallible human practitioner; you can trust Him utterly. So, "as for
you, you have only to remain under the hands of [this] Physician,
for He hates anyone who pushes His hands away" (*En 102* 5; see
also *Enn 21*, version 2, 4; *47* 4). Augustine is fond of this contrast
between the human and the Divine Physician Who, as Isaiah
proclaimed, created and formed us, hence knows infallibly how
to re-create and re-form us; and his conclusion is invariably the
same: we must place ourselves "fearlessly" and "unreservedly into
[this] Physician's hands" (*En 40* 6; *SMa 19* 2).

God's Maternal Care

We have seen more than one instance in which Augustine employs
the term *fovere* as though its meaning contrasted with the more
painful forms of divine "care" implied in terms like *urere* or *secare*.
That contrast encourages me to embroider my translation of *fovere*
by adding an adverb, like "gently" or "tenderly." For God's care
for us does not always take the painful forms Augustine associates
with the activity of fathers and doctors. Indeed, we have already
seen that God Himself could be "mother" as well as "father";
now it is time to balance the picture, to show that *fovere* seems to
have associated even more naturally, for Augustine, with images
of a feminine and maternal cast.

The Wings of the Soul

We have already observed that, while weighing the possible senses
of the term *fovere* in his major commentary on Genesis, Augustine
dwells sympathetically on the image of the Holy Spirit as comparable to a mother-bird, incubating her chicks. In the course of that
same discussion, he adverts to the fact that Christ used a similar
image of Himself: He longed to take the children of Jerusalem
under His wings, as a protective hen does with her chicks. That
image of Christ as mother-hen made a deep impression on Augustine; he betrays as much both in his preaching and in his *Confessions*. But that impression became all the more indelible because
of its resonances with the stock Platonic image of the soul as
having, somehow, "lost its wings" and fallen into the world of
bodies. That fall leaves it with a mute yearning to grow those
spiritual "wings" once more, and to fly upward to the higher
contemplative world that was once its home and remains its

authentic native habitat, what the Aristotelian physics encased in the *Omnia* image would term its "natural place."

The image of the wingèd soul in Augustine's early dialogues regularly betrays the more Platonic side of its heritage[5]: the relatively intellectualist cast of the recent convert's thought encourages him to hope that the soul, like *Philocalia*, "drawn down from her heavenly abode by the sticky birdlime of lust" (*visco libidinis*) and shorn of her "wings," will be empowered to rise again by means of those *exercitationes animi* prescribed by her elder sister, *Philosophia* (*Acad* 2.7). In the same way, he and his two young students must "flee" the entire lower world of "sense realities" whose "sticky birdlime" keeps their "wings" from bearing them aloft and escaping to "their native air" (*in auras suas evadere*) (*Sol* 1.24). So he urges them to take their philosophical discussions seriously: for such "disciplines" will strengthen their minds to leap beyond (*transilire*) even the demonic "spirits of the air," leaving them behind (*supervolare*) in their upward flight (*Acad* 1.21). He himself is tempted to regard the training exercises Reason is putting him through as slow and "roundabout," but that is because he is still "insufficiently exercised" to rise to the "vision of that Reality" he longs to behold (*Sol* 2.34). This lofty regard for the contemplative "flight" is what inspires the fulsome thanks he showers on his former patron, Romanianus. For he considers Romanianus as truly an instrument of God's Providence in laying the groundwork for his recent conversion: he it was who, playing the role of "mother-bird," had so generously "cared for the nest, as it were, of my [earlier] studies" (*quasi nidum studiorum meorum foveras*) (*Acad* 2.3). Now, however, as if in answer to Monica's prayer—*Fove precantes, Trinitas* (*Vita* 35)—it is divine *Philosophia* herself who "nourishes and cares for me" (*nutrit et fovet*). Moreover, she promises to "show forth," with perfect clarity, the God Whom she deigns, even now, to "disclose as though through the luminous clouds" the apostles beheld on the mount of Transfiguration (*Acad* 1.3).

That telltale image, already linked with the pregnant term *fovere*, points to the deep current of continuity which runs through Augustine's lifelong manner of imagining his conversion process. That profound continuity alerts us in its turn to the intensely "erotic" cast of Augustine's intellectualism; his was an authentically Platonic eroticism with an unmistakable religious stamp (*Sol* 1.22–23). The upward flight may appear to be overly intellectualistic, particularly in the early "disciplinary" stages Augustine thought were required for "exercising the mind" to comprehend higher, immaterial realities; but the fuel of the ascent is a contemplative *eros*, just as the term of the ascent is an equally "erotic" union-by-vision with God.

Hence, it was not so revolutionary a step as it might otherwise seem when Augustine began to show a decided preference for speaking of the soul as being borne aloft to this union by the "wings of charity." For charity remains essentially the "appetite for beatitude" (*beatitatis appetitus*) (*Mor* 1.18), and (as we shall shortly see) the ascent it fuels still empowers the soul to pass upward from faith, through the stage of spiritual "understanding," to blissful union with God in immediate vision. Augustine can still portray God's providential "care" for us, accordingly, whether mediated by the Incarnate Christ or by "mother" Church, in imagery that remains remarkably consistent with that contained in his earliest works.

So, for instance, he can illuminate one of his favorite Psalm texts (54:7): "Who will give me the wings of a dove, and I shall fly and be at rest," much as his early works would suggest. The Psalmist, he explains, "finds himself without wings, or perhaps with wings that are bound. If wings are lacking, let them be given him; if bound, let them be freed: for even one who frees a bird's wings [is correctly said to] give, or give them back, to him" (*aut dat aut reddit pennas suas*). Notice, however, that those wings are the wings of a dove; and "the dove is depicted here as the symbol of love," and it seeks the same "rest" as Paul did: to "be dissolved and be with Christ" (*En 54 8*).

But the first sermon of *Enarratio 103* is even richer. Augustine starts from his cherished *Philocalia* theme: we see all about us the beauties of His creation, but we cannot "yet see the inestimable beauty of their Designer." Let us love Him, nonetheless, though we cannot yet see Him, "so that by our love's meriting we shall at last come to see Him" (1). That love, however, is nothing less than the "Charity of God that has been poured forth into our hearts," the Holy Spirit, the very God Who "protects" and "lifts us up" (*sublevat*) toward the heavens from which Christ sent forth the Spirit (10). Hence, the Psalmist's phrase "He ascends above the wings of the winds" (the "winds," Augustine claims, symbolizing "souls") must be understood as portraying the "wings of souls . . . whereby they are raised aloft." Such wings are (obviously!)

"the soul's virtues, good works, right actions." But wings always come in pairs; just as "all the commandments are contained in two," the two commandments of love, for God and for neighbor. Hence, "Whoever loves God and neighbor has a wingèd soul, its wings unbound, flying with holy love to the Lord. But whoever is entangled in carnal love has birdlime in those wings" (*viscum habet in pennis*); they are tied down (*obligatas*) from ascending (13).[6]

Plainly, the "spiritual physics" of his *Omnia* image is at work here. "Just as impure love causes an inflammation of the soul, and summons it to the desire for and pursuit of perishing earthly realities, sends it hurtling downward among the lowest, and plunges it into the depths" of the cosmos, so "holy love," on the contrary, "lifts it toward the highest; it enflames and excites it in the direction of eternal realities, those that never die or pass away, lifts it from the depths of the lower world [*profunda inferni*] up to heaven. For every type of love has its proper propelling force [*vim suam*] . . . ; it cannot but conduct" the soul in one direction or the other. "The soul that is bound down by earthly love has birdlime, as it were, in its wings; it cannot take flight. But once cleansed from the filthy love of temporal things, it takes flight . . . on those two wings, those two commandments [enjoining] love for God and love for the neighbor" (*En 121* 1).

But his *peregrinatio* image can also function as a backdrop. "Sion," he tells his hearers, "was a single city, which fell," so that holy people have been known to "dwell temporally" in the earthly remains (*reliquiis*) of her fall. But "the true Sion, the true Jerusalem, . . . is eternal, in heaven: she, she is our mother; she gave us birth, she is the Church of the saints, she has nourished and reared us [*nutrivit*]. She is partly on *peregrinatio*, but the greater part of her remains in heaven," represented by the "bliss of the angels." Those who toil in "this life," therefore, and "long for that homeland, run, run out of love, but [as Omnipresence thinking requires] not with bodily feet: they do not look for ships" to travel by, "but wings," the "two wings of charity," love of God and love of neighbor (*En 149* 5). That same logic of Omnipresence can prod Augustine to warn (in the familiar tag from Plotinus) against taking the "wings" image too literally: we "approach God, even if from afar, not by walking on foot, or riding in any sort of vehicle; not with the swiftness of any animal," and not even by "rising on wings, but through purity of affections and probity of saintly comportment" (*En 58*, sermon 2, 1).

Growing Wings Again

But our soul's fall, like that of the legendary *Philocalia*, has left us bereft of spiritual wings; like newly hatched chicks we need to keep to the safety of the nest (*nidus*) where, nourished and protected by the mother-bird, we may safely grow the wings that will eventually enable us to take flight to the upper airs. That "flight" regularly represents, for Augustine's imagination, the mind's upward climb from faith in authoritative teachings, to more mature understanding of those teachings, and ultimately to direct and immediate vision of the God from Whom all such truths radiate. His earliest dialogues have already begun to portray that initial stage, of faith in authority, by means of infancy images: it is like life lived in a cradle (*cunabula*) (*Ord* 2.26) or in a "nest" (*Acad* 2.3). Or, as we shall come to see, it is a time spent suckling "milk" at the maternal breast.

All those images undergo rich development in Augustine's preaching. Psalm 83, for example, appears to distinguish the "home" the sparrow finds from the "nest" where the dove places her young ones. A "nest," Augustine explains, is a transitory dwelling, much like the tents and inns befitting the human *peregrinus*; the nest the Psalmist here refers to symbolizes first the Church, then the "faith" practiced in her; but at the same time that nest recalls the liminal and passing character of all temporal good works, even when performed in the "nest" of that Church. Our ultimate "home" will be a life of unbroken contemplation (*En 83* 7–8).

More frequently than on the "nest," however, Augustine focuses on the mother-bird herself, and particularly on her protective role toward her chicks. At times, he gets so carried away spinning out rhetorical variations on this motif that he seems suddenly to catch himself and, half-embarrassed, to justify his enthusiasm for the figure by reminding us that the Christ of the Gospels used it of Himself. In *Sermo 264*, indeed, Augustine seems unable to have done with this image: once it enters in the second, it then (through four subsequent and lengthy paragraphs) repeatedly fades, then reappears, now slipping offstage, then tripping on again, like some ingenue actress whose doting director is helpless to make her behave. In sermon after sermon, the image of the hen evokes the same network of associations. Let us bless God, Augustine never tires of saying, for, like the hen who gathers her chicks under her wing, He has made us "safe." "Our enemy may not turn us," when secure beneath those sheltering wings, "from the Way." For He (She?) it is Who "cares for us" (*fovet nos*), shelters and protects us, so that "we do not wander away from beneath His [Her?] wings, attempt to fly prematurely, with the result that [our enemy] captures us, still mere chicks, unfledged." That protective metaphor can, however, abruptly shift into a "nourishing" one. If the Christian "would be strong [*firmus*], let him be nourished by this maternal warmth." Let believers enter, therefore, under the "wings of this Divine Wisdom," the Incarnate Christ, Who "on behalf of Her chicks became weak [*infirma*], to the point of dying" for them. This brings Augustine to portray Christ as Father and Lord, the Church as Mother and Servant (*ancilla*) of Christ, and ourselves as "sons of that *ancilla*." So, from the Gospel image of the hen, Augustine has darted to Paul's kindred image (Eph 5:29) of the "marriage" between Christ and His Church—the Church which, like His own flesh, He "nourishes and cares for" (*nutrit et fovet*) (*En 88*, sermon 2, 14).

Augustine positively revels in this paradoxical image of God's own Wisdom and Power become "infirm" in order to share, and ultimately cure, our sinful "infirmity." This paradox, he feels, is what proves the exquisite appropriateness of Christ's comparing Himself precisely to a mother-hen (*gallina*). For no other bird acts the way the mother-hen does when her chicks are ailing. Granted: they all give birth, warm (*calefaciunt*), and protect their young, but none of them so dramatically shares their infirmities: the hen, exactly like the Divine Wisdom Who loves us, "becomes totally changed through her affection for her chicks" (*En 90*, sermon 1, 5). Her cries "become hoarse," her "whole body becomes shaggy, her wings droop and her feathers become disheveled: why, you can see her become in a manner sick for her chicks." But what accounts for this marvelous transformation? The *gallina*'s "maternal charity" for her offspring, Augustine replies. So with Christ: He took on our infirmity, even our death, in order to "gather His chicks under His wings like some mother-hen sharing the sickness of her chicks"—a "maternal infirmity" Augustine hastens to add, "entailing no loss of His [Divine] Majesty" (*En 58*, sermon 1, 10). The Psalmist's several references to God as protecting us "beneath the shadow of His wings" regularly conjure up this image of the mother-hen (*En 62* 16; *SD 13* 5–6) and inspire Augustine to urge his hearers to "acknowledge their own infirmity" and flee to the safety to be found "under the wings of this Wisdom-Mother, Who Herself [*ipsa*] became infirm on our behalf" (*En 90*, sermon 2, 2).

But despite his fondness for the mother-hen, the legend of the pelican inspires Augustine to outdo himself entirely. His hearers must be familiar with that legend, surely: how pelicans actually kill their young soon after they are hatched, then mourn their death for three full days; then the mother-pelican pierces her own breast, allows her blood to bathe the dead chicks, and thereby wakens them back to life again. Ah well (was there a jaundiced eye or two in the basilica that day?), Augustine admits, this may be just a legend after all. But if it is true, he returns to the charge, it applies nicely to Christ "Who brought us to life by His Own blood." It fits Him, for man though He was, "He brought His children to life with the flesh of a mother. Yes," Augustine insists, "it fits Him well enough. For He called Himself a mother-hen," thereby reminding us that "He had both the authority of a father and the affection of a mother." A paradox? But that same paradox is also verified in the Apostle Paul, who did not hesitate to tell the Corinthians (1 Cor 4:15) that he had "begotten" them as their father, and the Galatians (4:19) that he was once again enduring the maternal pangs of "giving birth to them" (*En 101*, sermon 1, 8).

But to appreciate Paul's "maternal" role fully, we must acknowledge that it was Paul's "charity" that begot and gave birth to those Christians. "Listen," Augustine urges, "listen to the charity that gives birth to them, the charity that fitted Paul to deal with his children with a heart both fatherly and motherly." And in the very next moment Augustine has prodded us into realizing that Paul's charity was the very "Charity of God" Himself, which "has been spread abroad in our hearts through the Holy Spirit Who has been given to us." This realization brings us back to the mother-bird whose affect of charity, we saw, was principally responsible for the "hatching" effect at Creation. Now, however, that same Spirit of Divine Charity "gathers together those whom It conceived and birthed" so that they are now "interiorly sons, and safe; they will fly forth from this nest of fear" to heavenly and eternal bliss (*En 147* 14).

But that nest, Augustine reminds us once again, in which we are protected from all the surrounding enemies that make us fearful, is also the nest of "faith": "Enduring in faith, therefore, it is faith itself that is nest for [God's] chicks" (*En 83* 7). For it is faith, as we shall see, that "nourishes" the growth of our spiritual wings, enabling us in time to fly upward toward more "adult" understanding of God's word to us, and promising in the end to return us to the unmediated vision of God we once enjoyed.

MOTHER AND NURSE: SCRIPTURAL ROOTS

That "nourishing" process, however, Augustine most frequently portrays in the tender image of a human mother, or of a wet-nurse, suckling the child entrusted to her care. One text that was partially responsible for the spell this image cast on his imagination was Paul's self-description to the Thessalonians: he had been among them "like a nurse, who cherishes [*qui foveat*] her children" (1 Thess 2:7). The first explicit citation of that text in Augustine's works (*Adim* 25)[7] indicates that he has already firmly associated it with Paul's complaint that he was compelled to give the Corinthians "milk to drink, not meat," since they were like "little ones," not adults, "carnal" and "unable as yet" to take in truly "spiritual" teaching (1 Cor 3:1–2; also 2:6). Such spiritual doctrine, Paul explains, would have been "beyond their understanding" (1 Cor 3:14–15). The author of Hebrews, whom Augustine identified with Paul, employs the same metaphor: the Hebrews have grown so "slow in understanding" that they have "gone back to needing milk, not solid food"; they are like "babies" who could not be expected to digest the "solid food" appropriate to "mature men" (Heb 5:11–14). We have also seen how the assertion from Ephesians (5:29) that Christ "nourishes and cherishes" (*fovet*) His Church could also evoke, however paradoxically, this same image of maternal care. The fruit of this associative activity is this: that Augustine's imagination frequently tends to "translate" the term *fovere* as meaning "to suckle at the breast," as a nurse, or mother, would give milk to her child.

UNFURLING THE MOTHER IMAGE

The mother–nurse can, accordingly, be virtually anyone. Most obviously the figure fits Paul, who boldly depicted himself that way. But *Sermo 88* 24 shows that the same figure can apply to Moses, who pleaded on behalf of the Israelites with "maternal love," or, rather, out of "bowels both maternal and paternal," to the God Who Himself was both mercy and justice. Or it can apply to Augustine himself, telling the recently baptized that he has just "performed the sweet offices of a nurse" on their behalf (*S 353* 1). Or the mothering agency can be the Church. We shall see that in the *Confessions* it can be Monica, or the wet-nurses who suckled Augustine as an infant.

All such identifications are true on the surface; at bottom, the true mother–nurse is Incarnate Wisdom, or just plain God. For all those others are agencies and precisely that, creatures through which God's Omnipresent Providence, providential Omnipresence, is mediated to us. Augustine is constantly coaching us to "see" that Mother-God not only acting in and through all of them, and acting in a variety of ways, but always with a single design: to suckle us weak and carnal "little ones" on the milk of faith, but then to wean us, prod us into "growing up." For if we grow up, we shall in time become fit and "strong" enough to *vacare*: to "be still" and come—contemplatively—to "know" God as God. For that contemplative union, anteroom to eternal vision, is the "food of spiritual grown-ups" God yearns to offer us.[8]

Against the Manichees with their contempt for the Catholica's requirement that we begin from submissive faith, Augustine naturally stresses the need we have for beginning at that stage. For we are all, as *Sermo 12* 5 puts it, still "wayfarers," and faith is the first step we must take in "walking" toward the ultimate "vision" we long for. Hence, he urges his hearers as "God's faithful ones and true sons and daughters of the Mother-Catholica, let no one deceive you with [the promise of] poisoned foods"—the Manichee "food" of "reasoned" knowledge—while "you are still [at the stage] requiring milky nourishment. Walk now, perseveringly, through your faith in Truth," and you will arrive securely at that vision. For the humble Christ, Augustine concludes, took a body from a woman in order to become our *firmitas*, the "strength" on which our weakness may safely rely; for He is God's Omnipresent Word (*S 12* 12). "Behold," he says in *Sermo 216* 7, "behold it is the womb of Mother-Church, behold it is she who gives you birth, bringing you forth into the light of faith, groaning in her labor. Do not, in your impatience, kick against her womb, and narrow the doorways of your birthing."

All this is true enough, as far as it goes; but a few lines later we are told to "praise the Lord" Himself, for it is *He* "Who creates you. You are being suckled, praise Him; being fed, praise Him." But to what end, this suckling and feeding? "You are being

nourished," Augustine replies, "so advance in age and wisdom."
Now he alludes to Paul, that "kindly nurse of little ones," who
warns us (*admonet*) not to "remain little boys [*pueri*] in understanding, but little children so far as wickedness is concerned, while
becoming perfect in understanding." We are summoned to grow
up, therefore, and "gladden . . . our Father by our advance in
wisdom, and not sadden our Mother by our failure [to do so]."
That Father, Augustine goes on to make clear, is God Himself;
that Mother is the Church, whose role is to help us on our
pilgrimage to the Heavenly Jerusalem. There, the Father will
clothe us, like the Prodigal, with the *stola prima*, the original
spiritual body we forfeited by pridefully wandering away from
our Father's house (*S 216* 7–11).

Assuredly, while still "infirm," the believer remains child of his
"Mother" the Church; but this implies, Augustine insists, that "so
long as he stands in need of milk and clings to the breast, he is not
yet child of his Father. Until now, he is carried in the bosom of
the Church, and is unable to sit down to the solid food served at
the Father's table." "Animal and carnal" rather than "spiritual"
and capable of "spiritual judgment," the Christian at this initial
stage of growth "draws food from his mother's breast." This is
what Paul implied by saying he had to act as a "mother unto you
[Corinthians]." But all such mothering care is aimed at helping us
grow up until we are able to pass from maternal "milk" to the
"solid food" the Father offers us at His table (*En 49* 27).

It is important to realize, however, that whether milk or solid,
these are two forms of the same, identical Divine food. Augustine
sees his God as "nourishing me so that I may become capable of
eating the food You feed the angels. For here, He Who has
promised us heavenly food nourishes us with milk; to do so, He
employs a mother's compassion. For just as the nursing mother
takes [from the Father's table] the same food as the infant is unfit
to digest, and passes it through her own flesh, pouring it out as
milk," so Our Lord, "when He came to us robed in flesh, turned
His Wisdom into milk for us" (*En 30*, sermon 1, 9). But this,
Augustine goes on to explain, implies that we ought not to remain
mammothrepti, little boys who "suckle for a longer time than is
proper," insisting that their food always "be passed through the
flesh" of this or that human intermediary. No, God desires us
"little ones" to "open our mouths wide, [but] at *His* table."

But how does God school us to pass from the maternal breast

to the paternal table? Now Augustine answers by introducing a new variant of the "suckling" image: God acts just as mothers and nurses do; they sprinkle wormwood on their breasts, and He does the same by sending the bitterness of suffering and disappointment into our lives. By doing so, He strives to "wean" us from the pleasures of this passing life, and make us long for the delights of eternal union with Him (*En 30*, sermon 2, 12). Notice once again how even God's "maternal" care has begun to take on a distinctly "paternal" character.

For the temporal life we live here, Augustine is convinced, is bitter, is hard (*S 311* 14). And yet, ironically, we are loath to "migrate from it" to the eternal delights the Father promises us. We are like those little tykes who "cling annoyingly" to the breasts of their mothers or nurses, until they "spread something bitter about their nipples, to repel the youngster so he will no longer ask for milk." So too, Augustine reminds his hearers, "God has filled this world with all manner of bitterness"; why then, "if the world has become so bitter to you, do you still suckle away at it?" Why is it that "your mouth still gapes for it, you throw yourself upon it, you suckle away at it?"

And yet, even those eternal joys God promises are maternal in character: even our accession to the "food of grown-ups" takes the form of suckling: at the "glorious" and "consoling" breasts of that Heavenly Jerusalem who both is and is not Yahweh "Herself," the eternal "fountain" of enduring delights. Just as our food, whether milky or solid, is all one food, so Augustine cannot "see" his "paternal" God except as maternally paternal, cannot "see" God's tender suckling action in its infancy phase without already glimpsing, affectively, and through that very image, the culmination to which it tends: the infinitely tender culmination portrayed in Isaiah's thrilling poetry.

ISAIAH'S MOTHERING GOD

For there is abundant evidence to show that the prophet Isaiah provided a generous array of illustrations for Augustine's "maternal" image of God. It may have been that the *fovere* images he found in the New Testament made Augustine especially sensitive to the procession of maternal images Isaiah employs; but one is tempted to think that Isaiah's images might have been powerful and moving enough to have fertilized Augustine's imagination even without such reinforcement.

But what do we know of Augustine's readings in Isaiah? Augustine himself informs us that, while at Cassiciacum, preparing for his baptism, he had asked Ambrose to suggest appropriate Scripture for his readings and meditations during that period of preparation. He goes on to tell us that Ambrose replied by proposing the prophet Isaiah. But Augustine claims to have found Isaiah so difficult to "understand" at the time that he soon laid the book aside, resolving to come back to it when he was more experienced in the understanding of Scripture (*Conf* 9.13). How soon, though, did he take up Isaiah once again?

The second book of his *De libero arbitrio,* most probably written some two or three years after his conversion in A.D. 386, gives us a telling clue toward answering that question. For there, as in the *De magistro,* written shortly afterward, we see him already blazoning the phrase from Isaiah 7:9 that soon became the motto for his entire subsequent intellectual quest: *Nisi credideritis, non intelligetis,* "Unless ye believe, ye shall not [come to] understand."

That translation, however, was based on the Greek Septuagint version of Isaiah, which Augustine long favored. Meanwhile, during the early years of Augustine's literary activity, Jerome was laboring in Bethlehem on his translation of the Old Testament, basing it on the original Hebrew rather than the Greek of the Septuagint. His return to that original language of Scripture made it plain that the Septuagint translators had found themselves confronted, in Isaiah 7:9, with a rich and complex play on words. The prophet has been sent to speak to King Ahaz, who is in panic before the threatened invasion by Razon the Syrian. "Be still," or "quiet," Isaiah counsels him; "let not your heart be afraid." Ahaz must place his faith, in the sense of trust, in Yahweh, for if he does not "believe" in Yahweh's power to save his people, he shall not *permanere*: shall not "endure," "continue," or "stand firm." But the Hebrew for "believe" or "trust" can also be rendered as "stand" or "take a stand" *in* or *by* the Yahweh being trusted: hence, the line taken by most contemporary translations of the entire phrase, "if you do not stand by [or in] Me, you will not stand at all."

Now, Augustine's appeal to Isaiah 7:9 from the year A.D. 388 onward may be taken as an indication that he had, by that year at least, returned to reading that prophet. Furthermore, the crucial importance of the motto "Unless ye believe, ye shall not under-

stand" highlights the paradox that this text, in precisely that
translation form, never once occurs in his *Confessions*!

The paradox is removed, however, if one notices the repeated
use he makes of that same text, but in the translation that more
accurately reproduces the original Hebrew pun. So, for example,
he counsels us in *Confessions* 4.8: "stand with Him and you shall
stand; rest in Him and you shall be quiet," or, "you shall be
still"— exactly as Isaiah had assured Ahaz. So too, in 8.7, the
maternal figure of Lady Continence challenges him: "Why do you
stand in yourself, and [so] not stand at all." The term *stare*, "to
stand," has come to replace both the *credere* and the *intelligere*, the
"believe" and "understand" of the translation Augustine had
earlier favored; "standing in God," Augustine means, is our only
hope of standing at all. But consenting to stand "in God" and not
"in ourselves" is tantamount, as we shall see, to "casting our
cares" on Him, allowing Him to be our *susceptor* and "take us
up," as a doctor would his ailing patient, or a caring mother
would her fretting child.

Both *Confessions* and preached works show that Augustine's
study of Isaiah did, in fact, powerfully influence the way he came
to imagine, and imaginatively understand, God's working on his
soul during the long process of his conversion. We have already
seen him adapt Isaiah 43:7, where God proclaims that He had
"created" and "formed," and "made"—hence (Augustine infers),
He Himself would "re-create," "re-form," and "re-make"—the
Israel He looks on as His child: "*Ego . . . Ego . . . Ego.*" Augustine
reproduces the prophet's own emphasis (*En 45* 14). He will do the
same (*Conf* 6.26) with the "*Ego . . . Ego . . . Ego . . .*" of Isaiah's
poignant image of God maternally "carrying" Israel (46:3–4); he
had earlier evoked that same repetition by thrice confessing that
"*Tu portabis . . . tu . . . tu*" (*Conf* 4.31). Image, language, thought,
affect: the linkages are unmistakable.

Ego feci et Ego feram et Ego portabo et Ego salvabo, God proclaims:
"*I, I* have made you, and *I* shall bear you, and *I* shall carry you,
and *I* shall save you" (Is 46:4). But the synthesis of these two texts
also hints at how capital Isaiah's moving images of God as
"mother" turned out to be in Augustine's imaginative mode of
understanding God's workings. The editors of the Bibliothèque
Augustinienne edition of the *Confessions*, in their notes and Scriptural Index, provide ample confirmation of that; but closer comparison of Augustine's text with that of Isaiah's prophecy suggests

that there is more to that story than even their alert scrutiny succeeded in uncovering.

A Mother Remembers

Doubtless the most familiar of those texts is the one which Isaiah applies to Yahweh, but which is so strikingly applicable to Monica. I shall cite Isaiah's text in a slightly modernized form of the Vulgate, adapted where required to match the version Augustine was familiar with.

To begin with, then, I submit that it is *a priori* unlikely that Monica's son would have failed to resonate with those heart-rending lines:

> Can a woman forget her infant
> so as not to have pity on the son of her womb?
> And if she should forget,
> yet will I not forget you [49:15–16].

But Augustine has associated that text with the "hymn" from Isaiah 42 where Yahweh portrays Himself (Herself?) as a mother suffering the pangs of birthing a child:

> I have always held my peace [*tacui*],
> I have kept silence [*silui*], I have been patient,
> I will speak now as a woman in labor,
> I will destroy, and swallow up at once [42:14].

"You are silent," Augustine says to his God: *taces* (*Conf* 1.28). But "will You be forever silent?" That echo of Isaiah, though, heralds the explosive image-fusion which occurs at 2.6–7, where he describes himself as "forgetful" of the God he now knows never forgot him. He thought of that God as "silent" (*tacuisse te*), but was He truly "silent"? No, Augustine's mother, Monica, was "worried" about him; she admonished him, or, rather, through her God Himself "sang" (*cantasti*) admonitions to refrain his lusts, admonitions the young Augustine spurned as so much "woman talk" he would have blushed to heed. Those words came from God; but, Augustine insists, he "did not know that" at the time, and "thought [God] silent and her the speaker, but through her [God] was not silent, and [Augustine's] contempt for her was contempt of [God]."

The irony here is masterful. Just a moment before, God was portrayed as paternal; Augustine "could not evade [God's] whipping" him, "merciful in fury." Suddenly God becomes maternal, "sprinkling on all [Augustine's] illicit delights the [wormwood] of bitterness" to wean him from them (2.4). Now "She" becomes the Yahweh of Isaiah's "hymn": a mother groaning in labor, but keeping "silence." Yet Augustine's "forgetfulness" of God only counterpoints with the image of the human mother (and her Divine counterpart) who cannot forget the child of "her" womb. And all the while, in the foreground, scurries Monica, herself in spiritual labor over her son (see 5.16!), and womanly mouthpiece of the mothering God Who, though silent in "judgment," refuses to be silent in another register: for He teaches and admonishes untiringly through prophets, Scripture, and agents like Monica. For this, Augustine's preaching assures us, is his standard interpretation of the "silence" Isaiah's hymn attributes to Yahweh (*Enn 34*, sermon 2, 12; *49* 6; *82* 2; *93* 7).

THE MOTHER WHO CARRIES HER CHILD

Despite the "silence" She resolved on in Her "hymn," however, Yahweh immediately goes on to promise that She will

> lead the blind into a way they know not [*nesciunt*];
> and in the paths of which they were ignorant [*ignoraverunt*],
> I will make them walk;
> I will make darkness light before them,
> and crooked things straight [42:16].

To follow that "way" and "walk" in those paths, though, we must rely on the Yahweh Who is both our eyes and our strength; that theme spurs Augustine to connect the image above with one which Isaiah had used just shortly before. There, Yahweh was portrayed as the One Who

> gives strength to the weary,
> and increases force and might in them that are not.
> Youths shall faint and labor,
> and young men shall fall by infirmity.
> But they that hope in the Lord shall renew their strength,
> they shall take wings as eagles,
> they shall run and not be weary,
> they shall walk and not faint [40:29–31].

Whereas shortly afterward, Yahweh addresses Her people in the same vein, as

> You who are carried by My bowels,
> are borne up by My womb.
> Even to your old age I, *I* am the same [*Ego ipse*].

We have already remarked that the force of that repeated *Ego* was not lost on Augustine the preacher. Isaiah continues:

> And to your gray hairs *I* will carry you:
> *I* have made you, and *I* will bear,
> *I* will carry and will save you [46:3–4].

And *Tu portabis, Tu portabis,* Augustine echoes him:

> You, You will carry us, You will carry us,
> Both as little ones and to our gray hairs
> You, You will carry us,
> Because when You, You, are our strength,
> then are we strong,
> but when that strength is our own,
> then it is weakness [*Conf* 4.31].

And again,

> Behold, You are present to us,
> and free us from our wretched wanderings,
> and set us up in Your Way, and console us, saying:
> "Run, I, *I* shall carry you [*Ego feram*],
> and *I* shall lead you there,
> and once there, *I* shall [still] carry you" [*Conf* 6.26].

The editors of the *Confessions* have already pointed to the presence of the images from Isaiah's chapters 42 and 46. I am suggesting here, however, that it seems to have escaped them that the image from chapter 40 is also present; it has been magnetized, as it were, by the maternal character of its two companions, so that Augustine spontaneously pictures the Yahweh Who sees us "weary" and "stumbling" and "renews" us to walk, then "run" in His paths, as a mother looking fondly on the child she has "carried" since the time she gave birth to him.

THE BREASTS OF THE MOTHER-GOD

Another Isaian image, which scholars have detected in the *Confessions*, occurs in the glorious description of Jerusalem's "resurrection": "You shall suckle," Yahweh assures his people,

on the milk of Gentiles,
and be nursed by the breasts of kings:
and you shall know that I am the Lord your Savior [60:16].

That identification is far from incorrect; for in 4.1 Augustine pictures himself, when "all is well" with him, as an infant "suckling on [God's own] milk, and enjoying [God] as [his] food." Yet *Sugens lac* tuum, *fruens* te *cibo*: not on kings or Gentiles, but, Augustine is boldly claiming, he is suckling at God's own breast. And, significantly, he goes on to ask:

And what man is any sort of man [*quis homo est quilibet homo*],
since he is but a man?
But let the strong and powerful [*fortes et potentes*] laugh us to scorn,
but let us, the weak and needy, confess to You [4.1].

There is, I want to argue, a far richer store of image-material in *Confessions* 4.1 than Isaiah 60:16 can account for, particularly if we recognize that Augustine is embarking there on a fugal development that runs unbroken to the second paragraph of the next book. For, first of all, the startling claim that Yahweh Himself (Herself?) is doing the suckling recalls Yahweh's ironic question:

Shall not I, that make others bring forth children,
Myself bring forth? says the Lord.
Shall I, Who give generation to others, be barren [66:9]?

That same claim additionally reminds us that in the very next verse the prophet launches into his call that all who love Jerusalem "Rejoice for joy with her, all you who mourn for her,"

That you may suckle, and be filled
with the breasts of her consolations,
that you may milk out, and flow with delights,
from the abundance of her glory.
For thus says the Lord:
Behold I will bring upon her as it were a river of peace,
and as an overflowing torrent the glory of the Gentiles,
on which you shall suckle;
you shall be carried at the breasts,
and upon the knees they shall caress you.
And as one whom the mother caresses,
so will I comfort you,
and you shall be comforted in Jerusalem [66:10–13].

Furthermore, the mention of those "strong and powerful" who "laugh to scorn" the little ones content to suckle at God's breast

forcibly reminds us of the terms in which the "scoffers and rulers"
of Jerusalem are depicted as mocking the prophet's message:

> Whom shall he teach knowledge?
> And whom shall he make understand his hearing?
> Them that are weaned from milk,
> and are drawn away from the breasts?

To which the prophet replies:

> With the speech of lips
> and with another tongue,
> [Yahweh] will speak to this people
> To whom He said: "This is My rest [*requies*],
> Refresh the weary [*reficite lassum*],
> And this is My refreshing [*refrigerium*]":
> And they would not hear [28:9–12].

A PARENTHESIS ON "METHOD"

It should be clear by now that Augustine was more than something
of a poet, was imaginative enough to read and respond to the
poetry of Isaiah with a fellow-poet's lively sensibility. Hence, to
appreciate the poetic synthesis he has wrought of Isaiah's poetic
materials, it would be hopelessly inept to analyze that creative
achievement by executing a series of wooden philological compar-
isons, matching verbal sequences in the *Confessions* against similar
verbal sequences in Isaiah.

Take, for instance, the image of suckling we started with, from
Confessions 4.1. There can be, first off, no warrant for claiming,
or tacitly assuming, that the moment one such suckling image has
been located in Isaiah, we have automatically hit upon the only
one that Augustine had in mind when he evoked that image; there
are simply too many other images of suckling in Isaiah to be
examined as rival candidates. But, secondly, given what we have
already seen about the way in which Augustine's imagination can
interrelate, combine, and even fuse several associated images into
unitary symbolic complexes, by what right may we exclude even
one of those various candidates?

Consider the question, now, purely from the standpoint of
Isaiah's imagery: in the prophet's triumphant resurrection paean
in chapter 66, do the "breasts" he speaks of belong to Jerusalem,
or to Yahweh? Follow the development of the image closely, and
at a certain point Jerusalem's breasts have somehow become Yah-

weh's own! But then we realize that for Isaiah, it was never, even from the beginning, a question of either–or; in the peculiar logic of his intensely poetic imagination, Jerusalem's consolation of her returning children *always was* consolation that came straight from Yahweh Himself.

Or should one say, from Yahweh "Herself"? Again, both replies are correct, and their simultaneous correctness partially accounts for the deeply moving, the unforgettable power of this passage. But we have seen that Augustine's imagination and affect can move along those same paradoxical lines: God–Father can *become* God–Doctor, and, just as swiftly, God–Mother–Nurse within the space of a line or a few words; the mother-hen can be Paul, Christ, and the Holy Spirit by turns. We must not be surprised, then, that any single mother-image from Isaiah may instantly fuse with any other, even several others, without Augustine's asking our permission for such illogical behavior.

A FUGUE OF CONVERSION IMAGERY

Ideally, this would be the moment to trace the entire catena of *fovere* images Augustine has been deftly linking together since the opening paragraphs of his *Confessions*; but that would amount to presenting virtually a full-scale interpretation of the work. In lieu of that, now turn back to the suckling image in *Confessions* 4.1; accept momentarily as a working hypothesis that Augustine has sounded there the opening bars of a fugal development on the various motifs implied by his *fovere* theme; then, I submit, simply tracking the sequence of images running in relay from *Confessions* 4.1 to 5.2 will succeed in laying bare the powerful synthesis of Isaian images Augustine has succeeded in weaving.

Augustine begins, as we saw, with a recall of those Isaian "mockers" who undoubtedly figure the Manichees who arrogantly fancied themselves "men," grown-ups who scorn the Catholica's insistence on the need for becoming a believing "little one," an unweaned infant "suckling" at God's breasts (4.1). Soon afterward, he experiences the desperate anguish inflicted by the death of a cherished young friend (4.7–11); he is inconsolable; he "carries" his tormented heart about, but that heart refuses to be "carried" by him; on his own, he can find no place to "put" it, no place where it can find "rest" (4.12). Isaiah's promised "rest" has adroitly been reset against the background of the *Omnia* where nothing can truly "rest" unless it be "carried" to the "place" appropriate to its "weight"!

He is "wearied" by the diet of Manichee falsehoods (the "poisoned food" we noticed earlier) that make it impossible for him to conceive rightly of the God on Whom he has turned his back; but only in that God, he realizes now, could his heart have found a "place of untroubled peace" (4.16). "Return," he exclaims with Isaiah, "return, you sinners" and "cling" to that God; and now, in the new version of Isaiah 7:9 he has come to prefer, "stand with Him and you shall truly stand, rest in Him and you will find rest," for in this "region of death" (again, in *Omnia* terms), no "rest" can be found (4.18).

Instead of vaunting his intellectual accomplishments in arrogant Manichee fashion, now he no longer scorns, but almost envies those "slower minds" who were content to be "little ones," and "grow wings of charity, safe in the nest of the Church, being nourished on the food of a healthy faith." He brings Book 4 to an end with the touching Isaian prayer we have already noticed, begging God to "protect" and "carry" us, "carry us, both as little ones and until our hairs are gray" (4.31).

But the fugue runs on into Book 5, as Augustine unfurls the image of the Mother–God who must first carry her child, then help it stand, then coax it to walk while she supports it. Only later will she urge it to "run," and even "fly." Eventually, the converted sinner's "mouth is turned about to [God]"; he rises up from his "weariness" and finds at the breast of that nursing God "refection [literally: re-making] and true strength" (5.1). Now it becomes plain that Augustine pictures sinful humans as so many querulous children, vainly striving to flee from the enveloping Omnipresence of that paternal–maternal God, tearing themselves away from Her "gentleness" only to "hurtle against" His paternal "righteousness," and scrape their knees on the "rough places" only He can smooth. But if they turn back to Her, realize they are but children and thereby become "little ones" in the true, spiritual sense, "tossing themselves upon [Her] and wailing in [Her] lap," then God's response is exactly as Isaiah had described it would be. Isaiah had put it this way:

> And the Lord God shall wipe away the tears from every face.
> . . . And they shall say in that day:
> Lo, this is our God. . . .
> We shall exult and rejoice in His salvation [25:8–9].

Augustine's analogue runs:

> Sweetly You wipe their eyes of tears,
> until they wail even louder now,
> but with tears of rejoicing,
> because You, Lord, You . . . ,
> Who made them,
> now re-make [*reficis*: feed? refresh?] and console them [5.2].

Here Augustine has succeeded in orchestrating virtually every one of the image-motifs announced by the ensemble of Isaian mother-images we surveyed above: Yahweh is a Mother-God Who is unable to forget the child of Her womb, even when that child has turned his back and forgotten Her; She is "silent" in judgment, but not in "admonition"; She has made, borne, and will continue to "bear" him. "Blind" and "ignorant" though he is, She will enlighten his darkness, "lead" him in the "way," the "paths" of return She has appointed. She will "carry" him, "weary," "weak," and "infirm." She suckled him in his infancy, and as he grows up, She will perform all the other offices any caring mother would: help him to "stand," support him while he learns to "walk," then urge him to "run." Perhaps transcending what a human mother could achieve, Yahweh will even, by "renewing" his strength, enable him eventually to "fly" with the "wings of eagles." Even then, She can be relied on to support him, from helpless infancy to the "gray hairs" of enfeebled old age. For, having "formed" him, She alone—*Ego, Ego*—can reform him; having "made" him, She alone can *reficere*: feed, re-make, refresh him, can "fondle him in Her lap," "comfort him like a son comforted by his mother," "console" him on Her "glorious breasts," and guarantee the *refrigerium* and "rest" (*requies*) his weariness yearns for.

Fovisti caput nescientis: THE UNITY OF THE *Confessions*

In this fugal development running from Book 4.1 to Book 5.2, Augustine has gone a good way toward suggesting the proper manner of translating that marvelously polyvalent expression from Book 7 *fovisti caput nescientis*. But by narrowing our focus in hopes of isolating the Isaian elements of Augustine's maternal image, we were compelled to prescind from those elements of his *fovere* image which are either non-Isaian or at least less obviously Isaian. It is time, now, to compensate for that distortion of perspective. For the fact is that, however rich the Isaian lode turned out to be, Augustine managed to "set" its contribution into that larger ensemble we were surveying before narrowing our focus.

To exemplify what I mean: we saw that Augustine envisaged, as one important form of God's *fovere* activity, His often "cruelly kind" treatment of us as *medicus* and "surgeon." We also saw how frequently the "hand" of God became the healing, sometimes burning and cutting, hand of a surgeon; we were urged to trust Him, because He "knew," while we (too often) "did not know" what He was about. *Fovisti caput nescientis*: could Augustine be alluding to God's medicinal care of him, a care exercised on one who "did not know" what his Divine *medicus* "knew": that He had to cut, burn, make His patient suffer, in order to "heal" him?

Once that possibility is entertained, a number of suggestions from the *Confessions* immediately surface. How many times, for example, does Augustine allude to his *infirmitas*, and leave us wondering whether to translate that term by "weakness" or "illness." How deftly, too, in the midst of the fugal development in Book 4 he describes the venerable *medicus* Vindicianus placing his hand on his "fevered" head, but not, alas, to "heal" him (4.5). Only now does he recognize the sufferings endured on the occasion of his friend's death as God's medicinal care for him (4.7–11). For God's healing hand is not repelled by the "hardness" of man's sinful heart; instead, God "melts" that hardness as He wills, whether with maternal "mercy" or paternal "vengeance": for there is "no one who can hide from Your heat" (5.1).

Later, through Ambrose, God's medicinal hand still works to heal the eyes of his spiritual vision (6.6), and later still, God continues to work, to "reform [his] deformities," reduce his "swelling," and apply with "secret medicinal hand" the "scalding lotion" that Augustine's spiritual eyes, swollen to closing, require (7.12). He is being readied to receive that decisive "admonition" embodied in the "platonist books" he read at Milan in A.D. 386: that admonition that will enable him to "see" what he was formerly "blind" to, the reality of the "spiritual" world. So, Augustine *may* have meant us to understand (with deliberate ambiguity!) that the treatment of the Divine *medicus*, Who "knew" what He was doing while Augustine "knew it not," was a series of painful "fomentations" applied to his "eyes" and "head," designed to transform His patient from "un-knower" to "knower": to one who had finally come to "understand" the

patient "care" God had so long been exercising in his behalf. If
that be the case, then perhaps that troubling verb *fovisti* should be
translated in appropriate medical terms.

But should the choice of such a medical translation necessarily
exclude our opting for a "maternal" translation *as well*? Again, we
have been brought to face that same question: Does Augustine's
imagination work in terms of an "either–or" kind of logic? He
himself seems to have answered our question by the very way he
continues to interweave paternal–medical with maternal imagery
throughout the development that climaxes in the *fovisti caput*
phrase.

For the fugal development that climaxed in the second paragraph of Book 5 is by no means the last word Augustine has to
contribute on the maternal image. In 5.13, for example, he
compares Monica with the mother-pelican, bringing her child
back to life by means of the "blood" of her own "heart." For like
Paul over the Galatians, she is spiritually "in labor" again over her
son (5.16). But Augustine remains incapable of taking the decisive
step required of him, that of "throwing his cares" (6.20) on the
God Who strives to "set him on His Way and console" him,
crying in the Isaian terms we have already noticed: "Run! *I* will
bear you, *I* will bring you there, and even there, *I* will bear you
[still]" (*et ibi Ego feram*) (6.26).

His efforts to come to a proper conception of God and of evil
are still frustrated; but now, in a striking reversal of the image, the
"silent groans" of his increasingly contrite heart, which itself is
"in labor" now, fly upward to (Isaiah's equally silent and groaning) Mother-God, yet he finds no "rest" from the phantasms that
like the mosquitoes that plagued Egypt, cause his spiritual eye to
fester and swell (7.11): and suddenly, the maternal image has
shifted into the paternal–medical key (7.11–12)!

But the result is that the combined momentum of both maternal
and medical images, or, more precisely, the interweaving of the
two into a single image-complex, launches Augustine into his
account of the vital Neoplatonic *admonitio* which encases the *fovisti
caput nescientis* expression. That resulting image-fusion does not
require, it does not even entitle, the translator to choose between
a maternal and a medical translation; indeed, for the "ideal"
translator, it would preclude any such exclusivity. But in doing
so, of course, it would challenge the translator to search out a
vernacular equivalent of that volatile term *fovere*, one that can

simultaneously evoke *both* medical and maternal associations, and so explode on the reader with the atonishingly rich ambiguity Augustine has achieved. But that is doubtless a challenge to accomplish the impossible.

Genesis of an Insight

Instead of taking up that challenge, let me essay the more modest task of presenting a paraphrase-explanation of the sudden insight Augustine hoped we would come to at the moment he flashed that bedazzling phrase on us.

Augustine has made it clear in the preceding books that in order to gain any clarity on the nagging Manichee question about "whence" evil came into our universe, he had first to transcend his phantasmal way of envisaging God's "omnipresent" relationship to that universe: he must learn to think of God in authentically "spiritual" terms. Even more fundamentally, he needed to undergo a profound change of attitude: he must become "humble and contrite" enough to stop complaining against, "contending with," God. He has detailed a series of contemplative insights (the "food of grown-ups") to which he came through reflection on those famous "platonist books" (a reflection aided by the God Who "took him up" (*assumsisti me*). But now, before claiming to have attained to the crucial Omnipresence insight, he takes a reminiscing step backward. He explains, for one last time, why the question "whence" evil came lured him into Manichaeism, and why, even after abandoning that sect, his sensist mode of thinking blocked him from answering it satisfactorily.

Now, at last, he confesses to his God, *fovisti caput nescientis, et clausisti oculos meos ne viderent vanitatem* (*Conf* 7.20). Take the elements of that phrase singly: first, Augustine is stressing that he was a *nesciens*, an "un-knower"; he is like an "ignorant" patient being treated by the Divine *medicus* who "knows" what He is doing. Or, secondly, he is like an infant who does not understand the care, so often a mixture of fondness and severity, his mother is lavishing on him. Either, or, better, both are true. And both of them give rise to appropriate translations of that term *fovisti*: God "fomented" and perhaps "soothed" his head (and particularly his spiritual eyes) as a doctor would, or "fondled," "caressed" it as would a mother comforting, consoling, her querulous infant. Both activities have the object of "closing his eyes," thus turning

his gaze away from the "vanities" of the temporal world that have
plagued him with so many "cares," and kept him from "seeing"
(in peaceful, contemplative *vacatio*) that only God is truly God.
Now, his eyes closed, he relaxes somewhat, stops his fretting and
squalling, "lets go," as it were, at least to some little extent (*cessavi
de me paululum*). This is not, as yet, that full *vacatio*, that complete
relaxation into the arms of the Mother-and-Doctor Who is ready
to "take him up" if only he would "toss his cares" entirely upon
Her, but it is a step toward some such Isaian release from both
self-reliance and self-concern. So, *consopita est insania mea*: his
insania, which complained so wildly against the "evils" of our
lower world, has been "lulled to sleep"; he is coming to see all his
anxieties and disappointments as evidence of God's paternal,
medicinal, but also deeply maternal care for him.

Now that God has closed his eyes as carefully as any doctor, as
tenderly as any mother, would, the clangor of the outside world
is stilled; he sleeps the healing sleep of the sick, the pacifying sleep
of the hyperactive infant. Then he "awakes" and finds himself
enfolded in God's arms (*evigilavi in Te*). But he understands that
"enveloping" power of infinite Omnipresence differently now
(*aliter*), "sees" It as the Omnipresent Providence that, all those
past years, surrounded him everywhere, as relentless and indefat-
igable as a mother's love. Isaiah's prophecy has been fulfilled:
having consented this far to believe and trust, Augustine has been
"lifted up" to the level of "understanding." Yahweh has brought
him to "walk" in the "paths of which he was ignorant" until now,
and to "know [Him] as Lord and Savior" (Is 7:9b, 42:4–16. 60:16).

PRELUDE TO SURRENDER

But *paululum*: Augustine wants us to know that his surrender was
not yet complete; his trust was not yet unreserved: it needed to
grow. So, after an interval of pondering on those "platonist"
books, he had to learn to accept not only that the Son of God and
Wisdom of the Father was the eternal "food for grown-up" souls,
but that He had "humbled Himself" to become that "solid food"
now "mixed with," filtered through, "flesh," as every nursing
mother filters it, so as to "suckle" us. If "weary, we cast ourselves
upon Him," He will receive us back, and "raise us up" to
"nourish" us until we are able to digest that solid food (7.24).

Augustine describes that final act of self-surrender as occurring in the garden at Milan. The scene is climaxed, unsurprisingly, by the apparition of a womanly figure, the Lady Continence. "Serene and joyful" she is, "alluring" as any mistress, "but nobly so, honorably"; "mother," too, of "joys" without number. She beckons him to "come, and hesitate no longer," "reaches out her hands" to "take him up [ad suscipiendum] and embrace him," smiles a smile both chiding and encouraging. Can he not do what her numberless other children have done? But then, she reminds him, they accomplished what they did, not of themselves, but only "in God."

Now her urging becomes thoroughly Isaian: "Why stand you on your own, and stand not at all? Toss yourself upon Him! Have no fear; He will not back away and let you fall! Toss yourself upon Him with full confidence, He will accept and heal you" (7.27).

His heart torn to ribbons, Augustine sobs like a child. Then he hears a child's voice, obeys, takes up the volume of Paul's letters that lies to hand, and reads the very same message on the page before him: "make no fleshly providence for your concupis-cences," which Augustine understood to mean: "from this mo-ment on let God be your only providence." And like a man long sick who has finally found a doctor he can trust implicitly, or like a weary infant who casts all his cares on his mother, making them her cares and his no longer, Augustine finds all his hesitations have vanished. His heart is flooded with a feeling of immense "secur-ity" (8.49).

Toward Final Rest in the Mother-God

Nor is that the final *fovere* image in the *Confessions*, not by any means; tracking that image and its variants through the closing five books will better remain a task for another day. For when writing that work, Augustine was convinced that our "conver-sion," like our *peregrinatio*, does not reach its term until our maternal-paternal God has enfolded us in the Isaian "peace" and "rest" of His, or Her, eternal Sabbath (13.50–53). Then we shall be "gathered" once again into the "peace" of the Heavenly Jeru-salem, at once our "fatherland" (*patria*) and our "mother most dear" (12.23). In those "heavens" we shall behold the Wisdom that God gives to "little ones," and so "perfects His praise in the mouths of infants and sucklings" (13.17). There we shall live in that maternal-paternal "bosom of Abraham" and "place [our] spiritual mouth to [God's] fountain" and "drink in Wisdom, as much as [we] can, endlessly happy" (9.6). All these images have been drawn from the Gospels, the Psalms, the Old Testament Wisdom literature; what bonds them together, though, is Augustine's assimilation of Isaiah's searing, transfixing vision: of a God Who baffles our too facile, too flaccid antitheses—mother and father, masculine and feminine, merciful and just.

NOTES

1. For fuller detail on the occurrences of this term and its cluster of images in Augustine's early works and in his *Confessions*, see my "*Ennead* VI, 4–5 in the Works of St. Augustine," REA, 9 (1963), 1–39; *Early Theory*, pp. 65–86; "St. Augustine's Images of God," *Thought*, 57 (1982), 30–40; "Isaiah's Mothering God in St. Augustine's *Confessions*," ibid., 58 (1983), 188–206; and *Imagination*, pp. 16–26.

2. *Conf* 7.20 and 13.22. In the latter locus, Augustine quotes 1 Thess 2:7, the Pauline text which principally inspires his resort to this image.

3. See chap. 1, above, at note 21.

4. See his "Christ the *Medicus humilis* in St. Augustine," AM II, pp. 623–29, and (under virtually the same title but with added detail), *Traditio*, 10 (1954), 1–28. The point of Arbesmann's study is, however, quite different from the one pursued here.

5. See the forty-odd texts collected in Pierre Courcelle's article on "Flügel der Seele" in *Reallexikon für Antike und Christentum*, 8, Fascicule 57 (1969), cols. 29–65. Also, on the Senecan tradition behind that image, see Jean Doignon's "L'Apologie de Philocalie et de Philosophie chez saint Augustin (*C. Acad.* 2, 3, 7)," in REA, 30 (1984), 100–10.

6. The conscientious outside reader for the Fordham University Press insists that this image is inconsistent with the one Augustine employs in *De utilitate credendi* 1.2: there, the fowler spreads *viscum* on tree branches in order to lure his prey. Hence (he argues), Augustine cannot be saying here that the *viscum* is "in" (or "on") the birds' wings. The *illatio* may be impressive, but the *factum* is that the text says otherwise.

7. See Mlle La Bonnardière's *Biblia Augustiniana: Les Épîtres aux Thessaloniciens, à Tite, et à Philémon* (Paris: Études Augustiennes, 1964), pp. 15–16. This entire series is an invaluable aid toward "tracking" the growth of Augustine's various image-clusters. The process almost always consists in his starting with an image drawn from one or two texts, then associating that initial image with the same or analogous images drawn from other texts. Since the texts in question are most often (not always) from Scripture, the successive text-clusters Mlle La Bonnardière has uncovered regularly represent the chronological stages in the process of image-amalgamation.

8. Tarcisius Van Bavel, in his "L'Humanité du Christ comme *lac parvulorum* dans la spiritualité de saint Augustin," *Augustiniana*, 7 (1957), 245–81, detects a "problem" (p. 255) in this exigency to pass beyond the need for "milk." But his manner of grappling with it (pp. 258–64) seems to me flawed by his failure to distinguish accurately, and then grasp the dynamic connection between, the *three* stages involved: faith, under-standing, and vision. But he is correct in observing (pp. 266–67) that Augustine *later* recognizes and strives to attenuate the difficulty his earlier systematic has created. One can, Augustine comes to see, be a "first-class" Christian without necessarily passing to the stage of "spiritual understanding," much less to the stage of "vision" which he prized so highly in his earlier thinking.

II • VARIATIONS ON THE PEREGRINUS IMAGE

4

The Peregrine Prodigal

SOME YEARS AGO, Leo C. Ferrari contributed an article on Augustine's use of the Prodigal Son parable in his *Confessions*.[1] Ferrari was astute enough to divine the importance of searching other texts for keys to understanding the sometimes cryptic allusions to this parable which Augustine makes in the *Confessions*. One of the most enlightening of those texts is certainly the one to which he assigns a pivotal role in his overall interpretation: the *Libri duo quaestionum Evangeliorum*, which Augustine published in the year 400 or thereabouts. The year, as Ferrari observes, is of particular interest: for Augustine would seem to have completed his *Confessions* either in or about A.D. 400. One would expect, therefore, the interpretation given there to have close bearing on understanding his use of this parable in characterizing his own prodigal *peregrinatio*.

But instead of taking Augustine's little exegetical essay on the parable as providing the headings for his interpretation of its employment in the *Confessions*, Ferrari does something closer to the opposite. He starts from what would seem, and has seemed to regiments of scholars before him, an obvious assumption concerning Augustine's intention: he wished to present the reader with the story (albeit "theologized") of his own individual *peregrinatio animae*, a *peregrinatio* which must (of course) have begun with his birth into this world. This assumption then encourages Ferrari to select from Augustine's exegetical essay only those elements which serve to illustrate the stages of such a "this-worldly" *peregrinatio*; this selection, in turn, permits him to leave out of consideration a number of other indications Augustine himself gives about how he understood this parable.

We have seen, however, that Augustine plainly understood the soul's wayfaring, or *peregrinatio*, as having taken its departure from the supernal "house of God," and as ideally returning there;[2] hence, we would fully expect that same circularity to hold for his understanding of that very model of the Christian *peregrinus*, the Prodigal. We would be safer in assuming Augustine's own understanding of the Prodigal story, and not some "this-worldly" interpretation more acceptable to our modern minds, when we go about the task of searching for, and interpreting, those elements of the parable he uses to describe his own "career." In this connection, a first thing to remember would be that the Prodigal story occurs in the fifteenth chapter of Luke's Gospel, in close company with those two other parables of strikingly similar import: the parable of the lost sheep, and that of the lost "drachma." But Prodigal, sheep, and coin—all three are instances of things that were not merely lost, but actually "*got* lost," and then were found *again*.

But perhaps an even safer course would be to loosen our hold on all such assumptions, and open our minds and pay careful attention to the interpretation Augustine himself gives in his little work aimed at clarifying such "Gospel questions." How did his essay of A.D. 400, then, interpret the Prodigal story?

THE STORY OF ALL HUMANITY

Augustine's two books on "Gospel questions" have a somewhat professorial, a livresque flavor suggesting the academic exercise. It is almost as though Augustine had been asked to furnish a handy vademecum for the novice preacher, a text-book to consult when looking for sermon ideas. He moves through each Gospel passage he takes for consideration in almost wooden, point-by-point fashion, bent on extracting a "lesson" from virtually every word or phrase. Not every point is of equal importance, even to him; hence, we shall not need to explore each single application he makes. But we shall quickly come to see that there are several such applications, which Ferrari omits, that do have greater importance to Augustine than would seem immediately obvious to a modern reader of the Gospels.[3]

"A man had two sons": Augustine would have us understand this as reminding us that God had two "peoples," like two stocks of the "human race," the elder of which (the Jews) "remained faithful to worshiping the one God," whereas the younger (the Gentiles) "deserted God to the point of worshiping idols." But, Augustine warns, our "consideration" of this parable ought to take up from the very inception of that entire portion of creation made up of "mortals" (*ab ipso exordio creaturae mortalium*). Luke is telling us, in other words, about the very beginnings of the "mortal," hence sinful and fallen, human race and of its two principal branches: the Jews (symbolized by the elder son) and the Gentiles (by the younger).

The younger son asked the Father to give him the "part of [the] substance which touched [pertained, was due to come to] him" (*quae eum tangeret*). Now, in what might initially appear to be a switch in Augustine's interpretation, the younger son suddenly figures the "soul which delights in its own power," or, perhaps more accurately, its assemblage of powers: of "living, understanding, remembering, and excelling by keen ingenuity" (*ingenio alacri*). These are all "divine gifts" (*munera*), but the younger son "received [them] into his own power through [an act of] free choice." That is, the "soul" freely chose to take possession of them, and to exercise autonomous dominion over them: as though they were rightfully its own to employ as it chose, and not God's gifts to be employed under God's direction. Then the younger son took them along with him and set out to a "distant region." This departure and journeying Augustine interprets as symbolizing his "bad use of his natural goods." That use was bad, Augustine specifies, for the precise reason (*eo ipso*) that he "deserted the Father out of desire to enjoy created realities, having left the Creator behind" (*patrem deseruit cupiditate fruendi creatura, relicto ipso Creatore*).

The parable tells us that this departure for a "distant region" occurred "not many days afterward." But "after" what? "Not long after the establishment [*institutionem*] of the human race," Augustine replies, and we are invited to equate that "human race" with the "mortal creatures" (*creatura mortalium*) whose beginnings (*exordium*) Luke is recounting. That is when "it pleased the soul [of the Gentile portion of humanity, at least], through free choice, to bear off with it a certain power of its nature, as it were [*quamdam velut potentiam naturae suae*], and desert Him by Whom it was created [*condita*], trusting overmuch in its own forces" (*praefidens viribus suis*). Here Augustine seems to be implying a distinction between the "creation" of the "soul" and the (subsequent) "establishment" of the "human race" (*condere* is the term he regularly uses for the act of creation).

From this point on, however, Augustine's interpretation of the parable gives the appearance of focusing more on the history of the individual human soul. The soul expends (*consumit*) its forces all the more rapidly, the more completely it deserts Him Who gave them. Hence, Scripture calls this kind of life *prodiga*—prodigal in the sense of "wasteful"—since it "loves to pour out [*fundere*] and spread itself out [*spatiari*] in external show, while emptying itself interiorly" (*intus inanescentem*). (Here we recognize key elements of Augustine's *vanitas* image.)

In slightly different terms, the soul which has fallen from the interiority of contemplative bliss into the realm of temporal activity is condemned to chase after what "proceeds from" itself, after its own external productions. By the same token, it has "abandoned Him Who is interior to it," and keeps running away from the God Who remains interior to itself, in its pursuit of exterior delights. The reader will recall that "soul," in Neoplatonism, is responsible for all the beauties of the sense-world; one of the ironies of its "fallen" condition consists in its "forgetting" that, and, so, mistakenly regarding the products of its own forming powers as more "wonderful" than itself. The ironic result is that it engages in a constant "pursuit" of what it has, itself, produced. Plotinus explains this paradox in *Ennead* 5.1.1, which we know Augustine read; he encased the same insight in the climactic sections of his own *De quantitate animae*.[4]

As one might expect, therefore, Augustine interprets the "distant region" to which the Prodigal wanders off as signifying "forgetfulness of God," while the hunger experienced in that region stands for a "lack of the word of truth," or, better, lack of the Divine "Truth," identical with God's creative "Word." In the original contemplative bliss from which it has fallen, the soul "fed upon" this divine "Heavenly Bread," and even in its alienated condition still hungers for It. Now, however, we begin to detect that the Prodigal has come to represent much more directly our individual souls, though still connoting, indirectly, Gentile humanity in its entirety.

The parable then tells us that the Prodigal "attached himself" to a "citizen" of that region: this must mean some "ethereal prince belonging to the devil's soldiery"; hence, the pigs the Prodigal was sent to feed stand for "unclean spirits under his command." The "husks" he fed to those pigs refer to

> secular teachings, resounding with sterile vanities which proclaim in prose and poetry the praises of idols, and fables pertaining to the gods of the Gentiles: in these the demons take delight. Hence when [the Prodigal], sated by them, wished to find something solid and

righteous pertaining to the life of happiness, he could not: this is what Scripture means by saying, "And no one gave him anything."

RISING, AND RETURNING

In se autem reversus: "having returned to himself." The Prodigal has at last turned away from those "exterior things which lured and seduced him, and turned his attention once again [*reducem*] to the interior realm of conscience" (*in conscientiae interiora*). He thinks of the (heavenly?) bread enjoyed even by the hired servants in his Father's house (*in domo patris*). But how was he able to know that, Augustine asks, so profoundly forgetful as he was of God, as all idolaters are? That *recogitatio*, he answers, that return from forgetfulness to "thinking-once-again," is clearly the achievement of someone who is "coming *back* to his senses" (*resipiscentis*). And such a re-turn would be possible only if the Gospel were being preached to him (*cum Evangelium praedicaretur*). (Augustine is evidently recalling Paul's "How shall they hear, without a preacher?" [from Romans 10:15].)

But St. Luke's mention of "hired servants" (*mercenarii*) now suggests a curious reflection: the preaching which served to "remind" the Prodigal of his Father must have been done by those heralds of the Gospel whom Paul stigmatizes (Phil.1:17) as preaching from less worthy kinds of motivation. They were not "heretics," since they preached what St. Paul himself preached. But Luke is right in calling them "mercenaries," drawn as they were by hope of "temporal reward." Scripture tells us that such as these "have their reward" here on earth; hence the Prodigal's cry (for he was famished for *heavenly* food) "Here I am dying of hunger."

It was only subsequently, *deinde*, that the Prodigal resolved to "arise"—obviously, Augustine interprets, he must have been lying prostrate, *jacebat*—and "go" on his lengthy journey (*longe*) away from the prince of pigs to his Father's house. Thus far, however, he has only meditated on, only promised to do penance upon his return: for "rightful and fruitful confession" can only be accomplished after one has returned to the Father, that is, after being established in the Church through faith.

"Rising up" (*surgens*), therefore, he returns to his Father; but while he was still a "long way off," that is, "before he came to an understanding of God, but was nonetheless piously seeking," his Father saw him, beheld him with love, came to meet him, and "fell upon his neck." This means that God "reached down, and in this embrace humbled" His own "arm" (*brachium*), Who is none other than the Lord Jesus Christ. "And He kissed him," for "to be consoled by the word of God's grace and so hope for the forgiveness of sins is nothing else than for someone returning [home] after distant journeying to merit [*mereri*] the kiss of love from the Father."

Now the Prodigal, established in the Church, begins to "confess" his sins; he is not worthy to be called his Father's "son," but he wants that (transformation into sonship) to come about "through grace," inasmuch as he is "unworthy of it through merits."

At this point the Father commands that the *stola prima* be brought and placed on the returned Prodigal. The Roman *stola* was a garment of respectability, even of honor; the Gospel term *prima* was intended to mean "first" in the sense of "finest." But Augustine understands *prima* as literally meaning "first": the "garment" the Prodigal had *originally* worn before his departure. That *stola*, Augustine explains, stands for the "dignity that Adam lost," the dignity (we are left to infer) that Prodigal humanity enjoyed before Adam's fall, and (apparently) its fall in Adam's fall.

The "fatted calf," Augustine tells us, represents the "Lord Himself," Incarnate and suffering, Whom the Father orders to be "brought," that is, "preached," and so made to enter the "thirsty" Prodigal's "insides, emptied as they are from starvation." That calf is now everywhere "eaten" at the Eucharistic feast of Christians, and so nourishes the "whole house."

Now it becomes plain that the Prodigal can symbolize both our individual souls *and* the "corporate" soul, so to speak, of Gentile humanity. For the elder son figures the entire people of Israel "according to the flesh." That people had remained "not in the house" but "in the field," doing "earthly works," as the bulk of the Israelites did. (Notice the implication here, that both Jewish and Gentile portions of humanity originally left the Father's "house," the soul's eternal home.) Now the elder son leaves the field and approaches the temporal version of God's "house," the Church of the New Testament. He questions one of the house-servants (a Christian preacher, obviously), but refuses to enter.

But when all the Gentiles have entered in, the Father will go out again, invite the elder son, and the nation of Israel too will find salvation. For now, however, the elder son reproaches the Father for his treatment of the younger son, who had "wasted his substance among prostitutes," that is, amid "superstitions." For "having abandoned the one legitimate marriage [*connubium*] with the Word of God, he fornicated, out of the foulest of lust, with the mob of [many] demons."

But, the Father remonstrates, "All my things are yours" (*omnia mea tua sunt*). This refers first of all to those spiritual riches we shall possess in "common" with saints and angels, riches that each of us can possess in their entirety, without any "crowding," without excluding others from the same integral possession of them.

But, *omnia*: to Augustine's mind that expression evokes the entire panoply of the real, from highest to lowest. "For when we have come into possession of that blessedness, higher realities will be ours to contemplate [*videre*]; equal realities, ours to rejoice with; and lower realities, ours to exercise dominion over."

Ad dominandum inferiora: Augustine has deliberately chosen the term employed in the Genesis creation-story, implying that the dominion we shall exercise when "returned" is a restoration of the *same* dominion that was (ours, because) Adam's, before his (and our) fall. Our souls, therefore, will once again attain to the ideal "mid-station" between higher spiritual and lower bodily realities that they should originally have preserved.

THE HUMAN SOUL'S *Peregrinatio*

This exercise in exegesis, then, presents us with a number of details which simply will not harmonize with the assumption that Augustine understands the Prodigal parable as typifying no more than the story of his own "earthly" *peregrinatio*. Not only is it true, as Knauer and Pépin both saw,[5] that the human *peregrinatio* terminates in our arrival in the *domus* of the Father; that *peregrinatio*, whether of the individual soul or of humanity in its totality, is perfectly circular, both beginning in the Father's house and (ideally) ending there.

But we have also noticed the shift Augustine's interpretation makes, from having the Prodigal first symbolize the entire Gentile branch of "humanity," then symbolize, a few lines further on, the "soul"—apparently the individual soul—and its God-given powers. Is there some inconsistency here? To answer that question, we need first to remind ourselves that, for a Platonist of Augustine's sort, the soul is what the human being authentically "is." Once that is clear, then the most obvious way of clearing Augustine from inconsistency would be to understand him as implying that each individual human being committed the same kind of sinful free-will act as did all of its companion "mortals," the entirety of the "human race." (Think, here, of how he insists on the "social" character of his adolescent "theft of pears" in the second book of his *Confessions*.)

But there is another possibility also: that Augustine here means "soul" as standing for the single collective soul which is "common" to all humanity before its "fall," and which is individualized only as one consequence of that fall. I have tried elsewhere to prove that this was indeed the view he came to adopt.[6] In any case, there is no solid reason for thinking Augustine's interpretation was necessarily inconsistent.

The Prodigal in Augustine's Preaching

But all this may have been true of the Augustine who composed his work on the "Gospel questions" in A.D. 400. Is it, though, his constant and unvarying interpretation of this parable? Quite the contrary. There are few Scriptural passages that exercised so strong a fascination for him, and very few whose rich suggestiveness allowed for his adapting them in such versatile fashion to his shifting theological and pastoral concerns. A study of the various readings Augustine gives of the Prodigal story turns out, to a remarkable extent, to be a record of his evolution as a theological thinker. Only a more comprehensive examination of that record will permit us to situate the exegesis we have just summarized.

What seems to be the earliest sermon where Augustine refers to the Prodigal is *Enarratio 24*, which scholars date to the year 392. Since he was ordained a priest in 391, he is new at the job. What we have of this sermon seems to be little more than a terse memorandum, as it were. In it, Augustine interprets the Psalmist as speaking for the Church (1) in terms drawn from the Prodigal parable. "Dismissed by You from paradise," he has the Church pray to God, "and having gone on *peregrinatio* to a distant region, I cannot go back on my own unless You come to meet me, straying [*erranti*] as I am; for my return has waited for Your mercy throughout the whole tract of secular time" (*toto tractu temporis saecularis*) (5). Here the Prodigal stands for the Adam who was "dismissed," but at the same time for all of us humans now incorporated into the Body of Christ; for we, too, appear to have been "dismissed" with, or perhaps "in," Adam.[7] That dismissal, furthermore, seems to have endured through the entire *saeculum* that followed, until God (in Christ) came to "meet" us, and to aid us in our return to paradise.

Sometime around the year 397, Augustine alludes to the same parable (*S 330* 3). He is addressing the soul which no longer "stands" in itself because it has gone out from God by its love of "exterior" goods (*foris*) like money. "You do this," he explains, "because by dismissing God and loving yourself, you have gone out from yourself as well." "You have come to value exterior realities as worth more than yourself: go back to yourself," Augustine urges, go *sursum*, rise "upward." For going back to oneself is the first step of return, but that step once taken, "you must not remain in yourself" but pursue that upward journey that culminates in your "remaining in Him Who created you."

"Imitate that younger son [the Prodigal], because you are, perhaps, him" (*quia forte tu es*). Now Augustine explicitly refers to that identity of individual and corporate souls which puzzled us a moment ago:

I say this to the (entire) people, not to one man only [*Populo dico, non uni homini*]. Even if all can hear me, I say this not to one, but to the human race [*humano generi*]. Go back, therefore; be that younger son who fell into want, his substance dispersed and lost through living riotously, who fed pigs, and, wearied by hunger, caught his breath again, cherished again the memory of his Father,

and by returning to his Father returned to himself as well. But *surgam*, said the Prodigal, "I shall arise." So, Augustine infers, "he had fallen" (*ergo ceciderat*). But he "rose up," and that movement of rising did not terminate until he was once again able to "abide" in the God Who had created Him.

Around the year 400, the year in which he seems to have composed his *Questions on the Gospels* embodying the interpretation we began with, Augustine gives one of the most extended treatments of the Prodigal parable to be found among his preached works (*SC 2* 11). It is scarcely surprising that, except for a detail here and there, these two contemporary interpretations resemble each other closely. So, the man with the two sons is God, the sons being two "peoples," the "elder" Jewish people and the "younger" Gentiles. The "substance" asked for by the younger son stands for the powers of "mind, intellect, and memory—whatever God gave so we could understand and revere Him." The "distant region" to which the younger son traveled stands for "forgetfulness of God." And he "dissipated" his substance, living riotously, that is, "pouring out [*erogans*] and not acquiring"—in other words "wasting his talent on pleasures [*luxuriis*], idols, and all manner of base cupidities, which [the Word of] Truth calls by the name of prostitutes" (2).

The "want" into which he fell was not a want of visible bread, but a "want of invisible Truth." The "prince" of that region he met up with was the devil: he is the one all *curiosi* come up against, for all "illicit curiosity is pestilent want of truth." The swine-husks he nourished himself with were "secular teachings that . . . make the devils rejoice, but do not justify believers" (3).

At long last, he came to see "where he was, what he had lost, whom he had offended . . . , and he turned back to himself" (*reversus est ad se*); "first to himself, and so to the Father." For it was necessary, Augustine explains, that he "first go back to himself, and thus come to know he was far from the Father," for Scripture says rightly, "Go back, liars, to [your] heart" (*redite praevaricatores ad cor*). Having turned back to himself, "he discovered that he was wretched," and began to think of the abundance of his Father's house. "How could this ever have come into his mind," Augustine asks, "unless the name of God was already being preached" (4)?

Now Augustine inserts the curious touch we noticed earlier: the mention of hired servants, "mercenaries," coupled with the Prodigal's "here I perish with hunger," prompts the observation that though it was the "bread" of God's word that was being preached to him, it was nonetheless preached by some who possessed it in the wrong spirit (*non bene tenentes*). For they preached the Gospel for the sake of gain, and "seeking their own good"; such as they are rightly called "mercenaries."

And yet, strangely enough, their preaching has a good result: the Prodigal rises up, *surgit*, for up to now "he had remained lying down and fallen" (*iacendo et cadendo*). He returns, and receives mercy at his Father's hands: "how close is God's mercy to the contrite of heart," and how close to this man even while in that distant "region of want." For even when he had it only in mind to rise and return, his Father knew his thoughts from afar, and came to meet him; indeed, when he was still "a long way off, his

Father, moved to mercy, came to meet him," and fell upon his neck, which means he "placed his arm upon his neck." What is that arm (*brachium*)? His Son, of course: "He gave him Christ to carry, that burden [*sarcina*] which does not weigh down [*onerat*] but bears up [*sublevat*], for 'My yoke is sweet, and my burden light' " (*sarcina mea levis est*). So light is Christ's *sarcina*, it not only does not press us down (*premat*), but even lifts us up (*allevet*). How is such a thing possible? An everyday comparison may help. Look at the birds; they "carry" their own wings, wings that might be thought a burden to them, and yet it was just such a burden the Psalmist prayed for when he begged to be given the "wings of a dove, and I shall fly, and be at rest" (5–6).

And now "The Father bids that they bring him the first garment, which Adam lost by sinning, . . . the hope of immortality [conferred] in baptism." Again, Augustine takes that term *prima* quite literally: it means the garment of "immortality" which God "first" conferred on man in paradise, which Adam had lost not only for himself but for all of us as well, and which now, in "hope" at least, has been restored to the "younger people" who (like Adam? in Adam?) had deserted and strayed away from the "house" where they originally dwelt (7).

OUR FIRST GARMENT: *Stola Prima*

Augustine focuses on the *stola prima* in another sermon (*SMa 94* 5), which dates anywhere from 393 to 405. He is explaining the "eighth" day of creation-history, which, he tells his hearers, "also means the first" day. For it refers to "Eternity, which by sinning we deserted in our origin, in our first parents [*in origine primorum parentum*], and so came down [*devenimus*] into this mortality." The eighth day therefore represents our recuperation of that first eternal day; we "make our way back to it [*repetimus*] . . . after the resurrection [when] this corruptible [body] will put on incorruption, this mortal body put on immortality, and the [Prodigal], going back [*rediens*], receives the *stolam primam* which is given back to him [*reddatur*] after the miseries of his *peregrinatio*."

Enarratio 44 9, dating from 403, urges us to "give back to God what is His," and not "wish to go further away, having received part of your *patrimonium*, and riotously waste it among prostitutes, and feed pigs." For "It is said of us, as well: 'He was dead, and is alive again; was lost, and is found.' "

In 407, he returns to the *stola prima* motif, in the eighth sermon on the First Epistle of St. John. The story of Daniel reminds us to keep our mid-station in the *Omnia*, for if we remain subject to God above, the lions, who are below us in the created order, will remain subject to us. Then,

> when we have escaped from all these snares of mortality, when the times of trial have passed away [*transierint*], and we shall receive back [*receperimus*] that *stola prima*, that immortality which we lost by sinning [*quam peccando perdidimus*], when this corruptible [body] has put on [*induerit*] incorruption . . . and our mortality put on [the garment of] immortality,

the original subordination of beast to man will be restored, and "every creature will acknowledge us as sons of God already made perfect." Then there will be "no more need of our being tried or scourged" by such things as danger from lions; "all things will be subject to us if here [in this life] we are subject to God"(7).

A MEDLEY OF THEMES

Around this same time (407/408), Augustine refers to men who worshiped *simulacra*, by which he seems clearly to mean idols. No wonder they did, he comments, since (like the Prodigal) "they fed pigs." For the Prodigal's feeding pigs he now interprets as referring to his adoption of Gentile "superstitions" and his worshiping of demons" (*En 95* 5). Worship of idols, Augustine frequently explains, is really a worship of demons.

Psalm 131 tells us "we shall enter into His tabernacles"— meaning God's "tents"— shall enter, both to "dwell" there and to "be dwelt in" by God. Interpreting this text sometime between 401 and 407, Augustine focuses on that term "dwell": "For you enter into your own house [*domus*] to dwell in it, but into God's house to be dwelt in" (*ut inhabiteris*), by the God Whose indwelling makes you happy. For "if He dwells not in you, you shall be wretched."

Consider the case of one who refused to be dwelt in by God:

> That son who said "Give me the portion of the patrimony which belongs to me" wanted to be in his own power [*in sua potestate*]. His patrimony was kept well secure by the Father [*apud patrem*], lest it be squandered [*dissiparetur*] among prostitutes. [Yet] he was given it; it was made over into his own power [*facta est in ejus*

potestate]; he set out for a distant region, poured everything out [*effudit omnia*] among prostitutes.

At long last he fell into want, remembered his Father (*recordatus est*), and turned back (*reversus est*) in order to be satiated with "bread." "Enter, therefore, so that you may be dwelt in; and be not your own, as it were [*quasi tuus sis*], but His."

The second sermon in the Wilmart collection, preached sometime before 410, develops the related theme of wrongly directed self-love. "Behold, you have chosen to love yourself: let us see if you can even 'abide' in yourself. No, you cannot; you do not abide there. Fallen from God, you fall from yourself as well [*a deo lapsus, et abs te laberis*]. . . . See, you have drawn away from God, and become lost to yourself as well" (*et a teipso peristi*). Again, the Prodigal is the classic example of such behavior: "What is left, but that you pour out [*effundas*] your mind's entire *patrimonium*, living riotously with prostitutes, that is, with lusts and various cupidities, and are compelled out of want to feed pigs, that is, unclean demons feed on you because unclean avarice has taken possession of you."

But, Augustine goes on to say, that son, starved and needy, "once returned to himself" (*reversus ad semetipsum*) said, "I shall arise, and I shall go . . . to the Father. Already returned to himself, but still prostrate" (*iacens*), he says, in effect, "I will not stay prostrate, will not remain so." This, then, is the rule of proper self-love: you must "arise" instead of lying prostrate, for by arising you stretch upward, as it were; you "love a better than yourself, and you love yourself." Love God, Who is by nature higher than the soul; "fasten yourself there" and you love yourself rightly. For Scripture says "It is good for me to adhere to my God." The counterpart of that maxim is found in another text, "You have allowed everyone to perish who has fornicated away from You." Adhering to God, Augustine interprets, is what is meant by "not fornicating away from" Him, and (by love's wonderful "osmosis") whoever "adheres to the Lord is one spirit [with Him]" (4).

About this same time (406–408) Augustine is expounding the phrase "water without substance" (*En 123* 9). This means the water of sinners, for sins have no substance to them: "they have scarcity, they have want." In just such waters "that younger son lost his entire substance." Remember how he went on *peregrinatio*, and asked his Father to give him the portion of the "substance" that came to him. "But why is it you want it for yourself? It is kept in better security by the Father [*apud patrem*]. It is yours, but you want to bring it to ruin; you want to journey farther away." But he sets out nonetheless, lives riotously with prostitutes, loses his entire substance, knows want and feeds pigs; then, "in his want [*egestas*] he remembers [*recordatur*] the Father's riches. Had want not knocked on his door, he would not have come to long for that satiety." But the "sweetness of this *saeculum* tastes sweet while we are swallowing, but it turns in our stomachs to a great bitterness." As with the Prodigal, so it is with us. Imagine that we have made a fortune in money, but lost our faith; what have we truly gained thereby? For invisible goods are far more precious than their visible counterparts (9). Why not, then, hold on to those invisible goods which you cannot lose against your will (10)?

Let those who pray this Psalm "exult" therefore, and "receive back [*recipiant*] their substance. They lost it, living riotously, but was their Father made any poorer? Let them go back [*redeant*], and find there the riches that they wasted with prostitutes on their distant *peregrinatio*" (11).

AVARICE AND SPIRITUAL FORMATION

Sermo 177, preached between the years 410 and 412, shows Augustine breaking slightly new ground. He is urging his hearers to be wisely "avaricious," by loving the God Who is their highest Good and author of all the lower goods that threaten to tempt them away from loving Him. God alone can truly satisfy our longing, but does He, Augustine asks, "suffice for the sinner?" No, for "wanting to have all things, he lost all things more completely, for [as Paul says in 1 Timothy 6:10] 'The root of all evils is avarice.' " Here Augustine cites God's words to the "sinner fornicating away from Him," as uttered through some "prophet" who (if he ever existed) is unknown to us: "You thought that, if you withdrew from me, you would have something more ample."

Again, the Prodigal perfectly illustrates that paradox of loss and gain:

> But like that younger son, see, you have fed pigs; see, you have lost everything; see, you have been left in want, and you went back, tired out, later than you should have [*sero fessus redisti*]. Now at last

understand that what the Father was giving you, He Himself kept in greater security. . . . O sinful soul, rife with fornications, become foul, become stained, become unclean—and still, so loved! Go back, therefore, to the Beautiful One, in order to go back [observe the "osmotic" transformation once again]) to [your former] beauty. Go back [*redi*] and say to Him Who alone suffices you, "You have allowed everyone who fornicates away from You to perish," [and] "It is good for me to adhere to my God."

For the root of all evils, once again, is "avarice": "In Adam himself, too, the root of all evils was avarice. He wanted more than he [had] received, because God did not suffice to him" (9).

THE SIDES OF THE NORTH

The "sides of the North," the *latera Aquilonis*, Psalm 47 told Augustine, "are the city of the Great King." He commented on this Psalm in the year 412. Those "sides of the North," he tells us, refer to the Gentiles, whereas Sion, housing the Jewish believers, was situated in the South. But why *latera*, Augustine asks, except that by "serving images [*simulacra*], adoring demons," they "adhered to the devil" (*inhaeserunt diabolo*). For all who cohere to anyone (*alicui cohaerent*) are said to be his "sides." And from that North

> came that son, also, about whom we heard just recently, he who was dead and came to life again, had been lost and was found. For, setting out to a distant region, he came even as far as the North, and there, as you heard, he "adhered" to one of the princes of that region. He became a "side of the North," therefore, by adhering to the prince of that region.

But the "city of the Great King," the city of God, to be built from both Jews and Gentiles, "is gathered" (*colligitur*) not only from the inhabitants of Sion but "also from the side of the North." Accordingly, that younger son, representing the Gentiles, "having returned to himself, said, 'I shall arise, and I shall go to the Father.' And the Father came to meet him, the Father Who says of him, 'He was dead, and has come to life again, had been lost, and is found.' "

Now comes a variant, commanded by the tenor of this novel interpretation: "That fatted calf" that was then slain and eaten "was the cornerstone," the Christ Who joined both Jewish and Gentile "walls" into a single structure. It was to be expected, therefore, that the Jews, figured by the "the elder son" who was at first "unwilling to share the feast, urged by the Father, finally entered in also; and now the two 'walls,' like those two sons coming to the calf, made up the city of the Great King" (*En 47* 3).

DEPARTING FROM THE OMNIPRESENT

Psalm 138, which Augustine commented in 412 or 413, was one of the Scriptural texts that most richly nourished his spirituality. Its central focus, for one thing, was God's Omnipresence, a theme Augustine never tired of meditating, deepening, and orchestrating for his hearers. It is significant, as we shall see, that the task of interpreting this Psalm occasioned an extended development on the Prodigal motif.

"While I am still in *peregrinatio*," Augustine confesses to God, "and before I come to that *patria*, You knew my thoughts" and knew them "from afar" (*de longinquo*). That word leads him naturally into the story of the Prodigal: "Consider that younger son; for he too has become the Body of Christ, the Church coming from the Gentiles. That younger son had of course gone far away" (*in longinquum*), unlike his elder brother, who figures the "saints" living according to the Jewish "law"; they remained working in the Father's field. But the (part of the) human race which veered off (*deflexerat*; this could be a corruption of *defluxerat*: "flowed downward"[8]) into the cult of idols, had "gone on *peregrinatio* to a great distance"—for how much farther can one get from God than some figment made by human hands?

That younger son, then, went on his distant *peregrinatio*,

> carrying his substance with him . . . and squandered it by living riotously with prostitutes. And, suffering from hunger, he attached himself [*applicuit se*] to a certain prince of that region; that prince put him in charge of feeding the pigs, with whose husks he desired to be satiated, but could not. After labors, suffering, tribulation, and want, the Father came to his mind, and he willed to return. "I shall arise," he said. . . . "I shall arise," because he was sitting down, for the Psalmist prays to the God Who knew both his "sitting down" and his "rising up": "I sat down in want, but I rose up with the desire for Your bread. I had set forth to a distance, but Him I had deserted, where was He not?"

God "knew his thoughts from a distance" and thus, as the Gospel says, the Father "came to meet him as he was coming." He had deserted the Father, as though he could be "hidden from the eyes of the avenging one" who was responsible for the sufferings he came to endure. For why should these things have befallen him, "except that the Father willed to scourge him at a distance, in order to receive him back, close to Him" (*ut reciperet propinquum*).

He is like an "apprehended fugitive" now, for, after all, where could he have fled from the Father's eyes? Journey though he would, God was already wherever he went (5). God not only saw, He foresaw (*praevidisti*), every path he trod, and so he prays:

> You permitted me [*permisisti*] to go my ways in labor, so that, if I chose not to labor, I might go back into Your ways. . . . I withdrew from You, though when I was with You all was well with me, and it was for my own good that, lacking You, all went badly with me. For had it gone well with me without You, I might perhaps have been unwilling to go back to You.

This, Augustine stresses, is the proper posture of "confession," the salutary recognition that we are justified, not of ourselves, but through the grace of Christ (6). The threat of Pelagianism is making itself felt.

"Lord, You knew all [my] *novissima et antiqua*": "all my most recent, and most ancient doings," Augustine translates. His most recent, when he fed pigs; his most ancient,

> when I requested part of my substance from You. Those ancient doings were the beginning of my most recent evils; the ancient sin, when we fell [*antiquum peccatum, quando lapsi sumus*], and our most recent punishment, when we arrived in this laborious and dangerous mortality. Would that this be the last of our punishments, which it will be if now we will to go back

and so avoid the eternal punishment of hell. "For we, brothers, have up to this point deserted God; let this life's mortality be labor enough for us. Let us remember the bread of our Father; let us recall the bliss of our Father's house. Let the husks of swine, the teachings of demons, not delight us."

"You fashioned [*finxisti*] me," the Psalmist continues, and "placed Your hand upon me." God "fashioned" us in our mothers' wombs, but, Augustine interprets, that meant fashioning us "in this mortality, and now for the labors to which each of us is born" in this world of punishment. For that is what the Psalmist means when he says "You placed Your hand upon me": "an avenging hand, weighing down the proud" (*vindicem manum, gravantem superbum*). God's fashioning us in our mother's womb was a punishment for our pride, a pride which, one must infer, we displayed "before" being so fashioned (7).

"Your *scientia* has become wonderful": "You are become an object of wonder," Augustine comments;

> I do not comprehend the You with Whom I used to be. How gentle was the Father's visage to me, when I said: "Give me my substance, [the substance] that belongs to me." And see, I set out for a distant region, and [my wayfaring] has become too much for me, worn out as I am with hunger; my labor is always before me. I am unable to perceive what I dismissed [*dimisi*]. . . . My sin has made Your *scientia* [now, Augustine's *own* knowledge of God!] a wonder from me [*ex me*], it exists as incomprehensible to me. For it was easy for me to contemplate You, before out of pride I left You,

but now, *non potero ad illam*: "I am unable to come to it"—of my own power, that is, *ex me*. "When I shall be able, therefore, I shall be able only *ex te*," empowered by You (9). For God alone can equip us with those "wings of charity" we once lost through our "cupidity," those wings whereby we may fly upward (12–13) from the Babylonian captivity, symbolized by our "mother's womb," to that "light," the Heavenly Jerusalem of unabating day (18). Meanwhile, as long as we are on this distant *peregrinatio*, let us groan continually, until we come finally to "that vision of peace, which is interpreted Jerusalem, which is [the *true*] mother of us all, the eternal city in the heavens" (29).

Enarratio 114, preached at Hippo Regius in A.D. 414, begins with a burst of praise. "Let the soul sing praise," Augustine urges his hearers, while she "is on *peregrinatio* from God; let that sheep sing that had wandered away; and let that son sing who was dead and came back to life, had been lost and was found; let our soul sing praise, my dearest brothers and children." For Prodigal, lost sheep, our individual souls—to Augustine's imagination they all share the same predicament, but God's forgiving care extends to them all (1).

AVARICE, PRIDE, AND FORNICATION

Augustine seems to have composed the second sermon of his second version of *Enarratio 18* sometime around that same year, 414. He is interpreting the Psalmist's expression "I shall be cleansed of the great sin" (*a delicto magno*). That "great sin," he tells us once again, is pride, *superbia*. For it is the root and cause of all other sins, the sin that turned angel into devil. The same preacher who told us shortly before in St. Paul's words that "avarice" was the "root of all evils" now insists, following Ecclesiasticus 10:9–15, that pride is the "beginning" of all sin. But (still citing Ecclesiasticus) the "beginning" of pride itself is the "apostasy," the "standing away," from God, the refusal to serve Him. So, "the soul [*anima*] goes into darkness, . . . so that it also squanders its substance living riotously among prostitutes, and, through want, becomes a feeder of pigs—[the same soul] who was once companion of the angels" (*qui erat socius angelorum*) (15; see also 3).

THE LOST SHEEP, THE PRODIGAL—AND ADAM

The first sermon of *Enarratio 70* seems to have been composed during the years 414 or 415. There Augustine apostrophizes Adam in the following terms: "Where did you flee Him, Adam, when you hid yourself among the trees of paradise? Him Whose face now you feared, when you had formerly been accustomed to rejoice in it? You went away, and you got lost." And yet, says Augustine now in a striking turnabout, God did not "dismiss" Adam; instead, He "dismissed" the ninety-nine other sheep and went searching for the lost one. Of that lost sheep, Augustine tells us, Scripture says that "He was dead, and has come to life again; was lost, and is found" (5). Now it is the Prodigal, lost sheep, and Adam that are all one to Augustine!

The second sermon from that same *Enarratio* helps to explain Augustine's appeal to that identity. He depicts Adam addressing God: " 'I,' " says "Adam the wretched, and Adam is every man" (*et Adam omnis homo*[9]), " 'when I will perversely to be like You, see what I have become. . . . I fell from You' " (*cecidi abs te*). How, then, are we to be rightly "similar" to God? "Let man convert himself to Him Who created him," Augustine replies; for (in the language of the *Omnia* theme), "by drawing away from God, he became cold; by drawing near to God, he becomes fervent; drawing away, he became darkened over; drawing near, he is enlightened."

Now Augustine once again forges the connection between Adam and the Prodigal: for that "younger son, who willed to have his substance in his own power, that substance which was being kept perfectly safe with the Father, set out for a distant region . . . [and was finally] 'corrected' [*correctus est*] by hunger, he who proudly departed out of satiation" (*qui saturitate superbus abscesserat*). "Hence," Augustine draws the moral,

> let anyone who wishes so to be similar to God as to "stand" up to Him [i.e., enjoy conformity with Him [*ut ad illum stet*], let him, as it is written, "guard his strength unto Him" [Ps 58:10], not withdraw from Him: cohering to Him, let him be imprinted with a seal as wax is by a ring; affixed to Him let him bear His image, doing what Scripture speaks of, "It is good for me to adhere to my God" [Ps 72:28].

For if, on the contrary, one chooses to imitate God perversely, so that "like God, he has no other by Whom he is 'formed,' no other by Whom he is ruled, such a one wants so to use his own power [*potestas*] and live as God does, no other forming or ruling him. What is the result for him, my brothers," Augustine now shifts into the *Omnia* register, "except to become torpid by withdrawing from His heat, to become vain by withdrawing from His light, and by withdrawing from Him Who exists in the highest and unchangeable manner, to be changed for the worse and come to be in lesser fashion" (*in deterius mutatus deficiat*) (6).

THE GRACE OF RETURN

During this same period (414–415), that summary of God's historic dealings with Israel, Psalm 77, occasions Augustine's comment on the expression "And He remembered that they are flesh, spirit that goes and does not return" (*spiritus vadens et non revertens*) (Ps 77:39). The anti-Pelagian cast of this sermon is obvious; it is significant, therefore, that Augustine finds it useful to revert to the *Omnia* image: "How is flesh to return," Augustine asks, "thrusting itself down to the lowest and furthest of realities by the weight of its [sinful] merits" except by God's graced election? For God's gift of grace is utterly free, so that

> the lost sheep goes back, not by its own forces, but carried back on the shoulders of the shepherd. It had power to lose itself when it freely chose to wander away, but it was unable to find itself; nor would it ever have been found unless it were sought out by its shepherd's mercy. And that son who, returned to himself, said, "I shall arise, and I shall go to my Father" also refers to this sheep. By a hidden call and inspiration, he too was sought and brought to

life again, by none other than Him Who gives life to all things. He was found, by whom? By no one but Him [Who came] to save and seek out what had gotten lost.

This wandering spirit, then, could never return on its own power; it must be called back (*revocatus*) by grace (24).

Sermo 96, preached in 416–417, reminds us that man's original perdition arose from a love of self which chose not to obey, not to remain subject to God; man wanted, rather, to "do his own will" (2). But this implies that man chose to love what was "outside" himself (*foris*) rather than love himself rightly. This turn made, Augustine issues a challenge in terms of that familiar "standing" image from Isaiah 7:9: "stand in yourself, if you can." But you will find that you cannot; for once you have begun to love external realities, "you have lost yourself," become "vain among things vain, and in a manner poured out your forces [*vires suas . . . erogare*] like a prodigal." Augustine seems to be offering this portrait of self-exhaustion as the reason why the Prodigal no longer had the strength to "stand"; but there is more to it than that. For, he continues, "he is emptied, is poured out [*effunditur*], has been reduced to want, feeds pigs. And laboring in this care of pigs, at last he "calls to mind" the plenty of his Father's house. "He poured out [*effudit*] everything among prostitutes," indeed, but that exhaustion of his powers was the consequence of the prior sin of pride whereby "he willed to have power over what was kept well safe with the Father; he chose to have those [powers] under his own will, and ended up *inops*." Augustine's hearers must have delighted in the word-play, for *inops* can mean either "in want" or "impotent, powerless"; one is tempted to translate *inops* by "in-operative." How the soul once gloried in its powers, and now it does not even have the strength to "stand"!

What does Scripture say of him? " 'Having returned to himself.' But if he has now returned to himself, he must have gone out of himself. Because he fell from himself, and went out of himself, he first goes back to himself, in order to go back to where he fell from himself." But it is not enough for him merely to "remain in himself"; He must now go back to the Father, for his "fall from himself was a falling from the Father." He must become once again subject to Him, truly find himself by "denying himself" in renewed submission to the Father. Hence, when he says "I shall arise," he immediately subjoins "and go to my Father." This shows that once returned to himself, he does not stop there, but "goes on [*pergit*] to the Father." He must now restore the original subjection he had overturned; hence, he must "draw" or "raise himself up" (*subducat*) but in such a way as to "adhere" once again to the Father (2).

<h2 style="text-align:center">FINAL INTERPRETATION</h2>

Augustine set himself to commenting the lengthy Psalm 118 at some time after the year 422. Hence, these thirty-two sermons represent virtually his last word on the Prodigal parable. Sermon 5, 2 begins as little more than a faithful paraphrase of Luke's Gospel account; the "younger son" is sketched allusively as having "poured out" (*effudit*) his "substance" among prostitutes; his resulting "hunger" Augustine now interprets as a longing for "the bread of the Father," meaning God's Truth. But he then suggests a possible interpretation, which he has come to prefer, whereby the "elder" son stands for the Pauline "old man" who "bears the image of the earthly" Adam, whereas the younger son figures the "new" man, bearing the image of the "heavenly" Adam, Christ. For his "youth" may be thought to suggest the "newness" we receive when converted by the grace of Christ.

Sermon 8, 2 of this same series contains a meditation on loving God and loving one's neighbor "as oneself." No one, however, can love what is utterly unknown to him. This brings Augustine to stress once again that the Prodigal had to "return to himself" before rising up and returning to the Father: so distant was his *peregrinatio*, he had "left even himself." But, Augustine reminds his hearers, "he would not have returned to himself if he had been altogether unknown to himself" (*si omni modo nesciret se*); nor would he have resolved to rise up and go to the Father if he had been "thoroughly ignorant of God" (*si penitus ignoraret Deum*). (There seems to have occurred a subtle shift here: Augustine no longer sees the necessity of having Gospel preachers "remind" the Prodigal of God.)

The next sermon, 9, finds Augustine speaking of the "proud" who, out of pride, "turn away" (*declinant*) from God, "as they [Adam and Eve] did who begot us mortally [and so ushered us] into these evils" we experience. Does that mean we played no part in our fall? No, for God's question—"Where are you, Adam?"—was not seeking knowledge He did not have, but was a scolding "admonition" both to Adam and to us. It is aimed at bringing to mind not "only that sin of the first humans" but our own "turning away" as well. "All of us should be terrified by the example [of that sin and the curse that followed it] not to turn away from God's commands, so that, by loving justice throughout all time, we receive back even through our labors in this world what we lost [*amisimus*] amid the delights of paradise" (1).

The proud, he goes on to say, are mockers of the martyrs' sufferings, and even of Christ's. But the "medicine" of suffering is the only cure for that "tumor which inflated us so that we fell and, prostrate, swelled outward even further." That inflating tumor is, of course, pride, "the same pride" as caused our fall, "enduring still, and growing even greater." Consider that "younger son, who on behalf of the pigs he fed," that is, the unclean demons he venerated, "used to persecute what was formerly a particle of his [later, eventual] self [in the person of] a tiny number of Christians [*particulam suam in paucissimis Christianis praecedentem persequebatur*]. Now, however, that son who was dead has come to life again; he had been lost, and was found." By this, Augustine interprets, Scripture means that he has been so completely converted from his former ways that "now he preaches most religiously, and exalts with highest praise those he once despised and heaped with opprobrium, martyrs drawn from many a numerous Gentile nation" (2).

Sermon 23 on Psalm 118 contains what may have been Augustine's final meditation on the Prodigal. "My soul is ever in Your hands," says the more acceptable reading (in Augustine's view) of verse 109. For we are told in another place that "the souls of the just are in the hands of God." These are words spoken by "a just man, not an unjust one; by one going back [*redeuntis*] to the Father, not drawing away from Him." For we may think of that "younger son" as "wanting to have his soul in his own hands, when he said to the Father, 'Give me my substance which belongs to me'; but on that account he died, on that account was lost" (5).

IN VARIETY, A THREAD OF UNITY

The first impression one receives on reading this series of interpretations, spread over so many years, is that the Prodigal parable was a remarkably flexible instrument in Augustine's preaching. He was able to adapt it to a variety of concerns as the occasion demanded: the relation of Old Testament to New, of the Jewish to the Christian religion, of Christianity to paganism and idolatry; it even became, toward the end, a weapon against Pelagianism. Hence, it would be misguided to claim that Augustine was more consistent in interpreting every single detail of the parable than he actually chose to be. He could aim the metaphor of "feeding pigs," for example, to warn us against the dangers of the education in pagan letters which he himself had undergone, or redirect it as a missile fired against the worship of demons. The Prodigal himself, in turn, can be made to stand for the "younger" Gentiles as opposed to their Jewish counterparts, then for Adam, for the entire human race, for each of us individually, or for that mysterious entity "the soul."

Despite all this flexibility and apparent inconsistency, however, certain motifs recur insistently enough to warrant our speaking of a central skeletal structure that holds all of Augustine's various interpretations together.

The identity of the Prodigal, for instance, may not be as confusing as initially appears: he took his departure shortly after the "institution" of the "human race," Augustine has told us; hence, identifying him with Adam is a natural move of the mind. For it begins to become plain that Adam was, to Augustine's way of thinking, not only the "first" individual human, but the original font and embodiment of all subsequent humanity; his original condition was "ours" as well, and so was his "fall." Not only were we "in" him; in a very real sense we "were" him.[10]

But what was its original condition when the "human race" was first instituted? Were all of us in and one with Adam, as in some corporate entity that Augustine can express with that mysterious term "soul"? We were, clearly, originally "clothed" with the *stola* of immortality: this, Augustine also makes clear, is the spiritual, immortal body we hope to receive—or rather, receive *back*—after the resurrection promised us. It would scarcely be stretching the point to denominate our original condition, then, as that of "souls" in that single corporate "soul" named Adam, or "Man." And since Augustine stresses that this was the original "stock" from which both Jews and Gentiles sprang, his way of occasionally identifying the Prodigal more specifically with the Gentiles becomes less confusing: the unity of the human race, both Jews and Gentiles, has been safeguarded. The story of the Prodigal, like that of Adam, is typical of the "departure" and "return," the circular *peregrinatio* of every human "soul." We all started out from the Father's "house," and all hope to return there.

Augustine several times stresses that our departure was the work of our "free choice." But what form did that choice take? Most prominently, it was a will toward autonomy, of having our "substance"—our soul-powers—under our own "confident" control. Hence, it was an act of insubordination toward the God under Whose control we ought to have remained. The root fault in our choice was therefore pride. We have seen him refer to that pride as linked with what he terms *saturitas*, a term we shall see more of further on; but he is careful to remind us that, whatever that "satedness" means, it was a "proud *saturitas*."

On several occasions, too, he has obviously been impressed by Scripture's frequent condemnations of "avarice," and most particularly by Paul's warning (1 Tim 6:10) that the "root of all evils is avarice." He seems to have experienced a temporary uncertainty about how this sweeping generalization could be reconciled with the equally general expression from Ecclesiasticus 10:15 that "pride is the beginning of all sin"; that text, as we shall see, made an early and lasting impression on Augustine. But in the very same context, Ecclesiasticus itself is linking pride with avarice (10:7–15). This may well have encouraged Augustine to suspect that these two "root" sins were not really in opposition to each other after all: our initial sin of "pride" was an "avaricious" as well as insubordinate rejection of God in pursuit of a phantom "more" than God. In any event, the "pride" he sees in Pelagianism will confirm him even more strongly in his conviction that *superbia* is the root and "beginning" of all sin.

The first of Augustine's classic triad of sins, then, was pride; but our choice also made "creatures," the bodily and temporal creatures of this lower "transient" world, the objects of our "enjoyment" in place of God. We deserted the only legitimate "marriage" the soul was made to enjoy, and "fornicated away" from God. It was perfectly coherent, then, that this radical fornication should have bodily "fornication" with "prostitutes" as its natural consequence; our sin of pride inexorably flowed into that second form of Augustine's triad, sins of "fleshly concupiscence."

But desertion of God was a fall away from Him to lower and lower realities, and by the same token toward that asymptotic limit, nothingness. And what more unlike God than an empty "idol," the tangible and sensible work of our soul's productive powers, the falsest "image" of God that can be imagined? Our worship of such utter "vanities" is at the polar extreme from our original submission to Verity, the Truth He is; it represents the extremest form of taking the sensible and tangible as the unique measure of value and divinity. Hence, Augustine can say that the demons, who rejoice in our rejection of God and worship of idols, have thereby made us *curiosi*, victims of that third member of the triadic sin, "curiosity."

What was the soul's activity before its fall? It dwelt in the Father's "house," we know; but there is no salient detail in the parable that would prompt Augustine to be more explicit than that. We are, accordingly, compelled to put various fragmentary hints together in hopes they will produce a coherent picture. Since the Prodigal is the classic instance of the "peregrinating" soul, however, we may feel an initial confidence in hypothesizing that the "bliss of our Father's house" must have been the joys of contemplation which (we have already seen) are shared by the "community of blessed spirits" in the Heaven of Heaven. This hypothesis would make excellent sense of Augustine's insistence that the soul's "bread" and "food" is God's Truth, whether Truth be taken to mean His Eternal Word (the food of "grown-ups") or the reminding "words" (the "milk" of little ones) served up by "preachers of the Gospel." This would also explain why Augustine finds it relevant to confess how difficult it is to come to a *scientia Dei*, a "knowledge" of God, even for the soul that once enjoyed, and longs again to share, that "vision of Peace" represented by the heavenly Jerusalem.

Seeing contemplation as the soul's original activity also makes sense of Augustine's situating the fallen soul in the "whole tract of secular time," for time is the arena of "action," so that the soul's fall from Eternity into time is identical with its fall from the concentrated stillness of contemplation into the diffusion, the "spread-outness" of action. Hence, too, the appropriateness of the observation that the various segments of humanity, both Jews and Gentiles, need to be "collected," brought together from this fragmentation, in order to form the City of the Great King.

That same hypothesis is strongly supported by the description of our fallen activity: it consists in the wanton deployment of our powers in "productive" activities, followed by the eager pursuit of those "exterior" products of our spiritual forces. So fascinated do we become with the lure of possessing and enjoying these "exterior" productions, we "forget" the God Who still dwells in us "interiorly."

So, our souls could be described as on an unfettered spree of "pouring out," "paying out," "squandering" their interior riches like a Prodigal living riotously among "prostitutes." In one instance Augustine describes the soul in a remarkable Neoplatonic anticipation of that contemporary metaphor: it becomes "spaced out" (*spatiari*). No wonder it ends up "interiorly emptied" and suffering "want." Its original "marriage" was to the One God, but now it wastes its spiritual substance on the "many," whether Augustine chooses to specify those "many" as the "image-realities" the soul produces in the spatio-temporal realm or the "demons" holding sway over souls in that fallen state. Notice, in passing, how the images of pouring out, squandering one's interior resources, suggest both the metaphysical self-eversion of the contemplative soul into action, and the erotic emissions of fleshly concupiscence; Augustine's imagination has forged, once again, a profound consonance, a natural consequentiality, leading inexorably from the first to the second. And both end in self-exhaustion.

And so the Prodigal's extreme state can be described as "lying" prostrate or (in the words of Psalm 138) "sitting down" in "want" or "impotence." He has gone as "far" as he can go into "forgetfulness" of his Father and original home. But then, he is "reminded" of both, and by the same token reminded of "himself"—of who he is and where he started from. That reminder comes, Augustine twice interprets, from "hired hands" or "mercenaries": preachers of the Gospel, but whose motivation is flawed by hopes of secular rewards.

"HIRED HANDS": THE MANICHEE CONTRIBUTION

Now that is surely a curious turn for his interpretation to take. The mention of "hired hands" is there in the parable, granted; and so is the Prodigal's cry that "I perish here of want." But not every detail of the parable calls for equal interpretive attention, and it is puzzling why Augustine's should bring forth this precise interpretation when others were surely possible. Why not, for instance, link these hired hands with those whom the master of the vineyard hired, each for a penny?

I would suggest that there was a reason extrinsic to the words of the parable that suggested this reflection, and that the reason was autobiographical. Observe how Augustine twice refers to "feeding pigs" as figuring devotion to the "vanities without solidity" of pagan literary learning; it is the same accusation he levels in the *Confessions* at his own early education. A similar autobiographical fact might easily explain his interpretation of the "hired hands": I suspect Augustine is thinking of the Manichees. For they preached Christ to him, conspired (along with Cicero's *Hortensius!*) to "remind" him of Father and Home, but they fed him on foods that left him, in the end, still perishing from hunger. I offer that now only as a suggestion to be kept in mind; further confirmation of it may come later.

Reminded by this preaching, then, the Prodigal "returns to himself"; for the "memory" of who he is and whence he comes is intimately bound up with the memory of the Father and Home. He begins to "seek after God, piously," but he is still "far off" from having a true "understanding" of God. Again, Augustine's own experience shows between the lines, along with the paradoxical recognition that runs through the *Confessions* like a refrain: that God Himself was always "near" him even when he was "far off."

RISING UP, AND BECOMING ERECT

But now he "rises up": *surgit*. Whereas he was formerly either prone from exhaustion or "sitting" in want, he now assumes a "standing" position. What does Augustine take this to signify? We saw that "to stand" in the context of the *Omnia* image regularly means to be "solidly supported" on the "firmament" that is God's Truth. That Truth, however, is Eternal, "stable," unchanging, in contrast to the "flowing" transiencies of the lower, temporal world. In this context, then, to "stand" means to be supported by and (osmotically) transformed by "adhering" to God and so participating in His own Eternity.

But the Lucan parable provides a different context, one that significantly enriches that notion of "standing" with a cluster of different nuances. The Prodigal is depicted precisely as "rising up" from a non-erect to a "standing" position: how does Augustine interpret that change?

We have seen that the term *surgere* suggests to his mind its cognate, *sursum*, and the Christian invocation to "lift up your hearts." We, like the Prodigal, have been "falling away" (*cadendo*), and our fall has left us "lying down" (*iacendo*), either in exhaustion or in "adhesion" to the earthly realities we have chosen to enjoy instead of God. But now the Word has been preached to us: *sursum corda*, "lift up your hearts." What does that command imply?

It connotes several things, but they are intimately related in Augustine's imagination. The first of them emerges from our desire for happiness. Our Prodigal experience should have taught us that we cannot find happiness by clinging "prostrate" to the joys of earth; hence, we are being summoned to convert and redirect our once-earthly desires to the "higher," spiritual realities, and, notably, to the God, the Bread of Truth, Who alone can satisfy us.

But the *Omnia* theme teaches that our wrongly directed self-love has subverted the due order of our original subjection to God. In this register, we are called upon to recognize that to love ourselves rightly we must love a "higher" than ourselves, become once again "fixed" on Him so that we can in time "adhere" to Him. Then we will find Him once again governing us in the due subordination our departure overturned.

But our prostrate position comes to have another meaning also: our fall into time and action, our wearying chase after earthly satisfactions that constantly flee from our grasp, our paying and pouring out of our soul's energies, all this has left us prone—"inoperative"—with sheer exhaustion; we no longer have the "strength" to "stand." With no more strength of our own to rely on, we must beg for helping grace from the out-stretched "arm" of the Father. Only that *Brachium*, the Son, Who came to save what had gotten lost, can truly tell us to "rise, and walk," at the same time imparting the strength required to fulfill that command.

But in the context of all these three image-registers, the Prodigal's *surgit* conveys the same core-meaning. Rise up, and stand erect, stretch heavenward, and then, your mind and heart raised up to the spiritual world above, your desires redirected, your due subordination to God restored, and empowered by the strength that can only come from on high, you will be in proper posture to "seek" Him piously, and come in time to "understand" Him truly. Growing in that understanding, you will eventually be enabled, with His help, to "return" to the contemplative delights of the "house" you once left, and to the God to Whom it is "good" for you to "adhere."

And once you have returned, He will clothe you again with the *stola prima*, that "first garment," the immortal and spiritual body that the first Prodigal, Adam, forfeited. But the Prodigal is you. All of us were once "in" Adam and one with him; it is "we" who forfeited, and hope to receive back, that "first garment." Thus transfigured, we who were reduced to feeding pigs will once again be the "companions of the angels"; we shall be "like the angels in heaven," in the "Heaven of Heaven," God's "house."

But this remains Augustine's interpretation of the *stola prima*, our onetime "first garment" of spiritual immortality, only so long as he remains confident that our *peregrinatio* is a genuinely circular one. The theory of the human situation undergirding that interpretation, though, envisaged us as originally "souls," even if clothed—as the angels themselves appear to be—in immortal, "spiritual bodies." That theory explained our "fall" into this world of body, action, and time as the inexorable consequence of a "sin" we committed in that pre-existent state; that sin accounted for our "dismissal" from that supra-terrestrial paradise.

But there will come a moment, long after the composition of his *Confessions*, when Augustine is assailed by tormenting doubts about whether this view of the soul's story can be reconciled with the data of Scripture. When that moment comes, one of the first casualties will be the interpretation of the *stola prima* that had long seemed to serve him so well. The challenge to that interpretation will be thrown down mainly by Pelagius and his followers, sometime around the year 411/412. It may be significant that from the year 412 on, Augustine omits any mention of the *stola prima* in the sermons we have surveyed. It may be equally significant that many years later *Enarratio 118*, sermon 9, once again speaks serenely of our "fall in Adam," insinuating that Augustine may by that time have regained confidence in the theory that subtended his erstwhile interpretation of our "first garment." But those are only tiny fragments of a story much larger than we need go into here.

NOTES

1. See his "The Prodigal Son in the *Confessions*," RA 12 (1977), 104–18.

2. See above, pp. 80–81, 82–91.

3. All quotations in the following pages are from Augustine's *Libri duo quaestionum Evangeliorum* 2.33.

4. See especially the meditation on the ascending powers of soul in *Quant* 70–79.

5. On Pépin, see chap. 1; on Knauer, chap. 2, above.

6. See my *Origin*, esp. pp. 282–335.

7. For Augustine's use of *dimittere*, see above, pp. 63–65. The usual implication is that God "dismisses" the sinful soul; but we shall shortly see that the inner dynamic Augustine reads into the term allows (even requires) that the sinful soul reciprocally "dismisses" God.

8. See the Maurists' asterisk and corresponding note to this effect, *En 138* 5.

9. The Maurists print *in Adam* (*En 70*, sermon 2, 6), but their asterisk warns the reader that the *in* is absent from most manuscripts. Both Migne and CSSL editions follow suit. One can understand that this would be a *lectio difficilior* for some copyist along the line of transmission; the original very probably read "Adam" *without* the preposition "in."

10. Augustine's interpretation of the Prodigal corroborates, accordingly, the theory advanced in my *Origin*, passim.

5

The Christian Odysseus

IN HIS RICHLY EMBROIDERED CONTRIBUTION ON "The Platonic and Christian Ulysses,"[1] Jean Pépin traces a number of applications of the Ulysses image in patristic thought, comparing the import accorded that image by Christian writers from Clement of Alexandria through Ambrose to Maximus of Turin. That study, James F. Curley claimed, shows "*pace* O'Connell and others . . . that the Ulysses figure became at the hands of the Fathers a truly Christian image, and not just a veiled Platonic one."[2]

That judgment has its baffling aspects; it may have been based on some secondhand estimate of my studies on Augustine. But firsthand acquaintance, if garnered with some attention, would make this much clear: "my" Augustine was always determined to think as a Christian, even when using, and frequently transforming, the Plotinian philosophy he once thought would serve as a trusty ally in "understanding the faith." We moderns might have more doubts on Plotinus' reliability than he did, but even from the first Augustine himself was obliged to part company with the great man on several crucial issues: in short, whenever he detected a conflict between his admired *platonici* and the faith as he had received it, faith always won, and Platonism always lost.

If, therefore, he made use of the Ulysses image, as he did, he was firmly convinced that it was a Ulysses "baptized" he was presenting, and in that sense a "truly Christian image." But that image, he well knew, was also a "Platonic" one; it would have been absurdly futile for Augustine to attempt to "veil" that lineage from the cultured reader of his day; besides, he did not see the kind of opposition between *his* Platonism and *his* Christianity that some modern scholars have tended to stress—and on certain points wrongly stress—and he certainly saw no opposition between them on this precise point.[3] So, it was consistent with his entire project as a Christian thinker to demonstrate that the Christian faith was congenial to the deepest insights of pagan culture. One such point of consonance, Augustine thought, was the view of human life as a circular *peregrinatio*, an "odyssey" that could just as easily be sketched as a journey overland as a risky, uncertain sea-voyage.

Another baffling feature of Curley's judgment is this: Pépin scarcely touches on Augustine, and says exactly nothing of his treatment of the Ulysses/Odysseus image.[4] True enough, he salts his meticulous catalogue of texts from other authors with occasional generalizations about "fundamental differences" separating the lessons drawn by the Fathers from those presented by pagan Neoplatonists. The "hostile sea," he tells us, did not become for Christian thinkers the entire realm of change or "genesis"; nor does the Ithaca to which Ulysses longs to return become the "intelligible world" from which the soul originally departed. But no sooner has Pépin made such statements than he feels compelled to hedge them. For Ambrose, the "sea" is "not without affinities to the world of coming-to-be from which the Neoplatonists wish to rescue the soul"; whereas Augustine (he observes in a footnote) was later obliged to regret the equation he established in his early works between Christ's Kingdom "not of this world" and the Neoplatonists' "intelligible world"; and Maximus of Turin roundly characterizes Ithaca as the *patria paradysi de qua primus homo exierat*, "the paradisal homeland whence the first man departed."

All of this, Pépin says, warns us that the "distance" between Christian and pagan exegeses of the Odysseus myth "can be shortened." Indeed, Christian interpreters and Platonists assumed "substantially the same exegetical foundation." For both of them Odysseus must fight the "hostile forces . . . of the sensible world" for a salvation that is "conceived of as a *return* to the fatherland."[5]

It is perhaps understandable that in an admittedly incomplete study of this patristic theme Pépin's generalized conclusions should take on this hesitant, if not self-contradictory, character. But in the end he has raised more questions than he has resolved about the Fathers generally. His statement about Ambrose's sea-symbolism, moreover, might have been considerably more direct: *Quod autem mare abruptius*, Ambrose asks, *quam saeculum*: "What sea is more sudden [in its storminess] than the *saeculum*, so uncertain, full of movement [*mobile*], deep, and gusting with the blasts from unclean spirits?"[6] That characterization, to use his understated phrase, is not without affinities to Augustine's own equation of "sea" with the *saeculum*, the realm of Platonic "coming-to-be." But again, what is more to the point here is that Pépin has cast no direct illumination whatever on Augustine's employment of the Ulysses image. Augustine did, however, employ this image, and to considerable effect. Moreover, the import the image had for him is of lively interest for the interpreter of his imaginative style of thinking.

It is almost inconceivable that Augustine was encouraged to exploit the Ulysses image for Christian purposes by readings in the earlier Fathers Pépin chose as focus for his study; his slender knowledge of Greek would have stood in the way of that. What is quite possible, though, is that he drew encouragement from Ambrose's use of it in his preaching on St. Luke's Gospel. It could also be true that only part of what Ambrose may have suggested to Augustine's mind and imagination is contained in the published version of his *Expositio* on St. Luke's Gospel. In any event, Augustine will regularly connect his allusions to Odysseus with that other traveler, Luke's Prodigal; he seems to have found enough resemblances between these two types of the journeying soul that they call each other to his mind and associate so closely in his imagination as occasionally to overlap and almost fuse into a single symbolic entity.

AN INSTANCE FROM THE *Confessions*

One of the most striking instances of this image-fusion occurs in a now-famous text from the *Confessions*; it will be significant for us further on that this same text, as wielded by the hammering hand of Paul Henry, drove the firmest of nails into the coffin of Willy Theiler's thesis that Augustine could have read no Plotinus whatever.[7] For Augustine can almost be heard reciting, word for word, fragments from Plotinus' evocation of the Odysseus image in *Ennead* 1.6.8, "On Beauty":

> But how shall we find the way? What method can we devise? How can one see the "inconceivable beauty" . . .? Let him who can, follow and come within, and leave outside the sight of his eyes and not turn back to the bodily splendors which he saw before. . . . [W]e must know that they are images, traces, shadows, and hurry away to that which they image.
>
> This would be truer advice: "Let us fly to our dear country [fatherland]." What then is our way of escape, and how are we to find it? We shall put out to sea, as Odysseus did, from the witch Circe or Calypso. . . . [He] was not content to stay though he had delights of the eyes and lived among much beauty of sense. Our country from which we came is *there* [on high], our Father is *there*. How shall we travel to it, where is our way of escape? We cannot

get there on foot; for our feet only carry us everywhere in *this* world, from one country to another. You must not get ready a carriage, either, or a boat. Let all these (bodily) things go, and do not look. Shut your eyes, and change to and wake another way of seeing. . . .[8]

And, from Augustine's *Confessions*:

Not by feet or by passing through spatial distances does one go away from You [Lord], or go back to You; nor did that younger son of Yours [the Prodigal] seek for horses or chariots or ships; nor did he fly away on visible wings, or journey on legs. . . . And so, to be in lustful passion, that is what it means to be in darkness and to be far from Your countenance [1.28; cf. 8.19].

But "afterward," on his "return," Augustine tells us:

You "warmed" my head [*fovisti caput*], unknowing as I was, and closed my eyes so that they would not look upon vanity . . . and my madness was lulled into sleep; and I awoke in You and saw that You were infinite, but in an entirely different [from a spatial] way; and that vision was not drawn from flesh [7.20].

Once we have been alerted by the identity of linguistic terms in both texts—feet and horses, chariots and ships, fatherland and Father—we are brought to a closer examination of the remarkable kinship they manifest on more substantive levels. They both embody the same thought-drive, subtending and suffusing it with similar affect by strikingly similar imagery. The "distance" to be covered is not of the spatial kind familiar from journeys "here," in *this* world, so earthly means of locomotion are irrelevant. The eyes required are not our outward "fleshly" eyes, for the "vision" is of another kind entirely. We must turn our eyes away from the "vanities," images, traces, shadows, from the delights of outward eye, and from the beauties of sense that make their appeal to lustful passion. We must no longer look on them, not turn back to them; we must close our outward eyes, turn inward, and allow "another way of seeing" to be "awakened" in us.

Augustine has substituted the Biblical figure of the Prodigal for the Greek Odysseus; he has also substituted Biblical expressions for whatever linguistic turns he may have found in Marius Victorinus' Latin, but not in some mechanically literal manner, word by word. Plotinus' thought, imagery, affect, and language have entered his ear and mind and imagination as an organic whole, as what André Mandouze calls an indivisible "schéma spirituel,"[9] just as did the corresponding components later drawn from Scripture. It is from this deeper level that Plotinus' text could re-emerge, years afterward, both "Christianized" and (forgive the term) "Augustinized." And in the process the Odysseus of Greek myth became one with the Prodigal of Luke's Gospel.

REASONS FOR AN "IMAGE-FUSION"

How are we to account for this "fusion" of images? A first modest step might be to consider the striking similarities between the Prodigal (as Augustine interpreted his story) and Odysseus as Platonizing allegorizers viewed him.

First and most obvious, both Prodigal and Odysseus were seen as emblematic of the human condition, figures of the soul "wandering" far from its native "home." One of these *peregrinationes* was overland, the other on sea; we shall keep that difference in mind for what follows. But for now, it may be relegated to secondary importance, for both Homer's sea and Luke's "far country" betoken "this world" of alienation from our true home.

Second, both wanderers started out from home: Odysseus, from Ithaca; the Prodigal, from his Father's "house." Both had life much better at home: Odysseus, with his bride, the faithful Penelope, who still awaits his return; the Prodigal, in what Augustine calls the soul's *connubium* with God. Now they both experience a life of deprivation, hunger, and hardship, and it makes them yearn for the plenty, security, and rest that "home" represents to each of them. Both journeys, then, are circular: their end is also their beginning.

Third, they both went a "great distance" from home. In the case of the Prodigal, Augustine interprets this as implying a journey so "far" from God as to bring on a forgetfulness, an *oblivio*, of God that is also a forgetfulness of "self." The Greek interpreters relished this point particularly: notice how often Odysseus is tempted to "forget" the home he longs for, and so forget that he is "the Ithacan." Circe, Calypso, the Sirens and Lotus-eaters, even the helpful Phaeacians in their well-meaning way, all embody this twin temptation to forgetfulness. It is intriguing in this connection that Augustine, in De Trinitate 14.14, strives to justify his use of the term *memoria* as bearing on present realities like the soul; to do so, he chooses a quotation from the *Aeneid* precisely to illustrate Odysseus' resolute clinging to the "memory" of himself as "Ithacan." Needless to say, those verses from Vergil were familiar to him from his school days.

Finally, for both the Prodigal and Odysseus, the pleasures of fleshly "concupiscence" were among the most dangerous threats to this memory of self, and to their unbending resolve to return home: Augustine would swiftly have detected the obvious analogy between the Prodigal's "prostitutes" and the seductive charms of Circe and Calypso.

So much, then, for the kinships Augustine would have seen between the Prodigal and Odysseus: his apologetic intentions would have been eminently well served by an artful demonstration that the best insights of Greek thought were fulfilled in the Gospel. We must bear in mind, however, that whereas we moderns must deliberately steep ourselves in classical lore in order to descry these connections, they would have been more immediately discernible to the reasonably cultivated person of Augustine's day.

A Problem of Detection

But at this juncture we have to face a nettling problem. We have seen the kinships between Odysseus and the Prodigal; we may safely conjecture that they would have encouraged the process of image-fusion Augustine accomplished in his *Confessions*. But in this instance it was Plotinus' text, a "source" (ambiguous term) *extrinsic* to Augustine's work, that provided the clues indicating that the Odysseus of the Neoplatonist had been transformed into the Prodigal of the Gospel. But without that extrinsic clue, could we have come so confidently to this conclusion? Or, to put the question another way: granted that Augustine sometimes fuses these images into one, could not the fusion become so complete, could not Odysseus get so "swallowed up" and assimilated into the Prodigal, as to leave us with no grounds for claiming that Odysseus still persists as a distinguishable ingredient in the fusion? Once the imagination has worked its alchemy and genuinely fused these two images, do we have any process of analysis to confidently decompose the fused product and *prove* that this or that one of the original ingredients still persists and exerts its magnetic force?

To resolve this difficulty, a first way suggests itself: fix on those elements that are "proper" to the Odysseus image, and much less appropriate to the Prodigal, and apply them as the litmus paper, so to speak, for discerning when Odysseus still peers out from the shadow of the Prodigal. One of those elements, for example, might be the presence of sea-voyage images rather than images of land travel; another might be shipwreck imagery; a third might be imagery reflecting "toils" and "dangers": Odysseus, one might think, experienced these more saliently than did the Prodigal.

When we come to examine more concrete instances of Augustine's imaginative work, it will become clear that criteria like these work well enough in the vast majority of cases; the notion of a "perfect" image-fusion will turn out to be more theoretical and asymptotic than real. Indeed, re-examination of the very image that suggests this difficulty will show that there remains considerable "oscillation" from Odysseus to the Prodigal and back; there are enough indicators in the text, and they are reliable enough to facilitate our discerning when Augustine is working in the Prodigal register and when that register shifts into the Odysseus key.

But there are some further complications that make that answer an incomplete one. One reason is that our business forces us to deal with more than Odysseus and the Prodigal. When it comes to literary referents, we have to take account of Aeneas, of the apostles in the storm at sea. But, one might object, when it comes to the man's psychology, we must not confine ourselves to literary referents; we must take into account, for instance, those more primitive feelings about the sea that Augustine, that confirmed landlubber, seems to have entertained. One might be tempted to think that these alone, nourished by his personal memories of seafaring, could conceivably explain his personal penchant for endowing sea-imagery with associations of danger, hardship, and fierce exertion, and perhaps explain it more authentically than could any referents from literature. Moreover, one might add, a child who has gone through the trauma of nearly drowning will forever deal with literature of the sea, forever read the *Odyssey*, the *Aeneid*, and indeed the Gospels, in a vastly different way from others.

To illustrate the problem, take the example of Aeneas. Here, too, we have a vivid tale of seafaring with all its risks and hardships. Augustine explicitly evokes aspects of it in *Confessions* 1.21. He is recounting his early studies in the Latin classics; his account slides insensibly from the beauties of that literature to its erotic associations. What miserable foolishness, he exclaims, to weep over the death of Aeneas' sometime lover, Dido, and not over one's own death, "which occurs because he does not love You, O God, Light of my heart" and (the image is a daring one, to say the least), "manly Power [*virtus*] Who fecundates [*maritans*] my mind and the bosom of my thought. I was not in love with You and was fornicating away from You, and fornicator that I was I heard nothing but 'Well done, well done.' For friendship with this world," Augustine summarizes in a phrase that rings like a theological definition, "is fornication away from You" (cf. 4.2). But now, he assures us, all that is changed: he would prefer to "forget" all such poetic fictions "as the wanderings [*errores*] of Aeneas" than forget those basic skills of reading and writing. For (Augustine implies) the latter can at least be "used" in God's service.

Note how the Aeneas story starts in the same aesthetic-erotic atmosphere as permeated the Odysseus image in Plotinus and the Odysseus-Prodigal in the parallel sections of the *Confessions*. Note, too, the cluster of identical associations all three figures evoke: wandering, fornication, forgetfulness, then God's higher Light streaming into the inner eye of the "heart." One might be tempted to suggest that the Aeneas story is unlike the *Odyssey* at least in this: it is a voyage from Troy to Rome, hence not a voyage of "return." Immediately, though, that suggestion is negated by Vergil's curious insistence that, once Aeneas' true lineage becomes known, he finds himself, in fact, on a voyage of "return."[10]

Before I answer the objection we are dealing with, notice how much further it could be pushed. One could suggest, for example, that matters might stand at much the same impasse if we surveyed Augustine's exegeses of the Gospel story of the storm at sea: the sea is what it is for Aeneas and Odysseus, the *saeculum*, tempestuous with hardships, dangers, shipwrecks. The heavens are dark, no stars lend guidance to our outward eye; but the "inner eye" of faith has its own light: it knows that the Christ Who seems to sleep nonetheless keeps us safe (*SS 75* 2; *63* 1–2; *76* 1). These details are all adjusted to the contours of the story, granted: but it is essentially the same cluster of associations that appears. Odysseus, Aeneas, the apostles, and Christians more generally: it is all the same sea-voyage for Augustine. Even when portraying the Prodigal, he can slip by a kind of oscillation into sea-odyssey imagery; but does this entitle us to infer that the Odysseus or Aeneas image is at work? Not necessarily. The Prodigal *may* have spontaneously shape-shifted into the kindred Gospel image of the Christian embarked with Peter and the apostles; or the "earth" of "this world" may simply have fused with the "sea" of this *saeculum*.

APPROACH TO A SOLUTION

It was in the interests of methodological probity that I felt it necessary to pose and illustrate this series of objections to the task of discernment that lies before us. They bid us to advance cautiously. Let me repeat, though: there is an abstract cast, an aura of "worst-case scenario" about all of them, that may prove unjustified when we come to deal with most, if not all, of the concrete challenges Augustine's text presents us with. Furthermore, the illustrations that seem at first to support the objections actually tend to undermine them in a curiously indirect way. For they tacitly work from an assumption that wider familiarity with Augustine's works confirms as true: whether in his preaching or in his writing, he constantly betrays the fact that his imagination is almost always an incorrigibly "literary" one.

Even when obviously speaking from his own experience, or giving utterance to his primal feelings, Augustine manifests an inveterate tendency to clothe his thoughts and feelings in illustrations drawn from literary sources, whether that literature be poetic, philosophical, or Scriptural. This may be partly the result of his early training that shaped what Marrou has called the typical "lettré de la décadence"; it is also true that most of Augustine's production consists in the interpretation of texts of one sort or another; and yet, one gleans the irresistible impression that this was also the kind of man Augustine ineradicably was.

That much said to blunt these objections, however, this much must be said for them: they stand as salutary warning that one must not be too facile in applying analytic procedures that would purport to demonstrate that this or that image-complex in Augustine identifiably evokes Odysseus rather than, or even in consort with, his frequent shadow-companion, the Prodigal; we must stay alert to the possibility that other literary referents, or more primal feelings, may have prompted Augustine's imagination to send up the signal-flares we could otherwise read too lazily.

But take the question from another bias, and the more appropriate conclusion to be drawn is this: the very project of proving analytically what the components of a genuine image-fusion were, and still are, may be fundamentally ill-conceived. For analysis tends to move most comfortably along the rails of "either-or": this or that image represents *either* Odysseus, *or* the Prodigal—or Aeneas, the apostles, what have you.

The imagination, on the other hand, works with an opposite "logic": its more congenial law is the law of "both-and." And so Augustine can start by divining a kinship of two, three, or even more imaginative constellations, can oscillate from one to the others and back to the first of them, until they begin to coalesce into a single multi-layered image-structure. Some of this process transpires on the level of deliberate consciousness, certainly, but most of its power derives from deeper levels of the soul, depths traversed by passions and affects which often remain only half-obscure to the author himself. The frequent result is that, when genuine fusion has finally been accomplished, the author himself can often recognize only dimly the rich ambiguities of what he has created, and even less clearly the several fields of force that fed the creative process itself.

But the very richness of those ambiguities suggests a conclusion quite contrary to our mythical objector's: grant, for example, the possibility of a "perfect fusion" between Aeneas and Odysseus; grant the further possibility that in some such instance Augustine's sea and shipwreck imagery may have been inspired by Vergil rather than by Homer; then, one would be fully entitled to argue that the resulting *fusion* simply is, and must be acknowledged as, Augustine's finished version of "his" own odyssey-image (lower case), only one of whose original components was Homer's (upper case) Odyssey-image. And the same combinative logic of imagination would hold for other encrustations as well: the Prodigal, the Gospel's storm at sea, and so on.

EXAMINING AUGUSTINE'S TEXT

These, then, are the terms on which we may feel entitled to proceed; we are entitled to hope that concrete acquaintance with Augustine's text may banish any last fears that we can never be confident in identifying any particular image—in this case, the Odyssey image—as an active ingredient in one or other of Augustine's dizzyingly complex image-fusions. But that acquaintance will also indicate that the work of image-detection grows increasingly delicate as Augustine's writing and preaching career enables him to feed more and more diverse materials into his imaginative mill. The task may be somewhat easier, however, if we succeed in catching the fusion-process closer to its beginnings: then the diverse materials may stand forth with something close to their original distinctness from one another.

It is a happy coincidence that Augustine presents us with just such a pristine version of his Odyssey image. It is clearly the dominant image subtending the prologue to the *De beata vita*. Augustine is portraying his own life, and human life more generally, as a voyage on a stormy sea; the reader's attention is piqued by a series of familiar Homeric echoes, until an overt allusion to the Sirens confirms the dawning recognition that they are echoes from the *Odyssey* after all.

AN EXTENDED METAPHOR

It is essential to grasp from the outset that the entire account, running from the first to the fourth paragraph of the *De beata vita*, is set in the metaphorical key: this will keep us from missing the metaphorical force of certain of Augustine's expressions, and taking them literally. Neither Pierre Courcelle nor André Mandouze, in their valuable studies of this passage and of its parallels in Augustine's writings, has succeeded entirely in avoiding that trap.[11] I have derived genuine profit from both their studies, however; there are claims made by both men on which I remain somewhat skeptical and reserve judgment; but in what follows I shall restrict myself to indicating only where I am compelled to differ from them.

The metaphorical atmosphere is evident from the very beginning: writing to Manlius Theodorus, one of the leading members of the Christian Neoplatonist circle at Milan, Augustine wonders whether one can arrive at the safe "haven" (*portus*) of the philosophical life by the unaided forces of reason and will. This question brings him to another: How did we all come to be "tossed into this world [*in hunc mundum*] as onto a stormy sea, as though randomly, haphazardly"? Was it "God" Who tossed us here, "or nature, or necessity, or our own will—or some conjunction of these factors, or all of them [working] simultaneously?" The question, he avows, is a very obscure one, and yet Manlius has undertaken the task of clearing it up—as, indeed, any conscientious Neoplatonist would feel obliged to do.

For this was one of the most burning questions to which Neoplatonic philosophers saw it necessary to address themselves; they viewed the soul as originally native to the other, higher world: how, then, explain its presence amid the obvious evils of "this world"? And Augustine has listed all the factors they saw it necessary to consider: God, or perhaps some more impersonal agency like "nature" or cosmic "necessity," or possibly some choice of our own "will." Or could it be that one may not choose one or other cause to the exclusion of the others, but that several, or even all four, causes mentioned, made some "simultaneous" contribution to our souls' being "here"?

Augustine already has in hand the elements of the problem that he eventually hoped was solved by means of his *dimittere* insight; the answer is that all four factors operate "simultaneously" in an exquisite interplay: God tossed us here, but by "dismissing" us, by "handing us over" to the "weight" of our own will, as His own laws of nature and cosmic necessity demanded. Augustine has still a way to go before that solution dawns on him; but Manlius Theodorus seems to have gotten him to see in Neoplatonic terms the number of "givens" any adequate solution had to take into account.

Obviously, though, our situation "in this world" is no more enviable than that of Odysseus the wanderer; it is an arena of toil, hardship, and danger. Augustine's negative evaluation of the "sea" is already firmly in place, and from its earliest days it insinuates that its ancestry derives from Neoplatonism's exegesis of Homer. "How few [*quotusquisque*] are there who know," Augustine now asks, "whither they must strive to get to, or how to return" (*quotusquisque cognosceret quo sibi nitendum esset quave redeundum*)? Clearly, as for Odysseus, the voyage toward home is a voyage of "return," yet that "return" would seem possible only to a "few." Mandouze (*pace* Courcelle) interprets a revealing phrase from the analogous context in *Contra Academicos* 2.5 as confirming the "return" character of this voyage: *respexi . . . quasi de itinere*, Augustine writes: he "looked back from [his] journeying" which was (obviously) heading *away* from the "religion" of his boyhood.[12]

PROVIDENTIAL EVILS

Now Augustine makes a suggestion drawn from his own experience: we might never find our way to the "land of our longings" unless "some tempest, which a fool might deem an adversity, drove us, all unwilling, off the course we were striving to steer," so that "un-knowers and wanderers," we finally arrived at safe haven (1.1).

That conviction was important to Augustine; early and late he will portray the entire series of adversities and sufferings God sent his way as providential: they drove him "against his will" and "without his knowing it" (*invitus, nescientes*) to what he recognized, once he arrived there, as the "haven" of his deepest longings. The parallels with the *Odyssey* are remarkable: what must Odysseus have thought of the tempest that drove him against the Phaeacian coast? As just one more in a series of adversities, frustrating his heroic resolve to return to Ithaca? And yet that adversity turned out to be a boon: these were the people who would ultimately bring him home.

Three Classes of Voyagers

But Augustine's prologue continues: there are three general classes among the sea-voyagers (*navigantium*) "whom Philosophy can welcome" to herself. What differentiates them in Augustine's account is the distance their respective *peregrinationes* have placed between them and their tranquil homeland (*patria*), and, consequently, the ease or difficulty involved in their voyaging back to it. The most favored of them have only a slight and easy voyage home; but the most unfortunate class, "deluded by the entirely fallacious aspect of the sea, have chosen to advance to the middle of it, and dared [*audent*] to make a distant *peregrinatio* from their homeland and often become forgetful of it" (*obliviscuntur*). As though propelled (mysteriously, Augustine once again admits) by some following wind which they deem favorable, "they penetrate into the depths of wretchedness, proud and rejoicing" (*elati atque gaudentes*), flattered by the false serenity that comes with "pleasures and honors" (*voluptatum honorumque*). What these require is some ferocious "storm" to blow them back, "weeping and groaning," to where "sure and solid joys" are to be found.

Some individuals in this second class, however, may not have wandered off too far (*nondum longius evagati*); they may have been frustrated by ill fortune, or beset by "anxious difficulties in their trifling affairs" until, not knowing where to turn, they set themselves to reading the "books of learnèd and very wise men, and awaken, somehow or other, in safe haven" (*in ipso quodammodo portu evigilant*). Once they are there, the traitorous sea tempts them no more.

Now, this is a puzzling way to put the matter: the voyager would appear to have been sleeping, and then, quite unaccountably, (*quodammodo*) he "awakes" and finds himself in a safe harbor. What does Augustine mean to convey by this curious, but oddly suggestive series of expressions? We shall have to return to them in time.

But there is a third, intermediate class also; Augustine includes himself here: these "look back" (*respiciunt*), whether in earliest adolescence or after having been tossed about longer on the sea, and espy "signs of their most sweet homeland." They "call it to mind" (*recordantur*), and straightway set course to return to it (*repetunt*). Or, more often, they may still "lose their way among mists, or plot their course by stars that sink into the ocean, or, entrapped by some enticement or other, put off the time for safe navigation; they continue to wander [*errant diutius*], and are often endangered" by shipwreck. But for these, too, it is often some "storm" of seeming adversity that blows them back to their "quiet, and longed-for homeland" (2).

Even for those who have arrived in the haven of "philosophy," however, one mountainous danger lies in wait: the "proud quest of empty glory." This mountain has "nothing interiorly full and solid" about it, but is empty and "inflated." So, it gives way underfoot and snatches those it has allured back into the "darkness" that so recently engulfed them (3).

Now Augustine takes each of the (metaphorical) terms drawn from the intermediate class of "navigators" and applies them to his own spiritual odyssey. When he was nineteen (the "adolescence" mentioned above), his reading of Cicero's *Hortensius* so fired him with a love of "philosophy" that he seriously meditated, not simply studying it, but (as Courcelle rightly explains) "converting" to the philosophic style of life, the "contemplative wisdom" (*Trin* 14.26) that Cicero commended in that work. Courcelle's instinct, leading him to compare this "first confession" with Augustine's later masterpiece, is unquestionably on target: the image is precisely the one he uses in relating this episode in *Confessions* 3.7. The *Hortensius*, he realized early, offered him a backward glimpse of those "signals" from the "homeland" he had been sailing away from, and which he was then prompted to "recall." The *Confessions* describes how Cicero's book affected him, by invoking the Prodigal image: *et surgere coeperam, ut ad te redirem*, he "was beginning to rise up in order to return to" God. But the *De beata vita* seems to be expressing the same insight in a different metaphor: he "was made to stand up straighter": *factus erectior*. Here we have another expression whose import we shall have to examine further on.

Now he claims that, after the *Hortensius* experience, he could conceivably even then have steered straight back "home" without delay. But "mists" still intervened to throw his life's course into confusion, and (later) he followed "sinking stars" that led his bark astray. Those mists, as Courcelle has ably shown, refer metaphorically to the residues of the fideist "superstition," the demand for blind faith, he had found in African Catholicism: this still deterred him for a while from the kind of intellectual inquiry to which the *Hortensius* inspired him. Soon, however, *factus erectior*, he chose to invest his trust in men who "taught" (and promised some "understanding" of belief) rather than merely issued "orders" to believe.

But these teachers turned out to be worshipers of the visible light, taking it to be divine. This was a central motif of Manichee teaching; Augustine refers to it, metaphorically, as so many "stars that sink into the ocean" and draw the mariner off his course. Initially attractive, those teachings later proved deceptive. In terms of the odyssey metaphor Augustine is employing, the Manichees initially replied to his newly formed resolve to abandon blind faith and strike out on a voyage of "understanding." In promising to "teach," to appeal to his reason and not merely "command" belief, they depicted their teaching as a reliable cluster of navigational "stars" to steer by; only after further sailing did he discover they were "sinking" stars. And yet, he never says they brought him to shipwreck.

Taking the Metaphor Literally

At this juncture, I submit, both Courcelle and Mandouze introduce a series of extraneous considerations that seriously befuddle the issues. They both begin by correctly interpreting those "sinking stars" metaphorically: Augustine is referring to Manichee teaching. But, they go on to explain, his conversion to Manichaeism betrays Augustine's "rationalistic" bent: by describing himself as *factus erectior*, he points to his "audacious" option to leave faith behind and become a "freethinker." But now they shift abruptly into a literal key: Augustine's "sinking stars" metaphor refers to his interest in "astrology"!

Now, it is certainly true that Augustine's early philosophizing betrays a streak of "rationalism"; the *De ordine* is sufficient proof of that. It is also true that, starting with Book 4 of the *Confessions*, he admits to a growing interest in "mathematical" studies of stellar and planetary motions.[13] I contest none of this, but I do question that the "sinking stars" metaphor refers to any of it, or that the *factus erectior* metaphor depicts the Augustine of Book 3 as a "freethinker." To these features of Augustine's "first conversion" we shall return in time. And we shall come to see, among other things, that Augustine's sybilline *factus erectior* turns out to be a far more pregnant phrase than either Courcelle or Mandouze was led to imagine.

At this point Augustine admits to having made his boldest foray into mid-ocean (*in mediis fluctibus*); this refers to the flirtation with Academic skepticism that followed on his leaving the Manichees. His quest for understanding seems temporarily to have foundered.

It was after (now Augustine is speaking literally) crossing the Mediterranean sea, however, that a (metaphorical) fresh wind filled his sails. On his arrival at Milan, both Ambrose and Manlius Theodorus led him to the pivotal insight that his habitual corporeal mode of thinking was inappropriate for dealing with either the soul or God. That lesson, events would prove, struck at the heart of the sensist way of thinking which had previously mired him in Manichaeism, and had more recently made him vulnerable to Academic skepticism as it was "commonly" understood.[14] But even after attaining to that crucial insight, he was "held back" from "flying swiftly into the lap [*gremium*] of Philosophy by the enticements of marriage and honors" (*uxoris honorisque*). His intention was that once he had obtained both of these (*cum haec essem consecutus*), "then at last I would do what is permitted to a happy few, and, under full sail and pulling at every oar, bear myself away to that breast and there find full repose" (*in illum sinum* [*me*] *raperem ibique conquiescerem*).

But now a dramatic new element enters the situation: he reads several "books of the platonists," compares them with Scripture, and catches fire: (*exarsi*). He would have cut anchor right then, he tells us, "except that I was influenced by the favorable opinion of certain persons." That was precisely when a providential "storm" blew up, one he was initially tempted to regard as an "adversity": he developed a pulmonary illness that made him incapable of "bearing the burden [*onus*] of that profession" of rhetoric which "was, perhaps, making me sail toward the Sirens." "I gave up everything and steered my boat, battered and leaking, to the tranquillity I had yearned for" (4).

An Odyssey and Its Implicits

This entire passage is both highly interesting and, for our present purposes, crucially important. Its importance stems from its being so early a text, so fresh a record of how Augustine viewed his life and conversion: the Odyssey image stands out not only clear but also relatively pure of interferences from competing images.

This is particularly true of the Prodigal image with which it later becomes almost inextricably entangled: the fifth paragraph of the prayer that opens the *Soliloquies* demonstrates that the Prodigal image was very much alive in Augustine's imagination at Cassiciacum, but that fact only underlines its surprising absence from this particular prologue. Further highlighting of that absence comes from the third book of the *Confessions*, where the dramatic *Hortensius* episode is portrayed in purely Prodigal imagery. In the *De beata vita*, only the single phrase *longe . . . peregrinari* sounds the faintest echo of the Prodigal's story, but even that phrase fits very well with the Odyssey image. It fits even more perfectly with the Plotinian description of the soul's "long journey," which, we shall see, furnishes the metaphysical interpretation of that odyssey. There were several points broached in this text where touches of Prodigal imagery would have been quite appropriate—the mentions of pleasure, forgetfulness, or "rising up" to return, among them—yet Augustine eschews those touches entirely.

Finally, this shift from Odysseus to Prodigal imagery offers a much more natural explanation, *pace* Courcelle, why the "storm" image fails to figure in Books 6 and 7 of the *Confessions*. Book 8 does, indeed, portray a "storm" as overtaking Augustine in the garden at Milan, but that is a "storm of tears." Courcelle's equating that "storm" with the type of storm Augustine formerly used to figure providential "adversities" is mixing metaphors for fair![15]

It would be tempting to conclude from all this that the Odyssey image originally occupied a more primordial and fundamental place in Augustine's imagination than even the Prodigal, but that would surely be overstating things. What is clear, though, is this: a number of features we find later associated with the Prodigal/ Odysseus amalgam could, and at one time did, associate comfortably with the Odysseus image working autonomously and virtually alone. That, I suggest, is an index of the power this particular image wielded over Augustine's imagination at the time of his conversion.

But this text discloses some suggestive interferences from other image-registers, and it will be important later on for us to have noticed them now. Augustine twice evokes the image of *Philosophia* in distinctly feminine and faintly erotic terms: he writes of her as having "lap" and "breast" (*gremium, sinus*) to which and in which, evidently, she "welcomes" those who "fly" to her, enraptured by her charms. One might object that Neoplatonic interpretations of the *Odyssey* regularly contrasted the sensual attractions of Circe and Calpyso with the charms of the equally feminine Penelope, who represented "philosophy."[16] Again, ours is not an either-or question, and such objections are far from fatal. Penelope may figure vaguely in the background, as a reinforcing image; but closer examination would confirm, I suggest, that as a component in Augustine's image of Philosophy her place is secondary at best.[17]

But there are other interferences as well: the image of vainglory as an "inflation," an "emptiness" with nothing "solid and sure" about it, already anticipates the imaged contrast of "vanity" and "Truth" familiar from Augustine's more developed thinking; it does not seem to cohere naturally with, and very likely roots in an associative cluster distinct from, the Odyssey image.

The same must be said of another expression that peers out shyly from this text. Augustine writes that he finally "cast away everything" and "steered his boat" toward home. The verb *abjicere* is stronger than the *relinquere* commonly found in Latin versions of the Synoptic Gospels, but the language and context are suggestively reminiscent of the first apostles' leaving everything, including their boats, to follow Christ. The early Augustine seems to prefer *abjicere* to *relinquere* when speaking of the renunciation involved in conversion, and it is at least interesting that he pairs the verb *abjicere* with the Gospel term *relinquere* in portraying the imagined "conversion" of Romanianus' adversary at law (*Acad*

2.6). But this is by no means all that could be said on his use of this term.[18]

The reader may now be disconcerted by the weight about to be placed on a single word, but there are two final expressions Augustine uses whose import we shall be in a position to measure more accurately later on. We saw him speak of "bearing [himself] away" ([*me*] . . . *raperem*) from the enticements of wife and honors, and flying to the bosom of "Philosophy." That translation for the term *rapere* is deliberately chosen to evoke the saying from Matthew's Gospel (11:12), that the "violent bear away" the Kingdom (*rapiunt*). That saying furnishes a surprising key for understanding Augustine's conversion account.[19] But it is significant that Augustine applies the term here, where it scarcely fits the dynamic of the Odyssey image, and so betrays its Gospel heritage all the more unmistakably. It also testifies further to Augustine's conviction that the wisdom of the Gospels did not stand in opposition, but brought fulfillment to the wisdom of the Greeks.

The second such word is the one Augustine uses to characterize his profession: it was an *onus* to him, a "burden." He found Matthew's Gospel employing this term (11:30) to describe the "light burden" of Christ. Augustine's image of the "weighted" soul is already aborning.

Aside from these interferences, however—interferences which will each bear fruit in later image-fusions—the Odyssey image of conversion manifests all the main features one would expect of it. We, meaning our souls, find ourselves on the stormy sea of this world, wandering away from our homeland, confronting dangers of shipwreck from mists, sinking stars, and tempests; we have forgotten the homeland we left, and yet, we guard a certain vague nostalgia for it which prompts us to "look back" when we are given signals "reminding" us of it. (Augustine twice uses the pregnant term *admonitio* in this prologue. The lineage of that term merits a full-length study in itself.)

What accounts for our being here, and for the winds that drive us toward the further deep, remains mysterious to us; but our own will seems to be one of the factors in play. And since our lot is such a wretched one, the suspicion is that our will must have been "at fault." Though Augustine does not use the term precisely here, our souls seem to have "fallen" into this world. That fall, however, was a diversified one: some of us have journeyed farther from home than others; hence, the "return" voyage is easier and quicker for some than for others.

What could that voluntary fault have been? Augustine drops several hints to clarify that: there was a certain "audacity" (*audent*) involved in our making this distant *peregrinatio*, a proud gleefulness whereby even now some penetrate still further, *elati et gaudentes*, into the depths of greater misery. Little wonder, then, that our first temptation should be the last we will overcome: vainglory.

But somehow coupled with pride, audacity, vainglory, there is the lure of pleasure. It is important to notice that Augustine pointedly couples these two types of fault in his own case. It was the combined attractions of both marriage and honor (*uxoris honorisque*) that classed him with those souls he describes as audaciously pursuing not only pleasures but honor as well (*voluptatum honorumque*). This twinned temptation prompted him to put off the time for good sailing, and defer his voyage to the haven of philosophy. Indeed, even after the dramatic episode of his Platonic readings, it was "good opinion" that still held him back: it is unclear whether he refers to his own good opinion of others, or theirs of him, but the motive reduces to "honor" in either case. In any event, Courcelle's suggestion (that Augustine's own "high regard" was directed toward historical examples of men who had succeeded in being philosophers despite being married) seems forced and unconvincing. Augustine's main concern here is to stress the providential character of that final "storm," apparent adversity, the illness that finally persuaded him to cast off the burden (*onus*) of his profession. That profession, be it noted once again, was probably making him sail dangerously toward the "Sirens."

What do the Sirens' voices represent for him? The context leaves little doubt. Courcelle rightly remarks that wealth as such held no great appeal for Augustine, particularly after the *Hortensius* experience; his profession, though, was a necessary livelihood he felt he had to count on to support the wife his sexual hungers convinced him he could not live without. But it was more than that to him; it held out the ripe promise of even higher honors and distinctions than he already enjoyed. That was a siren-song to which he could not shut his ears. And that is also an aspect of Augustine's own conversion account which has not always been accorded the importance it deserves.[20]

One final question: what does Augustine tell us of the original homeland from which his odyssey took its departure? Since the voyage home is clearly a voyage of return, his port of departure must have the same characteristics as he attaches to his present destination; it must have been a place of "quiet" and "tranquillity," where joys were "sure and solid," a haven where *Philosophia* holds out a bridal welcome, and where the interior spiritual eye replaces the corporeal eyes that can never yield any true insight into that pivotal pair of realities, God and the soul. But this, once again, is what the Neoplatonist found figured in Penelope: the untroubled life of contemplative bliss, longed-for home and haven after the soul's exhausting life of action "here." The eye can already discern, behind Augustine's earliest sketch of his odyssey and conversion, the half-obscured underpainting of the soul's "fall" from contemplation into action, from Eternity into time.

NOTES

1. "The Platonic and Christian Ulysses," in *Neoplatonism and Christian Thought*, ed. Dominic J. O'Meara (Albany: State University of New York Press, 1982), pp. 3–18.

2. See James F. Curley's review in *Dialogue*, 25 (1982), 31.

3. See the compact survey of the literature on this question in Courcelle's *Recherches*, pp. 1–12.

4. Pépin mentions in note 51 Augustine's later expression of "regret" that he once identified Christ's "Kingdom not of this world" with the "higher" world of Platonism. But he had good reason for "regret."

5. All quotations are from Pépin's article, pp. 14–15.

6. Ambrose's allusions are from his *Expositio Evangelii secundum Lucam* 4.2–3; the "sea" image occurs in paragraph 3.

7. See Paul Henry, s.j., *Plotin et l'Occident* (Louvain: Spicilegium Sacrum Lovaniense, 1934), esp. p. 112.

8. *Ennead*, trans. A. H. Armstrong, Loeb Library (Cambridge: Harvard University Press, 1966), I, 257, 259; emphasis added.

9. This is André Mandouze's happy coinage for what I have called a "parallel pattern" of language, thought, imagery, and affect; see his *Saint Augustin: L'Aventure de la raison et de la grâce* (Paris: Études Augustiniennes, 1968), p. 679n1.

10. *Aeneid* 3.154–191. Reminiscences of Vergil's *Aeneid* in Augustine's works have received, understandably, considerably more attention than those of Homer's *Odyssey*. For generous bibliographical indications, see Wolfgang Hübner's "Die *praetoria memoriae* im zehnten Buch der *Confessiones*: Vergilisches bei Augustin," REA, 27 (1981), 245n1 (the contributions by Hagendahl and O'Meara are especially worthwhile). See also

Constance Bennett's "The Conversion of Vergil: The *Aeneid* in Augustine's *Confessions*," REA, 34 (1988), 47–69.

11. See Courcelle's "Quelques symboles funeraires du néo-platonisme latin," *Revue des Études Anciennes*, 46 (1944), 65–93, esp. 87–88 (henceforth "Symboles"); it is also incorporated in *Recherches*, pp. 269–90. See also Mandouze, *Aventure*, pp. 252–59. Courcelle's version in *Recherches* reproduces and adds only one sentence (p. 289, relative to the "tempête" in the Milanese garden) to his 1944 article, so reference to that article is unnecessary. One should, to begin with, consult what he has to say about Manlius Theodorus in *Recherches*, pp. 153–56. But one need not accept every detail of Courcelle's historical reconstruction to acknowledge the crucial role played in Augustine's conversion by Manlius Theodorus and his Neoplatonism.

12. See *Aventure*, p. 259*n*2.

13. See, on this topic, Leo C. Ferrari's "Augustine and Astrology," *Laval Revue Théologique et Philosophique*, 33 (1977), 241–51. Again, I mean neither to deny nor to subscribe to the thesis (of Ferrari and others) concerning Augustine's interest in astrology; my remarks bear precisely on the "navigational" import of the "sinking stars" metaphor. That navigational character will receive confirmation farther on in these pages.

14. In both *Conf* 5.19 (cf. 5.25; 6.6) and *Acad* 3.37–42, Augustine insists that the "common" understanding of the Academics as merely skeptics was superficial: they were guarding the secrets of Platonism from those sensists, the Stoics and Epicureans. He himself, he tells us, never went so far with skepticism as to doubt such "truths" as "seven plus three is ten." That claim is perfectly consonant with his (later) interpretation of Academicism.

15. See Courcelle, *Recherches*, p. 289. In that same connection see also Mandouze, *Aventure*, p. 261*n*2.

16. See Felix Buffière's comprehensive work on *Les Mythes d'Homère et la pensée grecque* (Paris: Les Belles Lettres, 1956), p. 389 (henceforth: *Homère*) for the allegorical treatment of the Penelope figure.

17. I have, in fact, largely completed a study which endeavors to show that Old Testament "Wisdom" images, all of them feminine, claim pride of place as components in Augustine's images of Wisdom and Philosophy in his early dialogues.

18. In *Acad* 33 we are supposed to *abjicere et contemnere* the boat that brought us to port, while in *Sol* 1.17 the kindred terms *dejicere* and *aspernare* are paired in a similar context (cf. also *Sol* 1.24: *haec venire in contemptum*). I have nearly completed a study which convinces me that Augustine was impressed by Paul's use of this term in Rom 13:12: *Abjiciamus ergo opera tenebrarum* etc. This verse was part of the decisive "conversion" *capitulum* which he tells us he *read* in the garden of Milan (though he does not *quote* its first two verses); see *Conf* 8.29.

19. This, again, is the focus of another study which I have substantially completed.

20. Compare Jean Doignon's suggestions in "Le Symbolisme des Sirènes dans les premiers dialogues de saint Augustin," in *Hommages à R. Chevalier* (Tours, 1986), pp. 113–20.

6

Augustine's "First Conversion": *Factus Erectior*

WE SAW THAT IN HIS PROLOGUE TO THE *De beata vita* Augustine employs an expression which we left for later inspection. He describes himself as *factus erectior*, "become," or perhaps "having been made," "more upright." This change, he tells us, occurred sometime around his nineteenth year, and (from the way he expresses it in the *Confessions*), around the time he read Cicero's *Hortensius*.

The connection is significant. For in *Confessions* 8.17 it recurs: just as he is approaching that final paroxysm of conversion in the garden of Milan, Augustine thinks back. He recalls that dramatic encounter (3.7–8) with the book that, he still insists, "changed [his] heart-set" (*mutavit affectum meum*), dampened all his worldly ambitions, and set him aflame with the love of "undying wisdom."

A line or two later (3.8), and we are given to realize that "wisdom," in that phrase, should be spelled with a capital "W"; for in an allusion to the Prologue of John's Gospel that he would have intended almost any Latin-speaking Christian of his time to catch, Augustine observes that the Wisdom he is talking about is *apud Te*. It is, in other words, the very Word of God Who, John assures us in the Prologue to his Gospel, is *apud Deum*. This complex of suggestive terms provokes us to re-read Augustine's depiction of this entire episode. Then we recognize that he has described himself in the very terms Luke applies to the Prodigal in his Gospel. *Surgere coeperam*, he tells us, *ut ad Te redirem*: "I was beginning to rise up in order to return to You."

What does Augustine mean to suggest by this image of "rising up," whether expressed by terms like *factus erectior* or *surgere coeperam*? For it is an image he permanently associated with the *Hortensius* experience, which Pierre Courcelle has rightly termed his "first conversion."[1] And, as I hope to show, the fact that Augustine so vividly recalls that first conversion on the very threshold of his conversion in the garden at Milan, tells us a great deal about how he hoped we would understand not only Book 8, but the entire sweep of his *Confessions*.

THE *Hortensius:* AUGUSTINE'S "FIRST CONVERSION"

Courcelle has devoted his talents to a study of that "first," *Hortensius* conversion. He finds Augustine alluding to it in the prologues he wrote to both of his earliest Cassiciacum dialogues: the *Contra Academicos* and the *De beata vita*. His explication of the latter prologue brings him to consider the very expression that interests us here.

The context is familiar: Augustine has told Manlius Theodorus how his reading of Cicero's *Hortensius* left him aflame (*succensus*) with "so great a love for *philosophia*" that he "meditated" changing over to the contemplative way of life Cicero was inviting his readers to adopt. For precisely this, the adoption of a life of study and contemplation, was what the term "conversion to philosophy" represented in those times.[2]

What was it that held him back from taking that step? Or, perhaps more in line with the navigational metaphor Augustine is employing in the context, what prevented him from directing his "odyssey" to that longed-for "haven"? Clouds, or mists, first of all, Augustine tells us, *nebulae*, which threw confusion into the "course" he steered. But to what does this "cloud" metaphor refer? It stands, he immediately answers our question, for the "puerile superstition" which "frightened" him away from all intellectual inquiry (*ab ipsa inquisitione*). And Courcelle has done us the service of demonstrating that Augustine here refers to the authoritarian kind of Catholicism he had experienced in North Africa: a Catholicism he understood as "commanding belief" without "teaching" the believer, or answering any difficulties he may have had about how his belief might be "understood."[3]

THE MEANING OF *Factus erectior*

That demonstration, however, only makes Courcelle's explanation of what comes next in Augustine's prologue all the harder to swallow. *Factus erectior*, Augustine goes on to say; he succeeded in dispelling that "mist," and came to the view that he should invest his belief in men who "taught" rather than merely "commanded" belief. *Factus erectior*—"having become" or "having been made more erect," or "more upright"—what does Augustine imply by that phrase?

Courcelle interprets as though Augustine were here describing himself as succumbing to a movement of intellectual pride, "audacity in scientific research"; he is leaving faith behind him and assuming an attitude of rationalistic "freethinking." And yet, Courcelle goes on to admit, this move seemed "legitimate" to Augustine at the moment he wrote the *De beata vita*, but *not* to the later Augustine who wrote the *Confessions*.[4]

Now, this is a baffling interpretation at best. There appears to be, at first blush, something to be said for it: The *Oxford Latin Dictionary*[5] shows that among its other meanings, the Latin term *erectus* can indeed convey the kind of "standing tall" associated with arrogance and pride. Add to that the usual interpretation put upon the move Augustine describes in the very same sentence; his conversion to Manichaeism, one might feel secure in thinking, was surely motivated by the pride and rationalistic attitude he later associates with their attacks on the Catholica's demand for faith. We have already seen, moreover, that Augustine has some damning things to say, in this same prologue, about pride, vainglory, and "audacity."

Despite all that can be said for it, however, there still remains something ill-fitting, tightly uncomfortable about Courcelle's interpretation. Why should Augustine refer to this move as casting off a "puerile superstition," as dispelling mists and clouds that confused his life-direction, and at the same time use an expression implying that his decision was motivated by pride? It does not dispel but only increases our confusion, when Courcelle paradoxically allows that in 386 Augustine considered the move he is about to describe a *progressive* step. This brings us to consult the Latin dictionary once again. Was there a meaning for the crucial term *erectus*, and its comparative *erectior*, that would fit coherently into that more positive view of the step Augustine is recounting here? And could that same meaning result in a smoother, more natural interpretation of the image of "rising up" which Augustine evokes in *both* the *De beata vita* and the *Confessions* accounts of his "first conversion"?

The *Oxford Latin Dictionary* gives the clearest of affirmative answers to that last question: for alongside the "proud" associations of "standing up" or "standing tall" which the term *erectus* would have conveyed to the Latin speaker, that term could have intimated a different set of associations as well. To be "upstanding" could also mean to aspire toward "high" or "lofty" ideals.

This (or something like it) *could*, therefore, have been the meaning Augustine had in mind when writing that phrase, *factus erectior*, and it might equally fit the image of "rising up" conveyed by the *surgere coeperam* associated with St. Luke's Prodigal. But we still have no firm assurance that he *did* intend the phrase that way. One would have expected that Courcelle, with all his astonishing erudition about Augustine's linguistic habits, would have conducted at least a cursory search into the man's works to settle this issue for us. But since he did not, we must do it for ourselves.

GOD MADE MAN "ERECT"

My own suspicions of Courcelle's interpretation were first aroused, I must confess, by the way Augustine repeatedly adverts, in his commentaries on Genesis, to man's "erect" bodily stature. In this respect he seems to be appealing to an ancient world commonplace: man is different from the rest of the animals, whose non-erect carriage leaves their senses pointed earthward.[6] That is entirely fitting for those sub-human creatures, since they are earthy in their perceptions and appetites, and earthy they must always remain. But *De Genesi contra Manichaeos* assures us as early as 389 that man, on the contrary, was made upright in body, able to gaze on stars and sun and heavens; his upright carriage was meant to symbolize and constantly remind him of the fact that his "mind also ought to be erect [*erectum*] toward its supernal [dimension], that is, eternal and spiritual realities" (*in superna sua, id est, in aeterna spiritualia*). For while it remains true that man was made to the image and likeness of God "chiefly because of his mind," nonetheless, "the erect form of his body is also witness to that truth" (1.28). The same interpretation of our erect carriage is stressed in (the presumably early) Question 51, 3 of the *Eighty-Three Diverse Questions*: "other animals are prone upon their bellies," whereas man's erect stature fits him, like no other animal, to "contemplate the heavens." The "incomplete" work on Genesis (60) rehearses the same theme. The insight was a durable one; it finds it way into the *De Genesi ad litteram* (6.22) years afterward.

But we have also seen it crop up in Augustine's interpretation of the Prodigal story: the young man's "rising up" can be from a "prostrate" or from a "sitting" position, depending on Augustine's preaching context, but the effect of the action is the same in either case: it raises him up from the "earth," stands him up straight so that he can focus once again on the higher realities with which he was originally at "home." At the same time, it "puts him on his feet" for that "pious quest," the first leg of his homeward journey. Augustine points out that the initial stages of this "quest" (*quaerite et invenietis*, the Gospel urges, "seek" [or "quest"] and "you shall find") must be traversed in faith. That "seeking" goes on "before" the Prodigal has attained "understanding" of God (*antequam intelligeret Deum*).

But Augustine is equally insistent that the seeker should aim to "find." Then his faithful seeking will bring him to some measure of the "understanding" of God that faith, precisely as faith, necessarily lacks. We must all *start* by believing, but *not stop* there. Now it begins to dawn that "rising up" to "erect" stature may well have to do with the exigency to pass from faith to the higher level of religious "understanding." Here we have additional evidence that Augustine quite possibly leaned toward interpreting the term *erectus* in line with the more positive set of associations the dictionary tells us it could evoke: to "stand erect" may well have meant to aspire toward loftier, nobler perceptions and ideals than could animals ungifted with the power of reason. It must also be kept in mind that, for Augustine, both faith and understanding will be shot through with aspiration and desire; so, the Prodigal is both enlightened *and* attracted to "return" to the *superna sua*, the spiritual and eternal realities that were once the source of the contemplative joys he deserted.

Those two indications, then, from Augustine's interpretations of Genesis on the one hand and of the Prodigal parable on the other, have put us on the track of a plausible hypothesis for understanding his image of "standing" or "rising" up to "erect" stature. To test that hypothesis now, we must explore whether it is confirmed by the frequent employment Augustine makes of the term *erectus* and of its various cognates. And, as luck would have it, his early dialogues furnish a teeming hunting-ground for that quest.

AUTHORITY AND REASON

Anyone who has read them has seen how importantly the relationship of "authority to reason," of "faith to understanding," features in those early dialogues. Augustine is evidently coming to terms with his own past experience of a Catholica which he once thought "commanded" blind faith with no promise of understanding, and of a Manichaeism that promised to "teach," loudly offered near-instant "reasoned" understanding of life's conundrums, and mocked the Catholica for so benightedly demanding that her adherents consent on faith to the mysteries she proposed (*Vita* 4).

Now, the Augustine of Cassiciacum has been entrusted two young students, Licentius and Trygetius; it appears to have been his principal assignment in their regard to conduct them through a reading of Vergil's *Aeneid*. But it does not ever seem to have been Augustine's way as a teacher to interpret his mandate in limited fashion; in any case, he makes it clear that he is bending every effort to interest his young charges in "philosophy" as well as letters. To that end he has persuaded them to read the very book one might expect: the book that had meant so much to *him*, at their age, Cicero's *Hortensius*.

The discussions that became enshrined in the text of his early dialogues hint at a number of other respects in which Augustine manifestly hoped to pattern the young men's introduction to philosophical reflection on the model that had been so rewarding for him. There should be no surprise, then, that the finally edited version of the little group's dialogue-discussions often deals with the same problems and follows the same pathways as his own personal reflections had traced over the preceding years.

That parallelism holds notably for their discussions of authority and its relationship to reason. And one of the key terms that recurs in those discussions is the verb *erigere*, its past passive participle being, of course, *erectus*.

That term occurs, as we shall see, in two distinct contexts. The first of them has to do with the "food" image that threads its way through all the Cassiciacum dialogues: for the soul's food, as the climax of the *De beata vita* discloses, is "Truth" and "Wisdom" in their Christian Trinitarian meanings, the Eternal Christ Whom John calls "Truth" and Paul the "Wisdom and Power" of the Father. The overriding task of *Philosophia*, both as process of understanding and as lifestyle, is to "raise the soul up" (*erigere*), foster its "ascent" so that it may feed upon this "heavenly food" and drink from this inexhaustible "font."

But there is a second context as well. One disposition that can hinder the soul's ascent is an indiscriminate reverence for authority: authority can represent a heavy "yoke" imposed upon the mind, bending it earthward from the "erect" posture that befits it, and so impeding its ascent to the supernal Truth Who has promised to make us "free." In contrast to any such oppressive burden of authority, His "yoke" was "sweet," His "burden [*onus*] light." Augustine's creative imagination will conjure with those associations and generate the paradoxical image of a "burden" that "uplifts" (*erigit*) rather than bends the mind downward, a "yoke" that positively raises the mind to "taste" the Lord and find Him "sweet."

Erigere IN THE DIALOGUES

The first inkling of this imaginative process is given us in *Contra Academicos* 1.7–9. The youth Licentius has thrown up the "authority" of Cicero against the proposition his fellow-student, Trygetius, has been defending. Has Trygetius no respect for the authority of the "ancients"? Not all of them, Trygetius replies; only the wise (7). Their discussion suddenly degenerates into a debate inspired, as Augustine diagnoses it, not by "desire for the truth" but only by "boyish arrogance" (*puerilis jactantia*). This is not the sort of intellectual brawl he has been "nourishing and educating" them for, he complains. Indirectly he has recalled to them that "education" is a process of "feeding" their "desire for truth," not pandering to their puerile lust for verbal conquest (8).

But now this "food of truth" metaphor abruptly yields to its counterpart: Christ's "yoke" is sweet; He is the "Truth" that makes us "free." Trygetius challenges Licentius to make his own reasoned evaluation of the proposition under discussion in the same spirit as he, Trygetius, has adopted; for "philosophy" has promised "freedom" to all of us, which is why Trygetius has shucked off the "yoke of authority." Licentius protests: his friend is urging him to agree that even a good man who devotes himself faithfully to the "quest" (*quaerere*) for truth cannot for all that be a happy man; Trygetius' stand is that only he who has "found" (*invenit*) the truth can be happy. "But it is my judgment," Licentius insists, "that God alone knows that Truth [*Veritatem illam*], or perhaps the soul of man [as well], when it has left behind this darksome prison of the body" (9).

Augustine has artfully achieved two ends in this last paragraph.

First, he has broadly hinted at the Trinitarian nature of the "solution" toward which the discussion is tending. For he means to show that God alone can fully know the "Truth" Who is the Son of God; but he also means to show that man's soul, once liberated from its imprisoning mortal body, is promised a participation in that "knowledge" of Divine Truth.

But, second, he has thrown down a challenge any Manichee would recognize: he reminds his adversaries in his early work on *De Moribus ecclesiae et Manichaeorum* (1.31–34) of their untiring attacks against the "Catholic" demand for a faith which (they complained) surrendered all its rights to understanding and bent its unprotesting neck to the yoke of authority. Those attacks, he specifies, were invariably buttressed by appeal to the Gospel dictum: *Quaerite et invenietis, pulsate et aperietur vobis*: "Seek, and you shall find; knock, and it shall be opened to you." Augustine will explicitly quote that saying in the opening paragraphs of the second book of his *Contra Academicos*, but only to confirm what the attentive reader will have already divined; the overarching question of the entire preceding book, and of the *De beata vita* also, has been shaped by that same Gospel maxim: Is it the "seeking" for Truth that makes man happy, or only its ultimate "finding"? This is how Augustine framed the question from the opening of their discussion: Can man be happy only when he has "found" the truth, or even while he is "seeking" it (1.5)? In other terms, can the life of "faith" make us happy, or does genuine happiness require that we pass beyond faith to some sort of "finding" and "possession" of Truth?

But at this juncture it has become clear why, to answer *that* question, Augustine and his companions consider the "authority *vs.* reason" question so pivotal to their reflections. For one could trust in authority and so feel confident of "seeking," in the sense of "being on the right road toward" truth. But only the use of one's personal "reason" could make one confident of having "found" it.

Augustine's former confrères from Manichaeism must immediately have recognized that this new Catholic was beaming his dialogue squarely in their direction. But they must have been surprised that the drift of the discussion seemed, thus far, to favor what they may have thought was a position exclusively theirs: that faith in authority made sense if, and only if, it was meant to prepare the ground for reason's judgment on whether the object of one's belief satisfied the demands of human intelligence. Could Augustine be claiming that the Catholica, too, proclaimed this notion of belief as leading to "understanding"? In any case, the question must have piqued their curiosity. But it may also have disturbed some conservative spirits among Augustine's co-believers—like Monica, and even, perhaps, the bishop Ambrose! But credit Augustine for having captured his reader's interest: both parties would almost certainly have read further.

ALBICERIUS THE PSEUDO-CHRIST

Had they done so, they would soon have come upon a discussion which initially strikes the modern reader as a bizarre interlude that any sensible editor would today beg Augustine to cut from his manuscript: these "quaint" North Africans introduce Cicero's classic definition of "wisdom" into their discussion—"the knowledge of things both human and divine"—and then go on to dawdle for six succeeding paragraphs, nattering about a chap named Albicerius. This was an obvious charlatan, notorious in Carthage for powers of clairvoyance that more than seldom accomplished astounding feats. Must they concede that Albicerius fitted Cicero's definition of a "wise" man (1.17–23)?

On closer examination, though, Augustine is by no means dawdling. It is somewhat secondary to my purposes here, but careful analysis would show that Augustine is archly reminding the Manichees, and others as well, that one must not too quickly repose faith in every authority, even those who, like Albicerius, perform wonders very close to what Christ Himself is reported as having performed. Faith is one thing, uncritical credulity quite another; and no *reflective* Catholic (Augustine is slyly suggesting) would advocate a credulous trust in unexamined authority.

A good deal of what I have claimed above finds expression in the summary Augustine appends (1.24) to the Albicerius episode: he reminds Licentius that he had replied to Trygetius' reasoned position by throwing the "weight" (*moles*) of Cicero's "authority" against him. The image Augustine is evoking is one in which Trygetius might easily have been laid low by this massive weight. That becomes clearer from the next sentence: Augustine now describes Trygetius as "immediately standing up," and the term we have been tracking comes into play: *se statim erexit*. Not only did he stand up, "become erect," but Trygetius also "leapt up to the summit of his liberty, and snatched back what had been dashed from his hands by violence" (*in verticem libertatis exsiliit, rursumque arripuit quod erat de manibus violenter excussum*). This he accomplished, Augustine further specifies, in a spirit of "noble pride" (*generosa quadam contumacia*). And the crucial move in Trygetius' victory of reason over authority consisted in his argument that only that man is "perfect" who "governs his life according to the law of [his] mind."

It is significant (and reminds one forcibly of Courcelle's interpretation of the term *erectus*) that Augustine here implicitly admits that some might view Trygetius' rejection of Cicero's authority as proud, defiant: "contumacious." But, his choice of terms suggests, that estimate would be wrong. The boldness involved was *generosa*; it was a noble "rising up" to lay claim on the "freedom" which Truth Himself, the transcendent "Law" of our "minds," has promised us.

Also to be noticed is the warrior image running through this passage: Augustine's imagination has forged a first link between the image of violence—apparently the violence one does to oneself by exerting strenuous effort—and that of standing erect; he further associates both those images with the manly exertion, not to mention the violence, required by martial exercise. Notice again that in the *Contra Academicos* the youths are engaged in a passage of arms: Licentius has "violently" struck Trygetius' sword from his grasp, but Trygetius replies with a soldierly move in which answering violence is clearly implied.

In the background one can glimpse that text from Matthew's Gospel (11:12) which Augustine twice evokes in the describing the final paroxysm of his own conversion in the *Confessions*: "the kingdom of heaven suffers violence, and the violent bear it away" (*rapiunt*). In the midst of the interior combat (*rixa*) he was then experiencing, he cries out to Alypius that "the unlearnèd rise up [*surgunt*] and bear heaven away" (*rapiunt*) and the next minute "tears himself loose" (*abripuit*) from his friend's company, plunging into the garden where the rest of the drama is played out (8.19). But our minds have been subtly prepared for this metaphor by Augustine's earlier description of the enthusiastic crowd responding to Marius Victorinus' baptism: they wanted to "bear him away [*rapere*] into their own hearts; and bear him away they did [*rapiebant*] with love and gladness: for theirs were ravishing hands" (*rapientium manus erant*) (8.5). A few paragraphs later

Augustine prays God to *rape*, but with the sweet violence of love: (*flagra, dulcesce*) (8.9). He can hardly think of conversion except to recall this theme of evangelical "violence": the first of the two soldiers whose story Pontitianus relates becomes "angry at himself" on reading St. Anthony's life and "burns" to "bear away" (*arripere*) the convert's lifestyle as his own (8.15). The human ingredient in conversion is a decision about which of several goods we shall "bear away" (*arripiamus*) (8.24) and which we shall "bear ourselves away from" (*me abripere*) (8.26). So, after his vision of the Lady Continence, Augustine "rose up" (*surrexi*) and left Alypius behind; when he had arisen (*surrexeram*), however, and parted from his friend, it was only to lie down again (*stravi me*) beside a "fig tree." On hearing that mysterious *tolle, lege*, however, he once again "arose" (*surrexi*) to "snatch up" (*arripui*) the codex of St. Paul's Epistles, and read that *capitulum* which struck him with such liberating power (8.29). And (we shall analyze this motif more closely further on) the decision he is now empowered to make is to enlist in the *militia Christi* (8.29; see 15)!

That connection beween "rising up" and violently "bearing away" goes back to Augustine's earliest images of conversion. We noticed earlier that he employs that same term, *rapere*, in the account of his conversion in the *De beata vita*, and in the same paragraph in which the *factus erectior* image also occurs (*Vita* 4). Now, in the *Contra Academicos*, he continues with the "violence" theme, but (it becomes even plainer as we advance) as embodied in the martial image of the *miles Christi*, the "soldier of Christ." Licentius has "fought back" (*pugnasses*), Augustine admits, more manfully than one might have imagined possible, even after his companion had "occupied his fortress" (*occupavit praesidium*), a fortress not unlike the "citadel" (*arcem*) held by the Academics (1.24). All of this replies to Augustine's hopes for his students, for his efforts are directed at "exercising" or training both their "nerves" and their "spirit" (*nervos, studia*) for such dialectical swordplay as will arm them against all comers (1.25).

An analogous skein of connections appears in Book 2.18 and following. "Come, come," Augustine chides Licentius, "gather your forces" (*vires*), lest (in Vergil's words) "fear should take hold of your members before the battle-trumpet even sounds," or the desire to let others do the fighting "makes you choose to be taken prisoner prematurely" (2.18). Back to the battle, now, "stronger and braver" than before (2.19).

Once again the martial metaphor leads into a reflection on authority and reason: it would be unpardonable, Trygetius seconds Augustine's urging, for them to bow to mere *fama*, what is generally believed, rather than pursue the truth by reasoning things out (*rationibus*) (2.20). Yes, Augustine agrees two paragraphs later, they must now leave "childish toys" behind them, and (again, in Vergil's words) "forge arms for a valiant warrior" (2.22); they must carry their discussion of Academic teaching further still.

Confronting the Academics by "Reason"

And so they do, Alypius summarizing that teaching, and Augustine questioning him on his summary. Alypius first proposes his personal view of Academicism, and then appeals to those great and famous philosophers who are of a similar mind. Ought we not, he asks rhetorically, to "bend our necks" (*praebere collum*) to their "authority" (2.30)? But, as events prove, Augustine is unwilling to submit to that yoke, or to permit his friends to do so, too easily; his reasoned view of Academic teaching takes up the remainder of the work, and eventually wins assent even from Alypius. Instead of "bending their necks" beneath the heavy yoke of authority, Augustine will persuade them, they should "stand up" like free men, ruled by the "law of their minds," and bravely decide such matters for themselves.

Rising to the "Food" of Truth

The image of "rising" or "standing up" takes on a different shading in the *De beata vita*, the chief reason being that this dialogue is dominated by the metaphor of "food." The food of the soul is truth—or, as becomes plainer toward the end of the dialogue—the supernal "Truth" Who is our "bread of life." It is not surprising, therefore, that the *erigere* image takes its coloration primarily from this, though secondarily from the martial metaphor.

Augustine has invited his friends to share an intellectual banquet celebrating his birthday; he will serve as host (*ministrator*). But they must not prolong their feast beyond measure, for there is gluttony of soul as well as of body; so, they spread the discussion over three days. In closing the first day's session, Augustine offers to sharpen the question they should consider the next morning.

At this proposal, all his companions "reached out their hands as though to grasp a serving platter held on high" (*elatum ferculum*). Augustine begins to form his question, and tells us that "they raised themselves up [*sese erexerunt*] even more eagerly, and, as though with hands outstretched, made to aid the server bearing" the promised food to them (13).

THE "RAPACIOUS" BANQUETERS

Augustine gives the question full expression now, and, "suddenly, they shouted out, as though bearing away the entire course" (*quasi totum rapientes*). *Rapui quidem vobiscum*, Licentius admits: "I bore it away along with the rest of you" (14). But *rapere* is once again functioning as the Gospel word for what the "violent" do with the "kingdom of God": they seize upon it, snatch at it, in order to "bear it away." When the discussion resumes on the following morning, Augustine stresses the allusion almost too heavily: he describes Monica's reserve as recalling the behavior of a guest who, "seated amid famished and rapacious guests [*rapacissimos*], hold themselves back from being rapacious in their turn" (*a rapiendo*) (16).

CONVERSION TO THE *Beata Vita*

The *De ordine*, of course, centers principally on the universality of Divine Providence. Augustine seems to be winning his personal battle to "convert" young Licentius from his enthusiasm for literature to devoting himself seriously to philosophy. He finds one of the youth's remarks "raising him up with a keener hope" than usual (*erectior spe alacriore*). Perhaps his fears that Licentius might "be snatched [or borne] away" (*raperetur*) from "philosophy" were groundless after all; and yet, the young man might still be tempted to "erect" (*erigere*) a "wall" between himself and "truth" (1.8).

Licentius replies to his fears with a verse from Terence, *Hodie perii*, "Today I was lost." But then, in what is probably a deliberate echo (on Augustine's part) of the Prodigal's "conversion" story, he immediately corrects that phrase to *hodie forte inveniar*: "Today, perhaps, I shall be found" (1.8). Later (1.19), Licentius is once again described as "raising himself up" (*sese erigens*) to answer a telling objection from Trygetius, which prompts Augustine once again to encourage him, in a paler version of the martial metaphor, to trust in the "forces" (*vires*) God has given "in order that [he] may return to Him even stronger" than he was before (1.20). "O God of powers," *Deus virtutum*, Licentius is soon singing (1.23), and goes on to describe his lively sense of having been "converted" to that God, after all. Augustine is gratified: Licentius may be on his way to the *beata vita*.

But *beata vita*; Augustine is now brought to reflect on that term "Happiness." Only "mention it" he tells the youths, and "all raise themselves up [*omnes sese erigunt*] and look to your hands [*attendunt in manus*] to see whether you have something to give to the needy" (*egentibus*) and afflicted. But some, alas, invited to rise to under-standing, fall back instead into the swaddling clothes of quasi-superstitious reliance on authority. How could one ever call them "happy" (1.24)?

AGAIN, RISING TO THE "FOOD" OF TRUTH

At this juncture the associations of the *erigere* image we saw in *De beata vita* 13 have become much clearer: Augustine is playing with several images from the Psalms. Chief among them is Psalm 144:14–16, which may even then have been used as "grace" before meals. It runs:

> *Allevat Dominus omnes qui corruunt,*
> *et erigit omnes elisos.*
> *Oculi omnium in te sperant, Domine;*
> *et tu das escam illorum in tempore opportuno.*
> *Aperis manum tuam,*
> *et imples omne animal benedictione.*

> The Lord lifts up all those who fall,
> And helps all who are cast down to stand.
> The eyes of all hope in You, Lord,
> And You give them food at the opportune time.
> You open Your hand,
> And fill every living creature with blessing.

There, once again, is the *erigere* term we have been tracking. It is God who "raises up," or *allevat*, "lifts up," "all" those (*omnes elisos*) who have "fallen" or "been cast down." But that "raising up" is associated, here as in the *De beata vita* text, with "hope" (*sperant*) and a yearning for "food" (*escam*). That food, moreover, comes when God "opens His Hand": for the Eternal Christ, Son of the Father, is both our "Food" and the divine "Hand" that lifts and raises and feeds us on Himself.

I strongly suspect that, in Augustine's imagination, these images from Psalm 144 were also resonating with those of Psalm 122, which evokes the "eyes of the servants . . . on the hands of their masters" and "the eyes of the handmaid . . . on the hands of her mistress." Other resonances may have derived from similar images from Psalm 24:14 ("The Lord is a firmament to those who fear Him") and its context; but the reader is free to verify or reject those suggestions at will.

But many of the elements we have seen thus far come together strikingly in the interpretation of the Prodigal parable we saw Augustine give in *Sermo* 2 11 of the Caillau collection. For in placing his "arm" upon the Prodigal's neck, God "gave him Christ to carry." But Christ is a "burden" (*sarcina*) which does not weigh down (*onerat*) but on the contrary "bears up" the carrier (*sublevat*). Augustine repeats the paradox: the "sweet yoke" and "light burden" that is Christ not only does not press us down (*premat*) but "raises us up" (*allevet*)—the very term he had found in Psalm 144, alongside its companion, *erigere*. There, we saw, both terms describe the action of the God in Whom we all "hope" (*sperant*) in order that His Hand "open" to feed us on His "food." That food, we can now be increasingly confident, is the supernal Truth which Augustine "hoped" to approach through faith, but feed upon through "knowledge," "understanding," and the certain possession whose culminating form is the "vision" that joins the soul with God. But the *Soliloquies* will soon provide final confirmation of all these connections.

RISING TO THE UNIVERSAL VIEWPOINT

Shortly afterward in the *De ordine*, Augustine once again reverts to the martial metaphor: he urges Licentius to "attack" the question of universal providence "with a mind raised even higher" (*erectiore animo insurgitis*). He himself promises, in turn, to play the opposition (*adversabor*), while hoping that his young adversary can "protect [his position] solidly and strongly with a defensive wall" (1.27). "Gather together whatever forces [*quidquid virium*] you can," he urges. Licentius begins to demur, modestly, but, *Deinde erectior*, he "straightens up further" and boldly expresses his thesis on the universality of divine order (1.28).

Here a spat ensues between the two youths, both of them
succumbing to what Augustine decries as "puerile" vanity. He
lectures them, and just as he has finished, Monica makes her
appearance. The reader remembers that it was Monica who earlier
berated Licentius for bellowing Psalm 79 while busy in the latrine;
that scolding had led to a private conversation in which both he
and Augustine agreed in characterizing the good lady's attitude as
"superstitious" (1.22–23). It comes as no surprise, then, that
Monica's entry now brings up the question of faith and reason,
and provokes Augustine to defend his allegiance to the kind of
"philosophy" which, like Christ's kingdom, is "not of this world"
(1.32).

As their discussion advances, Licentius takes the occasion to
offer his views—remarkably Plotinian as things turn out—of how
the "sage" can always remain immovably "with God," whatever
may happen to that "slave," his body. As for his own "slave"
body, he admits it sometimes "raises itself up" (*sese erigit*) in
rebellion against the rule of his mind. Again, Augustine has subtly
reminded his readers that he is perfectly aware that the term *erigere*
can have pejorative connotations also (2.7).

But he is very soon back to the term's more positive sense. Why
can our minds not always acknowledge the universality of divine
order? Our view, too often, is excessively narrow: if we could
"raise up [*erigens*] the eyes of our mind" and take a vaster view of
things, we would see that nothing is truly "out of order" in our
universe (2.11). To take that higher view, however, a measured
amount of learning is necessary to "nourish the soldier [*militem*]—
or even the captain [*ducem*]—of philosophy" (2.14). Let those
who—like Monica?—have no use for such learning (*eruditio*) cling
to their faith, for authority and reason represent between them the
duplex via, the "dual way" toward truth (2.15–16).

Augustine returns to this relationship between reason and authority some paragraphs later (2.26–27), then sketches the way
the reasoning mind can rise in ordered fashion to God. A wonderful program that, Alypius praises his friend. But, Augustine
replies, not original with me! It has been proposed by men both
great and near-divine in wisdom. He is saying that, he tells us, for
the benefit of these young men; if they were asked to depend
solely on Augustine's "authority," they might rightly feel entitled
to despise the program of studies he has just advocated! Far from
wanting to act the authoritarian, he says, "I do not want them to

believe me at all, unless I teach them [*docenti*] by giving reasons."
But he cannot but admire Alypius for having "snatched with such
eagerness" (*tanta rapuisti aviditate*) at these prescriptions for the
quest of wisdom, and "borne them away" (2.28).

The *De ordine* winds its prolix way to an end as Augustine
explains the sevenfold work of Reason in constructing the ladder
of the liberal arts. One of Reason's final triumphs consists in
proving the immortality of the soul. In daring this venture (*ausa*)
he stresses, Reason "raised herself up mightily [*se multum erexit*],
and showed mighty presumption" (*multumque praesumpsit*) (1.43).
But it is obvious that this "daring" and "presumption" are both
to be considered praiseworthy.

One can easily imagine that Augustine fired this parting shot
with cold deliberation: he wants to warn his reader one last time
of how strongly he feels about the Catholic's right to *se erigere*, to
"rise up" to understanding. "Audacious" it may appear, to some,
for human reason to "stand up" this way; some might even think
it "presumptuous," "contumacious," or, worse yet, downright
"puerile." But Augustine is firmly of another mind.

The Prodigal's Great "Hope"

Augustine opens his *Soliloquies* with the prayer of a fallen sinner
"returning" (*redire*) to the Trinitarian God (1.2). In terms reminiscent of Luke's Gospel, he depicts himself as a Prodigal who has
been a "runaway" (*fugitivus, fugiens famulus*), begging God to
"receive" (*recipe*) him back again. For, he pleads, even God's
"enemies"—obviously the Manichees—"took [him] in, stranger
though he was, when [he] was fleeing" from Him. Now he cites
the second member of their favorite Gospel verse: "Let Your door
be opened to me as I knock" (5).

Shortly thereafter, he employs the Lucan term from the same
parable. He has avowed his desire to "know" two realities only,
God and his own soul. Yes, he is assured, Reason "dares to teach
him in order that he may understand" those realities (*ut intelligas,
docere te audeo*). But does he hold them now as "true" or merely
"probable"? Replying to Reason's question, Augustine admits that
up to now they seem to him only probable; and yet, "I confess
that (like the Prodigal) I have arisen [*surrexi*] to a greater hope" (*in
spem . . . majorem*) (1.15), the hope, the context makes clear, of
attaining genuine "knowledge," of possessing the certainty that
comes with "understanding" those realities.

That theme of "hope" is what forges the most fundamental link betweeen this Lucan *surgere* and Augustine's use of the term *erigere*; for he has told us earlier that "faith goads us [*excitat*] toward God, hope raises us up [*spes erigit*], and charity joins us to Him." Then he proceeds to orchestrate all the themes we have already seen associated with the image of "rising" and "being raised up." He prays to the God Who "converts" us, "arms us," "leads us into all truth," "conducts us to the door," brings it about that the door "is opened to those who knock," and, finally, "gives us the bread of life" (1.3).

Factus erectior AND AUGUSTINE's "CONVERSIONS"

Courcelle's interpretation of the expression *factus erectior* was by no means unintelligent. We have seen how Augustine himself teases us with reminders of the pejorative connotations the phrase *se erigere* can take: the slave that is Licentius' body can rebelliously "raise itself up" to dominate his soul; and Latin readers could quite properly ask whether the mind that casts off the yoke of philosophical authority and claims to "raise itself up" in quest of personal reasoned insight was not being too "daring," "proud," or even "contumacious."

Those reminders of the negative meanings *erigere* can take, however, only serve to underline the positive meaning Augustine prefers to express by the term. A "yoke" or "weight" of authority that served only to "oppress" and make us "bend our necks," that merely "commanded" and never sought to "teach," that imposed a "faith" that must never "rise up" toward "understanding"—that kind of yoke, he was convinced, could never be Christ's. For Christ's yoke was sweet; His burden actually lightened and raised us up with the "great hope" of tasting His Eternal Self as "food" of Truth. The Truth Christ claimed to *be* would "stand us upright," make us "free" from having to "bend our necks" to any "law" other than Truth, the divine "law of our minds," to any kind of yoke other than His. Once "returned to himself" and on the road of "return to the Father," the Prodigal must still strive for an "understanding" of the God in Whom he has come to believe.

Undoubtedly, though, Courcelle found encouragement for his interpretation in the conventional wisdom that would portray Augustine's conversion to Manichaeism as little more than a temporary spiritual shipwreck. If the interpretation given here is sound, on the contrary, we are faced with the disconcerting corollary that Augustine consistently viewed that conversion as a progressive step. That corollary calls attention once again to that curious feature we noticed in Augustine's interpretation of Luke's parable: the Prodigal must acknowledge that he could never have made his spiritual "turn" unless the Gospel had been preached to him. This is true even if the preachers were *mercenarii*, "heretics" like the Manichees who, it must always be remembered, preached to Augustine in the name of Christ. And, whatever their shortcomings, this was to their credit: they found him already *factus erectior*, and (in theory at least) respected that newfound attitude. They refused to "command" his belief, merely; they promised, at least, to "teach" him, lead him to some reasoned understanding of that belief. For they took seriously, more seriously than any Catholic clergyman Augustine had previously met, those words of Christ's: "Seek, and you shall find; knock, and it shall be opened to you."

And, *factus erectior*, Augustine is boldly claiming that, prompted to choose between Manichaeism and the sort of Catholicism he had experienced, his conversion by these *mercenarii* was a step in the right direction! In time he came to find that their teaching was not so nourishing as they had promised; so, he was compelled to cry out, like the Prodigal, "Here I perish with hunger." But his interpretation of St. Luke's parable, written in the year 400, must loyally admit what the slightly earlier account in his *Confessions* never once denies: heretics though they were, the Manichees' "reminders" were still efficacious in prompting his "return" and eventual incorporation into the true Church. *Oportet haereses esse*, Augustine never tires of assuring us: for heresies serve the providential purpose of prodding us to "quest," and of making us more keenly savor the sweetness of Truth, once "found" (*Enn 7* 15; *54* 22).

We can too easily be tempted to view Augustine's joining the Manichees as a "loss of the faith" he had drawn in with his mother's milk, and (in Courcelle's terms) an audacious assumption of the rationalistic "freethinker" attitude. But the Augustine of 386 saw it differently, and, *pace* Courcelle, so did the Augustine who wrote the *Confessions*. The nineteen-year-old Augustine had, true enough, turned his back on the faith of his childhood; but it is vital to notice what *kind* of faith he tells us he left behind. It was the "blind" sort of faith he had evidently experienced in African Catholicism: these were the "mists" he claims to have "dispelled."

But in converting to Manichaeism, he converted to *another kind of faith*. It was, moreover, one he *then* felt entitled to deem an authentic version of *Christian* faith—*more* authentic, indeed, than the Catholic version of the Christian faith. Despite all its attractions for him, what he had found wanting in Cicero's *Hortensius* was precisely that the name of "Christ" was not there; but the Manichees, on the contrary, had that name forever on their lips (*Conf* 3.8–10).

Now, the Manichees were rationalists enough, certainly, to promise they would eventually make everything clear to Augustine's reason; but, just as certainly, not from the very outset. They presented him with teachings which he had at first to *believe*; at first, therefore, he tells us in *De beata vita* 4, "I did not assent, but kept thinking that they were hiding something very great underneath the clothing" in which they expressed their doctrine, something "which they would eventually disclose" (*aliquando aperturi*). It was this promise of eventual understanding that made, and for some years kept, Augustine a Manichee.

He will later repudiate the Manichee claim that they did not "command" faith, but appealed uniquely to "reason." In doing so, however, he points to the facts of his own experience: they required an initial act of faith, just as the Catholica did; they promised that understanding would come, in time. Augustine has no problem with either that requirement or that promise. His problem was precisely this: that when he strove to attain that promised understanding, it became plain to him that they had asked him to place his faith in a tissue of absurdities.

Notice, too, that when Augustine later proclaims the need first to believe, then to pass on to understanding, he is just as insistent on the latter as on the former: a faith that did not strive to pass upward toward understanding was, in his eyes, truncated, spiritually immature, religiously infantile. Hence, the author of the *Confessions* had no sympathy for the kind of churchman who, when asked what God had been doing before creating the world, would wisecrack, "creating hell for the likes of them as ask that sort of question" (*Conf* 11.14). This was the sort who would merely "command" belief, and offer his flock no help toward "understanding" that belief. *Intellectum valde ama*, he later exclaims in that celebrated *Letter 120*, to a Consentius who professed himself resigned to settling for a faith with no such prospect of understanding. And his *Confessions* presents a picture of his "first conversion" which is perfectly consistent with the high evaluation he placed on understanding in his early dialogues. The power of Cicero's *Hortensius* lay in the exhortation Augustine read there to seek, quest after, "pursue," not this or that philosophic position, but nothing short of supernal Wisdom. And the enchanting power of Ambrose lay in his ability to preach a Catholicism which allowed for, and even invited, understanding.

By talking of "rationalism," "astrology," and "freethinking" in connection with Augustine's "first confession," both Courcelle and Mandouze run the risk of obscuring that vital point. They write as though the Augustine of the *De beata vita* were confessing to an adolescent change of orientation which he later repudiated; but the very opposite is true. Read both works carefully, and remarkably enough they both insinuate that his conversion to Manichaeism was a *progressive* step. It was taken *after* the *Hortensius* had done its part to liberate him even further from the childish superstition of blind faith, and after it had further encouraged him to "rise up" and, having arisen, to embark on a quest for understanding that was the first phase of his "return" to God. Granted: the Manichee phase of that quest will eventually prove disappointing; Ambrose and Plotinus will have to step in to fill the breach. But their twin service will consist in showing, in providential concert, that Augustine's quest for "understanding" of the Christian faith was still what it always had been: a far more positive move, religiously, than either Courcelle or Mandouze is inclined to acknowledge. The reason for that evaluation, we shall shortly see, was exactly as he expressed it to Consentius: understanding was an intermediate stage toward attaining that "highest peak of contemplation" of which St. Paul writes, the immediate *facie ad faciem* vision of God (*Ep 120* 4).

But, *factus erectior*: we have been concentrating on that term *erectior*, but have we gotten to the bottom of what Augustine implies by that tantalizing *factus*? I suspect not.

Allow me, therefore, one final suggestion.

In both his *Confessions* and his *De beata vita* Augustine recounts his conversion to Manichaeism as occurring soon after his encounter with Cicero's *Hortensius*. But this was the book, he tells us in both places, which raised his heart and aspirations from earthly ambitions to a desire to "embrace" supernal Wisdom. From "lying prostrate" he "became" or "was made" to "stand more upright," and so pursue the understanding of his faith in Christ; now the *Hortensius* invites him to step upward to "vision." But was it just a series of chance events which had resulted in his becoming "more erect"? In his prologue to the *Contra Academicos* Augustine throws out repeated mentions of "chance," "accidents," and "fortune"; but then, later on, he suggests to his friend Romanianus that all such expressions might be mask-terms for the cosmic order ensured by God's universal Providence; this, we know, is the very theme he next takes up in his *De ordine*. The prologue to the *De beata vita* was very probably written with those suggestions to Romanianus already in mind; indeed, the entire prologue makes most sense when read as Augustine's "first confession" that, like the adverse "tempests" which eventually drove him into his home harbor, even that first step in his conversion process was due to the workings of divine Providence. *Factus erectior*: did he merely "become," or is he saying he "was made," more upright by the God he came in time to see had always been tirelessly at work to "inflame" him with undivided love for supernal Wisdom?

One needs only to frame the question and the answer becomes obvious. But if that be true for whatever agencies "made" him more "erect," it must be equally true for Augustine's encounter with Cicero's *Hortensius*. He came upon it, he tells us almost offhandedly, in the ordinary course of his studies. His description of the later encounter with those "platonist books" is comparable: the unlikeliest of men placed them in his hands. So, too, one might initially be tempted to think that the child's voice chanting its *tolle, lege* prompted Augustine to open to a *capitulum* which merely "chanced" to catch his eye.

As with those "platonist books," or with that *capitulum* from Romans, so with the *Hortensius*. To the end of his life Augustine considered that encounter immensely important; it was forever, in his eyes, one of God's most elegant providential tricks. It left him with an incurable nostalgia, an ache that no sensual delight or worldly success could ever anesthetize. That ache—or perhaps one should call it a hunger—had once been for the life of *philosophia*, a life of leisure and quiet, *vacatio, otium*, a peace in which clearer and surer "understanding" might yield, even here on earth, to what Augustine believed would be the closest foretaste of the eternal

Sabbath, the bright radiance of "vision," accessible to us here on earth.

But Simplician's account of the conversion of Victorinus, Ponticianus' story about Anthony of Egypt, the surprise in finding that contemplative monasteries dotted the countryside about Milan—all this was building to a climax. By the time he entered that fateful garden, Augustine had come to realize that for a Christian, the call to the contemplative life meant something fuller than he had once imagined. It still implied, as always, that hunger for contemplative understanding, and ultimately for the "food" of supernal Truth, beheld in direct vision; it still demanded the casting off of all temporal cares and occupations, hence embracing the unencumbered life of celibacy; but further, it entailed becoming what, at Cassiciacum, we saw him striving to make his students: *milites Christi*, learnèd and intellectually supple, standing tall and free.

The image of becoming "erect" can take, accordingly, a variety of forms; while they are all fundamentally related in Augustine's imagination, each of them has a primary "dynamic," so to speak, its lines of force evoking, more naturally than its partners, *this* rather than *that* cluster of associations. We have noticed several instances of the particular dynamic whereby the man become "erect" brings the *miles Christi* to Augustine's mind. That association has yet to disclose all its secrets. We will be well advised to dissect it more carefully on another occasion.

Meanwhile, the *factus erectior* image appears to have brought us a considerable distance away from the Homeric Odysseus who originally inspired this exploration. Or has it? Answering that may seem to involve us in a momentary detour.

But traveling side-roads has its unique charms, and in this instance the landscape offers some fascinating aspects that make the detour worthwhile.

NOTES

1. See his *Recherches*, pp. 269–90. Jean Doignon's criticism of an earlier version of this chapter reached me too late to be integrated into this work; see his "*Factus Erectior* (B. *Vita* 1, 4): Une Étape de l'évolution du jeune Augustin à Carthage," *Vetera Christianorum*, 27 (1990), 77–83.

2. Courcelle, *Recherches*, pp. 49–60; see also Marrou, *Culture*, pp. 161–86, and A. D. Nock's classic study, *Conversion: The Old and the New in Religion from Alexander the Great to Augustine of Hippo* (Oxford: Oxford

University Press, 1933; London: Oxford University Press), cited by Courcelle, *Recherches*, p. 59n1.

3. Courcelle, *Recherches*, pp. 272–74; see also Brown, *Augustine of Hippo*, pp. 42–45.

4. *Recherches*, p. 274.

5. Pp. 616–17.

6. For valuable suggestions on the likely sources of Augustine's interpretation of the *erectus* notion, see H. Somers, "Image de Dieu: Les Sources de l'exégèse augustinienne," REA, 7 (1961), 112–14.

7

Homecoming to Ithaca

WE SAW AUGUSTINE DESCRIBE his life's career in the prologue to the *De beata vita* as an odyssey of departure and return: he "sailed" off from his homeland, at one juncture seemed to be heading out toward the very middle of the deep, but then caught sight of signals from the homeland he had left behind, and changed course toward the haven of Philosophy. We saw also how the image of rising to "erect" stature symbolized, for him, assuming the posture of mature spiritual "understanding."

But Augustine employs several other striking images in connection with his arrival home; they may repay close investigation. Consider, for example, the picture he paints (in *Vita* 2) of the three classes of wanderers; the second of these classes obviously includes himself; this type sets to reading the works of "men both learnèd and very wise," and then "awakes, somehow or other, in the very harbor" of the happy, philosophic life (*in ipso quodammodo portu evigilant*).

That image can flit by without the reader's actually adverting to it; but once attended to, it is, I submit, both odd and, despite its brief compass, oddly elaborate. The wanderer reads, then (presumably) falls asleep, then awakens and finds himself *quodammodo*—somehow or other, in a way that he himself cannot account for—"home"! What could have possessed Augustine to confront Manlius Theodorus in the first place, but his wider readership as well, with so strange an amalgam as this?

ECHOES IN THE *Confessions* ACCOUNT

As a first step toward answering that question, notice how closely the later conversion account in *Confessions* 7.20 echoes this very image. It would seem, at first blush, that the abundance of navigational metaphors in the earlier books has now been replaced by the doubled doctor-*cum*-mother image evoked by that rich term *fovere*. Despite that, however, Augustine deftly recalls the string of adversities he was earlier tempted to complain about. *De beata vita* 1 depicted them as so many providential "storms" and "tempests" blowing him and voyagers like him, all unknowing, homeward (*in optatissimam terram nescientes*). Now he figures them as medicinal sufferings applied by the maternal God, unbeknownst to himself, to heal and open his spiritual eyes (*fovisti caput nescientis*). The earlier dialogue recounts how he had to stop his ears to the siren song of "honors and pleasures"; the *Confessions* metaphor depicts God as closing his eyes to the "vain" attractions of the temporal, sensible world (*clausisti oculos meos ne viderent vanitatem*). Then, Augustine says, *cessavi de me paululum*. Following Isaiah's counsel (7:9) to Achaz, he "quieted down," relaxed his frantic striving to "do it all himself," and—already anticipating, though only a "tiny bit" (*paululum*), what Lady Continence will later advise—"let go" and allowed God to "do it." (That series of touches does not overtly feature in the *De beata vita*.) Having already closed his eyes, God now quiets his plaintive squalling and "lulls him off to sleep" (*consopita est insania mea*); both accounts stress the need for accepting "chance" adversities as providential and beneficent. And both accounts include that odd parenthesis of "sleeping"!

Then, the *Confessions* tells us: *evigilavi*. That term and its "conversion" associations hold a special fascination for Augustine: *in ipso . . . portu evigilant*, he writes in *De beata vita* 2; *Evigila, evigila*, he urges Romanianus to waken from the torpid "slumber" which "this life" inflicts upon the soul (*Acad* 1.2); he then portrays Monica as *evigilans in fidem suam*, when she recognizes the Trinitarian import of his description of happiness (*Vita* 36).

The list could doubtless go on; but where does Augustine find himself upon awakening? *In ipso quodammodo portu*, the *De beata vita* puts it, in its chosen navigational image: in the very "haven" he had (unknowingly) longed to reach. But, "somehow or other" (*quodammodo*). There is something abrupt, unaccountable about the fact that he awakens and lo! finds himself "home." That element of surprise is muted in the *Confessions* account, but not entirely absent: *evigilavi in Te*, Augustine confesses to God. "I awoke in You" (in God's own "arms," the logic of the image has it!)," and I saw that You were infinite" after all, but (here was the surprise) infinite "in another way entirely" (from what I had previously imagined).

And, Augustine adds, "this seeing was not a fleshly" but a new, a radically "spiritual" mode of "seeing." To this juncture, and despite their employing basically different images, the "arrival" scenes from both the *De beata vita* and the *Confessions* correspond almost point for point. Again, it does appear that the *Confessions'* emphasis on "letting go" and allowing God to act is of far less overt importance to the earlier dialogue—the dramatic recognition of grace contained in the *Ad Simplicianum* is yet to come—but aside from that, the match is almost perfect. What, though, of this final note the *Confessions* strikes, about discarding sense-knowledge of "vanities" and imaginative ways of picturing God: does the *De beata vita* account omit all mention of this advance toward genuinely "spiritual" insight?

True enough, much is said on this decisive transition in subsequent portions of the Cassiciacum dialogues; and yet, such is the consistency one finds in the workings of Augustine's imagination that the absence of this vital feature from so artfully composed an image of "conversion" strikes a tinny note. Besides, this allusion to sleeping and waking was almost certainly inspired by Plotinus' counsel in *Ennead* 1.6.8 that the Odyssean wanderer who desires to return to his soul's homeland must "shut [his] eyes" and "wake another way of seeing," and since Henry's *Plotin et l'Occident* scholars are virtually unanimous in seeing that very paragraph, in fact, that very phrase from Plotinus' treatise "On Beauty," as having burned its way into Augustine's memory before his departure for Cassiciacum. Can it really have left no traces in the very Odyssean image where one might fully have expected to discern its presence?

A WORKING HYPOTHESIS

I should like to propose a working hypothesis now, one which, however risky, still holds a fascination that compels me to share it; it may just be the case (I hope and, more, I suspect it is) that one or other scholar has scribbled a half-distracted note about a baffling text which, after reading my suggestion here, could turn out to be a missing piece to help fill out this jigsaw puzzle.

This hypothesis began with an impression: how strangely like Augustine's homecoming is that of Odysseus in Book 13.[1] The Phaeacians take Odysseus aboard one of their ships, and almost immediately this man "whose counsel was as the counsel of the gods" falls into a deep sleep. Homer is curiously insistent: it is a sleep so deep that he calls it "next akin to death." Through the entire voyage from Phaeacia to Ithaca, Odysseus sleeps "in peace, forgetful of all he had suffered." Still "heavy with slumber" (the fourth time "sleep" is mentioned!), he is carefully placed on the shore of his own island.

His Phaeacian benefactors then surround him with all manner of gifts. They leave him there, still sleeping, and take ship once more for home. When Odysseus finally awakens on his native land, he "knew it not, having been long afar"; "each thing showed strange to him." Homer goes on to attribute this puzzlement in part to Athena; she had "shed a mist around him" and around his treasure to protect him from premature discovery. "So," the account ends, Odysseus "started up and stood, and looked upon his native land." Like the Prodigal who "rose up," or the Augustine who had first to become "erect," Odysseus had to "stand up" and ignore (literally "overlook") the Phaeacian treasure at his feet in order to behold his homeland!

NEOPLATONISTS AND *Odyssey* IMAGERY

Pierre Courcelle has amassed considerable evidence for thinking that there existed at Milan an active circle of (presumably Christian) Neoplatonist thinkers. How dearly one would love to know what that group made of this strange episode. We may safely assume their acquaintance with Neoplatonism's long tradition of interpretating Homer's revered "wisdom" allegorically.[2] The *Odyssey*, particularly, was considered a rich mine of suggestions on the trials and eventual triumph of the fallen and "wandering" soul. Vincenzo Cilento has shown in rich detail the sympathy Plotinus exhibited toward such exercises—the works of several earlier practitioners of the art constituted regular reading in his school.[3] Moreover, his leading disciple and editor, Porphyry, relates how enthusiastically one such effort on his part was acclaimed by Plotinus himself.[4] There may be some trace of self-advertisement here—Porphyry was not above such exhibitions—but in spite of that, there must be a core of fact involved. And the oracle that Porphyry attributes to Apollo on the occasion of Plotinus' death at least suggests how acceptable Homeric allusions must have been to members of Plotinus' school: the master is depicted in an Odyssean image as "having swum swiftly" away from the bonds of human necessity and "the roaring surge of the body" to the safety of that shore "where the splendour of God shines round . . . and the divine law abides in purity." For, as Porphyry comments on the oracle, this "god-like man . . . often raised himself in thought" to the God beyond all shape and form.[5]

Porphyry has also left several of his own works in this line, most notable among them his "philosophical" exegesis of the episode concerning the *Cave of the Nymphs*—which Homer recounts almost immediately after Odysseus' landing on the Ithacan shore. It is unfortunate that his exegesis on the *Cave* takes up the thread of Homer's story very shortly *after* Odysseus lands on his home island, awakes, and "stands up." Doubly unfortunate, there is a lacuna in one of our richest sources on such allegorizing interpretations, written by Heraclitus the "rhetor." That lacuna extends from Book 11 to Book 19 of the *Odyssey*, hence covering the account of Odysseus' landing which occurs in Book 13.[6]

This absence of specific information about how the Neoplatonists interpreted the Ithacan homecoming contributes a large measure of the riskiness that hangs about the hypothesis I am proposing. But it contributes in equal measure to its fascination. Just as we know so much about Cicero's *Hortensius* from what Augustine has told us, could it not just be that, by attentively reading these early prologues, we might find ourselves peering through one of those lucky knotholes into the history of ideas; what he tells us may permit us actually to reconstruct something of what Neoplatonists read into the "landing" episode.

Augustine and Neoplatonic Allegorizing

Some years ago, Pierre Courcelle demonstrated that familiarity with Neoplatonic ideas need not have required exposure to the technical treatises of the school.[7] Tableaux and inscriptions on a host of funerary monuments showed convincingly that those ideas, and the symbolic interpretations they inspired of mythical characters like Daedalus, the Sirens, and Odysseus, had penetrated broadly into the general culture. It could easily have been the fact, therefore, that symbolic interpretations of Odysseus' homecoming, complete with the trappings of sleeping, waking, and standing up to "see," were as much in the fourth- and fifth-century "air" as were the figures and episodes Courcelle has discussed.

But in addition to what may have impregnated the cultural atmosphere of the time, we know that Augustine enjoyed direct acquaintance with Neoplatonic writings; furthermore, I have already alluded to the evidence that there existed an active "circle" of Christian Neoplatonists at Milan. So, let me put my suggestion this way: since the Odysseus image was clearly Augustine's model in the prologue we have been examining, it might not be far-fetched to speculate on what he might have learned in this connection from those Milanese Neoplatonists. It is perfectly possible that they prompted him to see similarities between the Prodigal's "rising" and Odysseus' "standing up," as well as to detect echoes of Odysseus' sleep and waking in Plotinus' injunction that we must "close our eyes" to all the varieties of "bodily beauty" before we can "wake another way of seeing."

Recall, once again, that the Phaeacians had left a sumptuous array of gifts next to the sleeping Odysseus before they departed; those gifts were certainly as various in their "bodily beauty" as Plotinus' expression implies; but in the *Odyssey* Athena counsels Odysseus to leave them behind in the Cave of the Nymphs, *before* leading him further toward home. Significantly, Porphyry cites Numenius' interpretation of this episode, and it is entirely comparable to Plotinus' observation: philosophic wisdom (as personified in Athena) would persuade the soul to disregard all sensible beauties in order to fasten the mind's gaze on higher, spiritual beauties. Porphyry parenthetically inserts this citation from Numenius, moreover, in his *Cave of the Nymphs*,[8] thereby making it part of the written tradition of Neoplatonic interpretation. That interpretation, in its turn, could easily have been partner to an exegesis wherein Odysseus' "standing up" implied rising above the "mists" surrounding him, literally "overlooking" the bodily beauty of the Phaeacian gifts, and so beholding the higher beauty symbolized by his Ithacan homeland.

The possibility we are weighing becomes more plausible if one compares Augustine's imagery with what Plotinus writes in the opening paragraph of *Ennead* 5.9. Plotinus has just proposed a threefold division of mankind. Its purpose is somewhat different from the one Augustine outlines in *De beata vita* 2, yet his "third kind" is not unlike Augustine's first; it comprises those "godlike men"—we saw that Homer's frequent epithet for Odysseus occurs in this precise context—who,

> by their greater power and the sharpness of their eyes, as if by a
> special keensightedness, see the glory above and are raised to it as
> if above the clouds and mist of this lower world, and remain there,
> overlooking all things here below and delighting in the true region

which is their own, like a man who has come home after long
wandering to his own well-ordered country [5.9.1].[9]

In their edition of the *Enneads*, Henry and Schwyzer suggest, and
Cilento concurs, that the Homeric parallel to this Plotinian observation is *Odyssey* 5.37. But that is a single line of text in which
Zeus predicts no more than this: the Phaeacians will "send [Odys-
seus] away in a ship to his own dear country."[10] One wonders
whether Henry and Schwyzer ever even considered the Homeric
landfall in Book 13 as a possibility, and judged it in competition
with the text from Book 5. But, again, we are dealing with the
way imagination works, so we need not feel obliged to select one
possible parallel to the absolute exclusion of its analogues. But
were one compelled to place these two possibilities in competition,
notice how much more detail Plotinus' reminiscence appears to
have borrowed from the actual homecoming in *Odyssey* 13: Zeus
(in Book 5) makes no reference to Odysseus as "godlike"; nor
does he lay any stress on the "long wandering" which would keep
him long afar, whereas both Plotinus and *Odyssey* 13 do. Plotinus'
allusion to "clouds and mist," furthermore, may well reflect the
"mist" Athena had shed about Odysseus and the Phaeacian hoard.
Surely by now Plotinus' image of Odysseus as "raised" above
cloud and mist and "overlooking" all the "things here below" to
feast his gaze on the landscape of "home" begins to take more
definite shape as an allegorical interpretation of Odysseus' "starting and standing" upright, then, overlooking the material trea-
sures left him by the Phaeacians, gazing instead at his (spiritual)
"native land."

Perhaps it has come to appear a good deal less fanciful to discern
similar echoes in Augustine's answering depictions of himself. He,
too, we saw, confesses to a "long wandering," confused by clouds
and fogs. But in time he became, or was made, "more erect,"
more capable, though still not entirely so, of beholding the home
he left in the higher world. Finally, however, God closed his eyes,
and lulled him to sleep. Then, somehow or other, *quodammodo*, he
awakened to find himself at last "overlooking" the vanities of "this
lower world" and delighting in the "true region," the home of his
soul. And, like the Neoplatonic Odysseus finally arrived at his
Ithacan homeland, he enjoys a vision no longer drawn from the
"flesh" but of "another sort" entirely.[11]

A Spiritual Vision

Was this a "mystical" vision in the proper sense of that term? A number of commentators on this section from *Confessions* 7 would have it so. Augustine, they interpret, has attempted, and partially succeeded in, making the kind of "ecstatic" ascent to an unmediated vision of God that his readings in the "platonist books" encouraged him to strive for.[12] That interpretation, however, is obliged to spin off from a few paragraphs of Augustine's account, torn from their roots in the total context of that account. The result is unsurprising: the interpretation that emerges from that procedure is beset with all manner of difficulties. Besides, Augustine tells us, not once but twice, that the upshot of the personal reflections he made after reading the "platonists" was precisely this: he had been "raised up" to glimpse the *invisibilia Dei*, but to glimpse them precisely as *intellecta*, with the eye of the "understanding" (7.23, 26). And to make matters even less ambiguous, he adds (8.1) that this seeing was of the darkly "enigmatic" sort that Paul describes as through a "mirror." It is obvious from the language that in the former instance Augustine is quoting the expression drawn from St. Paul's letter to the Romans (1:20); but the "image" Augustine has of the act of "understanding"—for he *does* employ such an image—has not been sufficiently explored. We shall glean more light on that image slightly further on.

But the interpretation of *Confessions* 7 is complicated by the dynamic relationship Augustine has set up between faith, understanding, and unmediated "vision." The "quest" that starts with "faith" must move not merely *to*, but *through*, "understanding," in order to culminate in eventual "vision." That vision is of Truth, indeed, but Truth once "lost" and now "re-found." And if Neoplatonism's interpretation of the *Odyssey* was truly Augustine's philosophical guide for understanding his Christian faith, that Truth—however much Augustine later regretted applying the expression to the Platonic over-world—is located in Christ's "Kingdom not of this world." In order to "enjoy" that Truth in all fullness, the wandering soul must have "returned" from the "sea" to the shore of its "most peaceful homeland," from the distracting activities of time to the quiet stillness of contemplation. But that, the Augustine of the *Confessions* came to be convinced, will be our lot only when we have been reintegrated into God's own Eternity.

Parallels in Augustine's Later Works

But are there texts from Augustine's later writings which echo and confirm the presence of this Odyssean "homecoming" image in the *De beata vita*? The least one can say in answer is that the image-pattern traced above generally accords with the ways Augustine later employs the various facets of the seafaring metaphor. The figure of Odysseus, of course, is seldom if ever explicitly identified as such, but Augustine is obviously happy to find parallels where the Old and New Testaments concord with the best and deepest in pagan models. At other times Scripture can suggest extensions and corrections of the pagan model. In all such cases, though, Augustine is content to preach, or write, drawing his nomenclature from the Scriptural rather than the pagan source, leaving only the understructure of the image to betray any pagan origins it might have.

Life as a Sea-Voyage

So, for example, Scripture presents a number of passages encouraging Augustine to interpret the figure of a sea-voyage as symbolic of our human life in time. The Christ of the Gospels, for example, enters Peter's boat, preaches to the people, and then gives instructions that result in the miraculous catch of fish. Can we not discern, Augustine asks his flock, that the "sea" is this *saeculum*, tossed by "gales and storms of temptation" and filled with "dangers to navigators," in which "men, like fishes, devour one another" (cf. *En 39* 9) and one must "seek the way to the heavenly homeland on the wood of the Cross" (*S 252* 2)?

At times the parallels with the *De beata vita* prologue are striking: into this *saeculum*, "stormy, dangerous, and full of distressing shipwrecks" came the Word of God Himself, and those who chose to heed His call were "liberated from the burdens [*sarcinis*] of secular businesses, and with lightened shoulders followed after Him; they bent their necks to His light yoke . . . and found peace" (3).

But if there is an Homeric parallel working here, it is not quite that of Odysseus' final homecoming, but that other famous landfall from the fifth book of the *Odyssey* (228ff.). After Calypso helps him construct a raft, and Odysseus departs from her island, the angry Poseidon catches sight of him and raises a violent storm. A powerful wave sweeps Odysseus from his raft and shatters it; he struggles back and is left clinging to a single spar. At this point the goddess Ino comes to his aid, and Athena as well. The upshot is that he is persuaded to let go of the wooden spar to which he has been clinging and swim to safety on the Phaeacian coast.

Now, none of these elements is contained in the Gospel passage Augustine is commenting; so, the question naturally arises, could his evocation of storms, shipwrecks, and the need for "clinging to the wood" have stemmed from his memory of the Homeric analogue? The thing is possible, it may even enjoy a measure of plausibility; but (for the moment, at least) that is as far as the evidence will carry.

Sermo 75 2 deals with the Gospel story of the storm at sea. Again, the sea is this *saeculum* (see also *SS 76* 1; *251* 3; *En 23* 2),[13] this temporal life in which we are all *peregrini*, though not all of us, alas, equally anxious to "return to our homeland" (*ad patriam redire*). But in any case, through the storms of this life, we must remain "in the boat," that is, "be borne along on the wood" (*in ligno portemur*). For even the "brawniest of swimmers" are often "sucked under and immersed" by the violence of the sea.

Here the "Homeric" embroidery we saw above—storms, danger of shipwreck, clinging to the "wood"—might readily be accounted for by the elements present in the Gospel story itself. Again, though, it would be unsafe to argue that the workings of Augustine's imagination confront us with an either-or question. That allusion to "strong swimmers," moreover, is faintly suspicious. There is enough talk in Homer's episode of Odysseus' being submerged and sucked under to awaken such suspicions, but we also saw that Odysseus finally had to abandon the wooden spar to which he had been clinging, and swim for shore.

ECHOES FROM THE APOLLONIAN ORACLE

However that may be, this was doubtless the incident from the *Odyssey* that inspired the Apollonian oracle's reference to Plotinus as an equally "god-like man," one who,"strong in heart, . . . swam swiftly . . . to that coast."[14] There is also a possibility that Augustine is admonishing his flock by directing another of his numerous slants against the Neoplatonists' "presumption" that they could reach their homeland as Odysseus had, without clinging to the "wood." If this is the case, Augustine could think of himself as on solid ground, from several points of view. First, this was an incident to which, we know, the Neoplatonists directed considerable attention;[15] anyone acquainted with their Homeric interpretations would have recognized Augustine's allusion readily, so his point would have gone home. One more feature is suggestive: the Neoplatonists habitually stressed Homer's observation that Odysseus, while navigating his raft, kept his eyes unsleepingly on the Pleiades, Bear, and Orion (5.272–275); Homer characterizes these as constellations that, unlike those Augustine twice mentions in the *De beata vita* (2; 4), never sink (*mergentia, labentia*) into the ocean.[16]

But Neoplatonic interpreters also frequently pointed out that Odysseus came to safety only with the help of those two goddesses, Ino first of all, but then that goddess of "philosophy," Athena. Their interpretations might deal variously with this suggestion, but Augustine could be subtly reminding his philosopher friends that at least one prominent interpreter from their school had claimed that Homer was insinuating that even a "god-like" man stood in need of divine help in order to escape the sea and swim to the safety of shore.[17]

Here, too, the Apollonian oracle that Porphyry quotes on his master's demise is additionally suggestive: that oracle praises Plotinus for the reason that, like Odysseus "unsleepingly" beholding the Pleiades, "[s]weet sleep never held [his] eyes," despite the "heavy cloud that would have kept them closed." But, one might object, the reference to his "swimming swiftly" might seem to attribute his arrival to his own intellectual powers. And yet, the oracle insists that while Plotinus was "struggling to escape from the bitter wave of this blood-drinking life . . . in the midst of its billows and sudden surges, often the Blessed Ones showed [him] the goal ever near." But the next sentence makes this allusion to divine assistance even more peremptory: "Often when [his] mind was thrusting out by its own impulse along crooked paths, the Immortals raised [him] by a straight path to the heavenly circuits, the divine way, . . . so that [his] eyes could see out of the mournful darkness."[18]

Augustine's interpretation of the "waters without substance" of Psalm 123 (*En 123* 9) is curiously reminiscent of Odyssean motifs. These are the waters of sinfulness, he tells his listeners, into which the Prodigal fell and "lost all his substance." But the image of "waters" and that of the Prodigal lead him to the image of *naufragium*, shipwreck: those who escape from shipwreck, he reminds them, "lose everything in the sea, and all come out of it naked" (*nudi omnes exeunt*). Not only is this true of those who suffered shipwreck with Paul, but "lovers of this *saeculum* have also suffered shipwreck, and all came out of it naked"—as, we know, Odysseus did. Like sparrows escaping from the fowler's trap, the Psalmist puts it, we have come free; but "lest you think you are able to do this on account of your own strength," Augustine warns, pray that prayer: "Our help is in the name of the Lord" (10–14). For despite all the temptations we must encounter in the "sea" of "this world" (*mundus iste*), we must remember that God "made the sea" and has put a boundary to its "storms," which can go no further than the "shore" that, one infers, is the end of time (*En 94* 9).

There are, then, suggestive parallels between Augustine's imagery in his post-Cassiciacum works and the images exploited in Neoplatonism: the stormy sea is "this world" of temporal realities, constantly threatening the homeward voyager with shipwreck and drowning; he has need of "wood"—whether ship or raft or spar— to cross that sea and come to haven. He is also more generally in need of divine aid of the sort Odysseus received from Ino and Athena. Finally, when voyaging through the darkness of this world, the navigator must steer, not by "sinking" stars, but by stars which never disappear below the ocean horizon.

MIST AND CLOUDS

We have already noticed in this same connection that Augustine (like Homer) sees mists and clouds as obstacles obscuring his vision. In one of his moods, he is inclined to stress this obscuring function of "clouds." Only spiritual "eagles" like St. John can fly above them in order to catch direct sight of the Divine Light (*S 135* 8; *InJo 19* 5). Those clouds, Augustine tells his flock (*S 222* 1), may be thought of as those "spirits of evil" St. Paul refers to as "ruling this world of darkness." They are indeed located "in the heavens," but not in the heavens where those spiritual "stars," the holy angels, dwell and shine down upon us. They behold the "beauty of Truth" without any "murkiness of vision, or any interpolation of falsity" (*En 56* 17). The "evil spirits" inhabit, rather, "this murky dwelling of the lowest air, where clouds also mass together."

But we should remember that Augustine's imagination some-

times assigns a more positive (and apparently un-Homeric) role to
"clouds": though they frequently block our view of that higher
spiritual world, they can sometimes, on the contrary, become the
kind of "luminous clouds" (*lucidae nubes*) the three apostles experienced on the mount of Transfiguration; on such occasions the
Father's voice can be heard piercing through them (*Acad* 1.3; *S 79*
1).[19] Or, in the purely visual metaphor, clouds can become
intermediaries of the Divine Light, transmitting but at the same
time half-obscuring it in the transmission. So they can figure the
apostles, prophets, and preachers (*Enn 35* 18; *56* 17; *76* 19; *134* 17)
who mediate to us the Transcendent Word through human words
and figures; they are clothed with "this murky flesh" and so bear
a "hidden light" which can "flash forth" from within them. The
flesh of Christ Incarnate is a similar "cloud," "tempering" the
Divine Light on account of the weakness of our spiritual sight (*En
56* 17; *83* 7; *InJo 34* 4–5). Or, clouds can figure the Scriptures, or
the words and figures employed by holy preachers and writers
(*En 103*, sermon 1, 9–11). Finally, the clouds can stand for the
entire panoply of visible created realities, "things that are made,"
"through" which, Paul assures us, we can "catch sight" of the
"invisible" attributes of God by means of our "understanding."

The Prologue to St. John's Gospel

But much the most interesting set of likely Odyssean reminiscences occurs in the commentary on St. John's Gospel, and
particularly in *Tractatus 1* and *2*. It is significant that Augustine is
here commenting St. John's Prologue. This was precisely the
Scriptural passage which he held up, in his *Confessions* (7.13–15),
as paralleling what he learned from those "platonist books" which
exercised so blazing an influence on his conversion. There is
reason to suspect, accordingly, that some associative threads
might still link Augustine's feeling for St. John's Prologue with
memories of the Neoplatonic themes he once so confidently
thought he had found there.

Some scholars cling tenaciously to the view that it was the old
priest Simplician who, in a series of intellectual discussions on
these issues, helped Augustine to see that there was a profound
accord between John's Prologue and the teachings of these *platonici*. But there is no real evidence for that series of discussions,
and, in fact, all the evidence is against it.[20] Simplician's role in

Augustine's conversion was of a different nature, and attentive reading of *Confessions* 8 makes that plain. But this is not meant to attenuate the reality of what the *Confessions*, along with Augustine's other works, makes undeniably clear: *Tractatus 1–2* of the *In Joannem* only solidify the conviction that Augustine always viewed this Prologue as closely akin in content with, though differing in expression from, what was contained in his Neoplatonic readings. Was there someone in the circle of Milanese Christian-Platonists who coached him into taking this view? Perhaps; but in the present state of our knowledge we neither know that there was any such person nor we can confidently attach a name to him.

And yet, Augustine held to the view that the Neoplatonists should have recognized that John's Prologue purveyed the same message as their writings did. One consequence of that view was the profound and even embittered disappointment with those "platonists" which Augustine began to experience once he discovered that they refused to accept the Incarnate Word as the indispensable "way" of salvation. They admitted that the soul was fallen into the temporal *saeculum*, and beset with all the distraction and danger of that "sea"; but they persisted—out of pride, Augustine thought—in thinking they could return to the soul's homeland without clinging to the "wood" of Christ's Cross.

Augustine seems to have initiated his polemic against the platonists, whom he had earlier admired somewhat too unreservedly, sometime around the date of his *De vera religione*, in 389 or 390. That polemic attitude shows clearly on the pages of the *Confessions*, and more clearly still in the year 406 when he composed *Tractatus 1–3* of his *In Joannem*.[21]

NAVIGATION AND THE "MOUNTAINS"

His first anti-platonist salvo in this work comes from a masked battery: St. John, he assures us, was one of those "mountains" Scripture speaks of, one of those exalted souls who are "illumined by Wisdom Himself," so that they can pass on what they have thereby learned to the "hills," those lesser souls, "little ones" (*parvuli*) who live by faith (*1 2*). The image makes sense if one recalls the structure of Augustine's *Omnia*: the Divine Sun shines from above, but its rays fall most brilliantly on the mountain tops; we lesser souls, *parvuli*, situated further "down" in the valleys of the nocturnal "lower" world, must look upward to the mountains

to perceive the sunlight which shines directly on their flanks, but
has not yet reached our lower level. From where we are, we see
that sunlight only indirectly.

But there have been other such mountains, Augustine must
allow, who seemed impressive in the view of their fellow-humans:
these, however, "concocted heresies and schisms, and divided up
the Church" instead of bringing her the "peace" that unifies.
Augustine describes these "mountains" in a seafaring metaphor
which curiously recalls the De beata vita prologue; it could possibly
betray how he still associates John's Prologue with Neoplatonic
imagery. They are

> mountains that cause shipwreck, and whoever brings his ship into
> contact with them shatters into pieces. For when those in danger
> catch sight of land it is easy for them to make for it, as it were. But
> sometimes the land that is sighted is a mountain, and rocks lie
> hidden beneath the mountain; so, when one makes for the moun-
> tain he slams against the rocks, and so arrives not into haven but
> into a graveyard [1 3].

ESPYING THE DISTANT HOMELAND

Thus far Augustine seems to be limiting his assault to heretics and
schismatics. *Tractatus 2* will change that; but it begins by reminding us that John was a "man sent from God." But in one sense,
Augustine has previously told us, he "had already begun to be an
angel" (*1* 4) in that he "transcended all earthly peaks, the airy
spaces, the loftiest of stars, and even the choirs and legions of
angels" in order to make contact with the Word through Whom
all things were made (*1* 5). How can we mere humans imagine
what that contact must be like? Augustine now employs the image
of espying the distant homeland from a mountain-peak; it recalls
the near-identical image from *Confessions* 7.27, where it applied to
the *platonici*. There, however, the line of sight was overland; here,
suggestively, the image has literally suffered a sea-change:

> It is as though someone were to glimpse his homeland from afar,
> and the sea stretched broadly in between; he sees whither he would
> go, but does not have the means to get there. So we, we want to
> arrive at that stability of ours [*ad illam stabilitatem nostram*] where
> what is [truly] *is*, because it alone is in the same way always; [we
> want to arrive there but] the sea of this *saeculum*, over which we
> have to go, stretches broadly in between. And yet, we already know

whither we are going, whereas there are many who do not even see whither they are going.

The divine solution to this navigational problem is Christ Himself, Augustine now explains: "He laid down the 'wood' [*lignum*] by which we could cross over the sea. For no one can cross over the sea of this *saeculum* unless borne by the Cross of Christ." So it is that even a person whose (intellectual) "eyesight" is so "weak" that he cannot see the further shore (the higher world) he longs to get to need only "embrace" that Cross and it will lead him to his destination (2).

For the Christ Who as Truth unchangeably "is" has entered our changing world and "become" our "Way" to Himself, the "homeland" where we shall no longer have need of any "boat" since there will no longer be a sea for us to cross. Now Augustine makes a statement calculated to stun the Neoplatonist: "it is better, therefore, not to see [the Eternal] 'That Which Is,' and not desert Christ, than to see It with the mind and despise the Cross of Christ." But he must forestall the impression that he has given too much away; his old hankering for understanding and vision is still with him, and asserts its claims: "It is good and loftier than that [belief without seeing]; it is excellent, both to see, if possible, the Whither one must go toward, and [at the same time] to cling to that [Cross] which carries [the voyager] to his destination."

But is this joining of faith with "seeing" a human possibility? Yes, Augustine assures us, "the great minds of the 'mountains' were capable of this," illumined as they were by the Light of Justice; spiritual giants, of which St. John was one, were capable of it, and "saw That Which Is." But lesser mortals, "little ones" incapable of understanding what John saw and handed down to us, are "brought by the ship [Christ's Cross] to That Which they do not see, the very same ship by which those who see arrive" at That Which they succeeded in seeing (2 3).

WHAT THE "PHILOSOPHERS" SAW

The opening of his next paragraph makes clear what the attentive reader had begun to suspect: that in this second *Tractatus* Augustine has shifted his attention from the "heretics" of the first *Tractatus* and is now speaking of "philosophers of this world." For St. Paul assures us that those philosophers did, in fact, "catch sight" of the "invisible [attributes] of God" which they came to "understand" through created realities (Rom 1:20ff.). "They saw Whither we must go, but ingrates toward Him Who accorded them [that power] to see, they willed to attribute the fact that they saw to themselves" and to their own intellectual power. Having become that "proud," they "lost [out on possessing] what they were seeing" (*amiserunt quod videbant*).

Augustine is crediting these "philosophers," here, as in his *Confessions*, with an unmistakably lofty achievement: "they saw what John tells of, that all things were made by God's Word, and that God has an only-begotten Son, through Whom all things exist; for these [affirmations] are found in the writings of philosophers. They were able to see That Which Is, but they saw It from a distance," and went on to despise the Cross of Christ Incarnate which was "necessary" to bear them "safely" across the "sea" to the Eternal Christ they had succeeded in "seeing" (*2* 4).

These philosophers, then, were genuine "mountains," catching the light of the sun and reflecting it to the "little ones," those valley-dwellers who are incapable of sharing their vision. St. John was such a "mountain," but he consented to be borne across the sea to the haven both they and he had glimpsed. That consent was linked with his humble realization that he was "not the Light" he had seen, but only a "witness" to that Light. Great he was, in every respect: "marvel at him, yes, admire him: but as a mountain" who was not the Light, "lest by thinking the mountain is the Light you suffer shipwreck against that mountain."

ONCE AGAIN, THE *Erectus* IMAGE

True to the pattern laid down in his early works, Augustine now shifts into the *erectus* image: "Raise yourself up to Him [*erige te*] Who illumines the mountain, the mountain who himself was raised up [*erectus est*] in order first to catch the rays and announce them to your eyes" (*2* 5). Three paragraphs later, this will recall the image of "standing"; Augustine introduces it through an untranslatable word-play: "Do not fall down [*cadere*]", he urges us, "and [that Sun] will not go down [*occidet*] for you. If you fall down, It will go down for you; if, however, you stand [*stas*], [that Sun] remains present to you." He continues with an observation that recalls his *dimissio* theme: "But you did not stand [*non stetisti*]; recall to mind whence you have fallen [*recordare unde cecideris*], whence the [Satan], who fell before you, cast you down. He cast

you down, not by force, not by pushing [*non vi, non impulsu*], but
[by the workings of] your own will" (2 8).[22]

Augustine here supposes that his hearers will understand that,
very much like (perhaps even in the company of?) the devil
himself, they once enjoyed the vision of that Light of Divine
Truth, but, as John's Gospel says of Satan, "did not stand" in that
Truth. This, he goes on to imply, is what Paul means when he
tells us that we were once "darkness." Now we have become
"light," but light "in the Lord"—that is, with God's indispensable
help. We had become "darkness," meaning that our minds had
become weakened, the gaze of our souls had become sickly; we
were no longer fit (*idonei*) to "see" the Light of that Eternal Truth.
Truth Incarnate has come into our world of time because we *needed*
to be "illumined" (or re-illumined) by that Light Who "illumines
every man who comes into this world." But had mankind not
"come into this world," had man, in other terms, not "departed
from [God], he would not need illuminating" (*non esset illuminan-
dus*). As things stand, however, "he does need illumining, and
precisely on this account: he departed thence where man could
always have been [i.e., remained] illumined" (2 7).

Here Augustine is repeating what he originally affirmed of the
"philosophers": their pride as men who had "come into this
world" of time had been preceded by an earlier sin of pride; each
one of them had "swelled up with pride, and been cast forth far
from his homeland" so that "the way" back to that homeland was
"cut off by the waves of this *saeculum*" (2 4). The voyage "home"
remains, accordingly, what it was for the earlier Augustine, an
Odyssean voyage of "return."

PARALLEL IMAGE-CLUSTERS, EARLY AND LATE

The elements we have encountered in paragraphs 2 to 8 of this
second *Tractatus* are all familiar; they are, in fact, identical with
those we encountered in the prologue to the *De beata vita*: a sea-
voyage which turns out to be a voyage of "return" to the "homeland" we have left; storms, clouds, mountains that threaten shipwreck; the need of a boat or plank to make for the safety of shore,
the haven that offers the security of escaping from the *saeculum*,
the tempestuous realm of time; the act of becoming "erect" in
order to glimpse the Light streaming from the higher world.
Compare those elements with those embedded in *Confessions* 7

and 8, and the comparison will show that the elements are all individually the same. But more than that, the dynamic pattern they form is identical with the pattern formed in the *De beata vita*. And that pattern, in turn, seems to reflect what we know, and can reasonably conjecture, about the Neoplatonic interpretations of Homer which were current in the culture of Augustine's time.

DISCREPANCIES IN THE PATTERN

There are, however, two intriguing exceptions to be noted about the parallelism I have just traced. First, the *In Joannem* fails to feature the image of "sleeping and waking" in the way the earlier writings would lead us to expect. And, second, there seems to be a firm distinction between the *erectus* image of "standing up" and the *stare* image of just plain "standing": instead of the one leading into the other, as one might expect, they seem to be working in tension against each other.

In his earlier works Augustine explained that by "sleep" Genesis symbolizes the suprasensible "contemplation" or "secret vision" in virtue of which Adam attained to a "more secret wisdom" which requires the closing of fleshly eyes (*GenMan* 2.16). This interpretation would fit quite smoothly with the kind of sleep that preluded the spiritual vision both Odysseus and Augustine enjoyed at the moment of their homecoming landfalls. But it must be acknowledged that Augustine does not restrict himself to this symbolism for sleep. Elsewhere, for example, he interprets Christ as referring to His death on the Cross as a "sleep" (*Enn 3* 5; *56* 12). He also associates sleep with the kind of torpid state brought on by the weakness or illness we have incurred by our fall; in this last connection, Augustine sometimes sees an intimate kinship between sleep, mortality, and death (*S 98* 2). The "sleeper," exactly like the Augustine of *Confessions* 8, drowsily resists the call to "awake" and be converted, murmuring (like the croaking of a crow) that he will change his life *cras, cras,* "tomorrow, tomorrow" (*SS 82* 14, *224* 4; *En 102* 16). From such a sleep the apostolic preachers came to wake and convert us to holiness of life (*S 162* 3).

Modo, ecce modo, the Augustine of *Confessions* 8.12 will murmur somnolently; he seems to be recalling that sleepy protestation when, in commenting on Psalm 63, he urges conversion on his hearers, exclaiming, "Will it not happen today [*hodie*] if you will it? Will it not be now [*modo*] if you will it? What great expenditure must you incur in order to accomplish it?" Then, as though recalling the *Odyssey* image he once borrowed from Plotinus in this precise connection, he taunts them: "Do you have to make a sea-voyage to the Indies? What ship need you rig out? See, even as I speak to you, change your heart, and what you have so often and so long cried out to be done will be done" (*En* 63 19). "*Evigilate*: Wake up to your salvation, wake up while there is time," he urges them now (*InJo 12* 14). Let no one tarry on the path leading to God's temple, to the work of the Lord, to prayer without ceasing.

The original Plotinian association, therefore, of "sleeping" to the world of sense in order to awaken to a higher, spiritual vision has shifted under the pressure of Augustine's pastoral concern for his people; by sleep he now more often means the sickly slumber of fallen concern for "this world," and "waking" has come come to mean "conversion" to the good works of the Christian life. But closer inspection would also show that this shift was strongly encouraged by several Scripture texts, along with allusions to them in the Ambrosian hymns to which Augustine was exposed during the weeks and months preceding his own conversion. They caught his attention individually, but then coalesced to form a lattice through which he viewed conversion as a process of being "awakened" to the demands and rewards of living a thoroughly dedicated Christian life.

"Standing" *vs.* "Standing Up"

An analogous shift probably accounted for the tension that later inserted itself between the images of "becoming erect" and of "standing." Even as late as 417, "becoming erect" retains much the same value as it has in the early works: it betokens the act of "rising up" to "understanding," and still implies a shift from "outward" bodily to "inward" spiritual seeing. "God gave you the eyes of your body and the reason of your heart," Augustine reminds his flock (*S 126* 3); "arouse [*excita*] your heart's reason; raise up [*erige*] the interior tenant of your interior eyes; . . . let him inspect God's creation. . . . Raise him up, arouse him" (*erige illum, excita illum*). Nor should we think this quest for understanding is beyond us: *Non enim denegatum est tibi*, Augustine assures them. That counsel, furthermore, is still closely linked with what Genesis tells us of man's superiority over the beasts:

God made you a rational animal, set you over the beasts, formed you in His own image. Are you to use [those powers] as a beast would, to see only what you would take into your belly, not into your mind? Raise up [*erige*] the gaze of your reason, therefore; use your eyes as a man should; behold heaven and earth; . . . behold the things He has made, and seek for the Maker.

For, as the Apostle assures us (Augustine now quotes Romans 1:20 freely), "The invisible attributes of God are glimpsed [*conspiciuntur*] from the created world, through those things which have been made."

"Standing Up" to "Understand"

Once again, that allusion to Romans 1:21 betrays the presence of Augustine's favorite image for "understanding": the act which permits us to "glimpse" (*conspicere*) the Divine Light, not directly and immediately, but as mediated, filtered "through" the screen (or "luminous clouds") of created realities (see pp. 232–33 above).

Augustine envisages the act of "standing up" or "becoming (more) erect," accordingly, as culminating in this *mediated* "vision" of the spiritual world that lies beyond the luminous clouds of visible, created realities. The distinction he draws between a mediated and an immediate vision of God is, for him, of capital importance; and it is that distinction which accounts for the curious tension we have noticed between his applications of the terms *erigere* and *stare*.

"Standing" vs. "Understanding"

For we are able, Augustine is convinced, and even summoned to "become more erect," to strive for understanding even while buffeted about by the tides and storms of our temporal condition. But, he has come to see, nothing, absolutely nothing, in this temporal world can boast of genuine "stability," can arrest the flow of change and mortality in order truly to "stand." True *stabilitas* (or *soliditas*) is promised to the Church only when it has been raised above "all the storms of this *saeculum*"; it will be accorded to those Christians who do not place their love in "impermanent realities" but long for "stable and unchangeable Eternity" (*En* 23 2–4; cf. *En 32*, version 2, sermon 2, 4–6). Privileged souls may rise beyond understanding to direct contact with the Eternal, but that contact is always fleeting. For the moment that it lasts, we rise above and out of time, but that breakthrough lasts but a brief moment. We must not seek that fullness of "life" in "this *saeculum*"; for here "days pass hurrying by," each succeeding its vanished predecessor, and if "the days themselves never *stand*, why do you wish to *stand* with them" (*S 108* 5)?

The image of "standing" can recall Plotinus' allusion to Odysseus' homecoming, but the recall only accentuates the difference Augustine sees between *erigere* and *stare*. "When you stand [*stas*] in your God," Augustine tells his hearers, "and delight in the light of His Truth, you will not look for some spatial tract [*locum*] by which to approach Him." For the Psalm's injunction to "approach Him and be enlightened," like Plotinus' Odyssean counsel in *Ennead* 1.6.8, was "spoken to the soul, not to some vehicle; it was spoken of our affections, not of our feet. And when you stand in Him, you will suffer no commotion" (*En 144* 3)

Not only do our "days" keep flying by into the past, the truth is that we live here in a realm of "night" rather than of genuine "day." The "day" which is our "promised reward is *there*" (*ibi*), not here (*En 143* 11). Only in the "morning" which is to come, the Psalmist reminds us, will we "stand before [God] and see" (*En 5* 4). For "beclouded [*caligans*] amid the storms of this *saeculum*, [the Psalmist] knows that he does not see what he wishes to see [*videre*]. . . . But he understands why he does not see, because the night, the darkness merited by sins, has not come to an end." Only in the "morning" shall we "stand before God and see" (*astabo tibi, et videbo*); for then we shall no longer "lie prone" (*non jacebo*), "taking our rest on earth, that is, seeking our happiness in earthly pleasures," and "fastened [*inhaerens*] to earthly realities"— as the beasts are obliged to do (5). This is why the mind of a sinner is ineluctably "beaten back by the Light of Truth" and proves unable to "support the brightness of right understanding. Hence, even those who sometimes see" (*vident*) or, more precisely, "that is, those who understand the Truth [*intelligunt*] . . . do not long abide in that vision" (*non ibi permanent*). But when their sinful "night has passed . . . it will become morning, so that they will not only understand but fasten themselves [*inhaereant*) to the Truth" (6).

It will be a great thing for us eventually to "stand there, among the angels. For he who fell from there did not stand in the Truth; but whoever did not fall stands in the Truth; and he it is that stands who places his joy in the Truth" (*En 121* 3). And what are God's own "years, that do not pass away?" They must be years that "stand"—the years of One Who is ever absolutely the Self-same (*Idipsum*). Better, perhaps, call those "years" a single "day." But in any case, however you choose to think of it, *stat tamen*: God's reality is at an absolute "still-stand." And when we make up part of that "City" that "participates in the Selfsame," we too shall share in His *stabilitas*, "our feet *standing* in the courts of Jerusalem" (6). Then we too shall BE as He IS: for then we shall truly "see" Him (8), that is, see Him "face to face."

CONCLUSION, AND A FRESH BEGINNING

There are, then, numerous occurrences of seafaring and home-coming imagery in Augustine's later writings; they manifest strikingly similar features, and regularly occur in the same "conversion" context as the *De beata vita* prologue represented; they would seem to be patterned on a model drawn from Homer's *Odyssey*. But does all this succeed in "proving" that the model active in the early dialogue still retained its patterning force in the imagination of the man who wrote those later works?

That might be claiming too much for these pages. My real hope in writing them, however, is more modest. It could well be that others may be stimulated by these musings to rummage about in their bank of file-cards labeled "miscellaneous," or, better, "anomalous." Every researcher, especially into Augustine, should guard a number of such entries: when pursued, the anomalous texts often eventually yield a hundredfold of illumination on the deeper workings of the man's mind—and imagination. I have shown here what curiosity, luck, and happenstance have conspired to bring one isolated student of Augustine to see, or at least to think he saw. As a result, I find myself incapable of exorcising the suspicion that, somewhere, someone out there is in possession of the pieces that will fill in the blanks in this fascinating jigsaw puzzle. How much that could yield us in closer understanding of Augustine's thought none of us can confidently say. But even what little we have seen here gives us reason to hope that, if we work together, there must surely be fresh surprises in store.

NOTES

1. *Odyssey* 13.70–124, 187–216. All translations of the *Odyssey* are taken from the literal rendering by Samuel H. Butcher (New York: Macmillan, 1895).

2. See Buffière, *Homère*, pp. 25–31 (on Homer's "inspired wisdom"); pp. 393–582 (on the Neoplatonic tradition of Homer-interpretation); pp. 365–91 (on Ulysses in particular).

3. See his "Mito e poesia nelle *Enneadi* di Plotino," in *Les Sources de Plotin: Dix exposés et discussions*, ed. E. R. Dodds, Entretiens sur l'Antiquité Classique 5 (Vandoeuvres–Geneva: Fondation Hardt, 1960), pp. 243–310; see also Buffière, *Homère*, pp. 420–21 and 531–40.

4. See Porphyry's *Life of Plotinus* 14–15, in Armstrong's translation of *Enneads*, I, 39–45.

5. Ibid. 22–23; Armstrong translation, I, 67, 69.

6. See Buffière, *Homère*, p. 378 (on the lacuna in the *Allegories of Homer* by Heraclitus). Buffière concludes his work with a translation and commentary of Porphyry's *Cave of the Nymphs* (pp. 597–616); cf. also his interpretive remarks on pp. 419–59.

7. See "Symboles," 73.

8. See paragraph 34 of Porphyry's work, translated in Buffière's *Homère*, p. 615: "Homer tells us," Porphyry sums up Numenius' interpretation approvingly, "that we must put away in that cave all exterior goods, . . . reject everything superfluous, turn away from the senses; and then, enter into deliberation with Athena, seated with her at the foot of the olive tree. . . ." Athena, as the Homeric goddess of wisdom, bears comparison with Augustine's *Philosophia*.

9. Translation from Armstrong's *Plotinus*, V, (1984), pp. 287–89; I have inserted several commas for additional clarity.

10. *Plotini Opera* II, edd. Paul Henry, s.j. and Hans-Rudolph Schwyzer (Brussels:, 1959), note to line 21, p. 410. The Mackenna translation (*The Enneads*, 3rd ed. [London: Faber & Faber, 1962]) p. 634, fails to give any reference to Homer, whereas Armstrong, in loc., merely refers the reader back to the Homeric parallels in *Ennead* 1.6.8. Cilento, in the essay referred to at note 3, above, refers twice to this passage from *Ennead* 5.9 (pp. 279 and 287) but fails to see its probable linkage with *Odyssey* 13.

11. See the text (*Conf* 7.20) quoted earlier.

12. The most famous proponent of this view is Pierre Courcelle in his *Recherches*, pp. 157–67. His lead is followed in whole or part by DuRoy (*Trinité*, pp 81–88), Mandouze (*Aventure*, pp. 665–78), and others. For my criticisms of the assumptions behind this view, see *St. Augustine's Platonism* (Villanova, Pa.: Villanova University Press, 1984), pp. 9–15, and notes.

13. Cf. *En 32*, version 2, sermon 2, 10, where the *aquae maris* stand for the "embittered," *amaricantes*; so too *En 65* 11. In *En 76* 18, those same waters symbolize the various nations, *populi*. See again Rondet's "Symbolisme."

14. See Buffière, *Homère*, p. 418.

15. Ibid., pp. 386–91; see also, the references Buffière lists in Index I.

16. Ibid., p. 206. This convergence of evidence would appear to confirm my earlier suggestion (at chap. 5, note 13) that Augustine's metaphorical allusions to "sinking stars" in the Odyssean prologue of *Vita* do not refer to any astrological interests he may or may not have had.

17. Ibid., pp. 386–88.

18. *Life of Plotinus* 22; in Armstrong's translation, *Enneads*, I, 67–69.

19. I have offered an analysis of this image as it occurs in the *Contra Academicos*, in *Art and Christian Intelligence*, pp. 175–77.

20. I have argued for this proposition in *Early* Theory pp. 93–94, and (in answer to the contestations of Fr. Goulven Madec) in "*Confessions* VII, ix, 13–xxi, 37," REA, 19 (1973), 87–100. See also *St. Augustine's Platonism*, pp. 35–36n24.

21. See *St. Augustine's Platonism*, pp. 5–17 and notes.

22. M.-F. Berrouard, in *Homélies sur l'Evangile de saint Jean*, Bibliothèque Augustinienne 71 (Paris: Desclée de Brouwer, 1969), p. 189n3, correctly cites *Sermo 32* 11 in this connection: the devil *consentientem tenet, non cogit invitum*.

8

Deliciosae Lassitudines: Languorous Delights

STUMBLING ON THE ODYSSEY IMAGE in one of Augustine's earliest works was a rare bit of luck. But discerning that same image in his later works is a much more delicate task. Even in its pristine form, we have seen it already encrusted with images drawn from sources originally foreign to Homeric or even Neoplatonic preoccupations. That work of encrustation progresses exponentially as Augustine's preaching and writing career advances. We have seen only a few examples from the *Confessions*, but they have already hinted broadly at what we are about to discover: that almost any one of Augustine's leading images can coalesce and fuse with a startling variety of others, and at times fuse with them so thoroughly as to become almost perfectly camouflaged.

It would, once again, be quixotic to think we could always trace the stages in that process of creative assimilation with anything like "scientific" accuracy; if, indeed, any intellectual gem of such purest ray serene has ever been the lot of human researchers to uncover. How does a poet like Homer, and a poetic thinker like Plotinus, "influence" a fellow-poet like Augustine, particularly when their influence triggers resonances from an array of other poets—Isaiah, Jeremiah, Luke, the Psalmist, John the Evangelist, to name but a few of them?

Tracing that process is something like trying to map the contours of some massive undersea mountain-range when the only hints we can glean are from surface observation; we see a trail of islands meandering like an aimless straggle of dots across the sea's face; it strains our imaginations to envisage them as really mountain-peaks, to think of their surface disposition as a pattern resulting from centuries of pressure, tension, thrust, slide, eruptions, who knows what else. We behold an archipelago, the work of that battery of forces, but we have so little direct acquaintance with their actual workings.

A Revealing Image

Occasionally, though, our search may bring us, half by lucky accident, to a single island where those subterranean energies have left a record of their labors that speaks to our minds in terms that seem unmistakable. It may be just such a telltale island that the *Confessions* offers for inspection in Book 10 (53). There Augustine is portraying the artist whose activity is wrongly directed; he depicts such a one as failing to "guard his strength" for God, but "sowing" it instead "into luxurious wearinesses" (*in deliciosas lassitudines*). A striking image, surely. The point Augustine is making is clear enough from the context: the artist should "use" both the beauties of the sense world and the products of his activity in God's service; but why, and how, did he come to express that insight in so arresting a way?[1]

The Aesthetic Context

First off, a closer inspection of the context is in order. In Book 10, Augustine has been examining his present state of soul; he has taken as headings for that examination the triad of sins he found in the First Epistle of St. John (2:16), warning us against pride, concupiscence of the flesh, and the "concupiscence of the eyes" that he denominates as "curiosity." Under the second heading, Augustine has reviewed the delights of the various bodily senses, coming finally to the pleasures of sight.

It will be important to bear in mind that his focus is an aesthetic one: he observes that the eyes "love fair and varied forms, and bright and beautiful colors," and quite especially that "queen of colors," light, which "seasons this world's life for its blind lovers with an alluring and perilous sweetness" (*inlecebrosa ac periculosa dulcedine* (51–52). He contrasts those "blind lovers" with the blinded Tobias who saw God's own Light "with his eyes closed," as did the aging Isaac and Jacob when their bodily eyesight was failing them. One is reminded of the long tradition of allegorizing interpretations which dwelt on Homer's blindness: his inner, higher eye was only the more probing for that want of corporeal sight.[2] But the aesthetic context reminds us once again that Augustine's variations on the "sleep and waking" theme are often connected with Plotinus' injunction, precisely in his treatise "On Beauty," that we must "close" our outward eyes in order to awaken "another," higher kind of vision. That Plotinian allusion

in turn, we saw, may well be a reminiscence of Odysseus' homecoming to Ithaca.

It is thought-provoking in this connection that the truly "blind
lovers" Augustine excoriates are also contrasted with the Ambrose
who knew how to praise the *Deus creator omnium* and "take up
[*assumunt*] [this visible light] in a hymn to You, instead of being
taken over by it [*absumuntur*] in their sleep." The alert reader will
remember that Augustine has just finished recounting how powerfully the Ambrosian hymns had affected him (49–50), and that
he had earlier quoted the first two stanzas of the *Deus creator
omnium* (9.32), including its praise of the God "Who garbs the day
with lovely light / The night with the grace of sleep." That same
hymn will furnish him material for meditation in Book 11 (35ff.).
Notice for the present that the mention of "sleep" as a kind of
"grace" for the weary distantly recalls the sleep of Odysseus being
returned to Ithaca; but the fuller significance of these seemingly
random associations will become clearer as we go on.

Augustine now accentuates the aesthetic focus of his remarks:
he lists all the "various arts and crafts," including the fabrication
of "diverse images, far exceeding all necessary and moderate use."
"Outwardly pursuing what they make," these artists too often
"inwardly abandon their Maker," the divine "Beauty" which is
"above their souls." Him they must take as the norm for the
beauty of what they produce, but they refuse to take Him as the
rightful end toward Whom the "use" of those products ought to
be directed: for He is the highest and deepest object of the soul's
yearning toward beauty (53).

This is the juncture at which Augustine emits the observation
that interests us here: God is "there [*ibi*] and they see Him not."
Had they that vision, it would forestall their "going farther" away
(*longius*) as the Prodigal did, and urge them to "guard their
strength unto You, and not sow it into delightful (or luxurious)
wearinesses" ([*ut*] *fortitudinem ad te custodiant nec eam spargant in
deliciosas lassitudines*). The "more distant" journey we saw originally associated with Odysseus has now become explicitly identified with the Prodigal, but for the moment we shall be wise not
to infer that Odysseus is altogether excluded from Augustine's
deeper imaginative intentions.

"Guarding one's strength unto God": the phrase is taken from
Psalm 58:10. While we keep that in reserve for the moment, what

hints do the *Confessions* give about these mysterious *deliciosae lassitudines*?

AN EARLIER OCCURRENCE

The closest verbal counterpart occurs in Book 2.2. Augustine is recalling the "shadowy loves" of his adolescence; those lusts lured him to wander, like the Prodigal, "farther away from God." "Through my fornications I was tossed about and poured out, I boiled and flowed over": *iactabar et effundebar et diffluebam et ebulliebam. Iactabar*: a curious term in the Prodigal context, for its primary sense conveys the buffetings experienced in a storm at sea!

"Farther and farther," he repeats, "I went from you, into more and more sterile seeds [*semina sterilia*] of sorrows, in proud dejection and restless weariness" (*superba deiectione et inquieta lassitudine*). Here Augustine is talking the language of "concupiscence," but the very next paragraph shows how closely such erotic reflections slide over into aesthetics: he regrets that no one helped him "turn to good use the fleeting beauties of these lowest realities," and seek the joys of God's "embraces" (*amplexus*) (3). Instead, he "boiled over" (*efferbui*) and gave himself up to the "outflow" (*fluxus*) of his passions; so he remained, like the Prodigal, "far in exile from the delights of [God's] house" (4).

ODYSSEUS, SHADOW OF THE PRODIGAL

Confessions 1.28, however, illustrates how the visage of Odysseus can be descried, dimly peering out from behind the Prodigal. That text we have already examined above; the principal point of that examination was, however, to highlight the kinships between Augustine's Prodigal and the Odysseus of Plotinus' *Ennead* 1.6, "On Beauty." Note that for Plotinus, too, aesthetic observations regularly consort with moralizing counsel: the telltale phrase "inconceivable beauty" (a quotation from *Symposium* 218E) recalls the need for transcending "lower" *eros* (represented by Circe and Calypso) by yielding to the "higher."

ADDITIONAL FEATURES OF THIS IMAGE

But there are further elements in the *Confessions* text which merit closer attention. First, Augustine's own context is once again both aesthetic and erotic: he is recounting the charms and frequently immoral attractions of the pagan literature he was forced to study as a boy. Images of "flux" once again dot the page: "Woe, you river [*flumen*] of human custom!" he exclaims; "how long will you roll the sons of Eve into that vast and fearful sea, which even those who clamber aboard the wood [of the Cross] only barely succeed in crossing?" (25). *Odyssey* echoes abound: "O hellish flood, the sons of men are tossed overboard [again, *iactantur*] into you" by being forced to read of Jove's obscenities; "You beat resoundingly against the rocks that line your coasts," urging young students to sail gaily toward spiritual shipwreck (25–26). The image of clinging to the "wood," especially in this context, forcibly recalls the fact that Odysseus was twice obliged to make his way to safety, once on the raft Circe furnished him, another time on a piece of planking from his wrecked vessel. But whether or not Augustine intended us to catch that analogy, this much is clear: the introduction of the Prodigal image in 1.28 has been skillfully prepared by an evocation of a sea-voyager's odyssey! And again, whether the voyager be Homer's Odysseus or Vergil's Aeneas may remain a secondary question; primary is the fact that neither of those two personages is so opposed in Augustine's imagination that he, or they, cannot subtly fuse with the Prodigal.

"I was in love with lower beauties [*inferiora*], and was going (further) into the deep" (*profundum*), Augustine summarizes his personal odyssey, and then recounts the composition of his early work on aesthetics, the *De pulchro et apto* (4.20ff.). Those pages he no longer possesses: they have "wandered away" somewhere or other. But so did Augustine himself, in writing them: the intellectual acuity displayed in doing so availed him not to profit (*usum*) but only to ruin, for—now we switch abruptly into the Prodigal register—"I strove to keep so good a portion of my substance in my own power. I did not 'guard my strength' unto You, but set out away from You to a distant region to squander it among whorish lusts. For what did this good reality profit me, who was not putting it to good use" (*non utenti bene*) (4.30)?

Similarly, the imaged thinking of his Manichee period provokes a comparison with the literary images of "verses, song, and the flights of Medea." And Augustine's summary comes couched in predictable fashion: "I was [like the Prodigal] on *peregrinatio* far from You, barred even from the husks of the swine I was feeding on husks. . . . By what steps was I led down [like Odysseus, or like Aeneas] to the depths of the lower world" (*in profunda inferi*) (3.11).

There are other texts in a similar vein (2.18, 4.31), but they would only accentuate features of the Prodigal/Odysseus image already brought sufficiently into focus. Notice, though, that all the *Confessions* texts so far examined are taken from Books 1 to 7; we must leave the later books to another occasion. But for the present, we have seen enough to hazard a preliminary summary of our findings.

FEATURES OF THE PRODIGAL IMAGE

What did Augustine hope his reader would conclude from this constant oscillation, an oscillation between them that so frequently ends up fusing these several personages into imaginative identity? Keeping in the corner of our mental eye the close analogy Augustine sees between them, let us put in order what Augustine has told us when expressly describing the Prodigal.

1. The Prodigal once dwelt in God's "house," "cleaving" or "adhering" to Him, sharing God's "embraces." His was a "legitimate *connubium*" with the Beauteous Divine Light that, like a manly *virtus*, "fecundated" his mind and "bosom" (*sinus*). In another image, he was "filled," "satiated" with this abundant "bread" of Truth Himself which God alone can be for him. Both images refer to the contemplative happiness that (in extant allegorizations of the Greek myth) Odysseus once enjoyed in the "intelligible paradise" figured by his native Ithaca.

2. He "turned away" from, "deserted," God, "set forth" on *peregrinatio* "away from" Him. But why?

Augustine's most regular explanation comes in terms of pride, *superbia,* or "audacity," *audacia*: he came to desire a certain autonomy, independent from God. This took the form of willing that his "substance," his soul and all its manifold "powers," be given over into his own "control," to deploy simply for the "enjoyment" derived from deploying them: he no longer willed to "use" them for God's service, and in order to return to the "enjoyment" of God. We shall shortly see that Plotinus portrayed the soul in entirely similar terms, as "standing away" from its intelligible superior out of *tolma*, the "audacious" yen to test and delight in the deployment of its powers over the sense-world.

In a relatively fewer number of instances, however, Augustine ascribes the soul's departure to *saturitas*, or, as in one instance we saw, a "proud *saturitas*." The image suggests that the soul had been utterly surfeited, cloyed by the "bread" of Truth that was its food: which, translated, means it became wearied by "too much" of contemplating the same Reality without any variety. Even here, however, the note of pride, *superbia*, is almost always present in some form or another.

Indeed, the larger section of *Confessions*, Book 10, from which our problem-text is drawn, shows Augustine re-affirming what he had said a number of times earlier: that the "root" of all sin is pride. Its partners in his habitual "triadic sin," concupiscence and curiosity, clearly spring from that root. But there may have been a tradition in Platonism ascribing the soul's fall from its contemplative beatitude to something like the *saturitas* to which Augustine alludes, and it could have left traces in the Milanese circle.[3] Significant, too, is the fact that in his *De beata vita* he speaks suggestively of God as unceasingly furnishing us a banquet (*epulas*): it is we who often cease from eating it, "whether through weakness, or *saturitas*, or busy-ness" (*negotio*) (17). The prologue to that dialogue, as we have seen, stresses the importance of pride and vainglory; it is somewhat surprising to find no mention of it here.

3. That turning away from God Augustine describes not only as a proud "insubordination," but also as "fornication away from God" with the panoply of "darksome loves" that go to make up "friendship with this world" of "lower beauties." Again his point is that the soul chooses to make those lower beauties the object of "enjoyment" rather than "using" them to pursue its way of return to God.

It is precisely in terms of this metaphor that Circe and Calypso and the Prodigal's "prostitutes" play a very specific role: they represent the erotic objects of bodily concupiscence that prompt the soul to yield to the flowing "current" of its lusts, to "boil and spill over," to "pour out" its inner "strength" and thus "dissipate" or "squander" its very "substance." It scarcely takes a sinister imagination to read such expressions, along with the associated mentions of "seed" and "fecundation," as unmistakably suggesting the male's experience of coitus. It is not surprising, then, that this "pouring out" results in the "exhausted" feeling of "lassitude"—a lassitude that Augustine can rightly describe as "luxurious" and at the same time "unquiet."

EARLY COMPONENTS OF THE *Confessions* IMAGE

That summary, however, sketches the contours of Augustine's thinking at the time of writing the *Confessions*. It presents the *product* of a gradual development, not the pathways which that development followed. Hence, it cannot claim to get us to the root of his Prodigal/Odysseus image or to tell the whole story of its formation in Augustine's imagination. To ferret out a more complete answer to those connected questions, it would be wise to survey the materials on which Augustine's imagination set to work. To begin with, what Scripture texts figure most regularly in Augustine's embroidery of this image and its settings, and how much illumination do his interpretations of those texts provide to help us understand the mental processes that went into his elaboration of the *deliciosae lassitudines* image?

In addition to the obvious Lucan story of the Prodigal, the text we have seen Augustine appeal to most regularly is verse 10 from Psalm 58, where (as his version read) the Christian soul is made to proclaim: *Fortitudinem meam ad te custodiam*: "I shall guard (keep, preserve) my strength for (unto) You."

We shall shortly see, however, that Psalm 58:10 frequently "calls," in Augustine's mind, to Psalm 72, especially verse 27; but that verse in turn associates with its two neighboring verses. Psalm 72:26–28 read:

> *Defecit cor meum et caro mea, Deus cordis mei; Deus cordis mei et pars mea Deus meus.*
>
> *Ecce qui longe se faciunt a te, peribunt; perdidisti omnem qui fornicatur a te.*
>
> *Mihi autem adhaerere Deo bonum est; ponere in Deo spem meam.*

Adjusting the Vulgate translation to what we have already discovered about Augustine's linguistic habits, this would read:

> My heart and my flesh have become deficient [i.e., lesser in being-quality], God of my heart.
>
> See, those who put themselves far from You shall perish; You have made everyone who fornicates away from You to perish.
>
> But the good for me is to adhere to my God; to place all my hope in God.

THE PHENOMENON OF "RECESSION"

There are, however, texts which play a less obvious role in Augustine's finished orchestration of this image in the *Confessions*, whereas they play a far more conspicuous role during the earlier stages when that image is in process of formation. This tendency for certain texts to lie patent on the surface in one period, and to "go underground" in a later period, I have referred to as the phenomenon of imaginative "recession." One meets with it again and again in tracking the workings of Augustine's imagination. Again, one might be tempted to infer that any such text dwindles in power as it recedes, but such inferences could turn out to be naïve; one must decide the matter by examination of individual cases, but it could well be (so the imagination works) that a recessive text is exerting as much as or even more power from its subterranean position than when it shows clearly on the surface. In cases like that, any interpretation of Augustine's imaged language that ignores even the slightest trace of a recessive text could fail importantly at capturing his intention. It should also be borne in mind that Augustine's "intention" may, in certain instances, be an interweaving complex of differing intentions, not always mutually reconcilable, since they may emerge from different periods of development, recorded at different levels of consciousness. But examination of a concrete instance may illustrate these rather abstract "principles" more clearly than further theoretical discussion would.

ECCLESIASTICUS 10:9–15

The first text that comes to mind as an example of "recession" is from Ecclesiasticus 10:9–15; I give the crucial phrases in the selective way Augustine frequently quotes them:

> *Quid superbit terra et cinis?* (9) . . . *quoniam in vita sua projecit intima sua* (10). . . . *Initium superbiae hominis apostatare a Deo* (14). . . . *Initium omnis peccati superbia* (15).

Translating as Augustine seems to have understood the text:

> Why does earth and ashes pride itself? . . . For in its lifetime it has spewed forth its insides. . . . The beginning of pride is man's standing away from God. . . . Pride is the beginning of all sin.

Curiously enough, when quoting this series of expressions, Augustine more often elides that peculiarly "Augustinian" touch from verse 15: "Because his heart has departed from Him Who made him." An odd instance of recession, surely; but he uses a number of analogous expressions concerning the "heart" in connection with the Prodigal story; this should warn us that the unquoted portion may still be exercising a subterranean influence. For the fact is that Augustine does equate the heart's turning from God with both pride and "fornication" from Him, and the effect of that turn is regularly the same: man, or the soul, ends up "spewing forth his insides," his inner riches, forces, or powers. We are here, obviously, in the neighborhood of those erotic images of "boiling," "spilling over," and "pouring out" that caught our attention earlier. Could Ecclesiasticus have accounted in some more ultimate way for Augustine's penchant for such imagery?

This seems a track worth pursuing. But pursuing it requires a generous measure of patience. For Augustine's exegesis follows a meandering course that leads him into apparent byways as he ponders what Scripture means by each of the key terms used, or merely suggested, by the Ecclesiasticus text. How, for instance, are we to understand "earth," and "lifetime"? How does the image of "spewing forth" relate to "pride" as the "inflation" talked about in other loci, and how do both of those relate to the images associated with "fornication," and so on? The series of texts on the following pages may seem to branch off into so many byways as to lead exactly nowhere; but that is the disconcerting way the imagination sometimes works, and Augustine's lively imagination more disconcertingly than most!

To begin, then: his first known citations of this section of Ecclesiasticus occur in his *De Genesi contra Manichaeos* 2.6 and *De musica* 6.40. Both these citations occur in the midst of what I have elsewhere tried to show were descriptions of the soul's "fall" from Eternity into Time, from peaceful contemplation into the "disquiet" and "labors" of action in the temporal world.[4] My associated claim was that this use of Ecclesiasticus could best be understood as connected, in Augustine's mind, with *Ennead* 3.7.11, where Plotinus describes the soul's fall from contemplative Eternity into temporal activity, and employs strikingly similar imagery: if Time could speak and tell of its origin it would say that it had originally been

> at rest . . . with eternity in real being; it was not yet time, but itself, too, kept quiet in that. But since there was a restlessly active nature which wanted to control itself and be on its own, and chose to seek for more than its present state, this moved, and time moved with it; and so, always moving on to the "next" and the "after,"

and what is not the same, but one thing after another, we made a long stretch of our journey and constructed time as the image of eternity.

For because the soul had an unquiet power, which wanted to keep on transferring what it saw there [in the Intelligible world] to something else, it did not want the whole to be present to it all together; and as from a quiet seed the formative principle, unfolding itself, advances, as it thinks, to largeness, but does away with the largeness by division, and instead of keeping its unity in itself, squanders it outside itself and so goes forward to a weaker extension; in the same way the Soul . . . first put itself into time. . . .[5]

I have elsewhere tried to show that this description, which Augustine would almost certainly have read in the light of a kindred description of the soul's fall in *Ennead* 5.1.1, exhibits a convincing parallel "pattern" (or "schéma spirituel") with the two Augustinian passages in which the Ecclesiasticus text first appears.[6] Scholars are agreed that *Ennead* 5.1 figured among Augustine's earliest readings in Plotinus; here is how it begins:

What is it, then, which has made the souls forget their father, God, and be ignorant of themselves and him, even though they are parts which come from his higher world and altogether belong to it?

The beginning of evil for them was audacity [*tolma*], and coming to birth [*genesis*], and the first otherness and the wishing to belong to themselves. Since they were clearly delighted with their own independence, and made great use of self-movement, running the opposite course and getting away as far as possible, they were ignorant even that they themselves came from that world; just as children who are immediately torn from their parents and brought up far away do not know who they themselves or their parents are.[7]

Notice in these two texts the number of elements that both call to one another and closely correspond to Augustine's interpretation of the Prodigal story: the soul originally enjoyed the "quiet" of eternal contemplation, but now experiences "disquiet" or "unrest" in the world of time; it possessed the All but still chose to seek for "more." The reason may have been *saturitas*, or *tolma* (audacity), or the "busy-ness" (*negotium*) Augustine archly mentions in the *De beata vita*, or (more likely) some combination of these. In any event, the soul no longer wanted the All to be present to it all together; it had in it a restlessness that wanted to be on its own and under its own control; it made a long "journey," "forgot" its "father" and "home" and very self, and, in the most striking similarity of all, like a "seed" unfolding its potentialities, ended by "squandering" its "interior" powers to the "outside."

Assume for the moment, merely as an hypothesis to be tested and not yet a thesis to be accepted, that there is some plausibility in connecting Augustine's invocation of the Ecclesiasticus text with his memories of these kindred descriptions of the soul's fall into "time" or "genesis." Does his subsequent use of Ecclesiasticus counterverify or confirm that hypothesis? Or, in terms that bear more precisely on our present investigation, we are faced with the fact that Augustine describes the activities of the ill-motivated artist as "sowing" his inner "strength" into *lassitudines* which he then describes as "luxurious," on the one hand, and "unquiet," on the other. I shall take it that the reader finds this as much a psychological puzzle as I once did. I shall take it also that the reader agrees that these twin expressions must have been the product of a subterranean work of Augustine's imagination, but that we can come in *some* measure to a satisfying understanding of that imaginative process.

A Working Hypothesis

My hypothesis, then, is this: assume that the centrally important Scriptural inspiration for this image was the description of the "proud" man (or: soul) spewing forth his insides; assume also that Augustine's imagination had forged, early on, a connection between that text and Plotinus' twin descriptions of the soul squandering its interior riches in a fall from eternity into time: will this assumption help us arrive at the "satisfying understanding" we are looking for?

Ennead 6.9.9

Before proceeding to test that hypothesis, though, let me refer to one more text from Plotinus which, I am now persuaded, contributed importantly to the imaginative synthesis Augustine is about to forge. Others have suggested that it very probably figured among his early Neoplatonic readings;[8] the pages that follow may serve to confirm their conjecture. I give the essentials of Plotinus' image.

Plotinus compares the soul to the noble daughter of a noble father, indeed, a daughter sprung from the divinity Himself. Originally, she clung to her divine progenitor with the love, the higher Aphrodite of Plato's *Symposium*, which is connatural with her very being. But now she has come to be born into a human life, having been seduced by the deceptive allurements of this lower world; she has turned harlot, exchanged the higher for the baser, mortal Aphrodite, deserted her father, and fallen.

But here, our love goes out to mere mimic-realities, not the good our soul truly seeks; that authentic good is not "here" but "there" and only "there"—not to be clasped in bodily embrace, but genuinely possessed in the truest fashion possible. So it can happen that one day our soul comes to detest her shameful condition, strips herself of all earthly incrustations, searches for her father, and in Him once again finds peace and rest. And Plotinus sums up with a lapidary phrase: "Anyone who has seen knows what I have in mind."[9]

Da amantem et sentit quod dico: "Show me a lover and he will understand what I am talking about." That celebrated phrase from Augustine's sermons on St. John's Gospel (*InJo 26* 4) is often cited as one of his most characteristic coinages. It almost seems a desecration to suggest that it may have been "lifted" from *Ennead* 6.9. Nearly as famous is that paradoxical observation from *Confessions* 11.17: "What do we talk about more familiarly and knowingly than time? . . . What, then, is time? If no one asks me, I know; but if someone asks and I want to explain it to him, I do not know." Here, too, Plotinus may have anticipated him; speaking of eternity and time, he observes wryly that "we think we have a clear and distinct experience of them, as we are always speaking of them and using their names on every occasion. But when we try to concentrate on them . . . our thought runs into difficulties. . . . We think it sufficient, . . . when we are asked, to state the opinions of the ancients, and so be freed from the need of further research about them." That paradoxical observation occurs in the opening paragraph of the same treatise quoted at length above, *Ennead* 3.7. These must seem very slender indications that Augustine owed a debt to both those treatises; but perhaps those fragile clues will receive stouter corroboration as we attempt to map the pathways Augustine's imagination followed in gleaning the disparate materials which went into forging that striking image: *deliciosae lassitudines*.

THE ELABORATION OF AN IMAGE

In this instance, as in so many others, the richest resource for exploring the workings of Augustine's imagination proves to be his preached works. Indeed, the trouble is that the wealth one finds there turns out to be a poverty of riches: Augustine returns to variants on this image time after time, but with a liberty of interpretation that sometimes appears disconcertingly arbitrary, even whimsical. The reader should be warned; in the next score of pages, it will seem at times that we are hacking our way through a jungle of tangled undergrowth. Only at the end does some semblance of a pattern emerge.

Turning to the preached works, then, and following their chronology as well as our information permits, we soon find that *Sermo 351* 4, preached in 391, already contains an allusion to our Ecclesiasticus text; it is part of Augustine's early Scriptural armory, therefore, but it is not yet given any of the elaborate development it will later receive.

THE "STRENGTH" MOTIF

Enarratio 17, however, despite its terseness, announces a motif that will later figure in the process of imaginative association that concerns us. Augustine's theme is "strength": the *fortitudo* the artist will eventually "sow" outward. It is through God, our *virtus*, that Christ and the Christian are "strong," Augustine says: He is our *firmamentum* and protector, because we do not "presume" on ourselves, by "raising against [Him] the horn of pride" (2–3). Some paragraphs later (43), the Psalmist refers to sinners as so much "dust," and Augustine comments that "exalted and inflated with pride [*elati atque inflati superbia*] . . . [they are] borne away from the solidity and stability of the earth." *Elati, inflati, soliditas,* these were the same imaged terms we saw Augustine use to picture "pride" in the *De beata vita,* but they also have a rich future before them.

THE "FORNICATION" THEME

Sermo 216, which also dates from 391, comments on another motif of interest: fornication. But Augustine is not using that term in its usual sense; he applies it, rather, to that "first fornication, and ultimate avarice," the "slavery to idols" to which Paul refers as both "avarice" and "fornication." Fornication then consists, Augustine goes on, not only in pleasures of the body, but also in "outflow of the soul" (*animae fluxu*). Immediately Augustine gives his Scriptural warrant for that interpretation: does not Psalm 72 warn us that God "causes everyone to be lost who fornicates away" from Him by failing to heed the injunction that "It is good for me to adhere to God"? Psalm 72, therefore, has been brought quite early into play, and the "soul's" fornication is as much an "outflow" in its way as the body's is!

Since *Sermo 9* treats of the same theme, it calls for treatment here despite the fact that it is undated. We are to adore the "One God," Scripture tells us, but the sinner against this commandment (note the one-and-many theme) wants to "dismiss the one God Who is like the legitimate husband of the soul, and fornicate through many demons." (That allegiance to demons can take the form of consulting astrologers, fortune-tellers, and the like.) This type of "spiritual" fornication becomes adultery, however, if the sinner persists in claiming membership in the Church, thus "remaining in the husband's house" despite being unfaithful to Him (3).

Sermo 213 (from sometime earlier than 410) offers a variant on the same theme: Christ found the Church, which is now His bride, but found her a prostitute and made her a virgin. Why *meretrix*? "Because she fornicated after idols and demons." In this way "all were guilty of fornication of the heart; few may be guilty of it in the flesh, but all are guilty of it in the heart" (7).

"INFLATION," "SWELLING," *Tumor*, AND "TUMESCENCE"

Now for a related theme: in his treatment of the Sermon on the Mount, published in 393/394, Augustine describes the "proud" and "audacious" as "inflated, distended as though with wind"; this he connects with Paul's warning (1 Cor 8:1) that "knowledge inflates" whereas charity builds up. He then quotes the single verse from Ecclesiasticus designating "pride" as the beginning of all sin; we fully expect him to connect inflation and distention with "bursting" and "spewing forth," but neither here (3) nor in a subsequent citation of the same text (32) does he pursue the comparison to that point.

In *Sermo 353*, however (from 391–396), we can observe a subtle development on the inflation theme. Pride is full of paradox: like the "fallacious bigness [in the sense of swollenness] of those who are sick," it "throws down by lifting up, empties by inflating, dissipates by distending" (1). We are a first step on the way toward that "pouring out" imagery later used of the Prodigal, but Augustine makes no explicit connection here with the same imagery from the Ecclesiasticus text. But the connection with sickness needs bearing in mind.

Sermo 380, for which we have no certain date, dilates on the same theme: Christ came to us as humble, in order that man might not think himself great by "swelling up" (*tumescendo*) rather than by "growing up" (*grandescendo*). For that is what pride is: a (diseased) "swelling" (*tumor*), not true grandeur. And so, the humility of Christ the *medicus* was the very "medicine" He brought to heal that "tumor of the human race" (2). Inflation, the diseased kind of inflation suggested by *tumor*, then that ambivalent term "tumescence"—here is a lead toward the Prodigal's specific way of "pouring himself out" among prostitutes, but Augustine fails to bring it to explicit articulation. To what extent, though, was that association nagging at his subconscious? Perhaps the evidence for that will surface with time.

The thought, though, was dear to Augustine: he develops it in another undated work, *Sermo 123*. Christ's humility was "medicine" for man's *tumor*, for "man would not have perished (gotten lost) if he had not swelled up with pride" (*nisi superbia tumuisset*). For Ecclesiasticus tells us that pride is the beginning of all sin (1).

That text makes its next appearance in the incomplete work on Genesis Augustine wrote in 393. *Quid superbit terra et cinis*, Ecclesiasticus had exclaimed. How does this cohere with what Genesis means by *terra*, "earth"? For there it means the visible portion of creation as opposed to the invisible portion, called "heaven." "But the soul, also, which is invisible, is called 'earth' "—by the author of Ecclesiasticus—"when it swells out [*tumesceret*] with love of visible realities and is exalted by obtaining them" (9).

Sermo 97 (again, undated) extends the same theme somewhat by comparing humans to the devil. For it was to man that those words were directed, "Why does earth and ashes pride itself?". "The devil is proud," Augustine exclaims, "but he is not earth and ashes," but an "immortal spirit." But (there is a faintly sardonic note in this) "You are mortals"—hence, in that respect inferior to the devil—and yet "like the devil you are proud!" (2).

"DISSIPATION," "OUTFLOW," "SQUANDERING"

Sermo 2 11 from the Caillau collection dates from around the year 400. We have already examined its interpretation of the Prodigal parable, but it is worth reinspecting briefly for the theme that more precisely concerns us here. For Augustine interprets the Prodigal's "dissipating" his substance—his "mind, intellect, memory, ingenuity"—as *erogans, et non adquirens: expendens quod habebat*. He "paid it out," "expended" it; but how? *In luxuriis, in idolis, in omnibus cupiditatibus pravis, quas meretrices Veritas appellavit*: the word of Truth uses the term "prostitutes" to signify "licentious immoralities" and "all manner of base cupidities" (no surprise there), but the term refers to the worship of "idols" as well! Augustine, therefore, "sees" the worship of idols as somehow a spending, a squandering of those God-given gifts constituting our "substance."

ABANDONING CONTEMPLATION FOR ACTION

Letter 55, written to Januarius in 400/401, uses the Ecclesiasticus text to connect the theme of pursuing "exterior" realities with falling from contemplation into action, thus passing from an "enlightened" to a "darkened" condition. Augustine is commenting on the phrase where Ecclesiasticus says that "the fool changes like the moon." This refers to Adam, he writes confidently, "in whom all have sinned": *in quo omnes peccaverunt*, as Romans 5:12 assures us. "For the human soul, withdrawing from the Sun of justice, that is, from that interior contemplation of unchangeable Truth, re-directs all its forces to outside realities" (*omnes vires suas in externa convertit*), and so its interior and higher powers become more and more "darkened over." Those powers become enlightened once again when the soul "begins to go back" to that Sun, "withdraws its attention in some manner from earthly realities" and "dies to this *saeculum*." For, he goes on to explain, the soul is "changed for the worse by going forth toward exterior realities, and 'in its lifetime, spewing forth its insides' " (8–9).

"FLUX" AND "FLOWING"

Sermo 25 from the Mai collection (preached sometime between 393 and 405) is more than revealing on what the images of "flux" and "flowing outward" suggest to Augustine. He is commenting the healing of that poor woman with the flow of blood: a *morbus detestabilis*, the preacher tells his flock, yet while everyone holds in horror the bodily counterpart of that disease, what should we think when it happens to the "heart"? His meaning becomes clear in the next sentence: "I know not how, but the perversity of the indwelling soul that is turned toward its [bodily] dwelling [makes it] withdraw from itself. . . . The flow of blood as it affects the soul is *luxuria* . . . and the luxurious [immoral, licentious] are likened to a flow of blood." For while misers, on the one hand, "labor" in getting, the luxurious labor in spending, "paying out" (*erogando*). No matter, though, for either vice can kill (*utrumque occidit*) (2). *Erogare* was a verb we saw frequently describing the activities whereby the Prodigal ended up emptied, exhausted, and weary; this connection with "flux" and sexual immorality will be worth remembering.

"Prostitutes" and "Fornication"

Sermo 10 2, from the year 411, accords with the theme we have just seen: it tells us that both Church and Synagogue were "prostitutes" (*meretrices*) before Christ effected their conversion: "for every soul which delights in earthly filth, having deserted the Eternity of Truth, fornicates away from God." That includes the Jews; it also includes the Gentiles whose fornication went as far as worshiping idols. Here we have an interesting mélange: fornication is being used in the "spiritual" sense again, but while it can still refer to idolatry, it also conveys the more general notion of deserting God to take delight in "earthly" realities. When God is designated as Eternal Truth, however, there is a none too subtle suggestion that He is being viewed as object of the soul's original contemplative "delight": even without the letter to Januarius, we would be tempted to infer that the soul's "prostitution" consisted in abandoning that life of contemplation.

We have already touched on *Sermo 177* 9 (from 410/412) in connection with the Prodigal; we saw that Augustine there depicted God as berating the soul "fornicating away from Him" through the words of an unnamed "prophet" whom he quotes as speaking in God's name: "You thought that, if you departed from me [*discederes*], you would have something more ample." Where he found this quotation remains a mystery both to me and (to judge from their silence) to the editors of his works. It does not seem to come from Scripture, but its thought content is strikingly parallel to Plotinus' presentation of the soul's fall from Eternity into time. Could it be that Augustine is in fact drawing on a reminiscence from *Ennead* 3.7, and mistakenly attributing it to a Scriptural source instead? If so, the lapse is a significant one!

Sermo 162 remains undated, but it shows Augustine forced to defend his notion of "spiritual" fornication. He is confronted with Paul's distinction (1 Cor 6:18) whereby "fornication" (in the usual sense) is termed sinning *in corpus proprium* ("against one's own body") as opposed (apparently) to other sins which are *extra corpus*, "outside the body." Augustine draws a distinction of his own between "fornication" in the "special sense"—in which Paul is using the term—and in the more "general sense" spoken of in the familiar phrase from Psalm 72:27, that God makes to "perish" all those who "put themselves far" from Him, and so "fornicate away" from Him. This, as we saw, was the Psalm which encouraged Augustine as early as 391 to elaborate his notion of "spiritual" fornication; but we have also seen that he regularly reads its language as echoing (and interpreting) that of the Prodigal story.

His discussion here tries to argue, first, that "special" fornication is one case included in the wider classification of "general," or spiritual, fornication; the latter he explains in his usual way as failing or refusing to "adhere to God," by "adhering to the world" instead. He bolsters the legitimacy of this usage by appeal to the Epistles of Sts. John and James, and summarizes in a "definition" couched in their language: "one who loves the world cannot love God, and one who chooses to be a friend of the world is an enemy of God."

But now he replies to a sterner challenge contained in Paul's distinction: bravely he sets himself to prove that one must not take Paul's phrase as implying that other sins besides fornication in the special sense are *extra corpus*, in the sense of *not* being *in proprium corpus*, "against one's own body." This brings him to argue that "general" fornication is not uniquely "spiritual" after all; it, too, must be viewed as a sin *in proprium corpus*. For, he reasons, the *mundanus homo*, the "worldly man" who "adheres" to the world, "puts himself far from God, fornicating away from God Himself," in the general sense of the term; that much is clear from Psalm 72. But we must bear in mind that "the human spirit [*animus*] is attracted and distracted [*trahitur atque distrahitur*] by carnal sense and prudence, whatever be the temporal and carnal realities [it fixes on] through bodily concupiscence." Thus, it ends up "serving the creature rather than the Creator" in the sense that by "loving and desiring all temporal realities" (*omnia temporalia*) it becomes "given over and subject to carnal concupiscence for [that temporal] universe" (*universae concupiscentiae carnali deditus et subdi-*

tus factus). This is why we can say that the human spirit becomes "as though entirely" (*tanquam totus*)—both body and soul—"the servant of the creature and alienated from the Creator Himself, through that beginning of all sin which is pride; and the 'beginning of pride,' as it is written, 'is the standing away from God.' "

It is this "general" fornication, then, that St. John speaks of in his First Epistle, where he warns us against "loving the world" by that triad of sins, " 'concupiscence of the flesh, concupiscence of the eyes, and secular ambition.' " But this "love of the world" is as truly, even if not so intensely, a sin against one's body as fornication in the special sense is (3–4).

But why did this phrase from St. Paul cause Augustine so much concern? The reason was, I suggest, that Paul's distinction seemed to threaten the legitimacy of a usage to which Augustine had become strongly attached: if understood at face value, Paul's text would seem to be setting "fornication" in the usual sense in such opposition to other sins that it would invalidate Augustine's penchant for "generally" categorizing the soul's love of "temporal" and this-worldly realities as fornication "away from God." So, he goes to some pains to buttress his understanding of Psalm 72:27 by adducing two additional texts from Sts. John and James, and then sets out his argument that even the sins Paul was calling *extra corpus* were, on closer inspection, sins *in proprium corpus*.

The entire drift of his argument, then, its result if not its express purpose, is to restore the intimate kinship he has been supposing between general and special fornication, a kinship that Paul's distinction put at risk. That way he hopes to succeed in legitimizing his own interpretation of the soul's original "turn away" to temporal and this-worldly realities as "fornication away from God." Then, in a final flourish, he brings to bear his standard "triad" of sins by quoting the crucial text from St. John's First Epistle: his understanding of sin as triadic, he is telling us, is also legitimate, since each member of the triad qualifies as "fornication" both in the "general" sense and in the Pauline sense of being "sins against one's own body."

The argument is a tormented one; that may simply underline how important the notion of general, spiritual fornication still seemed to him. But it is interesting to note that in *Retractationes* 1.19.6, written years later, Augustine will find it necessary to abandon this position. Yet, if we can trust its dating, *Sermo 10*, from A.D. 411, indicates that he was still comfortable with it while writing his *Confessions*. That presumption will receive more solid confirmation further on.

"Inner" and "Outer," "Light" and "Darkness"

Letter 140, paragraph 61, returns to a theme we have seen before. Augustine advises Honoratus that the "poor will have their fill" and their "hearts will live" because of the Light that is "within," not by possession of "outward" realities, which are no more than "darkness." It is charity that will make them alive, not pride, for (he cites Ecclesiasticus) "the beginning of all sin is pride." This was the vice by which the devil "progressed irrevocably into exterior realities, and out of envy toward man threw him down [*dejecit*] by persuading him to [perpetrate] something similar." This is why Ecclesiasticus tells us that the proud "spewed forth his insides during his lifetime."

"Private" and "Proper" *vs.* "Common"

What does this "lifetime" mean? Augustine answers: *In vita sua, tamquam in propria sua, et quasi privata, qua delectatur omnis superbia.* His meaning seems to be that the soul's sin of pride took the form of choosing to live a "lifetime" of its "very own" (*propria*), a "private" life. Does he mean to contrast such a life with some sort of life the pre-fallen soul would have enjoyed in "common" with other souls in the intelligible realm? If so, the fall results in the soul's taking hold of this or that particular body to govern as its very own, hence forfeiting its share of that common governance of the entire sensible world it previously enjoyed. Augustine's text as it stands is somewhat too condensed to propose this interpretation with certainty, at least at this point in our investigation; suffice it to say that this interpretation would be perfectly consonant with Plotinus' view of the matter! In any event, this letter is usually dated as of 411/412.[10]

The "Labors" of This Mortal Life

We have already seen much of *Enarratio 138* in relation to the Prodigal theme; it was preached in the year 412. Notice, though, how importantly the *labor* motif figures. It is his "toil" (or struggles, hardships, distress?) that prompts the Prodigal to think back on his father (5); "You permitted me," Augustine prays in his place, "to go my ways *in labore*, so that if I chose not to *laborare*, I might go back into Your ways" (6). "Let the labor of this mortal life suffice for us," he urges his hearers, the *labor* for which God fashioned us (*finxerit*) in our mother's womb, fashioned us with an "avenging hand that weighs down the proud" (*vindicem manum, gravantem superbum*) (7).

We have already noted above (pp. 159–60) how the words of the Psalmist now bring Augustine to interpret the phrase "all my most recent and ancient" deeds as his sins. His most "ancient sin," he goes on to explain, occurred "when we [i.e. humanity] fell" (*lapsi sumus*). It thus became the fountainhead (*exordia*) of his (and evidently our) more recent sins. That "fall" carried with it a "punishment," which Augustine identifies with God's action when, with "avenging hand" He fashioned us in our mother's womb. This, then, is how "we arrived into this laborious and dangerous mortality." The laboriousness of this mortal life is, therefore, punishment for a common "fall" which occurred before God fashioned us in our mother's womb. "So did [God] cast down the exalted" sinner (*elatum*), "so that He might [find him] humble [and] raise him up" (7).

The "Ease" and "Rest" of the Contemplative Life

But, Augustine goes on, our *labor* is always still before us; it contrasts with the "ease" (*facilitas*) we once experienced in contemplating the *facilis* countenance of God (9). But the "rest" (*requies*) we long for cannot be ours until we cross this "sea," and arrive at the "end of the *saeculum*," the end of time (10). After these *labores* we shall possess that unfailing Light (16); but not so sinners, since they are swollen with pride (*intumescunt*), and "inflated with the [empty] name of justice" (26).

Once again, the Ecclesiasticus citation is embedded in a context describing us as fallen from the "rest" and "ease" of contemplation into the "labors" of the "sea," the temporal *saeculum*. That note of *labor* and *labores* may represent Augustine's way of painting the "secular" soul's life of action in somber colors; but it nonetheless coheres more naturally with the Odysseus than with the Prodigal image; it does not once, for example, enter into that comprehensive interpretation of the Prodigal which Augustine presented in his work on "Gospel questions." Furthermore, the image of the "sea" as scene of these "labors" makes it all the more likely that we have here a fusion of Prodigal and Odysseus images.

Enarratio 38, from 413/414, again stresses the theme of "labor," again connecting it with temporality and the *saeculum*. Augustine is portraying our life in Paul's metaphor of the toilsome footrace; "laboring here," we look forward to the homeland *mansio* where running will be at an end. But meanwhile, like Paul, let us not be proud. There is still much "wanting to us"; and the "inflation and swelling [*inflatio et tumor*] of the proud only imitates greatness: there is no health to it" (*non habet sanitatem*) (8).

This sets Augustine to meditating the evils of our life in time, the life proper to the "old man," the Adam in each of us, oriented (as God's curse in Genesis puts it) toward "sin, mortality, to times that fly by, to groaning, labor, and sweat" (9). Or, as Sirach expresses it, as long as we are "here, in this *saeculum*," all is vanity for the man who "labors" under the sun (10).

The fusion with the Pauline footrace is a new touch; but the mélange of various elements shows Augustine's imagination working at fever pitch. We are reminded of the terminal *mansio*, the "sick" inflation of pride, Adam's curse as ours to bear as well; then he forges the connection between sin, mortality, labor, and the temporal *saeculum*; finally, he adds that colorful touch, invoking the *Omnia* image, that all this transpires "under the sun."

THE "FALL" THROUGH PRIDE

Enarratio 35 18 (perhaps from 411, in any case from before A.D. 415) explains what the Psalmist must have meant by the *pes superbiae*, the "foot of pride": it is "on" this foot that sinners "fell" (*ceciderunt*), that is, "deserted God and departed." Augustine uses similar language of the Prodigal, as we have seen; he continues in that vein by saying that the proud man's "foot" is to be understood as his soul's "affection" (*affectum*). The serpent of Eden keeps watch on you, he tells his auditors, to see when the "foot of pride" comes your way, to see when you are "falling, so that he may throw you down" (*quando labaris, ut dejiciat*). Here Augustine is experimenting with a quite special variation on his *dimittere* theme (both Paul's *tradidit eos* and the *dimisit eos* of Genesis are cited in this same paragraph): it would appear that the devil can "throw down" only the soul that is already "falling," and falling through pride. For, he cites our text again, "the beginning of all sin is pride," the sin which brought on the devil's "fall" and "expulsion" from paradise, on the one hand, and Adam's fall and "dismissal," on the other.

PELAGIANISM AND GOD AS OUR "STRENGTH"

A similar use of Prodigal language but without express mention of the Prodigal occurs in *Enarratio 58*. This *Enarratio*, comprising two sermons, dates from the year 413; the Pelagian controversy is in full cry; it has developed to such a point that Augustine does something he had long deferred: he mentions his adversary by name (Sermon 1, 19). He gives a frankly anti-Pelagian interpretation of that favorite text of his, Psalm 58:10: "I shall guard my strength unto You." His new interpretation of that text is made clear from its opposite: "guarding one's strength unto God" means not "presuming on oneself," that is, not forgetting that the soul's "light" and "forces" (*vires*), all its "wisdom" and "strength," are not *ex se*, but derive from that "fountain" of both light and strength that is the "region of unchangeable Truth; the soul withdrawing from this is darkened over, but if it come nearer, it is enlightened." It is, then, God Who (as Psalm 26:10 puts it) "takes us up" (*suscipit*), finds us lying prone in sins, and "lifts us up" (*assumit*) so that we can stand "erect": His "strength" must be ours if we are to be strong at all (Sermon 1, 18).

The opening paragraph of Sermon 2 turns back to the same verse to sum up what was explained about it. Augustine's summary concludes:

> "I shall guard my strength unto You," because whatever we are able to do, unless we keep it with Him and unto Him [*apud illum et ad illum servemus*], we lose it by withdrawing [*recedendo*]. Our mind [*mens*] ought always be watchful lest it withdraw from Him; but even if it [has withdrawn and] was far away, [it must strive to] come closer, nearer and nearer, not [in the familiar tag from *Ennead* 1.6.8] by walking on foot, or by riding on vehicles, not with the swiftness of animals or the spreading of wings, but through purity of affections and uprightness of moral behavior.

Here we have a clear case of image-recession: the Prodigal is never mentioned, but his story is obviously uppermost in Augustine's mind. But just as significant is the fact that Augustine has been able to appeal to one of his earliest intuitions, encouraged by Plotinus, in battling this new heresy: for Pelagius' claim that our souls were naturally equipped for virtuous action was all too reminiscent of the soul's original "proud" and "audacious" will to be "on its own," trusting and even exulting in its "own power."

PRIDE, THE FIRST AND LAST SIN

The first version of *Enarratio 18* (which may have been composed as early as 392, but could also have been the product of rewriting in the years 414/415) asks God to pardon his "servant." This prayer does not extend, Augustine makes clear, to the "proud" man, the man who "wishes to be in his own power." This is the "great sin," for (as Ecclesiasticus tells us) there can be no greater sin than to "stand away from God, which is the beginning of man's pride. . . . This is the last sin of which those going back to God [*redeuntibus*] [are cleansed], as it was the first sin for those who withdrew from Him" (14). The notion that pride is both first sin and last was already present in the prologue to the *De beata vita*, but here we see Augustine giving it more formal expression.

The second version of the same *Enarratio*, which dates more surely from 414/415, expands somewhat on the same themes. Pride was the sin that made the angel into devil; it is the "head and cause of all sins," as Ecclesiasticus tells us. Pride is the beginning of all sins, and the beginning of pride is man's standing away from God. That *apostasia* from God, he goes on to warn, was committed by the "soul going into darkness, and badly using its freedom of choice, so that other sins followed after [that one]."

Now the Prodigal motif, announced only allusively in the earlier version's reference to being in one's own "power," is given fuller development: "Thus [the soul] squandered its substance, living riotously among prostitutes, and through want became a feeder of pigs, that soul which formerly had been companion of the angels." It was because of this pride that the Son of God humbled Himself and came to us as "medicine" for that "swelling" (*tumor*) (15).

ADAM, PRODIGAL, AND WE

Enarratio 70, sermon 2, 6 begins a lengthy meditation on Adam's choosing to imitate God "perversely": and "Adam," Augustine tells us roundly, "is every man" (*et Adam omnis homo*).[11] This brings Augustine to illustrate his theme by allusion to the "younger son," who, he now says, "proudly departed from [God] out of satiety [*saturitate*], but was corrected by hunger." Let him who would be genuinely "like God" do so by "guarding his strength unto Him," as Psalm 58:10 puts it, and "adhering to

God" as Psalm 72:28 advises. Why, then, did man eat of the forbidden fruit? Out of disobedience, Augustine answers. "He wanted to use his own power" and "be like God, with no one else having sway over him" (7). The dominant theme in the context is man's proud disobedience in violating God's command; the deepest motivation for that disobedience is the will to exercise one's powers independently of God; but this only makes it more intriguing that Augustine begins by connecting that form of pride with the seemingly unrelated notion of *saturitas*!

LIGHT AND STRENGTH

Enarratio 104 3, dating from 414/416 gives a slightly different twist to Psalm 58:10: guarding one's strength unto God consists in "coming to Him" in order to be "enlightened" (Ps 33:5), lest "out of blindness we fail to see what we ought to do, or out of weakness fail to do what we see should be done." But that "enlightenment" has ultimately to do with the face-to-face vision of God we must seek in faith and hope, a vision that, Augustine assures us, we shall endlessly enjoy *sine fastidio*—without any fear, one is prompted to gloss, of that *saturitas* to which we once proudly surrendered.

PRIDE, "INFLATION," AND THE "MANY"

Sermo 4 33 (410/419) returns to the inflation theme: the Donatists have "swelled up with the disease of pride," which shows they have no charity, for "charity," Paul assures us, "is not inflated." This prompts Augustine to make an ingenious application of the one-*vs.*-many theme: the Donatists' pride accounts for their being "put outside by their own weight" (*pondere suo*), excluded from unity and splintered into "division." Again, an early Plotinian insight has been pressed into service against the heretic: for the soul's primal "inflation" resulted in its passing from contemplation of the "one" and breaking apart in pursuit of the "many."

The inflationary image of pride is given another interesting twist in *Enarratio 112* 1, dating from 414. The proud, in their "empty bigness" (*vana granditate*), are unable to "enter by the narrow gate" as the humble (figured by the *puer*, in the good sense of "little one") can easily do. But now the register shifts; the Ecclesiasticus text is set into the *Omnia* key: "And what malice is worse than pride's, which wills to have no one placed over it, not even God. For it is written: 'The beginning of man's pride is the standing away from God.' " This was the pride that "rose against the divine precepts with swollen pates" (*tumidis cervicibus*).

Enarratio 7 4, evidently composed in 414/415, shows how varied Augustine's use of the "inflation" image can become. In doing so, it also presents another interesting example of imaginative recession. Augustine ends with a quotation of verse 15, then verse 14 of our Ecclesiasticus text: the image of "spewing forth" is not part of the quoted material. And yet, that image is subtly at work, and its power can be measured by the roundabout shifts whereby Augustine finally hauls it in. He explains the phrase *conculcat in terram vitam meam* as referring to the serpent's being told that he shall "eat earth," whereas Adam and Eve were told "You are earth, and shall go [back] into the earth." Hence, the *conculcat* points to the devil's "treading" Adam and Eve underfoot, thus making them into the "earth" he feeds upon. Furthermore, the "earth" to which the soul's "glory" is "brought down," Augustine interprets, is the "dust" spoken of in the same Psalm. But dust, as everyone knows, is what every "wind casts forth from the face of the earth." That wind is, obviously, the "inflating" wind of pride suggested by the missing member of the Ecclesiasticus text; it puffs the soul up like a dust-cloud lacking all solidity (*et inflata non solidata, tamquam ventus elatus pulveris globus*). Hence, the continuing danger of pride, that vice through which "the soul first fell" and which is (again) the "last" for it to conquer. And Augustine ends by quoting the two verses from Ecclesiasticus mentioned above (4).

Injustice and "Labor"

Some paragraphs later, Augustine is interpreting the verse *ecce parturivit injustitiam, concepit laborem* (Ps 7:15). The latter member he explains as reminding us that "seed is conceived," whereas what is "brought to birth" is formed from that seed. Injustice, therefore, is the fruit of the "labor" to which Adam was condemned in Genesis (3:17). Why "labor"? Augustine answers with a familiar commonplace: because whoever comes to love goods that can be lost against the lover's will is condemned to the "most wretched" toil (or distress) of striving to possess them, against the constant competition of others who are striving to do the same. This toilsome pursuit of exclusive (i.e., "proper") possession often gives birth to the "injustice" that takes the form of outracing another for some prize, or wresting it from him if he gets there first. Labor, therefore, is the "seed of iniquity," being in its turn conceived by that "first sin" spoken of by Ecclesiasticus, that of "standing away from God" (16).

That same connection between sinfulness and "labor" features in *Enarratio 139* 13 (from A.D. 414), but in a peculiar connection. The Psalm read *Caput circuitus eorum*: as though to say, literally, "their head is (going around in) circular paths." The head, Augustine interprets, refers to the "pride" of the impious whose "labor never ends" because they go "around in circles." We know the head refers to pride because we say the "head" of something to designate its "beginning," and Ecclesiasticus informs us that pride is the *initium peccati*. Furthermore, proud men are false, and false men lie; hence, proud men "labor" since truth is much easier to tell. Indeed, Augustine generalizes, there is "labor" in every work of evil (13).

WIND, DUST, AND THE "INVISIBLE EARTH"

The version of *Enarratio 1* handed down to us is almost certainly a reworking that dates from the year 414 or 415. It compares the impious to so much "dust" the wind scatters—not over, but— "from" the face of the "earth." This prompts Augustine to give an interpretation of "earth" quite different from the one we saw earlier: in its solidity it figures that *stabilitas* in God of which Psalm 15:5–6 speaks when calling God the "portion of my inheritance"; it is the "earth" which Matthew's Gospel says the "meek shall inherit." As such, it must be that "invisible earth" (the Omnipresent God) which "nourishes and envelops" (*continet*) the "interior man," just as the visible earth does the "exterior" man. The "wind" that blows the impious from the face of this invisible earth is, predictably, "pride, because it inflates."

Augustine now pictures the soul in its original contemplative bliss: he who "was being inebriated by the riches [*ubertas*] of God's house and was drinking from the torrent of His delight" expressed his wariness toward pride by saying 'Let not the foot of pride come my way.' " He now removes any doubts that the "earth" in question "pertains to" (signifies?) the "interior man," or that it was through pride that man was cast forth from that earth when he tasted of the forbidden fruit: for it is written, "Why has earth and ashes prided itself? For in its lifetime it has cast forth its insides." But the wording of the text does not seem to fit smoothly into the context of his argument. It would fit better if it said "he *was cast* forth" from the "earth" which Augustine has labored to equate with the "insides," the "interior man." Augustine brushes the objection aside with a show of linguistic ingenuity: "to *be* cast forth can be expressed without absurdity as casting *oneself* forth" (4).

He may have his own *dimittere* theme in mind here; it would make his reply somewhat less forced. Nonetheless, he seems to have made a curious leap from explaining the "interior earth" as figuring the (ostensibly) divine *stabilitas* which "nourishes and envelops" the soul in contemplative bliss, to explaining that "earth" as identical with the "interior man" himself. But imagination's logic can sometimes produce bizarre effects.

PRIDE AND "ELATION"

Psalm 37, explained in 415, presents Augustine with what at first seems a paradox: "For my iniquities have lifted up my head, and like a heavy burden weighed down upon me" (verse 5). Augustine's ingenuity shines brightest when faced with such challenges: the "wicked" man in question must be the "proud" man, "whose head is lifted up" against God Himself—as Ecclesiasticus tells us—in proud "apostasy" from God; an apostasy which is the *initium omnis peccati*. "It is an act of lightness [*levitas*] to lift up the head as though one had nothing to carry," he continues; hence, it is appropriate for God to compel the sinner to "accept a weight to press him down" (*pondus unde possit comprimi*). For in that way the proud man's "labor is turned upon his own head," as Psalm 7:17 elegantly expresses it (8).

Similarly, *Enarratio 82* (from 414/416) has Augustine contrasting the *elatio* of the proud with the majestic loftiness of God, Whose Lordship rules "over all the earth" and "all heaven" as well. That realization should "crush down all earthly pride." "Therefore let earth, meaning man, stop priding itself," or, as Ecclesiasticus puts it, "Why does earth and ashes pride itself" (14)?

Letter 186, to Paulinus, was written in A.D. 417 or thereabouts; it shows Augustine interpreting the Prodigal parable in familiar terms, but now plainly with anti-Pelagian point. He begins with that favorite text from Psalm 58:10: it is good for man to say to God, with all the *vires* of his free choice, "I shall guard my strength unto You." But this is precisely what the Prodigal failed to do: he thought he could "guard what [God] had given him without His help," but instead, wandering off and living riotously, "he burned it all up," "paid it all out" (*consumpsit, erogaret*).

Sermo 154 (from 418) sees Augustine return to the "inflation" motif: if consecrated virgins find themselves thinking how far above their neighbors they are, they must "fear the swelling" (*time tumorem*). Think, like St. Paul, of what is still wanting to you, then you will not become "inflated" (5). Pursue the charity that is "not inflated"; therefore; let this grow in you, and your "soul will be solidified, not inflated." Remember, too, that "knowledge" when without charity can "inflate," but charity will keep it from doing so (6). Question your soul, then, to find whether you see "inflation" there; for "where inflation is, there is emptiness" (*ubi inflatio est, inanitas est*) (8).

Spiritual Fornication Again

Sermo 15 was preached sometime after the year 418. It shows Augustine apparently confident that his notion of "spiritual" fornication still remains a valid one. Once again he quotes St. James scolding "adulterers," and interprets the phrase following as defining what he means by that expression: the "friend of this world" is the "enemy of God"; "adultery" therefore is "friendship with this world." That accusation is leveled (once again) specifically at Christian "friends of the world" since they are "joined in legitimate marriage" with the one God, but fail to keep "chastity of the soul." Pagan sinners, on the other hand, are "fornicators" in that they "in a manner prostitute themselves to many false gods," but they do not count as "adulterers" since they do not have God as their "legitimate husband." Hence, we can be confident that this notion of "spiritual" fornication stayed solid for him until years after composing the *Confessions*. Notice also that Augustine again calls attention to that contrast between "one" and "many."

Closing Interpretations

The latest interpretations Augustine gives of the words from Ecclesiasticus only serve to underline the exegetical opportunism and consistent inconsistency which characterized his exploitation of this text from the very beginning. *Tractatus 25* on the Gospel of St. John, for instance (from 419/421 or thereabouts), has brought Augustine to Christ's words "I shall not cast them outside" (*Non ejiciam foras*). He quotes our Ecclesiasticus text, including the words about the proud soul's "spewing forth its insides." The verb *projecit* Augustine now explains as meaning *porro jecit*: "threw outside." The soul, then, is described as "going outside" *a Deo*: from God (15). This is what Adam did, abandoning the Divine Fountain Which watered his mind from within (the contemplative metaphor again), and seeking "outward" riches like money, honors, and so forth. That outward turn Augustine explains as rooted in Adam's wanting proudly to "live by his own counsel." "Let not the foot of pride come near me," therefore, the "foot" by means of which Adam "went out," presumably on his prodigal's journey (17).

Perhaps our latest text, chronologically, comes from the fifteenth sermon of the lengthy *Enarratio 118* and dates from 422 or after. Augustine is commending humility as the virtue most fitted for this "night" which provides the setting for our *peregrinatio*. For "being proud" was the evil whereby man was expelled into this night (*in istam noctem pulsus est homo*). And he quotes Ecclesiasticus' portrayal of the beginning of man's pride as his "standing away from" God (8).

Sermo 142 corresponds substantially with the eleventh sermon in the Wilmart collection; but that correspondence has been of no help in the effort to date it. Augustine is urging his hearers to "learn" from their experimental knowledge of their penal condition (*experimento*) what an evil it was for the proud soul to "lift up its heart against God" and "fornicate away from the Lord by presuming on itself. O how good it is to adhere to the Lord, by always entertaining humble sentiments." That soul, he affirms, was in "health" before its fornication, whereas its present "infirmity" is obviously a penal one. Now he introduces the contrast between the One and the many: "Withdrawing from that simple and singular Good into the multitude of these pleasures here, and entering into love of the *saeculum* and of earthly corruptions, that is what it means to fornicate from the Lord" (2).

For "love of the world makes the soul an adulteress, and love of its Maker makes her chaste"; but unless she blushes at her corrupt state, "she does not desire to go back to those chaste embraces" she once enjoyed. Let her now confess her foulness, and long for her onetime beauty; she who went forth by pouring herself out [*effusa*], let her go back in confusion" (*confusa*) (3).

Augustine now develops the familiar theme: the soul's abandonment of God was an abandonment of itself as well. But how did it ever occur? To understand his image, one must picture the soul as originally rapt in the vision of God. But then, "She looked back [*respexit*] upon herself," Augustine explains, "was pleased with herself, fell in love with her own power. She withdrew from Him, did not remain in herself . . . and fell over [*prolabitur*] into exterior realities. She loves the world, she loves temporal realities, she loves earthly things." But even if it were only herself she loved, "to the disregard of Him Who made her, she would still [by love's osmotic effect] become lesser, would fall short [in being-quality: *deficeret*] by loving what is lesser" (3).

Now Augustine moves to the contrast of "within" and "without": "You disregard the fact that you have been fashioned," he berates such a soul, "and love what you yourself have fashioned; you love the exterior works of your activity; you disregard the work of God within you" (4).

This prompts a shift to the inflation image: the soul "had swollen up with pride, and by its *tumor* it could not go back through the narrow (gate). . . . She tries to enter, but her *tumor* prevents her. . . . The narrow (opening) irritates her *tumor*, the irritation makes her swell out even more." *Ergo detumescat*: "Let her, therefore, make her swelling come down. But how? By accepting the medicine of humility," a bitter cup, assuredly, but salutary. For at present she has no true *magnitudo*, since "bigness is solid, but *tumor* is mere inflation." Hence, again, *Detumescat*: in order to become "great, sure, solid," let her "make her swelling come down" (5). To that end, let her learn charity, for charity is neither "inflated" nor proudly "lifted up" (8).

ELICITING A PATTERN

The reader was warned: Augustine's imagination follows a meandering course; the associations he makes, even with the identical image-term, can differ wildly from one sermon to the next, for he is always facing a different challenge: whether from Manichaeism or Donatism or Pelagianism, from the sequence of verses in this Psalm or that, or from the variety of occasions on which he had to preach: feasts of martyrs or major feasts of the Church calendar, explanations of the Our Father or of the Creed, what have you. He often warns that any Scriptural image can take on a variety of meanings depending on its context; but he himself is not above manipulating his interpretations in order to point to some lesson he feels his auditors, here and now, must be brought to realize.

The sometimes unpredictable variety of his associations, then, should not surprise; what is remarkable, however, is the number of underlying threads of consistency to which one finds him returning, over and over. The texts we have surveyed here exhibit a variety that is close to bewildering, yet closer inspection shows how regularly, in detail after detail, the same general story-line unfolds.

The story reads as follows: the Prodigal, Odysseus, Adam, our souls, are all one to Augustine. "We," accordingly, once dwelt in blissful contemplation of the "One God," "adhering" to Him; we were "companions of the angels" in His "house," our true "homeland." Now we find ourselves emerged from a "mortal" mother's womb, infected with "mortality" and in pursuit of the "many." That "many" is "secular" and temporal; it once appeared to us as "more" than the One God we securely possessed, but everything temporal turns out to be fleeting, transient, elusive; enjoyment of it is frustrating, futile, fraught with "labor" and laborious distress.

We once knew "rest" and "ease" in contemplation of God, but we have plunged and at the same time been plunged—"dismissed"—into the realm "under the sun," a region of "vain" and unremitting "busy-ness," a restless "sea," cruelly buffeting and dangerously threatening.

So preoccupying is our individual "race" after private and "proper" possession and enjoyment, we have gone a "distance" great enough to make us "forget" both God and the true "self" that is marked by our celestial origins. We have abandoned our own "interior" selves to chase after the "exterior" products of our proud, insubordinate activity, "spewed forth our insides" like whoring sons who have forgotten their heavenly Father, or brides of One "legitimate" Husband turned away from Him into "fornications" and "adulteries" with the "many." So extreme has that fornication become, we have squandered our soul's powers in the fabrication of empty images of the God we deserted, then delighted the "many" demons by worshiping those idols.

What was it that brought us to desert our contemplative quiet and bliss, and "fall" into this frenetic round of activity? The ultimate root of our "ancient sin" was clearly pride: a *superbia* that was also *audacia*. We freely chose to rebel against our legitimate subordination to God, to be our own masters, delighting to have our soul's powers under our independent control. This was to be our perverse way of mimicking God's own sovereign autonomy, of assenting to the diabolical suggestion that we become "like gods."

While still duly subordinate, we governed the entirety of the sensible universe in common with other souls, but we foolishly thought that by departing from God we would come to possess "more"; our willful choice was to rule some "private" and "proper" kingdom of our very own, and the fulfillment of that desire has become, ironically, the perfectly adapted punishment for that choice. For God, with an "avenging hand," has fashioned our fallen selves in the womb of a mortal mother, and "weighed down" our souls with the burden of a mortal and corruptible body, the only kind appropriate to the lower world we chose to make the scene of our distant "journey" from Him.

That primal sin of pride "inflated" us; from the perfectly inextended souls we were, utterly concentrated in that timeless instant that is God's own Eternity, we have "swelled outward" into the relative "emptiness" and "vanity" of both space and time, into a false "greatness" that is as hollow and deceptive as any unhealthy "tumor."

We have deserted the "solidity" of Divine Truth, the "stability" of the "firmament" that once supported us so securely. There, our "substance" had been guarded more safely than we could ever guard it ourselves; we could have chosen to "guard our strength" for God, thus keeping safe the whole array of our soul's "forces" or "powers" by "adhering" to Him, but we made the opposite choice: no wonder, then, that we find ourselves on a tossing, menacing "sea" that offers no such solid support. No wonder, either, that in our empty greatness we ended up worshiping those ultimate representatives of empty vanity, those extreme and most distant "likenesses" to God, the demons and their cherished idols.

But one of the most familiar properties of an unhealthy "tumor" is its tendency to suppurate, to burst outward and spread its poison abroad. Our sickness is very much like the bodily "flow of blood" familiar from the Gospel story; at bottom, of course, it is our souls that have "swollen outward" in pride; but that swelling turned the invisible soul into what Genesis and Ecclesiasticus both call "earth."

Little wonder, then, that this spiritual "spewing forth" should take bodily form and expression in the incessant "outflow" of licentious immorality, *luxuria*. For while our prideful "fornication" away from God might initially appear a purely spiritual sin, it nevertheless constitutes a surrender of the "whole" soul, now mortally embodied, to "carnal concupiscence." It is profoundly akin to "fornication" in the more usual sense of that term, and just as truly a sin "against our own body." That fornicatory "love of this world," moreover, St. John's Epistle describes in terms of a triadic sin: pride, concupiscence of the flesh, and concupiscence of the eyes.

Why does Augustine so insist that "fornication" takes this triadic form, and that all three are sins "against our own body"? We cannot avoid becoming somewhat speculative at this point. It would seem that he was convinced that this triad must not be considered a mere "trio," as though they were three distinct and unrelated types of sin; they are organically linked one to another. For pride, he says repeatedly, is rightly considered the "head" or "root" of the other two; it sets into motion a dynamic of sin that inexorably moves from pride into the two concupiscences.

Augustine has left us a series of clues on how that "dynamic" operates. Take the case of "curiosity" first. Once we had abandoned the "One" Beauty we formerly gazed upon with the "inner" eye of the soul, it was right and inevitable not only that (as Augustine interpreted Wisdom 9:15) our "corruptible body" should "weigh down the soul," but also that our "earthly habitation press down upon the *sensum*," the external sense-manifold that, incapable of gazing upon the One, was condemned to "think upon the many" (*multa cogitantem*).

So did *curiositas* become the perfectly natural sequel to the pride that caused our fall. But a similar dynamic leads to "concupiscence of the flesh"; for it was equally right and inevitable that our rejection of due subordination to God should result in our mortal body's rebellion against governance by our souls; and nowhere, in Augustine's view, did the body assert its insubordination more fearfully than in the imperious urgencies of sex. "Spiritual" fornication, therefore, the soul's act of spewing forth its interior powers, has as its natural resultant and expression that bodily "boiling over" and "spewing forth," that luxurious "outflow" which represents the climax (Augustine is speaking principally as a male) of "fornication" in our accustomed sense. Clearly, too, Augustine is assuming that the readers and hearers of his time would look on the loss of seed as diminishing a man's virile "strength," and consequently leaving him (literally) "ex-hausted" (*lassus*).

So, we are told that the Prodigal "paid out," "squandered," expended, and wasted his "substance"—among prostitutes. That activity left him both "empty" and "weary." But we can readily imagine why his "weariness" was both "luxurious" and "un-quiet" or "restless." For if spiritual fornication leads inexorably to its bodily expression, he has been engaged in "sowing" or "wasting his strength," his spiritual potencies. And the inevitable result is that post-coital "weariness" one recognizes as, on the one hand, "luxurious" and "delicious," yet, on the other, "restless," because guilt-ridden and ultimately unsatisfying.

Why, then, does Augustine apply this same metaphor to the ill-intentioned artist? Part of the answer lies in the close kinship both he and Plotinus regularly imagine as bonding the aesthetic and erotic spheres: for both of them, the lure of sensible beauty set into motion the same "lower" *eros*, "vulgar Aphrodite," as oper-ated in sexual attraction. In this, they both were following Plato's behest (and, Augustine could add, Ambrose's as well) that we should leave all sense-beauties behind, "close our eyes" to them, and seek the higher, invisible Beauty which only the inner eye of the soul could hope to glimpse. One may guess that both of them responded all the more ardently to Plato's urging since they seem to have been acutely sensitive to the dangerous allurements of "Circe and Calypso."

But what Augustine found irresistibly appealing in Plotinus was a metaphysic that rhymed with and grounded this "ascensional" ethic. A "naturally Platonic" soul, he discovered in the *Enneads* what seemed the perfect explanation for his soul's incurable nostalgia for another, higher world in which the true was the good and both were radiant with unalloyed beauty. What we have watched him accomplish here is to produce a faithful replication of the thought and image patterns which, I would argue, he gleaned and skillfully combined from *Enneads* 1.6, 3.7, 5.1, and

6.9 at least, and very probably more. Clearly, he read the *Enneads* with eyes sensitized by Scripture; but one suspects that by the same token he read Scripture with an eye sensitized to possible analogues to the Plotinian themes that most impressed him. Typically, those analogues often took the form of brilliant philosophical imagery. Following the logic of those images, he was able to find both Scripture and Plotinus recounting the same odyssey of soul.

That odyssey image describes how once we dwelt in enraptured contemplation of the supernal Truth-Beauty; we still dimly "remember" It, and the abiding nostalgia fed by that memory is constantly being fired by the beauties of the sense-world. For they are distant "images," many and various, of that One transcendent Beauty; this is why they were capable of "reminding" us of the loveliness we had somehow lost. But even while reminding us, they tempt us, like Circe and Calpyso, to break off our journeying and stay, make a "home" with them, and so "forget" the Ithaca to which we deeply long to return.

The ultimate irony, though, was this: those beauties our souls are so powerfully tempted to admire, even to worship, are in reality productions of those very souls. For, Plotinus explained and Augustine believed, our primal movement from the restful contemplation of the One Beauty into the sensible world was prompted by the desire to form the realities of that sense-world into "images" of the Beauty we had "seen" in the world above; our fall from contemplation into restless activity was, for both of them, primarily and explicitly, a descent into the aesthetic kind of activity most properly characteristic of the artist. And the artist stood, for both of them, as the consummate exemplar of every fallen soul's inveterate temptation: that of pouring out its energies into the production of sense-images of the Higher Beauty, only to go chasing after them with an erotic passion that invariably ends *in deliciosas lassitudines*.

One final observation: that image of luxurious weariness must have recalled to the reader's mind another famous episode from Homer's *Odyssey*: the Lotus-eaters. Ambrose mentions it, and in direct connection with the Sirens. That habit of coupling the two and alluding to "Sirens and Lotus-eaters" had become, in fact, a kind of cliché among Latin authors: one finds Quintilian doing the same,[12] and Ovid as well.[13] Mention the Sirens, and allusion to its partner-image of the Lotus-eaters seems to have been a kind of reflex as natural to them as "Romeo" recalling "Juliet" would be to us.

Augustine, we have seen, makes mention of the Sirens, but, somewhat surprisingly, never explicitly alludes to the Lotus-eaters. And yet the somnolent languors of Odysseus' crewmen, their luxurious surrender to the "sensuous delights" which eating the lotus-flower figured in Neoplatonic myth-interpretation,[14] is significantly coupled with their "forgetfulness" of the duty to continue the toilsome journey to their Ithacan homeland. One naturally expects Augustine to evoke that image, too, in warning his readers against the bewitching lure of luxurious lassitudes. I have been unable to find any such explicit evocation; other searchers could well succeed where I have failed. What we have already seen suggests that this could conceivably be just another instance where an image in recession still exerts hidden force in eventually producing an imaginative complex. In any event, we shall have reasons for returning to that suggestion, and to the Lotus-eaters, in a future study.

NOTES

1. I made only a brief attempt to interpret this image in *Art and the Christian Intelligence*, p. 213n171.

2. See Buffière, *Homère*, p. 30.

3. Something like this *saturitas* motif is already present (alongside frequent mentions of *tolma*, "audacity") in Origen's *De principiis*, e.g. 2.8.3, where it connotes a weariness with contemplation. This notion could easily have penetrated the Christian-Platonist circle at Milan: we know, for instance, of Ambrose's indebtedness to Origen. In any case the importance of the "food" metaphor in Augustine's writings suggests that it probably derived from some source(s) alongside the obvious Scriptural ones (manna, Eucharist, etc.). I am unable to find any locus in Plotinus that would clearly account for it: but see *Ennead* 5.8.4.1–2, where Plotinus depicts "Truth" as being, for denizens of the overworld, "mother and nurse, existence and sustenance" to them. Augustine, we know, set himself to an eager reading of St. Paul almost immediately after reading the *platonici*. It may have been the impression left by Paul's contrast between the "milk" of faith and the "food of grown-ups" that lent that phrase greater impact than it might otherwise have had: see *Early Theory*, pp. 205–26, and especially 211–13. For more on this possibility, see above, on the *fovere* image.

4. See *Early Theory*, pp. 173–82.

5. Translation from Armstrong, *Enneads*, III, 337–39.

6. See note 4, above.

7. Translation from Armstrong, *Enneads*, V, 11.

8. See Aimé Solignac, "Introduction," *Les Confessions*, Bibliothèque Augustinienne 13 (Paris: Desclée, 1962), pp. 111*n*2 and 688–89; see also Du Roy, *Trinité*, pp. 69–70 and 141*n*3.

9. Since the Sixth Ennead in Armstrong's translation was not yet published when this study was being written, this paraphrase was confected from both Stephen Mackenna's translation and that of Elmer O'Brien in *The Essential Plotinus* (New York: Mentor, 1964), pp. 85–86.

10. I must confess to a slight puzzlement on this point: for reasons it would be too laborious to present here, it had become my conviction that this distinction between a "proper" and "common" soul-life assumed crucial importance for Augustine at a later phase in his discussions on the soul's origin; to find that distinction explicitly operative this early is somewhat surprising. But this could just be an anticipation of a distinction that was always in the back of his mind, but whose importance dawned on him only later. For fuller details, see the Index to my *Origin*, s.v.: Soul, *Propria vita* of.

11. For this reading, see above chap. 4, note 9.

12. See his *Institutio oratorica* 5.8.1, along with the judgment of Harald Hagendahl in *Augustine and the Latin Classics* (Goteborg: Universitetet, 1967), p. 676: it was "not unlikely that [Augustine] had some reminiscences" of this work. Quintilian sees both the Sirens and Lotus-eaters attracting to an odd mix of pleasure and empty glory.

13. See his *Remedia Amoris* 785–790, and Hagendahl's judgment, pp. 691 and 468–69 that Ovid was "hardly unknown" to Augustine, as Marrou had once opined. But we shall return to this text further on.

14. See Buffière, *Homère*, p. 378. Ambrose (*Espositio Evangelii secundum Lucam* 4.2) sees the temptation of sensual *voluptas* principally in the Sirens; but the Lotus-eaters' *suavitas baccarum* encourages him to connect the two.

Epilogue: Lines for Future Research

It is some fifteen hundred years since he laid aside his pen, and yet the meaning of so much that Augustine wrote remains elusive to us. The international *Congresso* held in Rome in 1986 occasionally illuminated his thinking, but more often succeeded only in dramatizing that elusive quality. How often, for instance, we still hold differing views about that central event of his life, his "conversion" at Milan! What precisely is he telling us he was converted *to*? And what was that conversion *from*? Both papers and discussions among that host of assembled scholars proclaimed the fact that, still bereft of satisfactory answers to those two simple questions, we cannot claim fully to understand other crucial facets of Augustine's conversion account, either.

This study was inspired and guided by a growing conviction that in order to find out *what* he thought, we still have much to learn about *how* Augustine's mind worked. It has always been obvious that Augustine's mind frequently operated along the well-worn pathways and in accord with the familiar categories of fourth- and fifth-century discursive thought; his resulting "view of reality" clearly took shape, in consequence, along the lines we saw sketched by Vernon J. Bourke in our opening chapter. Nothing in this study should be interpreted as contesting that accepted view. My claim is, rather, that there is more to be said than is said by the accepted view: a "more" that is complementary, not contradictory to that view.

For Augustine's thought frequently moves in *another* register besides the more manifest framework erected by conceptual and discursive thought-ways. He can often think more the way poets do: in images and imaginative symbols, and when he does so, he challenges us to adopt different interpretive strategies from the ones that served to illuminate his discursive thinking. My personal suspicion is that much, if not most, of what still remains matter of disagreement among scholars lurks in these dim-lit catacombs

of Augustine's poetic imagination, awaiting the Ariadne's thread
of poetic interpretation to conduct us through its labyrinth.

It is comforting, then, to learn that other scholars have urged
the adoption of a similar strategy to the one I have proposed both
here and in a series of earlier writings. I learned of Suzanne Poque's
having published her two-volume thesis on *Le Langage symbolique
dans la prédication d'Augustin d'Hippone* only when I had already
completed the research, and most of the writing, of this study. I
resolved not to examine the fruits of her labors until I had finished
mine: that way, the results of my work would remain as independent of hers as hers, her footnotes now assure me, were almost
totally independent of any suggestions from me.

That reciprocal independence, I submit, helps to strengthen the
claim being made by both our studies—and, implicitly at least, by
the host of earlier contributions to which both of us have avowed
our indebtedness in bibliographies and footnotes: that explicit
study of Augustine's imaginative thought-ways is both a legitimate and imperative approach toward casting light on a number
of loci where his meaning still resists our questioning.

Poque's study also reinforces the impression my own research
leaves me with: there is no dearth of matter for extending the kind
of research she and I have undertaken. In fact, we both agree that
one might continue almost indefinitely with this kind of inventory
and interpretation of Augustine's images; both our studies combined, added to all the others I have become acquanted with, do
little more than scratch the surface.

All that is true, moreover, despite the diverse entryways Mlle
Poque and I have taken, and the differing veins we have scouted,
from out of the rich lode that Augustine's imagination represents.
There remains an incredible wealth of images still to be mined
there, and one would hope that other scholars would take both of
our contributions as invitations to continue investigating those
depths and occasionally, no doubt, bringing both correction and
nicer precision to our findings.

It is always somewhat surprising, though, to discover what
different views any two minds will take of the same assemblage
of materials. In the interests of future research, a word should be
said about the diverse approaches Mlle Poque and I have taken.
She begins her first volume with a lengthy Introduction, summing
up selectively a number of conclusions one might draw from a
series of studies, most of them French, on the structure and

classification of symbolism and symbolic imagery (pp. xvii-xxx).
She claims to find a certain consensus shared by authors like
Eliade, Jung, Ricoeur, Bachelard, and Durand, despite some
marked diversities between them. This in turn prompts her to
adopt a division into more active "diurnal" or "heroic" images on
the one hand, and more passive, "receptive," or "nocturnal"
images on the other. Then she takes the decisive step of limiting
her study to the former group.

She begins, therefore, with a set of generalized assumptions
about the workings of the imagination; only then (apparently)
does she approach the particularities of Augustine's imagination,
already armed with a set of categories dictating, or at least
suggesting, what images and classes of images she should look
for.

I have tried in my own Introduction to explain why the approach followed here is preceded by no such methodological
determinations of a generalized sort. Compared to the elegantly
structured and tightly organized compartments one finds in Poque's successive chapters, consequently, the reader must frequently have had the impression that, wildly and untamed, my
particular Topsy "just grew." It moves from image to image, or
better, image-complex to image-complex, with all the rank irreg-
ularity of a weedy field or tract of jungle underbrush, whereas
Mlle Poque's creation unfolds in the formal patterns of a *jardin de
Versailles*. Whereas Poque restricts herself to the "diurnal" side, I
find Augustine more naturally developing his image-complexes
by constantly moving from diurnal to nocturnal and back again;
whereas she limits her field of study to the preached works, I have
found that it reveals more about how particular image-clusters
developed, to move (with what some Gallic spirits might deem a
cavalier disdain for methodical organization) from preached works
to early dialogues to the *Confessions* and back again, as the accidents of the textual terrain suggested.

The difference in our two approaches stems, I think, mainly
from the fact that I had undertaken my research with a fairly
precise, albeit half-acknowledged agenda list of puzzling images,
particular to Augustine himself, which I was determined to decode; my attention was already directly aimed beyond this study
toward a further task: that of uncovering how these images
"worked," and principally in that baffling work the *Confessions*.
This implicitly made the individual laws of Augustine's own

imagination my norm for selecting the cluster of images I chose
for study; further, it commended the analytic pathways I eventually found myself spontaneously following. I found myself striving to track each particular image-cluster, as far as possible, from
its seminal core through all the variety of its successive mutations,
yet never losing sight of the genetic unity running through those
variations.

So much for our differences in method; the difference between
Poque's results and mine, I think, comes to this: having drawn her
agenda from more systematic and generalized studies of the
imagination, she has a better guarantee, over time, of casting her
investigative net more comprehensively than I could hope to do. I
suspect that her method assures her, much more than mine would,
that her probes will reach to all the species and sub-species of
whatever image-family she is concerned with. I, on the other
hand, working with no such pre-set grid, but hoping to catch the
highly individual way Augustine's imagination gives birth to any
single image-cluster, then hoping to track that cluster as it grows,
spreads, speciates and sub-speciates, could more easily wind up
overlooking a family-member here or there. But, in the main,
research according to this more anarchic formula may succeed in
tracking all the *moves*, including whatever illogical leaps and twists
Augustine's imagination may perform. In that way, we may hope
to learn with far greater fidelity how Augustine's individual imagination works, and so uncover with closer precision what his
imaged language is trying to tell us.

I have already pointed to several instances where this difference
in approach could make a difference in results. I have suggested
that, in respect of the image of "standing" (*stare*), Mlle Poque's
method may have induced her to accord primacy to the military
sense (which Augustine *does* employ), of "standing one's ground"
in battle, whereas Augustine may well have accorded that primacy
to the sense of "standing solid" in, or supported by, God.[1] My
advantage, perhaps. And yet, I must admit, the frequency of those
"military" applications had eluded me and my less systematic
mode of approach: advantage, Poque.

But there are similar advantages balanced against disadvantages
in her treatment of the *medicus* image (pp. 176–89), and the image
of God as Father (pp. 194–231): her "entry" on both these
complexes is guided by a classification of technical instruments,
the surgical *ferramentum* in the former, and the *flagellum* in the

latter instance. That systematic classification "works," once again, to the extent that it provokes examination of two significant clusters of Augustinian images; but surely it introduces an odd bias into the way she inspects those clusters, selects what images belong in each of them, and then attempts to summarize the unitary import she claims to find characterizing the entire cluster (pp. 222–24). The least one can say is that she has scarcely traced out the "natural pathways" followed by Augustine's individual imagination. When it comes to the "Light–Darkness" (pp. 257–79) and "Earth–Heaven" (pp. 299–324) image-clusters,[2] however, her treatment and mine are more closely akin; the likely reason for this seems to be that images of such cosmic sweep allow for only one "natural angle" for approaching and inspecting them.

Future researchers of this relatively uncharted territory may find it useful to weigh the odds on these different approaches; but there is certainly no guarantee that they will find them to be either mutually exclusive or entirely exhaustive of the possibilities.

But they will find, as I have said, rich terrain to explore. If I were younger, and just starting out on such a venture, I would love to track the various images Augustine associates with such "wayfarers" as Adam, the lost sheep, the Samaritan and the man who went from Jerusalem to Jericho, as well as the Israelites traversing the desert and crossing the Red Sea. (Augustine's im-aged understanding of those desert and Red Sea episodes will eventually disclose, I am convinced, many of the secrets contained in his puzzling early fondness for the term *admonitio* and its cognates.) There is still much to be learned, as well, about the osmotic "binding" and "cleaving" aspects of his love-image, about further aspects of the multivalent *fovere* image and its varied consorts, about the fortunes of those suggestive linkages he forges between *habitus* and *habitatio* images, as well as between them and the *stola prima* the Prodigal first lost and then received back. From another line of approach, it would be fascinating to have someone collect, translate, and explicate the various preached works in which Augustine unfurls the same series of "conversion" images as fill page after page of the *Confessions*: such a collection would represent something very close to an "authentic interpretation" of numerous crucial, and often puzzling, passages of that poetic masterpiece.

One could go on and on with such suggestions; what a delight-ful prospect it would be to look forward to reading the results several battalions of young scholars might turn up on such a bundle of topics.

Why, I can hear an impatient reader ask, why don't you get busy and do these things yourself? Alas, the rivers of Babylon sweep us all inexorably onward; there just isn't time left for all the projects which any of us would love to tackle. So, my own intention, for the moment anyway, is to pass on from such general (and essentially liminal) explorations of Augustine's imagery, in hopes of completing a series of studies begun some years ago, on the "conversion" imagery he employs in his *Confessions*. It appears that Patrice Cambronne has produced a more comprehensive (and perhaps systematically overelaborate?) study on *Confessions* imagery more generally.[3] But I have not had access to that study; it still remains available only in micro-fiche format. That may be another happy circumstance for me, enabling me to accomplish this next phase of my task as independent of Cambronne's findings as I was of Poque's. Comparing our results will be all the more interesting for that, I hope.

Future researchers will undoubtedly find their data-gathering task greatly facilitated by the incredible short-cuts made possible by the progressive computerization of Augustine's texts. I would like to make a small wager on the basis of my own experience: I suspect that they will find it worthwhile to make a series of inventories of Augustine's allusions (not only his express citations!) to verses, briefer snatches—even to single words (like that provocative word *tumescens*)—which he associates with one or other image-cluster. Brooding over such inventories, I suggest, will almost certainly result in some novel maps of Augustine's imaginative thought-ways.

A final suggestion, if I may: much can be done to close the gaps in our knowledge of the chronology of Augustine's works, and particularly of his preached works. I have already explained why, in order to get *something* accomplished in the study of his imagery, I have eschewed complicating my task by striving to trace the development of Augustine's images chronologically. In the present state of our knowledge, attempting too much would result in accomplishing very little in the way of solid results. But (I am thinking now of the method Mlle Anne-Marie La Bonnardière has applied so fruitfully to Augustine's Scriptural citations) this should not discourage researchers from undertaking smaller-scale and more finely calibrated soundings, aimed at uncovering whether and how certain shifts in Augustine's use of some favorite image might illuminate chronological relationships among his preached works. Argumentation of this sort can tend to verge on the circular, granted, but circular arguments are not always avoidable; nor need such circles always be rejected as vicious.

In a word, I cannot refrain from suggesting that the prospects for future research into Augustine's imaginative thinking seem both solid and bright. I am tempted to envy those who will be lucky enough to climb this scholarly peak in Darien.

NOTES

1. See chap. 1, note 4, above.
2. See chap. 1, note 3, above.
3. *Recherches sur la structure de l'imaginaire dans les* Confessions *de saint Augustin*, 2 vols. (Paris: Études Augustiniennes, 1982) (in micro-fiche). See the review by Goulven Madec in REA, 29 (1983), 341–42.

Bibliography

Arbesmann, Rudolph, o.s.a. "Christ the *Medicus humilis* in St. Augustine." AM II. Pp. 623–29.

———. "The Concept *Christus medicus* in St. Augustine." *Traditio*, 10 (1954), 1–28.

Armstrong, A. H. "Plotinus." In *The Cambridge History of Later Greek and Early Mediaeval Philosophy*. Ed. A. H. Armstrong. Cambridge: Cambridge University Press, 1967. Pp. 236–58.

Bennett, Constance. "The Conversion of Vergil: The *Aeneid* in Augustine's *Confessions*." REA, 34 (1988), 47–69.

Berrouard, M.-F. *Homélies sur l'Evangile de Saint Jean*. Bibliothèque Augustinienne 71. Paris: Desclée de Brouwer, 1969.

Bourke, Vernon J. *Augustine's View of Reality*. Villanova, Pa.: Villanova University Press, 1964.

Brown, Peter. *Augustine of Hippo*. Berkeley: University of California Press, 1967.

Buffière, Felix. *Les Mythes d'Homère et la pensée grecque*. Paris: Les Belles Lettres, 1956.

Cambronne, Patrice. *Recherches sur la structure de l'imaginaire dans les* CONFESSIONS *de saint Augustin*. 2 vols. Paris: Études Augustiniennes, 1982. Microfiche.

Chevalier, Louis, and Rondet, Henri, s.j. "L'Idée de vanité dans l'oeuvre de saint Augustin." REA, 3 (1957), 221–34.

Cilento, Vincenzo. "Mito e poesia nelle *Enneadi* di Plotino." In *Les Sources de Plotin: Dix exposés et discussions*. Ed. E. R. Dodds. Entretiens sur l'Antiquité Classique 5. Vandoeuvres–Geneva: Fondation Hardt, 1960. Pp. 243–310.

Claussen, M. A. "*Peregrinatio* and *Peregrini* in Augustine's *City of God*." *Traditio*, 46 (1991), 33–75.

Courcelle, Pierre. "Flügel der Seele." In *Reallexikon für Antike und Christentum*, 8 (Fascicule 57, 1969). Cols. 29–65.

———. "Quelques symboles funéraires du néo-platonisme latin." REA, 46 (1944), 65–93.

———. *Recherches sur les* CONFESSIONS *de saint Augustin*. 2 vols. Paris: de Boccard, 1950. 2d ed., Paris, Boccard, 1968.

Curley, James F. Review of *Neoplatonism and Christian Thought*, ed. Dominic J. O'Meara. *Dialogue*, 25 (1982), 31.

Doignon, Jean. "L'Apologie de Philocalie et de Philosophie chez Saint Augustin (*C. Acad.* 2, 3, 7)." REA, 30 (1984), 100–10.

——. "*Factus Erectior* (*B. Vita* 1, 4): Une Étape de l'évolution de jeune Augustin à Carthage." *Vetera Christianorum*, 27 (1990), 77–83.

——. "Le symbolisme des Sirènes dans les premiers dialogues de saint Augustin." In *Hommages à R. Chevalier*. Tours: 1986. Pp. 113–20.

Ferrari, Leo C. "Augustine and Astrology." *Laval Revue Théologique et Philosophique*, 33 (1977), 241–51.

——. "The Prodigal Son in the *Confessions*." RA, 12 (1977), 104–18.

Fontaine, Jacques. "Sens et valeur des images dans les *Confessions*." AM I. Pp. 117–26.

Fugier, Huguette. "L'Image du Dieu-Centre dans les *Confessions* de saint Augustin." REA, 1 (1955), 379–95.

Hagendahl, Harald. *Augustine and the Latin Classics*. 2 vols. Goteborg: Universitetet, 1967

Henry, Paul, s.j. *Plotin et l'Occident*. Louvain: Spicelegium Sacrum Lovaniense, 1934.

Homer. *Odyssey*. Trans. Samuel H. Butcher. New York: Macmillan, 1895.

Hübner, Wolfgang. "Die *praetoria memoriae* im zehnten Buch der *Confessiones*: Vergilisches bei Augustin." REA, 27 (1981), 245–63.

Knauer, Georg Nicolaus. "*Peregrinatio animae*: Zur Frage der Einheit der augustinischen KONFESSIONEN." *Hermes*, 85 (1957), 216–48.

——. *Psalmenzitate in Augustins* KONFESSIONEN. Gottingen: Vandenhoeck & Ruprecht, 1955.

La Bonnardière, Anne-Marie. *Biblia Augustiniana: Les Épîtres aux Thessaloniciens, à Tite et à Philémon*. Paris: Études Augustiniennes, 1964.

——. "Le thême de la 'terre' dans le Psautier d'après les *Enarrationes in Psalmos* de saint Augustin." *Annuaire* of the Ecole pratique de Hautes Etudes, Section V, No. 78 (1970/1971), 293–96.

Madec, Goulven. Review of Patrice Cambronne, *Recherches sur la structure de l'imaginaire dans les* CONFESSIONS *de saint Augustin*. REA 29 (1983), 341–42.

Mandouze, André. *Saint Augustin: L'Adventure de la raison et de la grâce*. Paris: Études Augustiniennes, 1968.

Markus, Robert A. *Saeculum: History and Society in the Theology of St. Augustine*. Cambridge: Cambridge University Press, 1970. Repr. 1988.

Marrou, Henri-Irénée. *Saint Augustin et la fin de la culture antique*. 2 vols. Paris: Boccard, 1938, 1949.

——. *Retractatio* (Vol. II of *Saint Augustin et la fin de la culture antique*). Paris, Boccard, 1949.

Nock, A. D. *Conversion: The Old and the New in Religion from Alexander the Great to Augustine of Hippo.* Oxford: Oxford University Press, 1933. Repr. London: Oxford University Press, 1961.

O'Brien, Elmer. *The Essential Plotinus.* New York: Mentor, 1964.

O'Connell, Robert J., s.j. *Art and the Christian Intelligence in Saint Augustine.* Cambridge, Mass.: Harvard University Press, 1978.

———. "*Confessions* VII, ix, 13–xxi, 27. REA, 19 (1973), 87–100.

———. "*Ennead* VI, 4–5 in the Works of St. Augustine." REA, 9 (1963), 1–39.

———. *Imagination and Metaphysics in St. Augustine.* Milwaukee: Marquette University Press, 1986.

———. "Isaiah's Mothering God in St. Augustine's *Confessions.*" *Thought,* 58 (1983), 188–206.

———. *The Origin of the Soul in St. Augustine's Later Works.* New York: Fordham University Press, 1987.

———. *Saint Augustine's* CONFESSIONS: *The Odyssey of Soul.* Cambridge, Mass.: The Belknap Press of Harvard University Press, 1969. Repr. New York: Fordham University Press, 1989.

———. "St. Augustine's Criticism of Origen in the *Ad Orosium.*" REA, 30 (1984), 84–99.

———. *St. Augustine's Early Theory of Man, 386–391 A.D.* Cambridge, Mass.: The Belknap Press of Harvard University Press, 1969.

———. "St. Augustine's Images of God." *Thought,* 57 (1982), 30–40.

———. *St. Augustine's Platonism.* Villanova, Pa.: Villanova University Press, 1984.

O'Meara, John J. *The Young Augustine: The Growth of St. Augustine's Mind Up to His Conversion.* London: Longmans, Green, 1954.

The Oxford Latin Dictionary. Oxford: Clarendon, 1982.

Pépin, Jean. "The Platonic and Christian Ulysses." In *Neoplatonism and Christian Thought.* Ed. Dominic J. O'Meara. Albany: State University of New York Press, 1982. Pp. 3–18.

———. "Recherches sur le sens et les origines de l'expression *Caelum caeli* dans le Livre XII des *Confessions* de saint Augustin." *Bulletin du Cange,* 23 (1953), 185–274.

Perler, Othmar. *Les Voyages de saint Augustin.* Paris: Études Augustiniennes, 1969.

Plotinus. *Enneads.* Trans. A. H. Armstrong. 7 vols. Loeb Classical Library. Cambridge, Mass.: Harvard University Press, 1966–1984.

———. *Plotini Opera* II. Edd. Paul Henry, s.j, and Hans-Rudolph Schwyzer. Brussels: 1959,

Poque, Suzanne. *Le Langage symbolique dans la prédication d'Augustin d'Hippone.* 2 vols. Paris: Études Augustiniennes, 1984.

Puèch, Henri-Charles. *Le Manichéisme, son fondateur, sa doctrine.* Paris: Civilisations du Sud, 1949.

Rondet, Henri, s.j. *Original Sin: The Patristic and Theological Background.*

Trans. Cajetan Finegan, o.p. New York: Alba House, 1969. Repr. 1972.

———. "Le Symbolisme de la mer chez saint Augustin." AM II. Pp. 691–701.

duRoy, Olivier. *L'Intelligence de la foi en la Trinité selon saint Augustin: Genèse de sa théologie trinitaire.* Paris: Études Augustiniennes, 1968.

Solignac, Aimé. "Introduction." *Augustin: Les* Confessions. Bibliothèque Augustinienne 13. Paris: Desclée de Brouwer, 1962.

Somers, H. "Image de Dieu: Les Sources de l'exégèse augustinienne." REA, 7 (1961), 105–25.

Van Bavel, Tarcisius. "L'Humanité du Christ comme *lac parvulorum* dans la spiritualité de saint Augustin." *Augustiniana*, 7 (1957), 245–81.

Verbraken, Pierre-Patrick. *Études critiques sur les Sermons authentiques de saint Augustin.* The Hague: Nijhoff, 1976.

Zum Brunn, Emilie. *St. Augustine: Being and Nothingness.* Trans. Ruth Namad. New York: Paragon, 1988.

Indices

1. INDEX OF SUBJECTS AND NAMES

Numbers in boldface indicate pages containing major treatment of the topic.

2. SACRED SCRIPTURE

3. WORKS OF ST. AUGUSTINE
(In chronological, i.e., *Retractationes* sequence)

Contra Academicos

De beata vita

De vera religione

21	65	79	39
43	67n10	113	9413n
65	42		

Contra Adimantum Manichaei discipulum

25	119

De diversis quaestionibus

	83	51.3	200
2.33	144–50		

De diversis quaestionibus ad Simplicianum

223

Confessiones

De civitate Dei

11.23	8*n*20

Retractationes

1.19	265

Epistulae

55 8	262	140 61	266
120 4	216–17	186	275

Ennarrationes

1 4	44, 48, 273	32, version 2, sermon 2, 4–6	241
3 5	239	32, version 2, sermon 2, 6	75, 90
4 3	43	32, version 2, sermon 2, 10	45, 244*n*13
5 4	242	33, sermon 2, 6	38
5 5	242	34, sermon 2, 12	126
5 6	242, 243	34, sermon 2, 13	105
5 8	243	35 18	233, 268
5 10	64	36, sermon 2, 12	43
7 4	272	38 7	25
7 11	59	38 8–10	268
7 15	215	38 10	31
7 16	272–73	38 17–18	44
7 19	41, 50	38 21	73
14 1	76	38 22	31
17 2–3	259	39 8	59
17 8	274	39 9	229
17 43	259	39 28	22
18, sermon 1, 7	103	40 6	105, 112
18, sermon, 1, 14	270	42 4	59, 76
18, sermon 2, 3	161	44 9	153
18, sermon 2, 7	54, 102	45 9	107
18, sermon 2, 15	161, 270	45 9–15	107–109
21, sermon 2, 4	105, 112	45 11	107
23 2	45, 75, 230	45 12	108
23 2–4	241	45 14	108, 124
23 3–4	24	45 15	109
24 1	150	47	157–58
24 5	150	47 3	158
24 14	44	47 4	105, 112
25, version 1, 3	103	49 6	126
25, version 2, 7	103	49 22	88
26, version 2, 17	109	49 27	121
26, version 2, 18	109–10	51 2	45
26, version 2, 1–9	110	51 10	41, 50
26, version 2, 22	48	54 8	114
29 6	88	54 22	215
29, version 2, 10	51		
30, sermon 1, 9	121		
30, sermon 2, 12	122		

26 4	258	41 13	91
34 4	37, 55	67 1	35
34 4–5	233	77 1–2	28, 35
38 10	24, 42	77 4	28, 35
39 10	24	106 5	111
40 9	23, 31	124 5	42
40 10	73		

Sermones

4 33	271	96 2	49, 163–64
7 7	24	97 2	239,261
8 4	42	103 1	73
9 3	260	103 3–6	42
10	265	108 5	75
10 2	263	111 2	73, 75, 76
12 5	120	119 3	75
12 12	37, 120	120 2	37
15	275	121 4	109
20 1	111	123 1	261
20 2	111	125 5	41
22 3	103	125 7	47
22 8	43	125 9	47
28 1–5	36	126 3	56, 240–41
28 5	36	135 8	54, 56, 232
31 4–5	91	137 3	105
31 5	76	142 2	276
32 11	245n22	142 3	277
37 23	50	142 4	277
38 11	73, 75	142 5	277
40 6	58	142 8	277
45 4	75	153 14	46
47 30	36	154 5	275
49 6	105	154 6	275
50 11	76	154 8	275
55 5	64	157 4–5	43, 76
57 9	59, 64, 76	160 7	47
57 11	76	162 3	239
63 1–2	45, 74, 75, 181	162 3–4	264–65
69 4	39	166 2	35
75 2	45, 75, 88, 181, 230	169 1	51
		169 18	76
75 8	31	170 10–11	76
76 1	45, 75, 181, 230	170 11	53, 76
78 3	42	171 2	74
79 1	54, 233	171 3–4	65
82 14	239	176 2	46
84 2	59	177 2	76
85 6	36	177 9	156–57, 263
87 11	57, 58	180 3	62
88 4	105	189 2	75, 88
88 24	119	205 2	76
91 1	84	208	74
91 9	76	209	74

CPSIA information can be obtained
at www.ICGtesting.com
Printed in the USA
JSHW021458300620
6407JS00001B/11